SEEKING REFUGE

SEEKING REFUGE

Central American Migration
to Mexico, the United States, and Canada

María Cristina García

UNIVERSITY OF CALIFORNIA PRESS   Berkeley   Los Angeles   London

University of California Press, one of the most distinguished university
presses in the United States, enriches lives around the world by advancing
scholarship in the humanities, social sciences, and natural sciences. Its
activities are supported by the UC Press Foundation and by philanthropic
contributions from individuals and institutions. For more information, visit
www.ucpress.edu.

University of California Press
Berkeley and Los Angeles, California

University of California Press, Ltd.
London, England

Library of Congress Cataloging-in-Publication Data

García, María Cristina, 1960–.
  Seeking refuge : Central American migration to Mexico, the United States,
and Canada / María Cristina García.
    p. cm.
  Includes bibliographical references (p.) and index.
  ISBN 0-520-24700-0 (cloth : alk. paper). — ISBN 0-520-24701-9 (pbk. : alk.
paper)
    1. Political refugees—Central America.   2. Political refugees—Legal status,
laws, etc.—United States.   3. Political refugees—Legal status, laws, etc.—
Mexico.   4. Political refugees—Legal status, laws, etc.—Canada.   I. Title.
HV640.5.C46G37 2006
325'.21'09728097—dc22   2005050648

Manufactured in the United States of America
14   13   12   11   10   09   08   07   06
10 9 8 7 6 5 4 3 2 1

This book is printed on New Leaf EcoBook 60, containing 60% post-
consumer waste, processed chlorine free; 30% de-inked recycled fiber,
elemental chlorine free; and 10% FSC-certified virgin fiber, totally chlorine
free. EcoBook 60 is acid-free and meets the minimum requirements of
ANSI/ASTM D5634–01 (Permanence of Paper).

In memory of
Clemente García
(1926–1996)
and
Rosario J. Argilagos Rodríguez
(1910–1997)

CONTENTS

Preface and Acknowledgments   ix

List of Abbreviations   xv

Introduction   1

1.   The Wars in Central America and the
Refugee Crisis   13

2.   Designing a Refugee Policy: Mexico as Country
of First Asylum   44

3.   Refugees or Economic Migrants? The Debate over
Accountability in the United States   84

4.   Humanitarianism and Politics: Canada Opens Its Doors
to Central America   119

Conclusion: Shared Responsibility? Legacies of
the Central American Refugee Crisis   157

Notes   169

Selected Bibliography   235

Index   255

PREFACE AND ACKNOWLEDGMENTS

The idea for this project began in Austin, Texas, in the late 1980s, when I was writing my doctoral dissertation on Cuban immigration to the United States. Before I began my daily ritual at the computer, I allowed myself an hour at a local coffee shop to load up on caffeine and sugar (the graduate student's "fix") and to read the morning's headlines. A very different immigration story was playing out in the Texas state newspapers. I read about Central Americans who escaped civil war in their homelands and crossed vast stretches of territory to find safety and employment in North America. I read of shelters and halfway houses as far north as Buffalo, New York, where hundreds of people waited for their asylum hearings, their transportation to Canada, or the opportunity to return home. I read of the detention centers emerging along the US-Mexico border to house thousands facing deportation. And I read of "sanctuary workers" who willingly violated immigration law and risked prison to protest what they considered to be an immoral foreign policy. Following this morning ritual, I walked home to write my history of the post-1959 Cuban migration, a group that seemed so fortunate by comparison, despite their own poignant stories of separation and persecution.

Through research and lived experience, I became starkly aware of how politicized refugee policy can be. The US government assisted the Cubans because they fled a hostile communist government during the peak years of the Cold War. Laws were bent if not broken to accommodate them. The Cuban Refugee Program, first established in 1961, invested over nine hundred million dollars in these refugees by the mid-1970s, to help them retool for the US labor market but also to help local economies to accommodate the newcomers with as little strife as possible. The US news media were generally positive about these new arrivals (at least those who arrived during the first two decades). Articles in major newspapers and news magazines celebrated the Cubans' democratic and entrepreneurial values—their familiarity—and helped to convince Americans that they were worth welcoming. This moral and financial investment in their future on the part of so many institutions, chief among them the US government, played no small role in helping the Cubans to adjust to their new society and become among the more "successful" immigrant groups in the twentieth century.

The nation faced a totally different scenario with the arrivals of the Salvadoran, Guatemalan, and Nicaraguan immigrants. This time, the administrations of Reagan and Bush insisted that those who fled the civil wars in Central America were not true refugees, but rather economically driven migrants. During the 1980s fewer than 5 percent of Central Americans were successful in their petitions for asylum; and no government aid packages were granted to assist in their accommodation. This time it was certain sectors of the US population that argued that the United States had a moral obligation to assist the refugees. Debates over immigration and foreign policy took place in town halls, churches, and college campuses across the United States, creating a climate conducive to change. But ultimately, it was the federal courts that mandated changes in asylum policy and in detention and deportation procedures.

These two very different experiences inspired my research and writing these past years, and I had a personal connection to both stories. My family, like thousands of other Cuban families who arrived during the 1960s, benefited from the Cold War struggles between the United States and Cuba. It mattered little whether the doors to the United States were opened because of humanitarianism or politics. The goal was to escape the violence and paranoia of the revolution, and return to Cuba when it was safe. In the meantime, the United States offered peace, economic opportunity, and, more important, choices. Eventually, exile became permanent residence for many of us, a story that needed to be told. However,

I was also committed to documenting the experiences of my Central American neighbors in Texas: people who also fled the violence of a paranoid state, but who faced a much more difficult challenge gaining acceptance into the United States. I hope that I have done justice to both stories.

Like all authors, I face the difficult challenge of naming (remembering) all the friends, students, and colleagues who helped with the research and writing of this book, either through valuable criticism of one or more chapters, or through discussion and debate, or through the support and friendship that made the process easier. I hope they will be proud to be in some way connected to this work. I thank Teresa Palomo Acosta, Julia Kirk Blackwelder, Cynthia Bouton, Derek Chang, Sherman Cochran, Ray Craib, Nicole Guidotti-Hernández, Itsie Hull, Michael Jones-Correa, Carol Kammen, Michael Kammen, Walt LaFeber, Harold Livesay, Tamara Loos, Angel David Nieves, Mary Beth Norton, Dick Polenberg, Suyapa Portillo, Mary Roldán, Gabriela Sandoval, Joni Spielholz, Eric Tagliacozzo, Betty Miller Unterberger, and Hector Vélez. Portions of this work were presented at seminars and conferences, including the American Historical Association; the Comparative History Colloquium at Cornell; Princeton University; and the University of California at Berkeley. I thank the students and scholars who offered feedback and helped to make this a stronger work.

I am indeed fortunate to have had two wonderful academic jobs since I defended my dissertation: at the Department of History at Texas A&M, and now at the History Department at Cornell University. I thank my colleagues at both institutions for the intellectual exchange in meetings and seminars, cafés and dinner parties, and even hallways an exchange that has made me a better teacher and scholar.

During the writing of this book, Robert Morse Crunden, my dissertation director at the University of Texas at Austin, passed away suddenly. I want to acknowledge his mentorship over the years. Bob's enthusiasm for my topic and his encouragement helped me immensely during those difficult years in graduate school.

I thank the staff of the History Department at Cornell, especially manager (and good friend) Judy Burkhard, as well as Barb Donnell, Maggie Edwards, Jennifer Evangelista, and Katie Kristof, who make going into the office such a pleasure. Their stories, jokes (often at the faculty's expense), and parties make the History Department a unique place to be. In the Latino Studies Program, Marti Dense made my job as director so much easier. If I got any writing done during that three-year period as program director, it was thanks to Marti's efficiency, talent, and willingness to run interference. I thank the students—undergraduate and graduate—associated with LSP for their energy and commitment to the program, their probing questions and feedback, and their appreciation.

I could not have done my work without the assistance of many talented and resourceful persons at libraries and special collections in Mexico, the United States, and Canada: the staff of the John T. Olin Library at Cornell University; Nettie Lee Benson Latin American Collection at the University of Texas at Austin; Biblioteca Central, Universidad National de México; Catholic Archives of Texas; Immigration and Refugee Board, Documentation Centre, Ottawa; Lauinger Library, Georgetown University; Library of Congress, Washington, D.C.; National Archives of Canada, Ottawa; National Security Archives, George Washington University, Washington, D.C.; and the presidential libraries of Geroge H. W. Bush, James E. Carter, and Ronald Reagan. I want to single out three persons in particular—David Block and Ida Martínez at Olin Library, and Margo Gutierrez at the Benson Collection at UT-Austin. David located many important sources for me. Ida expanded the Latino Studies collection at Cornell, which assisted my research and teaching. Margo has helped develop what I think is the best collection of Latino/Latin American materials in North America, which is my research home away from Olin Library.

Financial support for this project came from a variety of sources. The initial research was made possible by a summer stipend from the Louisville Institute and a Faculty Development leave at Texas A&M. The Canadian Consulate General in Dallas, especially John Morrow, facilitated a research grant that allowed me to consult special collections in Ottawa. At Cornell, financial assistance came from the Return Jonathan Meigs Fund of the History Department and from university study and administrative leaves that provided the time to research and write.

This is my second book published with the University of California Press. The first publishing experience was so positive that I naturally turned to them with my second manuscript. Senior editor Naomi Schneider believed in the project and assigned two excellent outside readers, who offered valuable suggestions for revisions. It is a much stronger book thanks to their input. Assistant editor Sierra Filucci and production editor Jacqueline Volin have generously guided the project to its completion. I am also grateful to Robin Whitaker for her copyediting and to Chalon Emmons for her editorial assistance. Jimmy Dorantes of LatinFocus provided the wonderful photograph for the book cover.

Finally, but no less important, I thank my family for their love and support. My husband, Sherm Cochran, is the kindest and most generous man I know. My mother, Chary García, is my spiritual anchor. My brother, Joseph, and sister, Victoria (and my siblings by marriage, Renee and Eddie), are there for me in more ways than I can ever list. My aunts, Nini and Martha, are the best examples of what an aunt should be. The integrity and commitment of my cousin Antonio Pérez and his wife, Carol, are inspiring. My nieces and nephew, Isabelle, Natalie, Cristina, Allie, and Nick, fill my life with laughter and adventures.

I dedicate this book to my father and grandmother, who died within months of each other, as I began the research for this book. Whatever talents I have, they helped nurture. Whatever person I am, and hope to be, they inspired.

I know that I will remember more names after I send these pages to press. Please know that you all have my gratitude and appreciation.

ABBREVIATIONS

ANSESAL	Salvadoran National Security Forces
ARENA	National Republican Alliance Party
CCR	Canadian Council for Refugees
CCS	Comité Cristiano de Solidaridad
CEAR	Comisión Nacional para la Atención de Repatriados, Refugiados, y Desplazados
CEIC	Canada Employment and Immigration Commission
CIREFCA	International Conference on Central American Refugees
CISPES	Committee in Solidarity with the People of El Salvador
COMAR	Mexican Committee for Refugee Assistance
CONONGAR	National Coordinator of NGOs Assisting Refugees in Mexico
CRTF	Chicago Religious Task Force on Central America
DED	Deferred Enforced Departure
EVD	Extended Voluntary Departure

FDN	Nicaraguan Democratic Forces
FDR	Revolutionary Democratic Front
FMLN	Farabundo Martí Front for National Liberation
FSLN	Sandinista National Liberation Front
IIRIRA	Illegal Immigration Reform and Immigrant Responsibility Act (1996)
IOM	International Organization for Migration
IRB	Immigration and Refugee Board
IRCA	Immigration Reform and Control Act (1986)
NAFTA	North American Free Trade Agreement
NGO	non-governmental organization
OAS	Organization of American States
ONUCA	United Nations Observer Mission in Central America
ORDEN	Democratic Nationalist Organization
RSAC	Refugee Advisory Status Committee
TPS	temporary protected status
UNHCR	United Nations High Commissioner for Refugees
UNO	National Opposition Union
URNG	Guatemalan National Revolutionary Unity

INTRODUCTION

> To leave one's country in search of refuge, to save one's
> family, one's community, meant facing the unknown,
> and not knowing what would happen tomorrow or
> whether the place one had chosen as temporary refuge
> would open its doors and warmly welcome those fleeing
> terror and death.
>
> RIGOBERTA MENCHÚ TUM

The political upheaval in Nicaragua, El Salvador, and Guatemala in the last decades of the twentieth century had a devastating human toll. A quarter of a million people died during the period 1974–96, and over one million people were internally displaced, forced to find refuge in other areas of their own countries. Many of those who survived the warfare and the human rights abuses chose temporary refuge in neighboring countries such as Costa Rica and Honduras, living anonymously as illegal immigrants or as documented refugees in government-run camps. When the camps filled up, or when their safety or economic survival was once again threatened, Nicaraguans, Salvadorans, and Guatemalans traveled further north, to Mexico, the United States, and Canada. Over two million of those who fled Central America during this period settled in these three countries.

This book tells the story of that migration and how these governments responded to the refugees' presence. It also tells the story of the individuals, groups, and organizations that responded to the refugee crisis and worked within and across national borders to shape a more responsive refugee policy. During this period Mexico, the United States, and Canada were engaged in discussions of free trade but were more interested in facilitating the free movement of capital than in addressing the human migration that inevitably followed from such policies. Likewise, they and other nations in the Northern Hemisphere ignored the refugee crisis created by the revolutions in Central America until fairly late in the 1980s, even though some had played a role in exacerbating the political conflict and had become unwilling hosts to thousands of refugees. By the time regional leaders sat down to address possible solutions to the crisis, over three million people had fled their homes, crossed national boundaries, and stretched charitable resources in hundreds of communities. It was the pressure exerted by international non-governmental organizations (NGOs) and the grassroots organizations that worked firsthand with the victims, as well as the refugees themselves, that forced these states to address the crisis.[1] Collectively these individuals and organizations established domestic and transnational advocacy networks that collected testimonies, documented the abuses of states, reframed national debates about immigration, pressed for changes in policy, and ultimately provided a voice for the displaced and the excluded.

The Central American refugee crisis highlighted the bureaucratic inconsistencies in the immigration policies of Mexico, the United States, and Canada. Each country politicized the refugee determination system or failed to offer a legal status that adequately addressed the refugee crisis, in large part to discourage further migration to its territory. Instead of crafting a regional response that collectively shared the burdens of relocating and supporting the refugees, each government reacted to the crisis on the basis of its own state interests. Each was then forced to readjust its policies to deal with the consequences of its neighbors' policies. Passage of the 1986 Immigration Reform and Control Act (IRCA) in the United States, for example, created a "border rush" of Salvadorans who sought refuge in Canada to avoid deportation, and then forced Canada to redesign its refugee determination system. Likewise, the Mexican government's very different responses to the illegal Guatemalans and Salvadorans in Mexico influenced the character of the migration to the United States and forced the United States to redefine its border policies.

Surveys and public opinion polls conducted at the time showed that the Central American refugees did not rank high in domestic political agendas. However, in all three countries, a small, vocal, and disproportionately influential segment of the population successfully lobbied for a more humanitarian response. These individuals—students, academics, lawyers, trade unionists, journalists, religious and secular aid workers—created organizations and networks to defend the rights of the refugees and to demand an end to their countries' complicity in the political upheaval. Wherever they worked—in *comunidades de base* (faith communities), refugee camps, legal aid offices, sanctuaries, universities, or nonprofit organizations in Central or North America—refugee advocates relied on the information and support provided by each of the network's constituent parts. Human rights activists in Central America, for example, relied on journalists and NGOs to publicize their cause, mobilize support, and secure protection for the displaced. Likewise, lobbyists working in Mexico City, Washington, and Ottawa depended on the refugees and human rights activists for the evidence that might help them argue their case.

By 1980, advocacy networks existed in Mexico, the United States, and Canada, working within and across national borders to protest not only human rights abuses in Central America but also state policies that militarized the region, exacerbated the civil wars, and discriminated against the wars' victims.[2] Some groups operated solely at the grassroots level, informing and providing assistance to communities and lobbying local legislators. Others, like the United Nations High Commissioner for Refugees (UNHCR), Americas Watch, and the Church World Service, worked on a broader scale, collecting evidence, providing testimony at hearings and tribunals, and using their moral authority to press for policy changes from government bureaucracies. Whether at the local, national, or international level, these actors were bound together by their common concern about the social upheaval in Central America. They used international norms to criticize individual state behavior, collected and disseminated information that challenged official state discourses, forced accountability, and ultimately changed policy.[3]

Clergymen, missionaries, and aid workers in Central America played key roles in these networks; indeed, much of the information circulated about Central America was first acquired by these individuals, who worked on the front lines. Religious and secular aid workers tried to help communities in Nicaragua, El Salvador, and Guatemala have some semblance of a normal life amid the bombings, disappearances, and assassinations. But they also played critical roles in documenting the abuses and traumas of war, from recording the names of those who had disappeared to compiling detailed reports and chronologies of death squad campaigns. Together with the photographs and films taken by international journalists working in the field,[4] this documentation presented a very different picture of events from the one presented in Central America, where censorship of information was a keystone of repressive governments. These advocates also challenged the discourses about Central America promoted by the Reagan and Bush administrations, which played key roles in militarizing the region. Those who were eventually forced to flee the region helped to keep Central America on the front pages of newspapers. They wrote articles and editorials, testified before legislative bodies, spoke to civic, political, professional, and religious groups, and cofounded some of the organizations that became the backbone of the solidarity and advocacy network.

Advocates who were motivated by religious beliefs were particularly predisposed to challenging laws and nation-states during this period, because they believed they answered to a higher authority. Their acts of civil disobedience inevitably gained front-page coverage in newspapers around the world. Photographs of nuns and clergymen arrested for sanctuary work, or for chaining themselves on government property in protest of foreign policy, were more sensational than photographs of refugee camps and detention centers, and understandably garnered more attention. Likewise, the assassination of high-profile religious leaders such as Salvadoran archbishop Oscar Romero commanded more international media attention than the dozens of nameless citizens shot and killed at his funeral procession. Their vocal defense of the rights of the poor and their willingness to suffer imprisonment, torture, and death made them heroic figures in a region that seemed so lacking in heroes. They risked their own safety to raise consciousness about Central America. In the process, they also provoked national reexaminations about the role of religion in political life.

It is impossible to separate the refugee advocacy of the 1980s from the larger protests against state policies and human rights abuses in Central America. Mass migrations generally attract the involvement of NGOs, which in turn encourage a shift in international policy.[5] Those who became involved in the sanctuary movement, or who filed lawsuits on behalf of the refugees in camps and detention centers, or who lobbied their legislators for immigration reform did so in part because of their opposition to state policies that created a disposable population. Refugee advocates in the United States, for example, argued that the United States had a moral obligation to help the displaced because of the country's long history of economic exploitation of the region and the role it played at the time in supporting corrupt military regimes and death squads. For some advocates, it was their opposition to militarization that brought them to refugee work; for others, it was contact with the refugees themselves in churches, clinics, and legal aid offices that heightened their awareness of foreign policy. However the advocates came to know about Central America or its refugees, the two political initiatives became symbiotically entwined. When Americans lobbied or testified in favor of immigration reform, they always condemned the policies that had created the refugee crisis in the first place.

The advocacy networks used a variety of tactics learned from other social movements around the world, among them the labor, student, and environmental movements of the 1960s, as well as the US civil rights movement and Vietnam War protests. Refugee advocates organized petitions, rallies, and demonstrations. They organized conferences, published books, articles, and editorials, and produced films and documentaries. They organized letter-writing campaigns and fact-finding trips for scholars, legislators, and journalists. They set up halfway houses and sanctuaries for the refugees. They financially supported communities in Central America through the sale of cooperative-produced clothing and crafts. And they transported food and medical supplies in highly publicized "peace caravans." All these activities served to heighten awareness of the wars and its refugees.

At the same time, those who worked in Central America promoting economic development and political rights helped local communities to experiment with democratic institution building and political empowerment. By addressing the issue of human rights, activists also addressed a wide range of interrelated issues including poverty, agrarian reform, environmentalism, population growth, the rights of women and indigenous societies, and what in the post–Cold War era has become known as globalization.

The refugees played a role in their own advocacy. By relating their personal experiences in interviews, at legislative hearings, and at church and civic halls, they gave a human face to statistics. The refugees exerted a transnational influence on their countries of origin—not only through the *testimonios* that helped to change state policies, but also through the economic remittances they sent to family and friends. These remittances, in particular, became so important to the developing economies of Central America that at least one head of state is known to have pressured the Reagan administration to ease up on the deportation of co-nationals.[6] And once repatriation or travel to their homelands became possible, these migrants exerted a significant influence on the political and economic life of the communities they helped to rebuild. Their migration reflected—and contributed to—the devastation in their countries, but the influence they exerted in exile and repatriation was equally powerful.

A COMPARATIVE FOCUS

Central American migration provides the case study through which to examine the role foreign policy interests play in shaping immigration policy. Over the past two decades, a number of studies (among them Loescher and Scanlan 1986; Mitchell 1992; Pedraza 1985; and Teitelbaum 1985) have examined how US foreign policy has shaped population movements, especially in the Americas, where US interests and influence are most evident. The United States has also been the focus of much of the recent literature on globalization, transnationalism, and remittances. This study draws on and contributes to that literature by adding a cross-national focus, examining the impact that state policies have, not only on the character and flow of migration, but also on neighboring countries and the region as a whole. The United States cannot be totally decentered in this discussion, given the economic and political impact its policies have had on Central America. However, the study places the United States within a North American context to examine not only the impact US policies had on the region but also the influences that neighboring countries exerted on the United States. Thus, Mexico and Canada, two countries that played an important role in the regional response to the refugee crisis and ultimately in moderating US policies, receive comparable attention. Likewise, the study also examines the impact that sending countries had on the North American policies. El Salvador, Guatemala, and Nicaragua maintained an interest in their emigrants for both economic and political reasons: emigrant labor abroad provided much needed income in the form of remittances; and dissidents exerted enormous political influence through their lobbying and fundraising in host societies. Thus, pressure from Central American governments also shaped the ways Mexico, the United States, and Canada responded to this migration and the ways they accommodated the refugees.

This study also contributes to the growing literature on Central American immigrants to North America. During the first decade of the migration, a number of reports and monographs were published examining the root causes, character, and distribution of Central Americans. Aguayo 1985; Aguayo and Fagen 1988; Fagen 1984, Fagen and Aguayo 1986; Ferris 1987; Manz 1988 *(Refugees of a Hidden War);* Montes 1987; Montes and García Vásquez 1988; and Peterson 1986 were among the studies that chronicled the early years of Central American migration and the migrants' reception in different host societies. These studies complemented others by Bonner (1984), Coatsworth (1994), LaFeber (1993), and LeoGrande (1998) that provided regional histories explaining the civil wars. After the peace accords were signed and repatriation programs begun, the scholarship on Central American immigrants changed, focusing primarily on the social and legal incorporation of Salvadoran and Guatemalan immigrants in their host societies, particularly in specific cities in the United States, as well as the immigrants' transnational ties to their homelands. Several important studies, among them those of Burns (1993), Coutin (2000), Hagan (1994), Hamilton and Chinchilla (2001), Loucky and Moors (2000), Menjívar (2000), O'Dogherty Madrazo (1989), and Repak (1995), focused attention on these new Central American populations and contributed to the social science literature on "Latino" groups in the United States. My study owes a great deal to these important works. However, rather than focus on one group in one particular setting, it seeks to examine Central American migration in three different national settings in order to draw certain conclusions about this migration, in this case about the context of reception and the ways domestic and foreign policy interests shape how immigrants are received and perceived.

Finally, the study contributes to the growing body of work on nongovernmental actors and their role in shaping domestic and foreign policies. During the 1980s, a number of books were published on the culture of protest in the United States, especially the sanctuary movement. Studies by Coutin (1993), Crittenden (1988), Cunningham (1995), Davidson (1988), Golden and McConnell (1986), MacEoin (1985), and Tomsho (1987) examined the religious and civic motivations for American protests against the wars in Central America. My study draws on these and other more recent theoretical works by Boli and Thomas (1999), Fisher (1998), Keck and Sikkink (1998), and Risse et al. (1998), which discuss the changing role of NGOs within a global context. This study also contributes to this literature by examining the role of immigrant advocacy networks that operate within and across national borders.

One could argue that comparative studies are inherently prescriptive, but historians are generally reluctant to offer policy recommendations. Nevertheless, the history of Central American migration does offer various critical lessons, which in the post–September 11 world the United States and its neighbor-allies ignore. These lessons include, first, the need for regional responses to migration crises in which wealthier nations collectively share the burden of accommodating the displaced, rather than shifting the responsibility to poorer nations. Second, while foreign policy decisions often cause the displacement of populations, migration should not be used as an instrument for undermining or bolstering a specific regime. Finally, and most important, asylum seekers are entitled to certain protections, rights, and procedural safeguards, as specified by a number of international conventions on refugees. Likewise, immigration policy must be fair, consistent, and humane.

OVERVIEW OF THE BOOK

The following chapters provide a history of Central American migration in the 1980s and 1990s, government responses to that migration, and the advocacy networks that emerged to shape the policies of states. Chapter 1 provides a brief history of the wars in Nicaragua, El Salvador, and Guatemala to explain the causes of the migration. It discusses the reasons why people migrated and where they settled, following their migration within Central America to countries such as Costa Rica and Honduras, and explaining why thousands ultimately chose to migrate northward. Chapters 2 through 4 examine how Mexico, the United States, and Canada, the countries that received the largest aggregate number of refugees, each responded to the refugee crisis. It examines how refugee policy was made, the role that different agents and interests played in shaping that policy, and the impact that individual policies had on neighboring countries.

Mexico is known as an emigrant-producing nation, but this discourse denies its parallel tradition of accommodating exiles and immigrants from all over the world. During the 1980s alone, Mexico became host to an estimated 750,000 Central Americans, primarily from El Salvador and Guatemala; and over a million more transited through the country on their way to the United States and Canada. Chapter 2 examines the political debates within Mexico regarding sovereignty and international responsibilities as well as refugees and economic immigrants.

During the 1980s and 1990s, Mexico tried to assert itself as a middle power in hemispheric affairs, challenging the United States on its Nicaraguan and Salvadoran policies, and assuming a prominent role in the Contadora peace initiative. (The Contadora Group consisted of representatives of Mexico, Panama, Colombia, and Venezuela, who first met in 1983 on the island of Contadora, off the coast of Panama, to establish a blueprint for a negotiated peace settlement.) From the beginning, Mexico denied the US discourse that the wars in Central America were part of an East–West struggle and asserted the rights of Central Americans to challenge unjust structures and institutions in their own countries and to shape their own destiny. However, this position was threatened by the presence of thousands of refugees along its southern border, which exacerbated centuries-old tensions with neighboring Guatemala almost to the brink of war, and jeopardized the political stability of Chiapas, a state of key importance to Mexico's overall economic development. Mexico's challenge, then, was to assert and balance its international responsibilities without alienating Guatemala and the United States. Its refugee and immigration policy was conceptualized against the backdrop of these foreign and domestic policy debates.

Even though Mexico was not a signatory to the UN Convention and Protocol, it granted official protection, albeit reluctantly, to one of the largest groups of refugees in the region, in large part because of pressure from various non-governmental organizations and from the refugees themselves. With the help of the UNHCR, the Mexican government established camps in Chiapas, Campeche, and Quintana Roo that housed forty-six thousand refugees, mostly Maya Indians, and then later assisted them either to repatriate or to legalize their status in Mexican society. However, the majority of Central Americans living in Mexico did not receive any recognition or assistance from the state or the UNHCR. Churches and charitable organizations that had direct contact with the refugees estimated that as many as half a million Salvadorans lived and worked anonymously in the major cities, and as many as two hundred thousand Guatemalans preferred to live outside the UNHCR camps and settlements, even if it meant forfeiting assistance. The Mexican government justified its neglect by claiming that the Central Americans were *transmigrantes,* or economic migrants, traveling through Mexico on their way to the United States or Canada, even though evidence suggested otherwise. In the end, Mexico's neglect encouraged many Central Americans to move further northward in search of higher wages and better working conditions. As a result, by the late 1980s the United States actively pressured Mexico to do more to control its southern border and step up its deportation of Central American workers, and in the NAFTA era Mexico was willing to comply.[7] Once again, Central Americans became the pawns of foreign policy decisions.

Of the three countries, the United States hosted the largest number of Central American refugees. Those who entered the United States—most of them illegally—encountered a society that was less than enthusiastic about their arrival. Since the passage of the 1965 Immigration Act, the United States had accommodated millions of immigrants, refugees, and undocumented workers from a variety of countries, and Americans perceived the Central Americans as yet another drain on their economy. The influx of so many undocumented migrants in particular—from Mexico, Central America, and other regions—contributed to the anti-immigrant backlash of the 1980s that culminated in the passage of the restrictive 1986 Immigration Reform and Control Act, which imposed a variety of measures and sanctions to try to control the entry of undocumented workers.

But for a segment of the US population, the migration of Central Americans presented a moral dilemma. Its members believed that the United States had a responsibility to assist the migrants from Central America because of the role their government had played in escalating the violence. The Reagan and Bush administrations denied that the "feet people" were refugees, because to acknowledge this would have implied that the governments they supported with billions of dollars each year were terrorizing their own citizens—an action that would both alienate the United States' Central American allies and sabotage continued congressional aid for these regimes. In the 1980s, the Central America advocacy networks in the United States called for a reassessment of US foreign and immigration policies. Chapter 3 examines how these networks demanded accountability from the US government for its actions in

Central America and on the United States–Mexico border—first, through protest and civil obedience, lobbying, and the manipulation of the media and, ultimately, through the courts and the Congress.

Of the three countries, Canada did not have a long tradition of immigration from Latin America, in part because of its climate and geographic location, but also because of its limited diplomatic presence and trade relations within the hemisphere prior to 1970. During the administrations of Prime Minister Pierre Trudeau (1968–79, 1980–84), Parliament reevaluated its relationship with Latin America, increasing its embassies and consulates and creating a number of new institutions to oversee trade, investment, and development. Like Mexico, Canada tried to craft a foreign policy independent in tone and substance from the policies of the United States, partly in response to nationalist complaints that Canada was a "US territory" overly influenced by the culture and world view of its superpower neighbor. Canada's foreign and immigration policies, then, became means through which to distinguish its international priorities and assert its distinct cultural identity.

Canada's first experience with accommodating large numbers of immigrants from Latin America came in the 1970s, when it agreed to offer asylum to Chilean refugees fleeing the rightist military dictatorship. Less than a decade later, thousands of Central Americans migrated to Canada because of its more generous asylum policies. Unlike the United States, which prior to 1990 granted asylum to fewer than 3 percent of Salvadorans and Guatemalans, Canada granted asylum to up to 80 percent of applicants. The number of Central Americans increased significantly after the US Congress passed the Immigration Reform and Control Act, demonstrating the impact that the polices of neighboring countries had on the character and flow of migration. In response to IRCA, thousands of Central Americans, especially Salvadorans, arrived at Canadian border cities requesting asylum. The administrative backlog that it created pointed to the weaknesses in its refugee determination system. That Canada kept the door open was in no small part due to pressure from advocacy networks that forced a reexamination of national debates about Canadian identity and the country's role in the hemisphere. Chapter 4 examines the impact of Central American immigration on Canada's national debate on immigration, its identity as an open and multicultural society, and US-Canadian and hemispheric relations.

The concluding chapter examines the difficulties and challenges of crafting a regional response to migration, especially after the terrorist attacks of September 11. Despite the lessons learned from the Central American refugee crisis and from the subsequent international efforts to exchange information, coordinate policies, and share responsibility for the accommodation of displaced persons, US interests have dominated these regional discussions and policies. Safeguarding civil liberties, due process, and human rights is often trumped in the name of national security. Once again, it is the non-governmental actors that remain the asylum seekers' most vocal advocates, trying to force nations to examine difficult issues that in the post-9/11 era many are reluctant to examine.

I

THE WARS IN CENTRAL AMERICA AND THE REFUGEE CRISIS

[Central America is the] most dramatic and divisive
foreign policy issue since the Vietnam war. It has
dominated the front pages of newspapers for many
months; co-opted almost all of the prime moments
of national television news; fueled acrimonious exchanges in Congress; and ignited a national protest
movement, centered in the universities and the churches
but reaching into unions, professional associations, and
the cultural community.

MARK FALCOFF, *Commentary*

The revolutions in Nicaragua, El Salvador, and Guatemala were each the
product of decades of struggles over land, resources, and power. However,
what began as localized conflicts became international crises that affected
dozens of nations, including neighboring Costa Rica, Honduras, and
Mexico; hemispheric allies such as the United States and Canada; and even
Cuba, the Soviet Union, and the European Community. Thousands of
Central Americans died, and millions were uprooted as a consequence of
the domestic and foreign policy decisions of these various actors. But just
as local political conflicts became internationalized, so, too, did their eventual resolution. The negotiated peace settlements and the reintegration of
the displaced involved some of these very same actors, who through
diplomacy, investment, and aid tried to establish peace, social and political stability, and economic opportunity in the region.

THE SANDINISTA REVOLUTION IN NICARAGUA

In 1979, the Sandinista rebels overthrew the US-supported government
of Anastacio Somoza Debayle. The Somoza family—Anastacio Sr. and his
sons, Luis and Anastacio (Tachito)—had controlled Nicaraguan politics
since 1934, thanks in some part to the United States, which helped them
to consolidate their political control. From the Truman to the Ford admin-

istrations, the Somozas were regarded by the United States government as reliable allies in the Cold War[1] and were rewarded with millions of dollars in economic and military aid, much of which found its way to private coffers. US support also guaranteed the Somoza dictatorship millions of dollars in loans from the international banking community, as well as substantial investments in the nation's industries. US corporations, in particular, benefited from their government's relationship with the dictatorship. Not only did Nicaragua get most of its imports from the United States, but US corporations also controlled thousands of acres of Nicaragua's most fertile land and owned or managed the leading mines, the railroads, and the lumber and banking industries.

The extensive US presence in Nicaragua's national life never guaranteed the people peace or socioeconomic mobility. The majority of the three million Nicaraguans lived in extreme poverty, and high infant mortality, illiteracy, and unemployment were common features of day-to-day life.[2] Two percent of the farms controlled nearly half of the tillable land, and over two hundred thousand peasants were landless. In turn, the Somoza family's wealth was estimated at more than a billion dollars. The Somoza family was said to control one-third of the country's acreage; the nation's construction, meatpacking, and fishing industries; the national airline and major television station; and banks, radio stations, and various other businesses. American investors made handsome profits from their ventures in Nicaragua: US investments yielded hundreds of millions of dollars in yearly income that was exported back to the United States.[3]

The extreme disparities in wealth and the corruption in the highest echelons of the government raised the consciousness of the citizenry, especially labor organizers, university students, journalists, and public intellectuals. Prior to 1972, the US-trained Nicaragua National Guard helped to keep the opposition weak and disorganized by assassinating over thirty thousand of the dictator's opponents and driving thousands more into exile.[4] (A former US Speaker of the House once called the Guard "murderers, marauders, and rapists.")[5] However, after an earthquake devastated the capital city of Managua in December 1972, the forces of opposition expanded. Strikes and demonstrations increased in the months after the earthquake as Nicaraguans protested the blatant theft of international aid and the shameless corruption of government officials who financially profited from the devastation.[6] Inspiring the protests was the politically moderate editor Pedro Joaquin Chamorro, who used his small opposition newspaper, *La Prensa,* to meticulously document the corruption and abuse of authority.

The Sandinista National Liberation Front (FSLN) increased its support base at this time. Founded in Havana in 1961, the FSLN favored a revolutionary political and socioeconomic agenda.[7] Over the next eight years, the Sandinistas, as members the FSLN were popularly called, waged war against the dictatorship, kidnapping and ransoming prominent political officials and business leaders and attacking military garrisons, government offices, and other symbols of Somoza's authority. Determined to eliminate the FSLN, the Nicaragua National Guard increased its surveillance of the population as well as its campaign of imprisonment, torture, and assassination. The Guard especially targeted the northern provinces, where the Sandinistas were believed to have their greatest support. Even the political moderates came under attack: Chamorro was jailed and finally assassinated in 1978. This action, more than any other, turned the political tide. A two-week general strike calling for Somoza's unconditional resignation evolved into a full-scale, nationwide insurrection. By May 1979 the Sandinistas controlled the nation's major towns and cities, including parts of Managua.[8]

On July 17, 1979, Somoza fled to Miami with some of the senior commanders of the National Guard.[9] Rank-and file members of the Guard were left to protect what remained of the government, but without leadership the Guard easily crumbled. Many of the soldiers fled to neighboring countries, especially Honduras, to avoid the retribution that would inevitably follow. On July 19, a coalition of moderates and leftists took control of Nicaragua's government. Calling itself the Government of National Reconstruction, the coalition debated ways to rebuild the war-torn country, provide desperately needed social services, and encourage the consumer and investor confidence needed for economic growth.

The ideological cleavages among the coalition members proved difficult to overcome. While all were committed to agrarian reform and basic social welfare programs such as universal health care, literacy, and free public education, they disagreed on the roles that the private sector and the multiparty political system would play in the new Nicaragua—if any. The more radical members of the FSLN saw no role for such institutions in their socialist state. As this segment assumed control of the national directorate and the armed forces, moderates in the coalition, such as Violeta Barrios de Chamorro (the widow of the slain newspaper editor) and Alfonso Robelo (the founder of the Nicaraguan Democratic Movement), felt increasingly silenced and shut out of the decision making. Particularly disturbing to the moderates was a series of measures taken to consolidate the government's authority and protect against counterrevolution: the suspension of elections for six years; restrictions on the press, free speech, free association, and other civil liberties; the strengthening of the internal security apparatus; increased defense spending; the arrival of Cuban and East European advisers and Soviet arms shipments; and the export of arms to Salvadoran rebels.[10] By 1982 several moderates had resigned from the coalition or gone into exile, including former Sandinista Edén Pastora Gomez, the famed "Comandante Zero" who had led a spectacular and much publicized attack on the National Palace.[11] Many middle- and upper-class Nicaraguans also chose to exile themselves to the United States, Costa Rica, and other countries during this transitional period rather than live in what they perceived as an evolving communist state.

Most nations in the hemisphere, with the notable exception of Central American neighbors Costa Rica, El Salvador, Guatemala, and Honduras, cautiously welcomed the change in Nicaragua's government. Despite its thirty-plus years of assistance to the Somoza government, in the final year of the revolution Mexico offered the Sandinistas tactical support and then recognized the new government almost immediately. In the 1980s, Mexico became one of Nicaragua's principal trade partners, providing Nicaragua with most of its oil even though that strained Mexican relations with the United States and potentially sabotaged Mexico's own economic relationship with its northern neighbor. With a long history of challenging the United States and supporting leftist movements in Latin America,[12] Mexico became the region's most vocal critic of US policy in Nicaragua, but it also viewed itself as a "middle power" that could negotiate an easing of tensions in the region.[13]

Since the 1960s, Mexico's evolving status as a major oil producer had increased its diplomatic clout, and the Central American crisis provided an opportunity for asserting a new status in the hemisphere. As early as 1981, José López Portillo (president, 1976–1982) tried to arrange talks between the Sandinistas and the Reagan administration to discuss a nonaggression pact but failed to convince Washington.[14] López Portillo's successor, Miguel de la Madrid (president, 1982–1988), later launched the regional peace initiative known as Contadora. Mexico's philosophical position was best summarized by de la Madrid: "Every country in the continent must do its utmost to restore peace and avoid war by respecting and upholding the sovereign right of its people to decide their own destiny and by rejecting interventionist solutions of any kind."[15]

Canada's response, on the other hand, was substantively different. Ottawa officially welcomed the end of the Somoza era and even prohibited Somoza's entry into the country when he asked to relocate there, but postponed recognition of the Sandinista government.[16] Throughout the 1980s Canadian policymakers opposed US policy in Nicaragua and criticized the militarization of the region, but avoided any official condemnation of the United States that might strain US-Canadian relations, especially in trade and commerce.[17] Instead, they tried to use their diplomatic influence behind closed doors, with limited success.

As the most powerful nation in the hemisphere, the United States shaped the tone and content of the political debate over Nicaragua throughout the next decade. With billions of dollars in regional investments and a moral commitment to the expansion of democratic institutions, the United States had a geopolitical interest in containing revolution in the Americas. However, US policy shifted dramatically in a relatively short period of time. Immediately following his inauguration in January 1977, President Jimmy Carter declared US aid to individual Latin American countries contingent upon their human rights policies, and thus withdrew economic and military aid from the Somoza dictatorship.[18] Although his administration would have preferred—and tried to negotiate—a more centrist government in Nicaragua, Carter officially recognized the Sandinista government and hoped that it would offer its country peace, security, and basic civil liberties. The United States granted Nicaragua close to a hundred million dollars in emergency aid during 1979–1980; helped to restructure Nicaragua's massive international debt (estimated at 582 million dollars); and facilitated over two hundred million dollars in new loans and grants, all with the goal of maintaining positive relations and avoiding the mistakes the United States had made with Cuba twenty years earlier.[19]

The symbolic significance of such actions was considerable given the role the United States had played in supporting the Somozas and their National Guard during the previous forty-five years. However, in light of this history, the Sandinistas were understandably suspicious of any US involvement—a suspicion that was not completely unwarranted. Key figures in the Carter administration, among them National Security Adviser Zbigniew Brzezinski, were equally suspicious of the Sandinistas and the role Nicaragua might play in exporting revolution in Central America. They worked to steer US policy away from this more accommodationist position, and it was this philosophical perspective that ultimately dominated in the Carter administration. By the end of 1980, the administration had been forced to shift its attention to the Middle East and the hostage crisis in Iran, but the CIA worked behind the scenes in Nicaragua, funding a variety of anti-Sandinista organizations with the goal of eroding the Sandinistas' popular support.[20] Shortly before leaving office, Carter canceled the remaining aid promised the Sandinistas in protest over the shipment of arms to Salvadoran rebels.

US-Nicaraguan relations collapsed after Ronald Reagan moved into the White House in January 1981. The Reagan administration, particularly hard-liners such as Alexander Haig, Elliott Abrams, Jeane Kirkpatrick, and William Casey, acknowledged that the Sandinista revolution and the conflicts in Central America began as nationalist struggles for socioeconomic and political justice.[21] However, the Cold War framed the gathering of intelligence, the interpretation of the data, and ultimately the policymaking in this administration. They were determined not to let post-Vietnam guilt interfere with the containment of what they saw as a growing Cuban–Soviet–East European presence in the region. Congress accepted the administration's evidence that Nicaragua had become a base for exporting communism in the region and appropriated the funds that the administration needed to carry out its policy of containment. They supported the economic embargo on Nicaragua and redirected aid to the "Contras": *contra-revolucionarios* on the Honduras-Nicaragua border, whom the Reagan administration directed to stop the flow of arms from the Sandinista government to the leftist guerrillas of the FMLN (Farabundo Martí Front for National Liberation) in El Salvador.[22]

By the end of Reagan's first term it was clear that the administration was interested in more than just containing the flow of arms in Central America: it was using the Contras to destabilize—and overthrow—the Nicaraguan government.[23] Honduras and Costa Rica were critical to this campaign, and by the mid-1980s the United States had directed millions of dollars to both these countries for the establishment of camps and safe houses from which the Contra operatives could conduct their operations.[24] As in the CIA-sponsored raids in Cuba in the 1960s,[25] the Contras' military maneuvers were designed to force the Sandinistas to commit the Nicaraguan armed forces to domestic defense and to create a climate of political instability that would erode popular support and encourage revolt. The Contras were instructed to bomb industrial and other economic targets, but excerpts of a CIA training manual later published in the press revealed that they were also trained in kidnapping and murder.[26] By 1983, the CIA itself was directly engaged in sabotage—bombing Nicaraguan oil reserves and mining harbors, for example—in clear violation of international law and the United States' own Boland Amendment, which prohibited assisting or using the Contras to overthrow the Nicaraguan government or to provoke conflict between Nicaragua and Honduras.[27] Congress responded with the second Boland Amendment in 1984, which severed lethal aid to the Contras once and for all. Nicaragua filed a complaint against the United States in the World Court for the mining of its harbors, and two years later the court officially condemned the United States. However, neither domestic pressure nor international sanction deterred the Reagan administration from its foreign policy objectives: the administration turned to the illegal sale of arms to Iran in order to redirect the profits to its Contra protégés.[28]

The Reagan administration's policy in Nicaragua drew criticism at home and abroad. Critics argued that US policy only served to increase poverty and homelessness in Nicaragua, destabilize neighboring countries and producing a large-scale regional migration. NGOs such as Amnesty International, Americas Watch, Church World Service, and the International Red Cross documented the human toll produced by the militarization of Central America. While public opinion polls showed that most Americans could not locate Nicaragua on a map,[29] a vocal and influential minority protested US policy and ultimately forced Congress to monitor the administration's support of the Contras. Not since the Watergate scandal had Americans taken so passionate an interest in the activities of their government, and the administration received thousands of letters from Americans who warned that Central America would become another Vietnam.[30] Such popular pressure undoubtedly influenced the congressional and judicial scrutiny that followed the discovery of the illegal sale of arms to Iran.

In the years following the Iran-Contra hearings, the Bush administration continued to undermine the Sandinistas, albeit through more traditional pressure—the economic embargo, diplomatic isolation, and financial support of opposition groups. In 1989, when the Sandinista government finally agreed to elections under the terms of the Esquipulas II peace plan, most knew that their days in power were numbered. The United States funneled millions of dollars to the opposition parties to ensure the Sandinistas' defeat. In February 1990, Violeta Barrios de Chamorro, representing the National Opposition Union (Unión Nacional Opositora, UNO), a coalition of fourteen political parties, was elected president of Nicaragua by over half of the war-weary electorate (the elections had an 86 percent voter turnout). The United States finally lifted its economic embargo and provided millions of dollars to help rebuild the society that, only months before, it had tried to destroy.

The opposition's victory came at a high price for the Nicaraguan people: thirty thousand dead; fifty thousand wounded; and three hundred thousand left homeless. And over half a million Nicaraguans remained outside their country, the majority of them in the United States, waiting to see what type of society would evolve in their homeland.

DEATH SQUADS AND GUERRILLAS: THE STRUGGLE FOR POLITICAL CONTROL IN EL SALVADOR

As in Nicaragua, the civil war in El Salvador was rooted in the unequal distribution of power. An oligarchy of landed elites known as the Fourteen Families controlled 60 percent of the farmland, the entire banking system, and most of the nation's industry.[31] Eight percent of the nation's five million people controlled half of the nation's income, while over one-quarter of the rural population was poor and had been pushed off their land to make room for agricultural estates dedicated to the production of coffee, the country's principal export.[32] Since 1932, the country was ruled by a series of generals with close ties to the oligarchy, whose interests they protected, and they were equally zealous in weeding out any challenges to their authority. A peasant uprising in 1932, for example, led to *la matanza:* the murder of over thirty thousand Salvadorans by the army and vigilante groups.[33]

Nineteen seventy-two proved to be a landmark year in Salvadoran politics, as it was for Nicaragua. After the fraudulent elections of 1972, more and more Salvadorans engaged in strikes, demonstrations, and other acts of civil disobedience against the government of Fidel Sánchez Hernández. The Catholic Church played an indirect role in catalyzing such behavior. As one of the principal institutions in El Salvador (and Latin America), the Catholic Church had historically helped to maintain the unequal power relationships by encouraging the poor and the oppressed to passively accept their fate on earth in hopes of greater glories in heaven. However, by the 1960s, a more radical wing of the Catholic Church preached what it called a "theology of liberation": the fundamental idea that poverty and oppression were not God's will, and that God's children had the right to challenge oppressive institutions, structures, and conditions in every sector of society.[34] Moreover, according to liberation theology, the Catholic Church was obligated to condemn these unjust institutions and assist the faithful in their struggle for liberation. Across El Salvador, and throughout Latin America, the more radical nuns and clergy organized *comunidades de base* (faith communities) that encouraged villagers and townspeople to meet weekly for a closer reading of the Bible and particularly the social justice teachings of Jesus's New Testament. This theology was not new or radical, they argued, but rather a return to the original teachings of Christ.[35] To those who held power in Salvadoran society, this theology whether new or not was certainly radical enough to threaten their positions of privilege. Particularly worrisome was the fact that this theology was preached by even the highest-ranking clergyman of their society, the archbishop of San Salvador, Oscar Arnulfo Romero, who used his weekly radio sermons to condemn the abuses in Salvadoran society and to urge President Carter to withdraw military aid.[36]

Whether influenced by liberation theology or the Sandinista and Cuban revolutions, a number of groups emerged in El Salvador to demand social justice: organizations such as the People's Revolutionary Block, the Front of United Popular Action, and the Popular League of February 28. Each drew its rapidly growing membership from different segments of Salvadoran society—university students, teachers, trade unionists, as well as the urban and rural poor—and used a variety of tactics to challenge the authority of the elites, from traditional forms of civil disobedience to guerrilla warfare.[37] A number of guerrilla armies also emerged, such as the Popular Liberation Forces, the People's Revolutionary Army, the Armed Forces of

National Liberation, the Central American Revolutionary Workers Party, and the Armed Forces of Liberation.[38]

The protests continued even after October 1979, when a new military-civilian junta overthrew the violent government of General Carlos Humberto Romero. The junta, comprised of junior and somewhat progressive military officers as well as civilian representatives and church leaders, passed a number of modest reforms, including an agrarian reform program, a minimum daily wage, a ban on paramilitary groups, and tax and banking reforms. However, few of these reforms were ever enforced. Within months, the civilian and church representatives had resigned from the junta in protest, and the power continued to rest with the old guard. From 1979 to 1982, three junta governments attempted to enact modest reforms, with very limited success.

The principal agencies of Salvadoran national security tried to eliminate the rebels and dissenters. The centralized intelligence agency known as ANSESAL and its affiliate, the Democratic Nationalist Organization (ORDEN), a nationwide network of government informants and paramilitary groups founded in 1968,[39] used violent measures to control the civilian population. Protesters were arrested and beaten, expelled from the country, or murdered. The armed forces were assisted in these efforts by privately funded paramilitary groups such as the White Warriors Union, the White Hand, the Anti-Communist Forces for Liberation, and the Organization for the Liberation from Communism, among many others, whose interlocking membership consisted of soldiers, off-duty police officers, and "the sick young sons of affluent Salvadorans."[40] Indeed, the paramilitary groups received their funding from members of the oligarchy, some of them living in Miami.[41] These groups, appropriately nicknamed the *escuadrones de la muerte,* or "death squads," employed particularly gruesome tactics. Those believed to have ties to insurgent groups or who challenged the established order in any way—through labor organizing, sermons and public speaking, classroom instruction, publications and journalism—were tortured, raped, and killed. Thousands of mutilated corpses appeared in town sewers, garbage dumps, street gutters, and shallow graves, left by their torturers as a warning to others: eyes gouged, tongues and limbs severed, breasts, genitalia, and throats slashed. One group's signature method of assassination was twelve gunshots in the face at point-blank range.[42] So many Salvadorans were found dead or missing that the Catholic Church's Legal Office, the principal agency that documented the abuses, could not keep up with all the reports of the missing and killed. A favorite target of these death squads were nuns and priests, especially those affiliated with the more liberal Maryknoll and Jesuit orders that preached liberation theology.[43] Flyers circulated throughout the capital city of San Salvador, urging the population: "Be a patriot, kill a priest!"[44] According to Americas Watch, eighteen priests were killed in El Salvador from 1972 to 1989.[45]

Nineteen eighty was a particularly violent year: over eight thousand civilians were killed, and yet no one was arrested for the murders. Among the victims were some very prominent leaders whose violent deaths were meant to intimidate the opposition. In February, one of the more progressive civilian members of the government, Attorney General Mario Zamora, was assassinated during a dinner party at his own home, shot a dozen times in the face.[46] In March, Archbishop Oscar Romero was shot and killed while saying mass at the cathedral. At his funeral procession, the military fired into the crowd of thirty thousand mourners, killing thirty and wounding hundreds. In December, four US church workers, Ita Ford, Maura Clarke, Dorothy Kazel, and Jean Donovan, were kidnapped and murdered. Their raped and mutilated bodies were later found half buried in shallow graves. Throughout 1980, the military purged itself of its most progressive members to silence dissent: officers were demoted, reassigned to diplomatic posts, exiled, or assassinated.[47]

As in Nicaragua, the assassination of prominent leaders—in this case Zamora and Romero—served to unite reformers and revolutionaries. After the government failed to properly investigate death squad leader Roberto D'Aubuisson, believed to have ordered the assassinations,[48] the various political parties, religious organizations, trade unions, and peasant groups joined forces to create the Revolutionary Democratic Front (FDR) under the leadership of former junta members Guillermo Ungo, Roman Mayorga, and Ruben Zamora.[49] Five guerrilla groups also joined forces under the FMLN.[50] The FDR and FMLN eventually reached a compromise and united under the banner FDR-FMLN.

Public pressure at home forced the Carter administration to place a temporary embargo on military aid to El Salvador—an embargo that was lifted in the final months of his administration, when the FMLN launched a new counteroffensive against the Salvadoran government. As in Nicaragua,

Carter favored a more centrist government and tried to negotiate one under the direction of Ambassador Robert White. The administration applauded the junta's decision to appoint as president José Napoleón Duarte, the moderate Christian Democrat candidate who was denied victory in the fraudulent 1972 elections, imprisoned, tortured, and sent into exile. Carter—and later Reagan—regarded Duarte as someone who offered a political alternative to both the leftists and the rightists, and could help to rein in the more reactionary elements of the Salvadoran government. Through Ambassador White, the Carter administration also tried to convince the more progressive politicians to remain in the junta rather than join forces with the FDR–FMLN. However, Duarte proved ineffective in ending the violence. In 1981, the Catholic Church's legal office in San Salvador reported that the death squads and the government security forces killed 13,253 civilians. (In comparison, casualties at the hands of the guerrillas were always many fewer.)[51] Particularly shocking was the massacre at El Mozote. In December 1981, the Atlacatl battalion, regarded as the Salvadoran army's most elite group of US-trained soldiers, killed 936 villagers in the Morazán province, mostly at the village of El Mozote. Over half of the victims were children under the age of fourteen.[52] Despite the international press coverage, the United States denied the massacre until 1992, when forensic scientists began unearthing the mass graves.[53] Assassinations decreased by the end of 1984, as a result of US pressure, but the Salvadoran military increased its bombing of villages on which the guerrillas depended for shelter and food. Over seventy thousand were left homeless as a result of this campaign.[54]

US military aid to El Salvador continued despite the blatant human rights violations and intense international opposition, and despite the December 1980 United Nations resolution calling for an end to military support of the Salvadoran government. As in Nicaragua, the hard-liners in the Reagan administration portrayed the Salvadoran civil war as part of the East-West struggle, in which the United States had a moral duty to contain Cuban/Soviet expansionism.[55] Even their closest hemispheric allies were unable to influence US policy. As early as February 1980, Canadian and Mexican representatives met to discuss their mutual opposition to US intervention in Central American affairs. Canada cut off aid to El Salvador in November 1980, and along with Mexico and most nations in the hemisphere supported the UN resolution. In August 1981, Mexico and France extended official recognition to the FDR-FMLN, in an attempt to prevent "foreign military intervention in the Salvadoran conflict" and "allow the Salvadoran people to decide their own destiny."[56] The following year Mexico tried to negotiate a peace between the FDR-FMLN and the Salvadoran government, independent of the United States, but the initiative was unsuccessful.

In order to continue providing aid, the US Congress required evidence that El Salvador was making significant improvements in human rights. Members of the Reagan administration either denied or downplayed news reports of civilian casualties, claiming that only leftist guerrillas were caught in the crossfire. They assured Congress that El Salvador was taking significant steps toward democracy and ending the violence. In 1982, when right-wing forces regained control of the Salvadoran government, the Reagan administration convinced D'Aubuisson, now president of the National Assembly, to allow Alvaro Magaña to become president and at least give the appearance of a more centrist government. And in 1984, the administration facilitated the election of Christian Democrat Duarte in the country's most expensive election, so that he could immediately initiate peace talks with the FDR/FMLN.[57] Public statements by the hard-liners in the Reagan administration showed their willingness to lie about what was happening in El Salvador. Commenting on the murder of the four American churchwomen, both Secretary of State Alexander Haig and UN Ambassador Jeane Kirkpatrick brought up the women's alleged connections to the guerrillas. In one interview Kirkpatrick suggested that the women got what they deserved: "The nuns were not just nuns. The nuns were also political activists. We ought to be a little more clear about this than we usually are. They were political activists on behalf of the Frente. And somebody who is using violence to oppose the Frente killed these nuns."[58] Commenting on US policy, a US diplomat who served in Central America during the Reagan years stated: "Unless they see a guy like D'Aubuisson running a machete through somebody, they're inclined to ignore it. . . . There is absolutely zero conception of what these people are really like, how evil they really are."[59]

Congress found the administration's arguments and evidence compelling enough to continue sending aid. Throughout the 1980s, El Salvador remained on the list of the top five nations to receive aid from the United States. All in all, the United States provided six billion dollars in economic and military aid to El Salvador during its twelve-year civil war. The United States also facilitated the transfer of millions of dollars in aid from the International Monetary Fund, the World Bank, and the Inter-American Development Agency.

While the different parties struggled for control of the Salvadoran government, thousands of people were uprooted from their homes or murdered. By 1986, over half a million Salvadorans were internally displaced, dependent on the government for their survival, and over one million had fled to other countries.[60]

THE "SCORCHED EARTH" POLICIES OF THE GUATEMALAN MILITARY

In Guatemala, a state of war began in 1954, when a CIA-sponsored military coup overthrew the democratically elected government of Jacobo Arbenz Guzman and thwarted the country's decade-long campaign for agrarian reform.[61] For the next forty years, a series of military officers ruled the country. As in Nicaragua and El Salvador, opposition groups in Guatemala during this time frame challenged the institutions that concentrated wealth and power in the hands of a small percentage of the population. Two percent of the population controlled 72 percent of all private land,[62] while 60 percent of Guatemalans earned roughly two dollars a day harvesting export crops such as coffee, sugar, and cotton. Workers and their families endured inhumane conditions at home and at work: inferior housing with no running water, sewers, or electrification; and access to health care and education was limited. Workers were offered few legal protections, and attempts at unionization were violently discouraged.

The Maya of the highlands of Guatemala, who comprised half of Guatemala's population of eight million and were the backbone of the agricultural economy, were especially poor and victimized. Multinational corporations, with the encouragement and support of various dictatorships, confiscated Indian land for oil production, mining, and cattle raising. Consequently the vast majority of Maya families were either landless and forced to work for others, or farmed holdings of less than seven hectares (the bare minimum needed to support a family). Mayas had the highest infant mortality rate in the country (134 per 1,000 live births compared to 80 per 1,000 for the *ladinos*),[63] and their life expectancy was sixteen years lower than for *ladinos*. Only 19 percent of Mayas were literate as compared to over 50 percent of the rest of the population. They were a voiceless and heavily exploited majority, whose intense poverty made them, the government feared, prone to insurgency. As early as the 1960s, the army moved into the highlands and kidnapped and killed those suspected of trying to form agricultural cooperatives, unions, or political groups.[64] Between 1966 and 1976, fifty thousand people were murdered.[65] Colonel Carlos Arana Osorio, the "Butcher of Zacapa," who assumed the "presidency" in 1970, was among several of Guatemala's leaders who exemplified the strategy. He is reported to have stated: "If it is necessary to turn the country into a cemetery in order to pacify it, I will not hesitate to do so."[66]

Various guerrilla groups operated during the 1960s and 1970s to challenge the dictatorships. In 1982, the four principal guerrilla armies joined to form the Guatemalan National Revolutionary Unity (URNG). Their platform included agrarian reform and price controls; equality between Indians and *ladinos;* democratic representation; and civil liberties such as freedom of expression and religion.[67] The government tried to control the population and erode the guerrillas' popular base through special programs such as the euphemistically called *frijoles y fusiles* (beans and rifles) and *techo, tortillas, y trabajo* (housing, tortillas, and employment), which provided food and other aid in exchange for service in the *patrullas de autodefensa civil* (civilian defense patrols). At the height of the civilian patrol system, the *patrullas* counted nine hundred thousand members.[68] The violence against the opposition reached new levels of barbarism from 1981 to 1984, during the governments of Generals Romeo Lucas García, Efraín Ríos Montt, and Oscar Mejía Víctores.[69] The army burned fields and killed livestock to destroy the guerrillas' food supplies. Individuals remotely suspected of assisting the guerrillas, no matter how young, were viciously tortured and killed.[70]

The Mayas were especially targeted. Accused of harboring or supporting the rebels, entire villages were burned to the ground by the *kaibiles,* the government's elite counterinsurgency units, many of whom were young Indians forced to wage war against their own people.[71] Entire communities were slaughtered. Soldiers used guns, knives, and machetes, or doused their victims with gasoline and burned them alive. Bodies were mutilated before and after death: limbs and heads severed, women's breasts cut off and stuffed into the mouths of their dead children. Even fetuses were cut out of their mothers' pregnant bodies to ensure that there would be no survivors.[72] One scholar has appropriately called this period "the time of mass terror."[73]

As one example, on July 17, 1982, five hundred Guatemalan army troops entered the tiny Chuj Indian village of San Francisco, rounded up the men, women, and children, and brutally murdered roughly 350 villagers. The four men who survived the massacre did so by hiding in the mounds of corpses to await the chance to escape into the jungle, and into Mexico. "I was under about ten bodies," reported one fifty-seven-year-old survivor. "Then the soldiers began shooting again. . . . I lay still, my face covered in blood, and they lifted me and said, 'This one is done,' and threw me on a pile of bodies." Later that night he escaped the village and traveled nine hours on foot to reach the border of Mexico.[74] Throughout the early 1980s, Mexican *campesinos* in Chiapas reported that the rivers flowing from Guatemala were filled with so many corpses—many exhibiting the visible signs of torture—that it became impossible to bury them all. The smell of burning and rotting corpses became an everyday fact of life along the Guatemala-Mexico border.[75]

The army called such actions "scientific killings" designed to eliminate the rebels' base of support. (Many of these atrocities were chronicled by Nobel Peace Prize winner Rigoberta Menchú in her controversial memoir *I, Rigoberta Menchú*.)[76] Survivors and nearby villagers fled deeper into the mountains to avoid a similar fate, or crossed the border into southern Mexico, where they hoped to find refuge among kindred cultural groups. Those who appealed for amnesty or who were caught by the Guatemalan military and allowed to live were "reoriented": interrogated for information on the guerrillas and then subjected to "reeducation" classes for twelve to fifteen hours every day for several months, where they were lectured on the "falsehoods" of the guerrillas' political campaign. Finally, in strategic areas, the so-called *polos de desarrollo,* inhabitants of towns and villages, were relocated to heavily patrolled "model villages," where their actions were strictly regulated.[77]

The government's policy of indoctrination and cultural annihilation continued in the model villages. Residents were allowed to speak only Spanish, and Catholicism and indigenous rituals were strongly discouraged in favor of some form of evangelical Protestantism—particularly that espoused by Ríos Montt himself—that taught subservience to authority.[78] The traditional Maya government was replaced with army-appointed commissioners and the civilian defense patrols that spied on camp residents and controlled the movement of the villagers. As part of the government's rural pacification policy, the Maya populations were forced to engage in public works projects, including rebuilding the structures and communities that the army had so assiduously burned down.[79]

From 1978 to 1984, approximately 100,000 Guatemalans were killed and 40,000 "disappeared" (their whereabouts unknown and presumed dead); 440 villages were destroyed, and 750,000 people internally displaced. Over a quarter-million people fled the country.[80] The Catholic Church was one of the few institutions to denounce the human rights violations. In one of their many official protests, the Conference of Guatemalan Bishops denounced the "massive assassination" of Indians and *campesinos,* as well as the lack of democratic institutions that could guarantee the welfare of the Guatemalan people. "Guatemala has experienced, and continues to live and endure a grave crisis," wrote the bishops in one 1984 document, "and [the country] is sinking further into the abyss."[81] As in El Salvador, clergy, nuns, and missionaries became popular targets for the counterinsurgency units, forcing many to flee the country and form the Guatemalan Church in Exile.[82]

US aid to Guatemala shifted according to human rights reports and the domestic pressure that these elicited. Military aid was temporarily suspended in 1977, but the United States continued to train officers in the Guatemalan armed forces, facilitate corporate investments, and provide humanitarian and development assistance to those in power. After a meeting with General Ríos Montt in Honduras in 1982, President Reagan remarked that Ríos Montt was a man of "great personal integrity" whom human rights monitors had given a "bum rap."[83] Military aid was reinstated a few years later. But in March 1990, under domestic and international pressure, the Bush administration recalled its ambassador in protest over the Guatemalan government's failure to investigate and punish human rights abuses; and military aid once again ceased in 1992.

As with the rest of the United States' Central America policy, its actions in Guatemala drew international criticism, particularly from its neighbors. This time, Canada served as cosponsor of the 1982 UN resolution condemning Guatemala. But to the disappointment of many Canadians, that was as far as Ottawa went to distinguish its foreign policy from that of the Reagan and Bush administrations. Mexico, in turn, was surprisingly less critical of Guatemala's human rights violations than it was of El Salvador's rightist regime, much to the dismay of moderate-to-left groups within Mexico. The silence was inconsistent but pragmatic: the Guatemalan conflict was closer to home and threatened to spill over into Mexico's southern states. Thousands of Maya refugees crossed Mexico's southern border and sought safety in the state of Chiapas, also home to a large Maya population that was actively involved in legal disputes over land and labor. Local and federal officials feared that the refugees would conspire with domestic opposition groups, and debated ways to control the border. The Guatemalan army, in turn, charged that the refugee camps were guerrilla bases and, beginning in 1981, crossed the border into Mexico to kidnap or murder suspected guerrillas. Nationalists demanded that their government stop this brazen violation of their sovereignty, but the Mexican government sent contradictory signals: while filing official diplomatic protests, it assisted Guatemala in its hunt for subversives and deported thousands of refugees. Not surprisingly, much of the rhetoric coming out of Mexico City blamed the country's problems on the United States, but the government was pragmatic enough to avoid any direct confrontation with either the United States or Guatemala. Domestic concerns far outweighed ideological commitments. In this particular instance, Mexico's policy vis-à-vis Guatemala complemented Washington's.

THE REFUGEES

Before 1970, migration within Central America was common. People migrated within and across borders for temporary work in farming, construction, and domestic service. Salvadorans had the longest tradition of cross-border migration, particularly to Honduras, where 350,000 had settled by the end of the 1960s, lured by the higher wages offered by the banana companies.[84] In administering the most densely populated country in Central America, the Salvadoran government encouraged seasonal or permanent migration of rural workers and unemployed urban dwellers as a safety valve to avoid uprisings such as the one that occurred in 1932. In 1967, the Honduran government tried to discourage further Salvadoran immigration through legislation that restricted land ownership to the

Honduran-born and, by mid-1969, through the deportation of three hundred thousand Salvadorans. Hostilities between Hondurans and Salvadorans climaxed in the 1969 "soccer war": violence erupted at a series of soccer matches between the national teams of both countries, giving expression to the resentment that Hondurans had long felt toward the Salvadorans who had migrated illegally to their country and claimed land, especially in the disputed border territories. Thousands were killed and over a hundred thousand people left homeless. In the wake of the war, the countries severed relations with each other, and the Honduran government closed the border to further Salvadoran migration.[85]

Guatemalans, particularly Maya Indians, also had a migratory tradition, especially to Mexico's Soconusco region and Chiapas in general (which had been part of Guatemala until 1824). There they found a Maya and mestizo population that shared cultural similarities. As Mexican workers sought employment in higher-paying industries, the Guatemalans provided the labor critical to the region's agricultural industry: an estimated twenty thousand to one hundred thousand seasonal workers in Mexico each year.[86] Until the 1990s, illegal immigration was tolerated to maintain an abundant pool of low-wage labor for the harvest of coffee beans, sugarcane, and other agricultural products. The border was fluid, and trade, commerce, and family ties extended across national boundaries. Thus the historical, cultural, and commercial ties between Chiapas and Guatemala pointed to the artificiality of the political border.

Migration to more distant countries such as the United States and Canada was less common, although a few thousand Central Americans lived in cities such as Washington, San Francisco, New York, and Miami by end of the 1970s. As the wars escalated, these smaller northern populations served as magnets, encouraging further migration.[87] The 1980 census in the United States, for example, counted 94,447 Salvadorans and 63,073 Guatemalans, and close to half had arrived in the previous five years. The detention of undocumented Central Americans on the United States–Mexico border also increased. In 1977, the first year for which such statistics are available, more than seven thousand Salvadorans and over five thousand Guatemalans were apprehended.[88]

Despite a migratory tradition within the region, the Central American nations were ill prepared to deal with the refugee crisis of 1974–1996. The wars in Central America displaced millions of people and forced them to migrate internally and across borders. As with most migrations, people traveled wherever they had networks of family, friends, or countrymen that could take them in and assist them in finding jobs. They followed established patterns of migration: Salvadorans traveled to Honduras and Guatemala because they had done so for decades; and Guatemalans crossed the border into Chiapas. But with each passing year, populations emerged in less traditional areas of settlement: Salvadorans settled in Mexico, Guatemalans in Belize, and Nicaraguans in Costa Rica. The clustering of several Spanish-speaking countries in a small geographic territory made it comparatively easy for migrants to move and seek safer opportunities elsewhere.

The international press commonly referred to these migrants as refugees because political upheaval played a role in their migration, but their legal status was far from clear and varied from country to country. According to article 1A(2) of the 1951 UN Convention relating to the Status of Refugees, a refugee is a person who "owing to a well-founded fear of persecution for reasons of race, religion, nationality, membership of a particular social group or political opinion, is outside the country of his nationality and is unable, or owing to such fear, is unwilling to avail himself to the protection of that country; or who, not having a nationality and being outside the country of his former habitual residence as a result of such events is unable, or owing to such fear, is unwilling to return to it."[89] Even though most Central American countries were signatories to the UN Convention and/or the 1967 Protocol, and to several regional conventions,[90] the constitutions of most were not encoded with formal procedures through which to recognize refugees or grant asylum. These countries also demonstrated varying levels of commitment to the convention's principles of *non-refoulement* (no forced return) and refugee assistance.

Complicating matters, most Central American migrants did not meet the strict UN definition of refugee status, having fled their countries because of the generalized climate of violence rather than a "well-founded" fear of persecution for the listed categories. By 1980, the United Nations High Commissioner for Refugees (UNHCR) readily admitted that the Convention and Protocol were too restrictive, and advocated a more lenient response to the so-called *nonconvention refugees:* those who did not meet the strict definition of the term but who had fled their homes, crossed an international border, and were living in refugee-like conditions. In May

1981 the UNHCR recommended that all Salvadorans who had left their country since the beginning of 1980 be considered bona fide refugees under a prima facie group determination because they had been displaced by political events and were likely to suffer if physically returned to their homeland.[91] Three years later, the nonbinding Cartagena Declaration tried to offer further guidance in dealing with the Central American refugee crisis. According to the declaration, refugees were "persons who have fled their country because their lives, safety, or liberty have been threatened by generalized violence, foreign aggression, internal conflicts, massive violations of human rights or other circumstances which have seriously disturbed public order."[92]

Each country conducted its own domestic debate on what constituted a refugee, and what types of programs should be made available to those so designated (i.e., asylum or temporary safe haven; resettlement; work authorization; social services, repatriation, etc.). Most governments preferred to view the Nicaraguans, Salvadorans, and Guatemalans living among their populations as economic migrants because it freed them from any responsibility. Statistics compiled by state, private, and international agencies demonstrated how politicized the debate, and the collection and interpretation of migration data, became. In 1982, for example, the US Department of State estimated that 225,000 Guatemalans had been "displaced" by the political turmoil; the Roman Catholic Bishop's Conference of Guatemala, in turn, estimated that as many as 1 million Guatemalans had been displaced.[93] Ironically, agencies often arrived at different statistics using the same sources; for example, using data provided by the Mexican government, the US Department of State concluded that 5,000 Salvadoran refugees were in Mexico, while the UNHCR placed the number at 120,000, and other NGOs estimated as many as half a million.[94] Estimating the number of refugees and displaced persons was an inherently difficult task given the spontaneous and transient nature of this population; [95] but US government statistics were generally much lower than those compiled by the UNHCR and other NGOs because of their stricter definitions of refugee status. As the principal supplier of military aid to Central America, the United States was also reluctant to admit that its policies caused displacement and generated refugees. Instead, they categorized this migration as economically driven, and their statistics reflected this bias. Human rights organizations, in turn, were accused of inflating the numbers to promote their own political agenda, namely, increasing their operational budgets and critiquing state policies. Unfortunately, US government estimates were disproportionately influential in determining the amount of emergency aid available to those affected by the wars: by 1984 the UNHCR received one-third of its funding from the United States, and US contributions were adjusted according to the reports and estimates provided by the country's own State Department.[96]

The lack of protection offered by states, then, became one more means by which migrants became the victims and pawns of foreign policy decisions. Human rights organizations and other NGOs were at times the migrants' only advocates, urging a broader definition of their status that would facilitate their accommodation, and assisting in their temporary or long-term integration into host societies.[97]

In Nicaragua, the first large-scale migration out of the country began during the mid- to late 1970s, when the fighting between Sandinista rebels and the Somoza dictatorship was most intense. An estimated two hundred thousand Nicaraguans fled to other countries during this period, although the majority are believed to have returned after the Sandinista victory in 1979.[98] A second wave of emigrants left after 1979 because of the Sandinistas' policies and/or the upheaval caused by the Contra war. For those who chose to leave the country, wealth, language, availability of transportation, and historical patterns of migration all played a role in determining the country of first asylum. The majority of middle- to upper-class exiles, for example, who perhaps had once studied or vacationed in the United States and had the financial resources to return, traveled to cities like Miami, Los Angeles, and Houston, where they found employment in the large Latino enclaves. Those interested in supporting the counterrevolution were particularly drawn to Miami, where exile groups such as the Nicaraguan Democratic Front were working with the US government to oust the Sandinistas. Other exiles/refugees migrated to neighboring and more familiar Spanish-speaking countries such as Costa Rica, Honduras, and Panama.

The Salvadorans and Guatemalans followed a similar pattern. Those threatened by the warring factions were the most likely to leave. Salvadoran migration increased after October 1979, when the death squads intensified the campaign against the opposition. According to the UNHCR, half a million Salvadorans fled their homeland during the period 1979–1982.

By the end of the 1980s, one million people were estimated to have migrated, and over half a million were internally displaced.[99] In turn, Guatemalan migration increased during 1982–1984, when the governments of Ríos Montt and Mejía Víctores escalated their counterinsurgency campaigns. According to UNHCR estimates, over one million people became internal migrants or refugees in Guatemala during the 1980s. According to US estimates, only one-fourth of the Salvadorans and Guatemalans displaced by the war received assistance, mostly in camps and settlements in Honduras, Costa Rica, and Mexico. The UNHCR placed the number as low as 10 percent.[100]

The countries that bordered Nicaragua, El Salvador, and Guatemala suddenly found themselves reluctant hosts to thousands of refugees. Humanitarian concern for the refugees was tempered by political and economic considerations: politicians feared that comprehensive assistance would encourage the refugees to stay permanently within their borders and increase resentment among nationals, who would have to compete with the refugees for jobs, housing, and social services. The presence of thousands of dissidents and rebels could also potentially destabilize their own countries. Central American governments therefore tried to discourage large-scale migration, and isolated the refugees in rural areas far from their population centers, where they would draw as little attention as possible, and their movement and activities could be controlled. The UNHCR as well as NGOs such as OXFAM, Catholic Relief Services, and the Church World Service played a critical role in helping the region to cope with the refugee crisis. By 1990, an estimated hundred international NGOs and six hundred grassroots NGOs operated in Central America.[101] However, paramilitary groups often equated assistance to refugees and displaced persons with support for guerrilla insurgents, and interfered with the delivery of humanitarian assistance and harassed, arrested, and even murdered aid workers.[102]

The UNHCR advocated resettlement in neighboring countries because such an arrangement would facilitate eventual repatriation. The UNHCR provided millions of dollars in funding to local government agencies to establish camps and to provide emergency food and medical care. Unfortunately, the agency's budget, stretched by refugee crises around the world, limited the amount of assistance it could offer in Central America. The refugee camps that emerged throughout the region varied in quality and in the level of social services. Camps that were designed as a temporary measure became permanent housing; some residents remained in their camps for as long as ten years with limited opportunities for education and recreation. In many cases, camps housed thousands more than they were designed to hold, and individual countries restricted the refugees' movements outside the camps as well as their opportunities to engage in wage-earning labor. International NGOs experimented with "durable solutions"—projects designed to make the refugees self-supporting through farming, artisanry, or industrial shops—but budgetary constraints limited the quality of these programs as well.[103] Not surprisingly, most refugees bypassed these camps altogether. Instead they chose to live as anonymously as possible as illegal immigrants in major cities. Others decided to try their luck further north, seeking employment in the more developed economies of Mexico, the United States, and Canada.

Honduras and Costa Rica provide important—and opposite—case studies of the regional responses to refugee accommodation and assistance. Honduras became one of the principal refugee-recipient nations in Central America, in part because of foreign policy decisions that placed the Contra soldiers and their families in camps on the Honduras-Nicaragua border, but also because of traditional patterns of migration. The Honduran government recognized the UNHCR's principle of *non-refoulement* in its domestic legislation, but did not have formal procedures for determining refugee status.[104] The government (which had reestablished diplomatic relations with El Salvador in 1980) insisted that Salvadoran and Guatemalan refugees live and work in certain zones and not within the general population. The UNHCR established "reception areas" along the border, where refugees were met and transported to one of several camps or supervised settlements, which some likened to concentration camps because of the visible army presence patrolling the zones.[105] These camps included Colomancagua, La Virtud, Guarita, El Amitillo, Guajiniquil, Los Hernandez, and San Antonio, but the largest camp was at Mesa Grande, which offered the most protection from roving Salvadoran army units who frequently crossed the border to kill suspected rebels. By 1983, the camps and settlements housed 18,000 Salvadorans and 550 Guatemalans.[106] The security violations made life extremely difficult, as did the normal tensions, rivalries, and anxieties that accompanied the concentration of people in a small geographic space.[107] The inability to sustain themselves through agriculture, construction, or other trades made the refugees dependent on relief agencies, and this further decreased morale among the camp population. If the Salvadorans left these camps, they forfeited their refugee status and became subject to deportation.

Ironically, Honduran policy toward Salvadorans and Guatemalans stood in direct contrast to the government's treatment of Nicaraguan refugees. Thirteen thousand five hundred Miskito Indians, regarded as political allies in the US-Honduran Contra War, were allowed to settle on agricultural land or work in internationally funded refugee projects, as long as they remained in the Mosquitia region.[108] Nicaraguan *ladinos* were also more favorably treated: they lived in settlements, but unlike the Salvadorans, were granted freedom of movement. By the end of the decade, government sources showed that the number of official refugees from Nicaragua had increased steadily each year but the number of Salvadorans had not, reflecting Honduras's more generous policies toward the former. However, government sources estimated that as many as 230,000 Central Americans lived illegally in Honduras.[109]

The Honduran army carried out its separate immigration policy. Honduran families living along the border were warned by the military not to assist any refugees or aid workers, or they would face reprisals. On May 14, 1980, when four thousand Salvadorans tried to cross the Sumpul River into Honduras to escape the Salvadoran army's campaign in Chalatenango, they were met by the Honduran military and forced to return at gunpoint. More than six hundred people were then massacred by Salvadoran troops.[110] A few months later, in March 1981, seven thousand tried to cross the Lempa River into Honduras to escape the military actions in Cabañas, but as they crossed the river they were shot at by both Salvadoran and Honduran soldiers.

The UNHCR tried to negotiate minimum safeguards for the refugees with local civilian and military authorities, but these agreements were repeatedly violated.[111] Relief workers were continually harassed, and refugees were kidnapped, interrogated, and tortured by Honduran army officers, or turned over to Salvadoran authorities. On August 29, 1985, for example, Honduran soldiers entered the Colomoncagua refugee camp and kidnapped, raped, and murdered some of the residents. In February of the following year Honduran soldiers once again entered Colomoncagua, and this time set up machine guns around the perimeter of the camp, including the soccer field, as a means of surveillance as well as psychologically harassing the camp residents.[112] Hoping that international pressure would force the Honduran and Salvadoran armies to respect refugee rights, the Evangelical Committee for Development and Emergency in Honduras, working with various international NGOs, created a "visitors program": hundreds of volunteers from North America and Europe traveled to Honduras to live and work in the camps, serve as bodyguards, and act as witnesses to the human rights violations. Teams of volunteers patrolled the border and accompanied the refugees as they traveled to the various camps. No army incursions occurred in camps or villages where the international visitors resided; but when the program ended at mid-decade, the kidnapping and torture resumed.[113]

Costa Rica's experience, in turn, demonstrated the difficulties that even stable democracies faced when reconciling national interests with international commitments. Unlike Honduras, no military force patrolled the border of Costa Rica and repatriated refugees at gunpoint.[114] Many of the refugees entered the country with tourist visas, which had to be renewed every thirty days. However, Costa Rica had signed the UN Convention and Protocol,[115] and in 1980 passed a law outlining the criteria for and benefits ascribed to refugee status. According to Costa Rican law, refugee status was temporary but granted recipients basic rights and protections. Only documented refugees were allowed to seek employment, for example, and could lawfully do so as long as they did not displace Costa Rican workers (90 percent of employees in a given enterprise had to be Costa Rican, and receive 85 percent of the salaries). Documented refugees were also eligible for the same government services as nationals (medical care and education, for example). The government established the infrastructure to provide these services, but the cost was borne by international relief agencies. Thus, the Costa Rican government committed itself to humanitarian assistance while protecting its citizens and national resources. The National Commission for Refugees worked with the UNHCR and other international NGOs to coordinate refugee assistance, but was dependent on the financial support that these agencies provided. In 1985 when the UNHCR cut back drastically on its financial aid, the Costa Rican government was forced to make corresponding adjustments in its refugee assistance programs.

An estimated forty thousand Salvadorans and Nicaraguans were assisted in Costa Rica by 1989.[116] According to Hayden some twenty thousand Salvadorans entered the country, most of them arriving between 1980 and 1982, and as many as two-thirds obtained refugee status.[117] A dozen camps were established to house the refugees; international NGOS sponsored durable solutions projects, which were designed to make the refugees self-supporting.[118] Refugees were allowed to seek employment outside these projects but more often than not found the bureaucracy difficult to navigate—a process made deliberately tedious to discourage competition with nationals.[119] Not surprisingly, most refugees who came to Costa Rica bypassed the official refugee network, as they did in other countries; they preferred freedom of movement and economic self-sufficiency in the underground economy, even if it meant forfeiting rights, protections, and services. According to the UNHCR, by 1989, as many as 100,000 Salvadorans and Nicaraguans in Costa Rica lived undocumented. Government agencies placed the number as high as 290,000, 90 percent of which were believed to be Nicaraguan.[120]

As the strongest economy and democracy in Central America, Costa Rica offered migrants safety and opportunities for advancement regardless of their legal status. Thus, refugees who chose to settle here during the 1980s were among the least likely to return to their homelands once repatriation became possible.[121] In 1992, President Rafael Calderón Jr. signed a decree that allowed Central American refugees to legalize their status and apply for permanent residency if they could prove residence in the country for at least two years.[122]

Refugee-producing nations also became refugee-receiving nations. Guatemala, El Salvador, and Nicaragua all signed the UN Convention and Protocol but exhibited different levels of commitment to refugee assistance. An estimated 145,000 Nicaraguans and 70,000 Salvadorans lived in Guatemala by the end of the 1980s, but the government barred UNHCR participation. El Salvador, in turn, did allow the UNHCR to help, and by 1991 the UNHCR had assisted 750 Nicaraguan refugees; however, an estimated 20,000 Central American refugees lived illegally in the country, assisted primarily by the Salvadoran Catholic Church, the International Committee of the Red Cross, and other international NGOs. The Salvadoran Catholic Archdiocese, for example, operated several camps that provided haven for roughly six thousand refugees.[123]

Nicaragua had the most liberal policy: over seven thousand migrants, most of them Salvadorans, received official refugee status and were granted freedom of movement and work permits. With the assistance of the UNHCR, the Sandinistas resettled some three thousand to cooperatives along the Pacific coast. Even though the Nicaraguan government encouraged refugees to regularize their status and become permanent residents, and granted them a host of benefits unavailable in other countries, one study showed that 77 percent wished to return to their homeland, a rate comparable to refugees in other countries.[124] Some twenty thousand lived and worked undocumented during the 1980s, preferring to remain outside the reach of the government.[125]

By 1989, six nations—Costa Rica, Honduras, Nicaragua, El Salvador, Guatemala, and Belize—reported an aggregate eight hundred thousand immigrants, of which 10 percent were officially documented as refugees and received assistance from local governments and international agencies.

THE CENTRAL AMERICAN PEACE PLAN

Most countries in the Western Hemisphere rejected the Reagan administration's categorization of the political conflict as an East-West struggle, and opposed the administration's emphasis on a military solution. In January 1983, representatives from four Latin American governments—Mexico, Panama, Venezuela, and Colombia—met on the island of Contadora, off the coast of Panama, to try to draft a regional peace plan independent of the United States. In 1984 the so-called Contadora Group offered a twenty-one point proposal for a peace settlement that tried to address the concerns of the various parties involved. Included in its list of recommendations were the removal of foreign military advisers from Central America; an end of support to guerrilla movements; and the eventual institution of democratic, pluralist governments, with socioeconomic reconstruction.[126] The proposal was drafted into treaty form and circulated to the nations of the hemisphere for discussion. The following year Argentina, Brazil, Peru, and Uruguay formed the Contadora Support Group (or Grupo de Lima) to lend support for a negotiated peace settlement.

The Reagan administration publicly stated its support for Contadora but undermined the negotiations.[127] The Contadora proposal recognized the legitimacy of the Sandinista government and called for an end to US support for the Contras, which were terms that the administration refused to accept. Administration officials insisted that the Sandinistas could not be trusted to uphold the terms of the peace accords, and the United States would ultimately have to reestablish its military presence in Central America. The Unites States enlisted the aid of Honduras, El Salvador, and Costa Rica (the so-called Tegucigalpa Bloc) to help stall the peace process by challenging individual points in the proposed plan. By the end of 1985, the United States had succeeded in stalling the negotiations.

By 1987, however, a new political climate facilitated the renewal of diplomatic efforts. Throughout the 1980s, the US Congress had become increasingly critical of the Reagan administration's militaristic policies, and by 1987 had significantly reduced aid to the Contras and to El Salvador, eroding Reagan's national mandate. The Sandinistas, in turn, had been able to contain the Contras to the border of Honduras, albeit at great moral and economic cost to their country, and exacerbating the popular discontent that would eventually displace them at the voting booth. In Costa Rica, newly elected president Oscar Arias Sánchez was less willing than his predecessor to allow his country to be used by the United States in their geopolitical agenda. Arias took the initiative and resumed the regional peace talks in 1986 (for which he was later awarded the Nobel Peace Prize). The presidents of El Salvador, Guatemala, Nicaragua, Honduras, and Costa Rica met in Esquipulas, Guatemala. (Interestingly, Esquipulas is home to the shrine of the Black Christ, which attracts the second largest number of pilgrims in the Americas, after Mexico's shrine to Our Lady of Guadalupe. The choice of setting perhaps symbolized regional leaders' hopes—and prayers—for peace.) Finally, on August 7, 1987, the participants signed a peace accord appropriately entitled "Procedure for the Establishment of a Strong and Lasting Peace in Central America" (also called Esquipulas II or Arias Plan.) The peace plan addressed national reconciliation; democratization and free elections; the termination of aid for insurrectionist forces; the nonuse of territory to attack other states; arms control; economic development; international verification and follow-up by UN peacekeeping forces; as well as a timetable for fulfillment of these commitments.

As part of the negotiated settlement, the Contra leadership agreed to a disarmament plan, and the Sandinistas agreed to open and democratic elections and an amnesty program for Contra soldiers who wished to be reintegrated into Nicaraguan society. However, when both parties refused to act in good faith, the five Central American presidents were twice forced to reconvene—in Tesoro, El Salvador (in February 1989), and Tela, Honduras (August 1989), to discuss ways to overcome the impasse. As a result of these meetings, the Sandinistas agreed to move up the scheduled elections to February 1990; to allow opposition parties freedom to organize and campaign; and to allow international observers access to the country to guarantee the fairness of the voting process. In turn, the United States and Honduras were asked to immediately demobilize the Contras. Both nations agreed to cooperate; US cooperation was secured, in part, because of the international outcry that came after the 1989 murder of six Jesuit professors of the Central American University and their two housekeepers.[128] However, when the Contras refused to demobilize, the United Nations Observer Group in Central American (ONUCA), a 625-member peacekeeping agency staffed by Canadians, Spaniards, and West Germans, stepped in to assure compliance along the Nicaragua-Honduras border.[129]

The various multinational accords tried to restore peace and address some of the fundamental issues that had caused civil war. However, in 1990, Central America was worse off economically than prior to the civil wars.[130] Democratization and social and economic reforms have come slowly and unevenly, and some have argued that the accords only served to restore US hegemony in Central America. In February 1990, Violeta Barrios de Chamorro and her UNO coalition assumed the presidency of Nicaragua. The United States finally lifted its economic embargo and provided millions of dollars to help rebuild Nicaragua's war-shattered economy. But many of the social problems that produced war—intense poverty, unemployment, and illiteracy—have continued to plague Nicaragua into the next century. In El Salvador, the guerrillas and the government agreed to a negotiated settlement on December 31, 1991. The electoral process facilitated an FMLN presence in the Salvadoran legislature, but the right-wing ARENA party—the party of D'Aubuisson and other death-squad leaders—continued to dominate Salvadoran politics. In Guatemala, UN-led discussions between the URNG and the government failed until 1996, when a peace accord was finally signed. However, thousands continued to disappear or suffer political violence. In Guatemala there were 1,406 documented violations of human rights in 1996 alone: 112 unlawful executions, 785 assassinations, 302 threats, 179 attempted murders, and 6 cases of torture.[131] Years after the peace accords were signed, people continued to be murdered or "disappeared," among them Guatemalan Bishop Juan Gerardi, who only two days before his death released the Catholic Church's official documentation of human rights abuses during the country's thirty-six-year civil war.[132]

In the Esquipulas II accords, the Central American presidents agreed to address the problems faced by refugees, repatriates, and displaced persons. In May 1989, representatives from the five Central American nations, Belize, and Mexico, as well as the UN general secretary, the UNHCR, and over sixty NGOs working in the region, convened the International Conference on Central American Refugees (CIREFCA), in Guatemala City, to discuss refugee rights, repatriation and integration, and assistance to the internally displaced.[133] In preparation for the conference, each nation evaluated the assistance needed to either integrate or repatriate the refugees and illegal immigrants within its borders.[134] CIREFCA then discussed specific development and assistance projects and ways to attract international funding for these projects.[135] From 1989 to 1992, local and international NGOs channeled 238 million dollars in international funds to assist in the repatriation or reintegration of these populations.[136]

Although small numbers repatriated as early as 1983, full-scale repatriation to Nicaragua, El Salvador, and Guatemala did not begin until each nation had negotiated a cease fire and guaranteed basic rights, including the right to live in safety and without retaliation and the right to participate in the political process. For example, the majority of Nicaraguan refugees who chose to repatriate from Honduras, Costa Rica, and El Salvador did not do so until after the Sandinistas' electoral defeat in February 1990; 25,000 repatriated immediately following the elections, and 71,500 returned by 1993.[137] In El Salvador, 30,000 refugees had returned within a year after the negotiated peace settlement.[138] Similarly, while thousands of Guatemalan refugees had returned from Mexico by 1990, the vast majority returned after the peace accords in 1996.

2

DESIGNING A REFUGEE POLICY

Mexico as Country of First Asylum

> People arrived in long lines, tired, sweaty, pale and sick,
> seeking Don Toño, to ask him for shelter and a little
> food. Some stayed in stables, others at the foot of the
> mountains with makeshift tents against the rain: a multi-
> colored array of plastic sheeting was to be seen every-
> where; bins containing corn and rice were quickly emp-
> tied; there was no longer anything to eat and everywhere
> there were hungry, underfed people, with malaria, tuber-
> culosis and gastrointestinal disorders. They started to die.
>
> FELIPE SÁNCHEZ MARTÍNEZ, COMAR

> For this reason we want you to understand what we
> refugees have suffered, so that you will do us the favor
> and tell all that the murder of Guatemalan *campesinos*
> continues.
>
> GUATEMALAN REFUGEE, January 1984

> The presence of the Guatemalan refugees in Chiapas
> caused us Mexicans to turn our eyes deeper within
> Mexico, reminding us that we also have a southern
> border.
>
> LUIS ORTIZ MONASTERIO, COMAR

Mexico takes pride in its long tradition of accommodating the persecuted
and the displaced. In the twentieth century, over two hundred thousand
people fleeing persecution sought refuge in Mexico. These included Irish,
Turkish Jews, Spanish Republicans, Eastern Europeans, Lebanese, Cubans,
Chileans, Argentines, Brazilians, Dominicans, Uruguayans, and Ameri-
cans.[1] Given this tradition, a long list of intellectuals and political leaders
have exiled themselves to Mexico at some point in their careers: José Martí,
Leon Trotsky, Pablo Neruda, Rómulo Gallegos, Gabriel García Márquez,
Augusto Monterroso, Luis Cardoza y Aragón, Fidel Castro, Héctor
Campora, and Seki Sano. Even César Augusto Sandino and Farabundo
Martí, who inspired the Central American revolutionary movements, lived
for a period of time in Mexico.[2]

Guatemalans, Salvadorans, and to a lesser extent Nicaraguans and Hondurans, are the most recent groups to migrate to Mexico. Of these groups, Guatemalans have the longest tradition of migration, especially to the Soconusco region. There they have worked in the cultivation and harvest of coffee beans, sugarcane, bananas, and other fruits. Their labor has been particularly vital to the Mexican economy since the 1960s. As the young men and women of Chiapas have sought employment in higher-paying industries, the Guatemalans have provided the labor critical to the region's agricultural industry: an estimated twenty thousand to a hundred thousand seasonal workers in Mexico each year.[3] Until the 1990s, illegal immigration was tolerated and even encouraged, to maintain an abundant pool of low-wage labor. The border was fluid, and trade, commerce, and family ties extended across national boundaries. Given these connections, Mexico was a logical destination for the thousands of Maya and *ladino* refugees fleeing Guatemala during the 1980s: it was culturally and geographically accessible, offered safety and economic opportunity, and was close enough to Guatemala to facilitate a quick return once conditions in the homeland improved. These were the same factors that made Mexico an appealing choice for Salvadorans and other Central Americans during the 1980s and 1990s.

The Central Americans were distinct from other twentieth-century immigrants to Mexico simply because of their greater numbers: over two hundred thousand Guatemalans and half a million Salvadorans were believed to be living in Mexico by 1990. With the exception of a few hundred Guatemalan intellectuals who received asylum following the 1954 coup, the majority of Guatemalans who migrated to Mexico were Maya *campesinos*. It was a young population—63 percent were under the age of twenty—and fewer than a quarter of them spoke Spanish.[4] Because of the Guatemalan army's "scorched earth" policies, many arrived in Mexico malnourished, suffering from a variety of diseases and psychological trauma.[5] They settled largely in southern Mexico, especially in the state of Chiapas. The Salvadorans, in turn, were disproportionately young, single males from large towns and cities, who preferred to look for wage-earning opportunities in Mexico's largest cities. Like the Guatemalans, they viewed themselves as temporary residents who hoped to return one day to their homelands, but because of Mexico's restrictive policies, the Salvadorans were more likely to seek refuge further north, in the United States or Canada.

The Central American migration provided Mexico with one of its greatest challenges. For the first time in its history, it was forced into the role of country of first asylum for hundreds of thousands of people fleeing repressive conditions. Like Honduras, Mexico was not a signatory to the UN Convention and Protocol, and thus not bound to accept the Central Americans. It *was* a signatory to two regional conventions—the 1954 Convention on Territorial Asylum and the 1969 American Convention on Human Rights (or San José Pact)—but neither convention legally bound Mexico to accept refugees. The San José Pact did recognize the principle of *non-refoulement* if the refugee's personal liberty was in danger for reasons of race, nationality, religion, social conditions, or political opinions. It was the American Convention on Human Rights that Mexico theoretically violated when it deported thousands of Central Americans in the early 1980s.[6] However, government officials skirted the issue when they argued that the deportees were economic immigrants who had entered the country illegally, and thus were not protected under regional conventions.[7]

Nor did the Mexican Constitution offer a legal mechanism for granting refugee status. Mexican legislation only recognized the category of "persons granted asylum," but asylum was rarely granted—and then only to those who applied from outside the country and could demonstrate that they had been persecuted strictly for political reasons. None of the other UN categories—persecution based on race, religion, nationality, or membership in a particular social group—qualified an applicant for asylum as they did in other countries. In the early 1980s, only one hundred Central Americans were granted the FM-10 visa (asylee), but none were granted this status from 1986 to 1990.[8] An endorsement from the UNHCR (or any other international NGO) did not automatically secure recognition and protection. In 1982, for example, the UNHCR recommended 242 Central Americans for asylum, using Mexico's stricter criteria; of these the Secretaría de Gobernación (Secretariat of the Interior) allowed only 73 to legalize their status, and then mostly through the nonimmigrant FM-3 (visitor visa) or the FM-9 (student visa). Nor did Mexico's support for the Contadora peace proposal and the Declaration of Cartagena, which recommended adherence to the UN Convention and Protocol as a means of addressing the problems of refugees and displaced persons, lead to remedial legislation. However, despite Mexico's exclusionary policies, it accommodated one of the largest numbers of UNHCR-recognized refugees.[9]

It was the Central American refugee crisis—the questions it raised at all levels of society, as well as the pressure directed against the government by the church, the NGOs, and the news media—that forced Mexico's re-examination of its role as a country of safe haven. For decades, the United States–Mexico border and out-migration to the United States had dom-inated all national discussions of migratory issues. Bilateral diplomatic and trade negotiations always inserted some discussion of work visas, illegal immigrants, detention and deportation policies, and/or border control. However, the Central American refugee crisis—and specifically, the crit-icisms directed at Mexico for human rights violations—forced a reexam-ination of state policies. Mexico's credibility and moral authority in the Central American peace initiatives, as well as in migratory issues related to its northern boundary, became dependent on its response to the migra-tion across its southern border.

REFUGEES, "BORDER VISITORS," OR ILLEGAL ALIENS?

The first group of Central Americans to arrive in Mexico during the 1970s, albeit in comparatively small numbers, was the Nicaraguans fleeing the Somoza dictatorship and the Sandinista war. Most of those who com-prised this first wave returned to their homeland. A second wave arrived after 1979, fleeing Sandinista policies and the Contra war, but like their predecessors they received no official recognition or assistance from the Mexican government. Most sources claim that they were simply transit-ing through Mexico on their way to the United States. By 1990, how-ever, a few thousand Nicaraguans were believed to be living and work-ing without documentation in Mexico, particularly in Mexico City, relying on church groups and their networks of family and friends for assistance.[10]

According to UNHCR sources, the Guatemalan refugee migration to Mexico began in 1980. The refugees were mostly Maya Indians, especially Kanjobal, Chuj, Jacalteca, and Mam. They came from the heavily popu-lated departments of El Quiché and Huehuetenango, but also from Petén, San Marcos, Quetzaltenango, Totonicapan, Solola, Chimaltenango, Alta Verapaz, and Baja Verapaz. These departments were regarded by the gov-ernment as the seat of the guerrilla movement, and thus targeted by the counterinsurgency campaign. It was a communal migration: the surviv-ing members of families and communities migrated and settled together just across the six-hundred–mile Guatemala-Mexico border.[11]

During the first months, it was not uncommon for Guatemalan refugees to travel back and forth from their Mexican settlements to their villages (or what remained of them) to determine if it was safe to return to their homeland. But by 1982 and the escalation of Ríos Montt's counterinsurgency campaign, such trips became impossible. Instead, out-migration increased dramatically. In July 1982, the first month of Ríos Montt's counterinsurgency campaign, nine thousand families fled to Chiapas. One report estimated that by 1983 thirty-five thousand Guatemalans had taken refuge just across the border of Mexico, with an additional seventy thousand believed to be living deeper within the country. Another report estimated as many as two hundred thousand Guatemalan refugees in Mexico.[12] Most hid in the jungles of Guatemala until it was safe to cross the "armed curtain" of Guatemalan soldiers that by 1982 patrolled the Guatemala-Mexico border. With the support of Mexican villagers and small landholders who gave them tents, food, and clothing, they squatted on *ejidos* and private lands, creating their own makeshift settlements.

The historical, cultural, and commercial ties between Chiapas and Guatemala made this six-hundred-mile stretch of land an artificial border. Until 1824 Chiapas was Guatemalan territory, and its loss to Mexico wounded Guatemala's national psyche comparably to Mexico's 1848 loss of northern territories to the United States. Indeed, significant comparisons could be made between the two borderlands. Throughout the nineteenth and twentieth centuries, Guatemalans crossed easily into Mexico to work, trade, and intermarry, just as Mexicans crossed easily into the US Southwest. As in the United States, the migrants were either tolerated or deported, depending on economic conditions and pressure from local interest groups. However, Guatemalan migration differed in that it was a largely indigenous migration, and in Chiapas, migrants found a Maya and mestizo population that shared cultural similarities and a land that was not unlike that which they had left behind.[13] Historically, the border between Guatemala and Mexico was poorly guarded, in part because of diplomatic policy considerations and limited manpower and resources, but also because of pressure from Mexican growers, who depended on this exploitable labor force.

Because of their small numbers, the first refugees from Guatemala were believed to be part of the usual seasonal migration of undocumented agricultural workers. The Roman Catholic clergy and missionaries were among the first to witness their trauma and to recognize and assist them as refugees. As new settlements emerged in Chiapas, creating a type of "refugee zone" along the border, the different state and federal agencies debated policy and what measures constituted an appropriate governmental response. As one Mexican official told the *New York Times,* "We've never had to face something like this before and it has taken time to adjust."[14]

The refugees technically came under the jurisdiction of the Secretaría de Gobernación and its Servicios Migratorios (Migratory Services). Given the uniqueness of the situation, in July 1980 the López Portillo administration established a new interdepartmental office, the Mexican Committee for Refugee Assistance (COMAR), with a threefold mission: to oversee emergency assistance to the Central American refugees; to provide them with political representation; and to design temporary and long-term projects for employment and self-sufficiency.[15] In theory, COMAR represented and coordinated the interests and policies of the Secretariats of Foreign Relations, Labor and Social Welfare, and the Interior, and consulted with the Secretariat of Defense. In practice, however, each of these secretariats had its own agenda and maintained contradictory policies that were impossible to coordinate.

The Secretaría de Gobernación and Servicios Migratorios took a more hard-line position than COMAR and the Secretaría de Relaciones Exteriores (Secretariat of Foreign Relations). Officials in the Secretaría de Gobernación acted on the assumption that the Central Americans were economic migrants, and routinely used the press to accuse the refugees of taking jobs and land away from Mexican citizens. Their position was starkly exemplified by Diana Torres Arcieniega, the director of Servicios Migratorios, who blamed all of Mexico's social problems on the refugees, including the social disintegration, poverty, promiscuity, ignorance, delinquency, and violence in Mexican society.[16] COMAR, on the other hand, acted on the premise that the Central Americans were fleeing repressive conditions and deserved the generosity of the state. Likewise, officials in the Secretaría de Relaciones Exteriores argued that Mexico had "international responsibilities" and warned of the foreign policy implications of any official response.[17] During the early 1980s, the hard-line position predominated, in part because of Mexico's economic crisis, which made immigration an unpopular topic. Two thousand refugees were expelled from Mexico in 1981 and thirty-five hundred in 1982, violating the principle of *non-refoulement*. Refugees suspected of being guerrillas were routinely handed over to Guatemalan authorities.[18] By 1983, COMAR had been subsumed into the Secretaría de Gobernación, theoretically to better coordinate assistance to the refugees, but also to control any dissident voices that challenged official government policy.

The Mexican government initially resisted any involvement from the UNHCR and other international NGOs, citing its sovereign right to resolve its own domestic affairs. Financial pressures forced a reevaluation of this position, and in 1981, a cooperative agreement was signed stating that aid programs would be designed and financed with the assistance of the UNHCR but coordinated and channeled through COMAR.[19] Soon after, the UNHCR established an official representation in Mexico City. Over the next decade, the UNHCR provided millions of dollars in aid (e.g. food, construction materials, housing supplies, educational materials, and salaries for refugee assistance personnel) to the Guatemalan refugees in Chiapas, and assisted Central Americans dispersed throughout the country, albeit indirectly, by assisting the Mexican NGOs that provided them assistance in rural and urban areas.[20] But the UNHCR was careful not to speak against state policies, or challenge the government in any way, or sabotage the agency's already precarious position.

Mexico agreed to accept Guatemalans as long as they were approved and registered by COMAR, and remained in government-supervised camps and settlements in Chiapas. Those who did so were granted ninety-day renewable visas, the FM-8, which offered them the temporary, non-immigrant status of "border visitor." Under the terms of their negotiations, if the Guatemalans traveled beyond the 150-kilometer refugee zone, they received no official status and forfeited their rights to protection.[21] Central Americans outside Chiapas who contacted the UNHCR for assistance in securing asylum were interviewed and evaluated according to Mexico's stricter criteria, but Mexican authorities ultimately made the final determination, and these decisions were highly subjective. Although the news media and church and NGO representatives commonly referred to the Guatemalans as refugees, Mexico did not have the legal mechanism by which to grant this official status. And despite the continual arrival of refugees each week, the administrations of José López Portillo and his successor, Miguel de la Madrid (1982–1988), resisted drafting new refugee or asylum legislation or signing the UN Convention and Protocol, arguing that the Mexican Constitution offered its "border visitors" sufficient rights and guarantees. Ironically, since the word *refugee* did not appear in Mexican law, Mexico officially had no refugees within its borders, only "border visitors" and "agricultural workers."[22] And since there were no refugees, these border visitors had little chance of regularizing their status and becoming permanent residents.

The one issue in which the UNHCR seems to have exerted the most influence during these early years concerned a proposed relocation to third countries. The UNHCR opposed such a policy, except when a refugee specifically requested it, because it made the eventual repatriation of the refugees difficult, if not impossible. Given the uniqueness of the Maya refugees—many of whom did not even identify themselves as members of a nation-state—the Mexican government agreed that it was in their interests to temporarily accommodate them in familiar surroundings until they were able to return to their ancestral lands. As one COMAR director stated, "I believe that receiving and protecting indigenous groups has, and will have, enormous historical significance for Mexico and Central America."[23] During the 1980s, the UNHCR relocated a few thousand Central Americans to third countries such as Canada and Australia, but only those that requested the transfer.[24]

By 1984, ninety-two camps and settlements housed forty-six thousand refugees in Chiapas. Access to the camps was restricted: armed agents of Servicios Migratorios patrolled each camp, and only church and UNHCR representatives were granted permission to enter the areas.[25] The Mexican government restricted the involvement of other NGOs in the camps, claiming that assistance was adequately provided by the UNHCR and COMAR. Maintaining national sovereignty was an equally important consideration, as was buffering the government from international criticism. "In Mexico we are not accepting either direct or bilateral assistance from another government or from the NGOs," said COMAR coordinator Oscar González. "[The NGOs] wish to maintain a physical presence in the areas where refugees are assisted, and there's no reason for that. We function in a totally open manner and with an infrastructure that adequately allows the Mexican state to deal with the situation."[26]

The camps and settlements were located in three principal areas: the first area extended from Tapachula to Comalapa; the second included the municipalities of La Trinitaria, Las Margaritas, and Independencia; and the third area, the most populous, consisted of the municipality of Ocosingo.[27] The settlements in Las Margaritas and the Lancandón jungle were the most difficult to assist because of their geographic isolation. Aid was flown in by single-engine plane or transported by canoe, jeep, or pack mules. Conditions in all the settlements and camps were poor, reflecting the general poverty of Chiapas, the UNHCR's stretched budget, and to some extent, government policy. Refugee assistance personnel accused the Mexican government of deliberately making conditions as disagreeable as possible in order to discourage further migration. They also accused some COMAR officials of corruption, charging that UNHCR aid, especially food, was not reaching its intended destination (a charge that eventually contributed to a restructuring of the organization in 1983).[28] Clearly, domestic policy considerations played some role in the amount of aid that was directed to the camps. Government officials wished to prevent the resentment and conflict that would inevitably follow if refugee aid exceeded the amount of social services available to the local population in Mexico's poorest state.[29] At the same time, the government viewed repatriation as the long-term goal of refugee assistance, and thus little emphasis was given to projects that offered "durable solutions" or opportunities for long-term integration into Mexican society. Whatever the government's rationale, UNHCR personnel learned not to challenge the Mexican government. When Pierre Jambor, the UNHCR representative in Mexico, was viewed as too interfering, Mexico filed an official complaint with the UNHCR and soon after Jambor was replaced.

The refugees provided aid workers with a number of challenges. They arrived malnourished and with a host of gastrointestinal and respiratory illnesses. Infant mortality was estimated at two hundred deaths per thousand live births. Doctors, nurses, and midwives from regional clinics and hospitals volunteered and found a population in dire need of health care but distrustful of state-sponsored medicine. In order to halt the spread of disease, aid workers worked around the clock to build wells, sewers, and latrines in settlements that seemed to spring up virtually overnight.[30]

Refugees were directed to government-run camps, but COMAR also allowed refugees to establish their own settlements, usually consisting of individuals from the same village or language group, in order to encourage the survival of communities and traditional forms of self-government. Residents were allowed to play a role in planning and organizing schools, health care, and cultural and recreational activities.[31] However, the camps and settlements offered few opportunities for wage-earning labor, land cultivation, or vocational training. The refugees did not qualify for work permits, but in some areas local authorities allowed them to engage in wage-earning agricultural work, which unfortunately also exposed them to exploitation.[32] The Roman Catholic Diocese of San Cristóbal de las Casas reported that over the years the generosity demonstrated by the local Mexican population began to wane, and some *ejidatarios* (members of cooperatives) began to treat the refugees as servants and *peones,* punishing them by withholding wages.[33] Not surprisingly, the majority of Guatemalans who arrived in Mexico preferred to remain outside the government's reach, relying instead on their own networks for survival.[34]

The refugees also presented the Mexican government with one of its most serious diplomatic challenges of the late twentieth century. The governments of Romeo Lucas García and later Efraín Ríos Montt and Oscar Mejía Víctores claimed that guerrillas used the refugee camps and settlements to channel weapons, food, and medicine to their compatriots-in-arms. The Guatemalan government demanded that Mexico repatriate the refugees, or at the very least relocate them further away from the border zone. When the Mexican government failed to act decisively either way, the Guatemalan army expanded its counterinsurgency campaign into Mexico. From 1982 to 1984, the counterinsurgency units, known as the *kaibiles,* crossed the border to kidnap, interrogate, and murder alleged guerrillas and their supporters, and Guatemalan planes and helicopters strafed or bombed refugee camps and settlements to intimidate the population.[35] From May 1980 to May 1983, the Guatemalan army conducted sixty-eight incursions into Mexican territory: nine Guatemalan refugees and seven Mexican farm workers were killed; twenty Guatemalans kidnapped; and seven detained, beaten, and/or tortured.[36] However, the casualties were underreported, the Diocese of San Cristóbal claimed, because of the isolation of the refugee settlements and the Mexican government's militarization of Chiapas, which restricted access to the camps and to information. The raids occurred regularly along the border and sometimes several miles into Mexican territory, terrorizing the refugees and the local population, and forcing thousands to flee into the jungles or further inward.[37]

The Guatemalan army was assisted in its actions by Mexican allies, some of them on the government payroll. In 1982, for example, in Ciudad

Cuauhtémoc, Chiapas, the local director of Servicios Migratorios, César Morales, unilaterally decided to continue deporting Guatemalans en masse, whether or not they had protected status. Gobernación eventually transferred Morales out of the area but only after COMAR officials threatened to withdraw.[38] Refugees were often detained and starved and tortured while interrogated.[39] Soldiers, lawyers and prosecutors, and local police and security guards were implicated in these actions.[40] Local *caciques* (power brokers), many of them wealthy ranchers and growers, also conducted their own immigration policy. Fearing the impact leftist guerrillas might have on Chiapas's politics and economy, they funded their own paramilitary groups, popularly referred to as the Guardias Blancas (White Guards), to safeguard their interests. The Guardias kidnapped and murdered refugees, clergy, and aid workers suspected of guerrilla sympathies.[41] In March 1982, for example, the Reverend Hipólito Cervantes Arceo, the parish priest of Mapastepec, was found murdered, both thumbs tied behind his back and his head beaten in with a church statue.[42] Local government officials claimed that he had been a victim of robbery, but residents and church officials blamed the paramilitaries as well as the government that gave them carte blanche to operate. Over the next few years, dozens of clergy, nuns, and aid workers were threatened, kidnapped, and assaulted. In June 1984, for example, Mexican police kidnapped three aid workers from the Puerto Rico camp, a doctor and two nuns, and transported them to secret locations, where they were bound, blindfolded, and interrogated at length on their—and the church's—suspected ties to guerrillas.[43]

The Mexican government clearly feared the role the refugees might play in destabilizing the state of Chiapas, which in spite of its poverty was of strategic importance to Mexico's long-term development programs. Chiapas was the agricultural heartland of southern Mexico, producing coffee, corn, cacao, tobacco, sugar, fruit, vegetables, and honey for export. It was also a key state for the nation's petrochemical and hydroelectric industries. By 1990, 82 percent of PEMEX's petrochemical plants were located in southeastern Mexico; and 21 percent of Mexico's oil and 47 percent of its natural gas were extracted in the Chiapas-Tabasco region.[44] Fifty-five percent of the nation's hydroelectric energy and 20 percent of its electricity were produced in Chiapas. Corporations made enormous profits from the land and the labor, but contrary to the federal government's assurances, the wealth did not "trickle down" to the municipalities. In 1990, two-thirds of Chiapas's 3.5 million residents did not have sewage service, and half did not have potable water. Despite its energy production, only a third of the homes in the state had electricity. More than half of the schools in the state offered only a third-grade education, and seventy-two out of every hundred children dropped out of school by the first grade. There were more hotel rooms for tourists than hospital beds for the local population (seven hotel rooms per thousand tourists versus 0.2 hospital beds for every thousand inhabitants). Each year during the 1980s over fourteen thousand people died—most of them from curable diseases such as malaria, dengue, measles, and gastroenteritis—who could have been treated if there had been more doctors, clinics and hospitals, and paved roads to facilitate transportation.[45]

The indigenous people, numbering over half a million, were overrepresented in the poverty rolls in Chiapas. A 1983 study by National Bank of Mexico warned that the continued exploitation of the indigenous peoples would potentially lead to rebellion. As recent Central American history suggested, the unequal distribution of power and economic resources made Chiapas receptive soil for revolutionary movements—or so the elites feared. Its geographic proximity to the centers of revolution in Central America, and its large and historically exploited population, who saw in the refugees a mirror image of their own experience, contributed to Chiapas's potentially volatile state. (Not surprisingly, when the Zapatista rebellion began in Chiapas on January 1, 1994, demanding a variety of legal reforms, local officials initially blamed the insurrection on Central American leftists in the refugee population.)[46] Mexican journalists reported on the unequal power relationships as they played out in land and labor struggles involving the actions of big landowners, the corruption of agrarian officials, and the delays in implementing agrarian reform. Often these articles were juxtaposed with reportage on the wars in Central America as if warning the Mexican population of their fate.[47]

The federal and state governments, corporate interests, and local elites took a keen interest in containing the spread of revolutionary ideas, and in so doing, trumped Mexico's own revolutionary heritage. Indeed, Mexico's 1917 Constitution, regarded as a model in Latin America, enumerated social and economic guarantees and protections that were not extended to the refugee population. The government contained the refugees' influence physically, in state-monitored and geographically isolated refugee camps and settlements, but also symbolically, through intimidation and the threat of violence and deportation. In order to protect its international reputation, the Mexican government discouraged international observers from visiting the camps and settlements.[48] Army barricades were a common sight on the major roads and highways in Chiapas, and those few who were allowed entry to the refugee camps faced yet other discouragements, namely, the remoteness and inaccessibility of many of them. The limited information that came out of the region during the 1980s came largely from the Roman Catholic Dioceses of San Cristóbal de las Casas and Tapachula, which publicized the refugees' cause and provided the few journalists with contacts and information.

In 1983, the government assumed a more aggressive immigration policy. Under the direction of Mario Vallejo, who at one point headed both Servicios Migratorios and COMAR, more than a hundred additional immigration agents were sent to Chiapas to assist in the roundup of illegal Central Americans.[49] The requirements for tourist visas were also stiffened. As further sign of the government's concerns about Chiapas, the de la Madrid administration announced a new "development" program, Plan Chiapas: to construct new roads, ports, and a major airport and theoretically to increase production and trade, as well as opportunities for wage-earning labor and upward mobility. However, for many *campesinos,* who had never benefited from such programs in the past, development programs were simply another pretence of redressing exploitation. Not surprisingly, by the time the Zapatistas launched their war against the Mexican government ten years later, Plan Chiapas had failed to significantly change any of the socioeconomic indicators.

The administrations of José López Portillo and Miguel de la Madrid were pressured by a wide range of domestic groups each arguing for a specific policy response. In favor of limiting the number of refugees were the conservative news media (e.g., Televisa, *Impacto, El Heraldo, Summa, Ovaciones*); the major rival opposition party (Partido de Acción Nacional); and ranchers and growers in Chiapas, who increasingly associated the refugees with the Mexican *campesinos'* land reclamation efforts and the challenges to their authority. More than a few editorialists explored the destabilizing long-term influence the new immigrants might have on Mexican society. One editorial compared the Guatemalan migration to the colonization efforts of North American immigrants in Texas in the first half of the nineteenth century.[50] Also supporting immigration restriction was the Reagan administration, which feared not only the expansion of revolution into Mexico but also the Central American transmigration through Mexico to the United States.

Defending refugee rights, in turn, were the more liberal sectors of the Roman Catholic Church, particularly the Diocese of San Cristóbal de las Casas (the fourth oldest diocese in Mexico) and its bishop, Samuel Ruiz García. "Solidarity committees" such as the Movimiento Mexicano de Solidaridad con el Pueblo de Guatemala and the Comité Mexicano de Solidaridad con el Pueblo Salvadoreño emerged to lobby on behalf of the refugees. Four of Mexico's political parties made pronouncements in defense of refugee rights;[51] and the moderate-to-liberal press, especially Mexico City's *La Jornada,* published sympathetic articles and editorials reminding the government of its international responsibilities.[52]

Given the Mexican government's critiques of right-wing regimes, many found its reserve toward Guatemala surprising, especially in light of the incursions into Mexican territory and attacks on Mexican citizens. However, policy was tempered by the reality of a six-hundred-mile shared border: any diplomatic or military response would have domestic consequences. A military response would also compromise Mexico's leadership role in the regional peace initiatives. A diplomatic solution was made particularly difficult by Guatemala's long-standing grievances about territorial boundaries, trade, commerce, and labor.[53] One editorial in the Mexican press warned:

> We need to be courteous and even affectionate with our brothers to the south, but we must also treat them with kid gloves. We must support them in all reasonable causes in the international arena. We must give them preferential treatment so they can sell the few surplus products that we need here. We must facilitate the entrance of their tourists and their students so that they can continue to educate themselves here. But we should not invest in Central America, and above all we should not try to influence their internal affairs. We should follow the precept that we so readily proclaim: nonintervention.[54]

At first, Mexican officials avoided any public condemnation of Guatemala. When asked to comment on the border raids, for example, Luis Ortiz

Monasterio, the director of COMAR (1981–1983), simply noted, "We have established a causal relationship between reports of burnings of and attacks on villages and the arrival of refugees in Mexican territory."[55] Likewise, the government's failure to draft new legislation to offer the Guatemalans refugee status or asylum was an attempt to remain neutral, because such refugee assistance would be interpreted as a condemnation of the Guatemalan state. Protests were largely symbolic. Twice López Portillo canceled goodwill trips to Guatemala (one of the trips after threats of assassination by ultra-right-wing groups in Guatemala), which the Secretaría de Relaciones Exteriores called "postponements" to allow for the possibility of renewed diplomacy.[56] And in 1982, Foreign Minister Jorge Castañeda de la Rosa delivered seven official protests to the Guatemalan ambassador in Mexico City. In his fifth "state of the union" address, López Portillo commented on Mexican foreign policy, especially with regard to El Salvador, Nicaragua, Cuba, and a number of other countries, but conspicuously absent from his speech was any reference to the troubles with Guatemala.[57]

Officials in the Secretarías de Defensa and Gobernación sent equally mixed messages. At the same time that COMAR was establishing dozens of camps and settlements, Servicios Migratorios increased its deportation of undocumented Guatemalans, deporting between 250 to 1,000 each week via Talismán and Ciudad Hidalgo.[58] Under pressure from the governor of Chiapas, the Mexican army increased its helicopter surveillance of the region, but this offered the refugees and local population little protection or assurance.[59] Indeed, there was growing evidence that the Secretaría de Defensa was assisting the Guatemalan government in its hunt for subversives. In 1982, Guatemala's defense minister, General Oscar Mejía Víctores (who several months later replaced Ríos Montt), was invited to observe the Independence Day military parade, a gesture that supporters interpreted as cautious goodwill diplomacy and critics interpreted as complicity.[60]

In June 1983, partly in response to US pressure to improve its human rights record, the Guatemalan government announced an amnesty program and initiated a campaign to convince the refugees to return to Guatemala. Guatemalan radio stations broadcast news of the amnesty across the border, while the Guatemalan consul in Comitán broadcast his own messages on Mexican radio stations, assuring refugees that their safety would be guaranteed by the International Red Cross. Members of the Guatemalan civil patrols and missionaries of the fundamentalist sect Gospel Outreach (to which General Ríos Montt belonged) entered the camps and settlements to persuade the refugees to return home. However, there was no cessation of violence that might have persuaded the refugees to return. The *kaibiles* continued to intimidate, raid, and bomb on both sides of the border;[61] and Ríos Montt himself warned that if the refugees did not take advantage of the amnesty program, the state would "come in and get them." Not surprisingly, the campaign failed to convince any sizable number of refugees that Guatemala's "model villages" provided a safer alternative.

By 1984 COMAR publicly advocated that the government relocate the refugees to other parts of Mexico as a means of protecting them from continued attacks. The Dioceses of San Cristóbal and Tapachula and Mexican *campesino* organizations also supported the idea of relocation, but only if the refugees accepted the idea, and only to other parts of Chiapas, more distant from the border. Relocation to other states, they argued, would undermine cultural identity and community networks of the refugees.[62] In January 1984, COMAR secured government permission to relocate five thousand refugees from six border camps to the Ixcán camp in Ocosingo, and asked diocesan officials for help. These officials opposed the move on the grounds that the Ixcán population would grow to ten thousand: too large a concentration of people in a small and fairly inaccessible geographic area.[63] After months of debate between the different parties, COMAR abandoned this specific plan but continued to press the case for relocation.

On April 29, 1984, COMAR once again argued the point in a communiqué sent to the Secretaría de Gobernación. In a sad twist of fate, the very next day over two hundred Guatemalan troops (accompanied by an undetermined number of people dressed in civilian clothing) attacked El Chupadero refugee camp, one of the most violent attacks of the 1980s. The attack began at 2:10 in the morning and lasted five hours. According to one eyewitness: "Everywhere was confusion. The children—our children—fled to the hills. You could hear cries of pain. Our wives searched for the children while they, too, fled. Everything was dark and we kept hearing shots. The shooting continued, and we don't know when it ended, but we heard it for hours. We all fled to the *ejido* of Las Delicias, two kilometers from El Chupadero, because we knew that the *pintos* would not dare follow us there."[64] Seven of the camp's four thousand residents were killed and dozens injured. According to the press, the bodies of the victims were savagely beaten or mutilated. A boy was found shot in the head, his ears and genitals severed; a woman, eight months pregnant, and her elderly father were clubbed to death. Overnight the settlement ceased to exist when thousands fled to the Mexican *ejido* of Las Delicias, in the municipality of La Trinitaria, twenty kilometers from the border. Hundreds of Mexican citizens in Las Delicias, in turn, fled the area, fearing they might be caught in the crossfire if the Guatemalan military followed the refugees there. Mexican residents demanded that their government either increase its military presence in the region or relocate the refugees. In the days following the attack, refugees from other camps and settlements, including those at Nuevo Iztlán, Ciudad Cuauhtémoc, and Cienegüita, fled further inward to avoid the fate of El Chupadero.[65]

As was their modus operandi, the Guatemalan government denied any involvement, blaming the raid on the leftist guerrillas. The Guatemalan ambassador to Mexico cynically demanded that Mexico conduct an investigation: "A country that admits refugees from another nation is judicially and politically compromised to secure their safety."[66] The Mexican government was initially slow to respond, trying to prevent the escalation of tensions. But on May 5, with sufficient evidence of the Guatemalan army's involvement, President Miguel de la Madrid sent an official protest to Guatemala, demanding an immediate investigation of the case and the identification and punishment of the guilty parties. However, Guatemala scored an important victory: the Mexican government also announced that in the interest of national security and the refugees' own protection, the camps and settlements in Chiapas would be shut down and the refugees relocated to Campeche, Quintana Roo, and possibly Tabasco and Veracruz. New offices and checkpoints would also be established along the border to better assess and control the influx of Guatemalans.[67]

Relocation to Campeche and other states had its supporters. The new Guatemalan Commission on Human Rights announced that it supported Mexico's decision to relocate the refugees but warned that the move would not stem the flow of refugees escaping the military's repressive tactics. The Conferencia Episcopal Mexicana also declared its support for the new policy but urged the government not to close the border with Guatemala because "the social and political problems lived by the Guatemalans [had] not been resolved."[68] However, the relocation announcement pitted the Mexican government against the Roman Catholic Church in Chiapas, the

UNHCR, the refugees, and even some COMAR aid workers, who re-signed in protest. Of these, the UNHCR adopted the most measured response, recognizing Mexico's sovereign right to relocate the refugees, but opposing the use of force against those who did not want to move.[69] The Roman Catholic Diocese of San Cristóbal de las Casas and specifically its bishop, Samuel Ruiz García, were the most vocally critical—of Guatemala, the UNHCR, as well as Mexican government policy. After the attack on El Chupadero, Ruiz condemned Guatemala for trying to provoke Mexico into a military response: "As Christians, we cannot fail to condemn these actions for all they represent: aggression toward a peaceful people in the late hours of the night; a flagrant violation of our national territory; human degradation in the assassination and mutilation of even the youngest of victims . . . all of which easily presupposes the weakening and even nonexistence of respect for human rights in our brother country, Guatemala."[70] Ruiz also criticized the UNHCR's failure to condemn Guatemala and to defend the refugees' rights to remain in Chiapas, which rendered it, he said, a "useless body."[71] Joined by the bishops of Oaxaca (Bartolomé Carrasco and Jesús Alba Palacios) and Huautla and Tehuantepec (Hermenegildo Ramírez and Arturo Lona Reyes), Ruiz issued a public statement asking the Mexican government to reconsider the forced relocation of the refugees. As an alternative, these bishops once again offered to assist the Mexican government in identifying land in Chiapas where the refugees could become self-sufficient without dislocating Mexican nationals.

Representatives from over twenty religious organizations signed an open letter requesting that the government reconsider its new policy. The Movimiento Mexicano de Solidaridad con el Pueblo de Guatemala declared the government's proposal antihumanitarian, especially because it abolished the camps that could serve as a temporary safe haven for the refugees that continued to arrive each week.[72] The refugees themselves sent letters to COMAR, the UNHCR, the Secretaría de Gobernación, and President Miguel de la Madrid, asking that they be allowed to remain in Chiapas. In Campeche and Quintana Roo, they argued, their families, communities, and cultures would disintegrate, and repatriation would become impossible. They attached letters of support from Mexican *ejidatarios* and the *asambleas ejidales* to demonstrate the cooperation and support of local Mexican citizens.[73]

The government defended its policy in different ways to different constituencies. To a wary refugee population, Gobernación framed the policy discussions around the issues of preservation of family and community and the opportunities for self-sufficiency. In the safety of Campeche and Quintana Roo, officials argued, the refugees would be better able to preserve their families and their ethnic and communal values because they would have wage-earning opportunities that were nonexistent in Chiapas. The government would grant them one-year renewable FM-3 visas, which would allow them to engage in paid agricultural work or artisanry at much higher wages than they could earn in Chiapas. The governor of Campeche, Eugenio Echevarría Castellot, also sent his personal assurances that refugee labor would not be exploited. "In Mexico no one is exploited," he insisted.[74] Refugee leaders were urged to travel to Campeche and Quintana Roo to assess their new environment and meet with Central Americans who had settled in these states. Four hundred representatives accepted the invitation, but returned to Chiapas with mixed reactions. The majority resolved not to relocate because of the unfamiliar and inferior quality of the land, as well as lack of housing and basic social services.[75]

To their most vocal critics in the church, the government framed the discussion within the larger context of human rights: "Maintaining the refugee population indefinitely in isolation and inactivity constitutes a violation of their human dignity," said one letter. "Relocation allows their incorporation into a worthy and productive environment."[76] To the general public, Gobernación framed the discussion around nationalist concerns about employment and wages, security and sovereignty. The government assured citizens that the states of Campeche and Quintana Roo were in dire need of agricultural laborers, and thus the refugees would not compete with Mexican labor.[77] In a meeting with Mexico City newspaper editors, Secretary of Gobernación Manuel Bartlett underscored the threat the border settlements posed to Mexico's long-term security. It wasn't just the raids by the Guatemalan army that threatened the stability of the nation, he said. Dozens of settlements had emerged on Mexican soil that housed no Mexican citizens and functioned independently of Mexican authority. With no loyalty or ties to the state, such communities posed a potential threat not only to Chiapas but also to the greater national good.[78]

However, many citizens remained unconvinced by these arguments, and decried the lack of information. One editorial in *Unomásuno* stated:

This cautious and accommodationist policy toward the repressive Guatemalan military regime suggests a concept of national security that public opinion is obligated to question and debate: Do the Guatemalan refugees really present a burden for Mexico and a threat to national security? Does relocating them from Chiapas truly honor our political and humanitarian commitments and help to prevent actions against our country? How will the government respond to the new refugees who will most certainly arrive? Will we prevent them from settling here and through what means? Is the delinquent and repressive government of Guatemala a friend of Mexico and the appropriate delegate to determine the futures of these unfortunate beings? If not the Guatemalan military, who, then, violates Mexican sovereignty? Whose interests do these attacks serve? These are only a few of the many questions that Mexican authorities must answer before the public. Mexican sovereignty is in danger, and we must defend it with frank and open debate.[79]

A number of less-publicized considerations made relocation to Campeche and Quintana Roo an attractive solution for the government. These states were generally more conservative politically and of less strategic importance to the country's overall economic development, counteracting the radicalizing influence the refugees might potentially exert on local populations. Even the Catholic Church here was more conservative—a welcome change from the Diocese of San Cristóbal de las Casas. The bishop of Campeche, Héctor González Martínez, reluctantly accepted the relocation but urged the government to take steps to "prevent the infiltration of disintegrative elements that reject our national values and instead favor the disintegration of the homeland."[80] The decision to relocate the refugees also made sense in light of Mexico's role in the Contadora peace initiatives. Guatemala had warned that its participation in peace talks was in part dependent on the relocation and/or repatriation of the refugees from the border. Thus, in agreeing to relocate the refugees, Mexico's leadership role in the peace process was validated.

The government warned the refugees that they would be relocated by force if necessary. Their only other option was repatriation. In a meeting between COMAR director Oscar González and the camp representatives, González warned that COMAR would withhold all protection if they failed to relocate.[81] Among the first targeted for relocation were the residents of El Chupadero and Puerto Rico, which had been singled out by the *kaibiles*. Despite these warnings, most refused to relocate. Four thousand of the six thousand residents in the Puerto Rico refugee camp, the largest in Chiapas, crossed the Lacantún River and hid in the Lacandón jungle. Refugees from Chajul, Loma Bonita, and Ixcán followed them, while twenty-five hundred residents of Las Delicias fled twenty-five miles to San Caralampio Huanacaston.[82] When mediation failed to convince the refugees to relocate, the government used more repressive tactics: they prohibited Mexican *campesinos* from hiring refugee labor; withheld shipments of food and medicine to the settlements; established a blockade to starve the refugees out of the jungle; and threatened to deport en masse.[83]

The bishops of the southern Pacific dioceses issued another communiqué, this one accusing the Mexican government of "ethnocide."[84] Human rights organizations and other international NGOs sent letters asking the government to reconsider its policy. The news media criticized the government's strategies. One editorial justified the refugees' decision to stay in Chiapas:

> The Catholic Church and the *campesinos* that support them [the refugees] have offered numerous possibilities for relocation within Chiapas, for the exact reasons articulated by COMAR. For [those reasons], the refugees' refusal to leave Chiapas cannot be interpreted as stubbornness or whim. Nor is it ungratefulness, maliciousness, or the product of foreign inciting. On the contrary, it reveals very simple motivations that do not challenge Mexico's national interests or security: it is a rejection of the permanent uprooting from their homeland that is implied by a removal to areas that are different in climate, culture, and geography.[85]

In the end, proclamations by church officials, journalists, and NGOs did not change policy, but they did force the government to compromise somewhat, if only to preserve its international image. Between 1984 and 1987, eighteen thousand of the forty-six thousand refugees were relocated: six thousand of them to four settlements in Quintana Roo and twelve thousand to four settlements in Campeche.[86] The official record stated that the refugees relocated willingly and happily, but witnesses disputed these claims.[87] In many cases, the relocated arrived to find that neither state nor federal government had adequately prepared for their arrival. There were no houses or even tents to accommodate them and no support services.[88] Slowly the refugees built their town-settlements, with their own schools, health centers, storehouses, and recreational areas. They cultivated rice, beans, corn, sugarcane, vegetables, and fruits; and they also built apiaries and workshops, where they produced a variety of crafts for export.[89]

Reports on the success of the Campeche and Quintana Roo settlements vary in their assessment. In the celebratory twenty-fifth anniversary UNHCR publication, *Presencia de los refugiados guatemaltecos en México,* one UNHCR official called these projects "paradigms for refugee integration,"[90] and in 1989, the UNHCR terminated its food aid, claiming that these refugees had become self-sufficient. However, other studies disputed this assessment and claim and cited the many problems the refugees encountered: allotted land was insufficient; workers were discouraged from certain economic enterprises so that they would not compete with the local populations; and labor continued to be exploited.[91] Despite these challenges, the refugees of Campeche and Quintana Roo were the least likely to repatriate in the late 1990s, in part because many did establish themselves economically, intermarried with the local population, and raised a new generation who was bound more to Mexico than to Guatemala.

By the end of 1992, the UNHCR reported that the number of refugees remained stable, only now the camps and settlements were distributed in three states, and the most vulnerable border camps were closed down. As many as 150,000 Guatemalans were estimated to be living illegally in border hamlets and in towns and cities throughout the country. They could be found laboring in the coffee plantations of the Soconusco or working in construction or the service industries of the state capitals. Even though they outnumbered their co-nationals in the refugee camps, they received virtually no attention from the state, the NGOs, and even the social scientists that studied this migration, who had limited access to government data.[92] When pressed, government officials claimed that they were economic immigrants: *transmigrantes* on their way to the United States, or migrants who would eventually return to Guatemala. But by the end of the 1980s, the stability of their numbers suggested that many of them had made Mexico their home.

LOS SALVADOREÑOS

Mexico's response to the Salvadorans provides a contrasting case study. Many of the earliest arrivals from El Salvador—during the period 1979–1982—came by plane with six-month tourist visas (FM-T), which were easily provided by airlines and tourism agencies. When their visas expired, Salvadorans simply remained in Mexico illegally. In order to control this growing population, in 1983 the Mexican government tightened its visa requirements for all Central Americans, requiring them to apply for tourist visas only in Mexican consulates. The visas continued to be renewable, but the applications also had to be processed in the home country, which was impossible for those fleeing repressive conditions. The applicant had to prove financial solvency in Mexico; by 1986, a monthly income of a hundred thousand pesos was required (an amount that exceeded the average salary of Mexican citizens).[93] The new regulations had their intended effect: the number of Salvadorans arriving by plane and with tourist visas dropped significantly. The new regulations, however, did not stem the flow of Salvadorans but only redirected the traffic. After 1983, border communities noticed an increase in Salvadorans who entered the country via the Guatemalan and Mexican border towns of Talismán, Tecún Umán, Tapachula, and Ciudad Hidalgo.[94] Since they were now traveling on foot or by ground transportation, most of them took an average of two weeks to reach Mexico from their hometowns in El Salvador.[95] UNHCR officials recommended that all Salvadorans who had left their country since the beginning of 1980 be considered refugees by prima facie group determination, but the Secretaría de Gobernación regarded their migration—like that of most Central Americans—as economically motivated. The majority left because of the generalized climate of violence and repression in El Salvador, but they could not prove that they had been individually singled out for persecution.[96] Thus only thirty-five hundred Salvadorans were granted asylum during the early 1980s and assisted by the UNHCR.[97]

Unlike the Guatemalans, who were mostly agricultural workers, the Salvadorans came from urban areas and small towns. Young single males under the age of thirty were overrepresented in this migration, and they traveled unaccompanied or in small groups. Over half of all Salvadorans who migrated to Mexico arrived after January 1982.[98] The Diocese of San Cristóbal reported that most Salvadorans remained in Chiapas only a few days before they traveled northward.[99] They gravitated to large towns and cities, especially Mexico City, Guadalajara, and Monterrey, and settled in the poorest neighborhoods, which generally allowed them to remain undetected.[100] They searched for jobs that required few credentials: construction, janitorial work, and other service occupations. Those with the highest levels of education or skills settled in Mexico City, where, if fortunate, they could earn higher salaries for their credentials or experience.[101] Like most illegal immigrants, they tried to be as indistinguishable from the general population as possible, which meant disguising their origins by adopting new names and identities, linguistic accents, and customs and obtaining forged documents.[102] By "passing" they could avoid being detained by local police; but if detained and lacking the documents proving legal residence, they were immediately deported.

Unlike undocumented workers apprehended in the United States and Canada, those detained in Mexico were not entitled to legal counsel, release on bond, or any hearing in which they could plead their case. Article 33 of the Mexican Constitution allowed for the immediate expulsion of a foreigner without due process. Nor were they allowed contact with members of NGOs who might intercede on their behalf.[103] They were detained in a jail cell and, as quickly as transportation could be arranged, were transported to a Guatemalan border town and simply left there. Refugees with financial resources could often avoid deportation if they were "fortunate" enough to come across a corrupt policeman who demanded a *mordida*. But in most cases, they found themselves in Guatemala, dependent on the assistance of local churches until they were able to attempt the crossing into Mexico once again.

Before the agency was restructured in 1983, COMAR assisted both Guatemalans and Salvadorans who settled in urban areas. They provided the Salvadorans with medical care, food, and shelter, regardless of their status. COMAR also experimented with a variety of programs to integrate Salvadorans into urban and rural communities. In the states of Morelia and Jalisco, for example, Salvadorans were relocated to areas that needed manual or technical laborers.[104] However, when the agency was restructured in 1983, the government limited COMAR's role to the assistance of documented Guatemalans in the camps, in part to discourage further illegal immigration.[105] This forced Salvadorans to rely exclusively on the churches, the NGOs, and their own familial networks for assistance in finding jobs, housing, and social services. The private agency Servicio, Desarrollo, y Paz[106] became one of the principal refugee aid organizations in Mexico City, providing medical care, psychological counseling, and emergency aid to the Salvadoran refugees and other illegal immigrants. They were also assisted by the Comité del Distrito Federal de Ayuda a Refugiados Guatemaltecos, the religious-affiliated Seminario Bautista, the Centro de Estudios y Promoción Social, and the Dutch social agency Vluchteling.[107] These assisted hundreds of Central Americans, but only a small fraction of the forty thousand Salvadorans believed to be in Mexico City by 1984.[108]

NGO surveys conducted during the early 1980s revealed that almost three-quarters of the Salvadorans polled identified themselves as temporary residents who would return to their homeland once conditions improved.[109] However, the surveys failed to identify how many planned to move further north, to the United States or Canada, if they failed to find employment and safety in Mexico. The Reagan administration assumed that most Central Americans were simply transiting through Mexico and pressured the Mexican government to do more to control its southern border. Several early studies of the Central Americans in Mexico also concluded that the Salvadorans were on their way to the United States, in part because the economic climate in Mexico in the 1980s—the devaluation of the peso, double-digit inflation, price increases, and rising unemployment—limited wage-earning opportunities, made day-to-day life expensive, and encouraged a significant Mexican out-migration.[110] Over 75 percent of the Central Americans polled in Mexico City had no regular employment, suggesting that they would eventually make their way northward in search of better opportunities.[111] In 1984, the Salvadoran Embassy in Mexico estimated that a half-million Salvadorans were in the country, 40 percent of whom were believed to be in transit to the United States or Canada.[112] In 1990, an estimated half-million Salvadorans were still believed to be living in Mexico, but it was unclear whether these were the same residents from the early 1980s or if the population had simply replenished its numbers over the years.

Some policy analysts have written that while Mexico did little to accommodate the Salvadorans, it did not pursue an active policy of detention and deportation, in essence, "looking the other way." When illegal Salvadorans were apprehended by police, they were deported to Guatemala, *not* to El Salvador—in most cases delivered to Guatemalan towns just across the border—making their reentry to Mexico almost guaranteed. However, by the late 1980s and early 1990s, the Mexican government was more actively committed to the detention and expulsion of undocumented workers, in part because of pressure from the United States.[113] Mexico further restricted the issuance of tourist visas to Central American nationals, requiring applicants to demonstrate financial and personal ties to their homeland that would compel them to return (e.g., property ownership, bank accounts, stable employment, as well as family). The number of deportations increased each year, and at times far exceeded the number of deportations from the United States. In 1988, for example, the Servicios Migratorios deported 14,000 Central Americans; in 1989, 85,000; and in 1990, 126,000. The Immigration and Naturalization Service (INS), by comparison, deported 12,133 Central Americans in fiscal year 1989.[114]

SOLIDARITY AND SANCTUARY:
DEFENDING THE RIGHTS OF REFUGEES

Clergy, nuns, and lay church workers in southeastern Mexico were among the first to notice the steady influx of Central Americans into their communities. Through parish aid offices, they organized networks of parishioners and volunteers who visited the refugees in their makeshift settlements and provided them with medical care, food, and clothing. UNHCR personnel remarked at the generosity of Mexican *campesinos,* who, though living at subsistence levels themselves, shared their land and resources with those they considered even needier.[115] The Roman Catholic Dioceses of San Cristóbal de las Casas and Tapachula created organizations to consolidate these networks and oversee the distribution of aid: the Diocese of San Cristóbal's Comité Cristiano de Solidaridad (CCS) targeted the Guatemalan refugees in government-run camps, while the Dioceses of Tapachula's Comité Diocesano de Ayuda a Inmigrantes Fronterizos assisted Central Americans who did not receive government recognition or assistance. Other Catholic dioceses, among them Tehuantepec and Cuernavaca, collected and transported material aid for the refugees in Chiapas.[116] At first these NGOs concentrated on meeting the refugees' immediate housing, food, and medical needs, as well as providing pastoral counseling. As the refugee migration became a seemingly permanent aspect of life in the southeast, they concentrated on what the UNHCR called durable solutions.[117] They also assisted in the transportation of unrecognized Central Americans, the so-called excludable refugees, to other parts of Mexico where they might avoid deportation. These faith-based NGOs were among the few organizations the Mexican government permitted to work in the area, and although rarely credited in the official records, they provided COMAR with a model for refugee assistance and cooperated with the committee in a number of its projects.[118]

Bishop Samuel Ruiz García of the Diocese of San Cristóbal emerged as the most visible defender of refugee and indigenous rights in Mexico. Affectionately called *tatik* (father in faith) by the Maya population, Ruiz had served his diocese and the state of Chiapas since his appointment by the Vatican in January 1960. His pastoral vocation developed during the tumultuous years of the Vatican II Council (1962–1965), which transformed the Roman Catholic Church worldwide, and the Medellín Conference (1968), which further transformed the church in Latin America. The Medellín Conference, in which he participated, reinforced his commitment to liberation theology, the Gospel's "preferential option for the poor," and his pastoral work with indigenous communities.[119] He learned to speak a half-dozen Mayan languages (in addition to the eight other languages he already spoke) and became well versed in Mayan cosmologies and popular religion, which helped him personally interact with and serve the indigenous populations, including the refugees in his diocese.[120] He committed his diocese to meeting the physical and spiritual needs of the poor with the limited resources at their disposal. As in the state of Chiapas, diocesan coffers reflected the poverty of the region. But he became a tireless speaker and a prolific writer of letters, reports, and communiqués through which he drew international attention to the unjust institutions and policies in Chiapas and attracted financial aid. When the Guatemalan refugees began arriving in his diocese, Ruiz immediately wrote letters and reports documenting the poverty and trauma of the refugees, the Guatemalan army's attacks on settlements, and the failure of the Mexican government and the UNHCR to adequately respond to the crisis. Excerpts were published in newspapers, newsletters, and church bulletins throughout Mexico and abroad. Religious and solidarity groups, domestic and international, contacted the diocese offering to send volunteers, supplies, and funding. He attracted millions of dollars in donations from international NGOs, which preferred to funnel their contributions through local organizations rather than through government agencies, which they distrusted. By the mid-1980s, Ruiz was raising over a million dollars in emergency aid each year, and his Comité Cristiano de Solidaridad had coordinated the work of hundreds of local and international volunteers.[121]

Distrustful of all government and military representatives, the refugees regarded the Diocese of San Cristóbal as one of the few institutions in Mexican society that they could rely on. Corruption among government aid workers manifested itself in myriad ways, including the theft of UNHCR food and medical and construction supplies; the "taxing" of services and wages; and continual threats of deportation. Thus, the diocese's reliable and efficient distribution of aid was all the more critical, especially during the first half of the 1980s, when the camps and settlements were first created and their future in Chiapas uncertain. The Comité Cristiano de Solidaridad concentrated on three principal goals: the efficient distribution of emergency aid; the representation of refugee interests; and assisting refugees in integrating and becoming self-sufficient. Pressure from the CCS helped to end the deportations of the early 1980s.[122] The diocese represented the refugees' interests through the documentation of their experiences, through legal counsel, and by representing their interests in the news media and before public opinion. The diocesan newsletter, Caminante, distributed throughout Mexico and the United States, recorded the testimonios of the Guatemalan refugees and gave up-to-date information on conditions in Central America as well as in the camps and settlements.[123] The CCS helped to organize the refugees so that they could represent their own interests in meetings with government officials. Almost all of the settlements had their own elected leaders, and dozens of organizations represented specific interests. (Refugee women, for example, created several organizations, among them Mama Maquin, Nueva Estrella, and La Unión.) Efforts to organize the refugees culminated in the creation of the Comisiones Permanentes de Representantes de Refugiados Guatemaltecos en México, or the Permanent Commissions, in 1987 to represent the refugees' interests in the discussions on repatriation.[124] And contrary to government policy, the diocese, like the CCS, strove to assist the refugees in becoming self-sufficient until they could repatriate to their homeland. In 1984, for example, the diocese worked with Mexican landowners to create a land-lease program so that some of the refugee communities could produce their own food. Working with advocacy networks in Europe, Canada, and the United States, the diocese also found international markets for the refugees' crafts so that they would have another vehicle for self-sufficiency.

The Diocese of San Cristóbal challenged the official state discourses about the refugees. When Mexican officials expressed concern that the refugee camps might serve as bases for insurgency, the diocese refuted the claim. "The refugees know that they are in a foreign country and they know they have to be careful," said Bishop Ruiz in one interview. "They don't move within Mexican political movements and they keep their distance from the guerrillas."[125] When COMAR withheld aid in an attempt to force the refugees to relocate to Campeche and Quintana Roo, the diocese called on its international network for help. The July 1984 communiqué alerted the network of the gravity of the situation: "The lives of five thousand refugees are endangered. . . . The refugees are asking for emergency food supplies. They are asking that the representatives of the UNHCR in Mexico and Geneva, as well as of other international commissions, come and witness the terror that the Mexican military has unleashed."[126]

In his activism, Ruiz distanced the Diocese of San Cristóbal de las Casas from the generally conservative Roman Catholic Church in Mexico, which feared sabotaging its already precarious relationship with the state. Until 1992, the Mexican Constitution included a number of provisions designed to curtail the influence of religious groups, especially the Roman Catholic Church. Among these provisions was Article 130, Section 9, which stated: "Neither in public nor private assembly, nor in acts of worship or religious propaganda shall the ministers of the religions ever have the right to criticize the basic laws of the country, of the authorities in particular or of the government in general; they shall have neither an active nor passive vote, nor the right to associate for political purposes."[127] Thus, Ruiz's proclamations theoretically placed him—and the Catholic Church—on a collision course with the state. Ecclesiastical authorities distanced themselves from Ruiz's proclamations and warned Roman Catholics of liberation theology's potential manipulation by Marxist groups that cared less about doctrinal matters than about challenging Mexican institutions.

Ruiz's actions, however, both shaped and reflected a new shift in church–state relations that began in the 1980s. Partly in response to liberation theology, Mexican clergy were increasingly critical of the abuses of the state. Banned from political office by both the Constitution and the Vatican, they used their moral authority to shape public opinion and to organize their parishioners. Not surprisingly, some of the most vocal clergy and bishops worked in southeastern Mexico, where the distribution of power and resources was most blatantly skewed. Bishops Ruiz, Alba Palacios, Ramírez, and Lona Reyes, among others, routinely condemned the political disenfranchisement of the poor by the ruling elites; the failure of the government to enforce the provisions of agrarian reform legislation; the corruption at all levels of the Mexican bureaucracy; the contamination and environmental degradation of southern states by Mexico's oil companies; and the government's characterization of the indigenous peoples as "targets for development." But they also directed much of the criticism at their own church. In one interview, Lona Reyes criticized the church's failure to take a more proactive role in addressing the rights of the poor: "The church in Mexico is profoundly conservative. Only ten bishops carry out their duties as prophets, pronouncing the Gospel and denouncing social injustices. The rest [of the bishops] are complicit supporters of a system that is based on human exploitation and the expansion of over 300 multinationals that dominate the global economy."[128]

Ruiz's supporters regarded him as one of the most important church leaders in Latin America. His enemies called him the Red Bishop and a guerrilla-priest of the "parallel church," who cared more about revolution than the spiritual needs of his people (a charge that increased when the Zapatista rebellion erupted in January 1994).[129] Ruiz particularly clashed with the governor of Chiapas, José Patrocinio González Garrido (1988–1994), and the ranching class that supported him, who accused Ruiz of being the root cause of all the land and labor agitation in Chiapas.[130] In 1989, Ruiz helped to found the Centro de Derechos Humanos Fray Bartolomé de las Casas[131] to document the human rights abuses of the González Garrido administration. The center accused the government of Chiapas of illegal evictions and detentions, rape, assault, torture, and assassination. Government and NGO records supported the center's charges: according to the Secretaría de Gobernación, from 1989 to 1993, 2,290 indigenous people were imprisoned in Chiapas, of which only 914 eventually obtained their freedom. According to the Comisión Nacional de Derechos Humanos, under González Garrido the state of Chiapas ranked second in the number of human rights violations.[132]

In response, González Garrido declared war on the Catholic Church in Chiapas. He authorized police to investigate and detain clergy members, especially the Dominicans, the Jesuits, and others who espoused liberation theology or were suspected of labor agitation, political organizing, or ties to revolutionary groups. Nuns, priests, missionaries, and lay church leaders were followed, harassed, and detained, especially if they were foreign-born. In July 1990, Father Marcelo Rotsaert, a Belgian priest at the parish in Soyatitán, was arrested and eventually deported for allegedly encouraging the land reclamation movement and refugee support for the URNG. The following year, Father Joel Padrón González of Simojovel was accused of being a "guerrilla-priest" and sent to Cerro Hueco prison in Tuxtla Gutiérrez. When a meeting between the bishops and representatives of the state government failed to bring about his release, Ruiz and the Centro de Derechos Humanos launched a media and letter-writing campaign to attract international attention to his case.

Five hundred Mayas of various tribes organized a 123-kilometer protest march to Tuxtla Gutiérrez—which they wisely called a pilgrimage—to express their support for Father Joel by praying for his release. By the time the group arrived in the state capital, their number had grown to over eighteen thousand. When they arrived at the state capital, they attended a Mass at the Basilica of Our Lady of Guadalupe, presided by Bishop Ruiz, and then prayed continuously for three days. News that eighteen thousand Chiapans could organize at a moment's notice naturally worried federal officials. Making matters worse, the International Commission on Human Rights, an agency of the Organization of American States, launched a formal investigation of Father Joel's case, and letters of support arrived from all over the world. Over the objections of the governor, Father Joel was ordered released from Cerro Hueco after serving forty-nine days in prison. In retribution, the Guardias Blancas evicted hundreds of *campesinos* from their land, assaulted their family members, and/or destroyed their property.

However much the bishops tried to downplay their role in catalyzing the march, the state and federal governments associated the two. Not long after, a local newspaper uncovered a plot to assassinate Bishop Ruiz. Evidence also suggests that in 1993 the Mexican government, with the assistance of Monsignor Girolamo Prigione, the representative of the papal nuncio in Mexico, tried to convince the Vatican to remove Ruiz. In one interview with Mexican journalists, Prigione stated that Ruiz had made "grave doctrinal and pastoral errors [that] clashed with the church and offended the pope."[133] However, the campaign failed to yield the desired results: Prigione received thousands of letters and telegrams demanding his own resignation, and the government was forced to deny any involvement in the campaign.[134] Ruiz remained bishop of Chiapas until 1999, when he retired at the age of seventy-five, the church's mandatory age of retirement for clergy, but continues to represent the interests of the poor and disenfranchised through his speeches, writings, and mediation. In the late 1990s, he served as mediator between the Zapatistas and the government. In 2000, he was awarded the Nuremberg Human Rights Award for his work in "defending the poor and exploited" in Mexico.[135]

The Catholic Church in Chiapas respected the refugees' rights to seek safe haven outside the UNHCR camps and settlements. Churches helped to hide undocumented Central Americans from local police, and often arranged their transportation to other, safer locations. By 1981, a network of "sanctuaries" had emerged throughout the country, as far north as Matamoros and Nogales on the United States–Mexico border, to assist undocumented Central Americans in avoiding detection by police, in finding housing and employment, or in crossing over into the United States. Ironically, this network included the wives of several politicians.[136] When a sanctuary movement emerged in the United States in 1981, American volunteers traveled to Tapachula, Ciudad Hidalgo, and other border towns to inform church workers of the opportunities for safe haven north of the United States–Mexico border. Jim Corbett, regarded as one of the founders of the US sanctuary movement, traveled to Chiapas from his home in Tucson and provided aid workers with the names, addresses, and telephone numbers of churches along the United States–Mexico border that would shelter refugees.[137] Among these was the Casa Juan Diego shelter in Matamoros, where many Central Americans stopped before crossing into the United States, as well as Southside Presbyterian Church in Tucson, Arizona.[138]

A variety of international, national, and grassroots organizations played a role in refugee advocacy and assistance in Mexico. Some, like Amnesty International, Americas Watch, and Human Rights Watch, as well as the Mexican government's Comisión Nacional de Derechos Humanos, focused on the documentation of human rights abuses committed by both

Guatemalan and Mexican authorities. In March 1984, for example, Amnesty International published a forty-five-page report documenting the kidnapping and murder of Mexican *campesinos* and Guatemalan refugees in Chiapas and Oaxaca, and the use of torture to extract information: charges that the Secretaría de Relaciones Exteriores rejected as "inaccurate, distorted, and one-sided."[139] Additional evidence for Amnesty International's charges was provided a year later when the September earthquake unearthed several bodies exhibiting signs of torture in the ruins of the federal district attorney general's headquarters in Mexico City. Public outcry forced passage of legislation banning the use of torture in police investigations; and in a symbolic gesture to demonstrate the Mexican government's new commitment, Mexico became the second country to ratify the UN Convention against Torture in January 1986.[140] Nevertheless, throughout the 1990s the Mexican government was repeatedly accused of human rights violations, especially in Chiapas. Between May 1992 and May 1993, 157 charges were filed against state authorities in Chiapas, and violations increased after the Zapatista rebellion of January 1994.[141]

Other international NGOs such as Oxfam, Catholic Relief Services, and Vluchteling provided funding for emergency aid and durable solutions, channeling their funding through the church or through Mexican NGOs such as the Programa de Asistencia para los Refugiados Centroamericanos, the Servicio, Desarrollo, y Paz, and the Comité de Ayuda a Refugiados Guatemaltecos. Grassroots NGOs, in turn, monitored government policy and lobbied the federal government to draft new refugee and asylum legislation and sign the UN Convention and Protocol. Following Esquipulas II, fifteen NGOs united under the umbrella organization CONONGAR (National Coordinator of NGOs Assisting Refugees in Mexico) to better represent Mexico's interests in the CIREFCA conferences. By the 1990s, then, the Mexican NGOs, secular and faith-based, had become major figures in the shaping of refugee policy in Mexico and the discussion of regional solutions to the crisis of refugees and displaced persons. However, their work was largely dependent on funding from international NGOs, and when interest in Central America's refugees waned in the early 1990s, the funding, and their ability to carry on their work, was further limited.

On July 17, 1990, after years of lobbying, the Mexican Congress agreed to amend the General Population Law and provide new guidelines for the recognition and admission of refugees. Refugee status, as delineated by Article 42, Section 6, of the new law, drew on the definition offered by the Cartagena Declaration rather than the standard definition offered by the United Nations. It was the first time a state had included this more liberal definition in its legislation.[142] Under the new law a refugee was an individual who, "to protect his life, security, or freedom, threatened by generalized violence, foreign aggression, internal conflict, massive violation of human rights, or other circumstances that have seriously disturbed public order in his country of origin, is forced to flee to another country."[143] Thus, unlike the United States, which placed the burden on Central American applicants to prove persecution, Mexican law recognized that a climate of "generalized violence" was sufficient grounds to offer an individual or group protected status.

Aspects of the new law were immediately controversial and elicited complaints from the NGO community. According to the new law, those who wished to be considered for asylum had to file their request upon entry into Mexico. Excluded from consideration were those who entered the country illegally or in some other nonimmigrant status, such as "border visitor." Nor were police and government officials required to inform entrants of their rights. Once an application was made it was forwarded to a committee in the political asylum division for determination. According to CONONGAR, four years after the law had passed, no applications had been forwarded from a local delegation to the central office.[144] Even more controversial was the provision that imposed ten-year prison sentences and financial penalties on those who, "without legal permission from a competent authority, intend to bring, or bring illegally one or more foreigners to Mexico or another country, or house them, or transport them through national territory with the purpose of hiding them from migratory inspection."[145] According to the US Committee for Refugees, this provision was more likely to be enforced against the NGOs that assisted refugees than those who smuggled illegal immigrants, simply because of the corruption in the police force.[146]

In 2000, Mexico finally became a signatory to the UN Convention and Protocol.[147] Two years later, asylum procedures were streamlined: applicants were given fifteen days to file a petition for asylum in the nearest office of the Instituto Nacional de Migración, and within thirty days an "eligibility committee" would render a recommendation. If the petitioner received a negative verdict, then he or she had the right to appeal to an independent judicial court, the Tribunal Federal de Justicia Fiscal y Administrativa. Because the institute's offices were directed to expedite the deportation of illegal Central Americans, NGOs urged petitioners to file as quickly as possible.[148] Under the new guidelines the UNHCR continued to provide temporary assistance to successful petitioners, and refugees could request citizenship after five years. However, according to the NGO Sin Fronteras, asylum petitions dropped after these provisions were enacted, reflecting the distrust applicants generally had of the Mexican government and their reluctance to divulge their histories and concerns.[149]

By 2001 asylum seekers in Mexico represented two dozen nationalities from all over the world. Guatemalans and Hondurans were the Central Americans most represented in the rolls. UNHCR interviews with asylum seekers suggested that most were probably on their way to the United States or Canada: asylum seekers tended to file a petition only after they were detained by authorities; and up to 80 percent of successful petitioners relocated to other countries within a year of receiving refugee status.[150]

RETORNO: GUATEMALAN REFUGEES REPATRIATE

Throughout the 1980s, the Reagan and Bush administrations pressured the Mexican government not only to step up the control of its southern border but also to cooperate with the Guatemalan government in establishing a repatriation program that would facilitate the return of the forty-six thousand UNHCR-recognized refugees as well as tens of thousands of undocumented Guatemalans. The Mexican government insisted on several conditions before it agreed to participate in any organized repatriation: the return of the refugees had to be voluntary and their security guaranteed; and the refugees had to be allowed to return to their places of origin or to the location of their choice. Until 1987, refugees who wanted to return to Guatemala could notify COMAR about their intentions, and the UNHCR would arrange for their transportation to the border. However, once back in Guatemala, refugees had no official protection, since the UNHCR was barred from operating in Guatemala.

The Guatemalan government's terms for political and economic reintegration discouraged the majority of refugees from returning during the 1980s. Returnees were required to register with the army and petition for amnesty, which required admitting to certain "crimes" against the state and relocating to the model villages. Thus, prior to 1984, only a few hundred returned, but when the Mexican government announced its relocation program, the numbers increased. Refugees concerned about the disintegration of their communities and cultural values, and the "Mexicanization" of their children, decided to take their chances in Guatemala rather than move to Campeche or Quintana Roo. UNHCR and COMAR officials estimated that the refugee population decreased by as many as six thousand people in 1984, many of whom were believed to have returned to Guatemala.[151]

In 1986 a larger-scale repatriation became a possibility when Vicente Cerezo took office as the first popularly elected and civilian president of Guatemala in several decades. Following his inauguration Cerezo initiated another propaganda campaign to convince the refugees to return, and to demonstrate his commitment he established the Comisión Nacional para la Atención de Repatriados, Refugiados, y Desplazados (CEAR) to supervise the reception and transportation of and assistance to returning refugees. Much of CEAR's budget came from the UNHCR and other international donors, and consequently, in 1987 the UNHCR was finally permitted to establish an office in Huehuetenango to assist in the reintegration efforts and the distribution of aid. That same year the refugees established the Permanent Commissions to become the third party in the binational discussions on repatriation. The Permanent Commissions insisted on certain protections and guarantees for the returnees, among them that the repatriation be voluntary and have international accompaniment and that the refugees be guaranteed safety, freedom of movement within Guatemala, and access to land.[152]

The NGO community disagreed on how to best support the refugees in their repatriation efforts. NGOs in Mexico, for example, encouraged refugees to remain in the country until there was sufficient evidence of the Cerezo government's commitment to human rights, as well as a greater commitment on the part of the Guatemalan military and the URNG to a peace accord. The UNHCR, in turn, did not actively discourage repatriation, but it did not actively promote it either. The UNHCR agreed to assist those who *voluntarily* chose to return and, through its Support Program for Voluntary Repatriation in Huehuetenango, helped to coordinate an infrastructure to assist in their reintegration. Funding from the

UNHCR and the European Economic Community helped to upgrade schools, build health clinics, pave roads, and dig wells in Huehuetenango. The World Food Program provided the refugees with short-term assistance until their arrival in Guatemala, when CEAR theoretically assumed responsibility for their social and economic reintegration.[153]

However, the Cerezo government's failure to act on some of the refugees' demands, as well as the ongoing violence, limited the number of repatriates in the late 1980s. Army officers were not investigated or prosecuted, as the refugees demanded, and some even served on CEAR, suggesting that despite the symbols of a new democracy the true power continued to rest with the military. Members of the Cerezo administration publicly clashed with defense officials on issues of resettlement, political incorporation, and land use. The military continued to insist that the refugees be directed to the model villages to safeguard against the guerrillas who had infiltrated their populations, which of course violated one of the principal terms of the repatriate agenda. More alarming, human rights organizations reported that political killings, disappearances, and kidnappings increased sharply from 1988 to 1990, provoking even the US State Department to recall its ambassador in March 1990 in response to "the government's failure to investigate and punish those responsible."[154] Refugees in Mexico listened to Guatemalan and Mexican radio broadcasts to try to decipher what was happening in their homeland and how safe it was to return, but the best indicators were always the border activities of the Guatemalan army, the number of new refugees who arrived in their settlements each month, and the stories related by the "scouts," or those who returned to Guatemala to appraise conditions on behalf of their families and communities. Of these indicators, the last provided the most reliable evidence that little had changed in Guatemala and that repatriates could expect continued harassment from the military and the civilian patrols.[155]

Despite these setbacks the negotiations continued on and off for several years. In the meantime Esquipulas II and the subsequent CIREFCA conference of May 1989, in Guatemala City, provided the international mandate as well as the institutional framework for repatriation across Central America. Over a hundred thousand Salvadorans and Nicaraguans had returned to their homelands from Honduras and Costa Rica, encouraged by the negotiated peace settlements and elections that were beginning to take place in the early 1990s.[156] These developments helped to keep the channels of communication open between the Guatemalan government and the elected representatives of the Permanent Commissions.

Like his predecessor, President Jorge Serrano Elías (who took office in 1991) tried to demonstrate his administration's good faith. The Serrano administration made use of the new Human Rights Ombudsman established by the 1985 Constitution and the advisory Commission for Human Rights that appointed special prosecutors who investigated and forced the resignation of high-level officials implicated in human rights abuses. The government also established the National Peace Fund, a development project that channeled international aid to the areas most affected by poverty and violence. Finally, on October 8, 1992, the Serrano administration and the Permanent Commissions signed an accord that paved the way for the first organized repatriation of Guatemalan refugees. On January 20, 1993, the *retornos*[157] began: 2,480 refuges returned in a convoy of 75 buses accompanied by 240 international observers. Nobel Peace Prize winner Rigoberta Menchú Tum was among the delegates who greeted the refugees at the border. On January 24, the convoy reached Guatemala City, where several thousand supporters joined them for a rally in the main square. The returnees then traveled to Cobán, and from there they divided into smaller groups to travel to the towns and cities of their choice.

In the larger transit points, like Cobán, the refugees received their medical checkups and identification documents. Local churches and NGOs assisted them in their immediate needs. Once the refugees reached their final destination, CEAR was to provide them with the tools they needed to get through the first months: seed for the first harvest, building materials to build their homes, and food supplies to carry them over until they were self-sufficient. CEAR was also mandated to assist in the construction of schools and health clinics, the expansion of public utilities, and social services. But CEAR's failure to provide fast and efficient services became a major complaint of the refugees and the communities that reintegrated them. UNHCR personnel were often called on to serve as mediators with local politicians and bureaucrats, but especially the local populations, who after years of government propaganda were reluctant to live and work alongside those the military had labeled terrorists. In such cases, UN-funded development programs, such as the so-called Quick

Impact Projects (small-scale one-time investments), helped to diffuse the tension by responding to urgent needs in specific communities and benefiting existing residents as well as the returnees.

The refugees returned to the country's poorest, most militarized and war-devastated areas: hundreds of villages had been razed; tens of thousands had been killed, tortured, or maimed; land and property had been distributed to others or lay unproductive after years of neglect. The social inequities that had inspired revolution remained unresolved, distrust of civil society continued, and the violence seemed never-ending.[158] The Guatemalan Human Rights Commission reported 482 extrajudicial executions, 381 assassination attempts, 37 kidnappings or disappearances, and 83 attacks on populated areas in the twelve-month period prior to the first *retorno,* despite the return of democratic government.

Local and international support for the negotiations offered the returnees the only hope that the terms might be upheld. Despite the continued risks to their members, dozens of new NGOs emerged at the local level to assist in the reintegration and to pressure CEAR to live up to its mandate. Twenty-five Guatemalan NGOs and cooperatives united under the umbrella organization Coordinación de ONGs y Cooperativas para el Accompañimiento de la Población Damnificada por el Conflicto Armado Interno[159] to assist the refugees in their immediate and long-term needs, and to counter the military's negative publicity about the *retornos.* Hundreds of observers from European, Canadian, US, and Mexican NGOs accompanied the Guatemalans in their overland journey and sometimes remained in their communities for a period of time to assure their safety and assist in their initial adaptation.[160] "Without international accompaniment," said one refugee, "the people are like worms the army can just step on."[161] However, as late as 1995, Guatemalan soldiers continued to assassinate returnees.[162]

By the end of 1996, when representatives of the government and the URNG finally signed a peace accord, as many as thirty-six thousand Guatemalan refugees were believed to have returned to their homeland, either spontaneously or with UNHCR assistance. Hundreds continued to return each month. However, some fourteen thousand of the recognized refugees expressed a desire to remain in Mexico, at least in the short term. Some did so out of fear that the terms of the peace accords would not be upheld, preferring to wait a period of time to see what transpired. Others opted to remain in Mexico for economic reasons, feeling that they had a better chance to earn a stable income in Chiapas than in the war-devastated departments of Guatemala. Still others had intermarried and raised their families in Mexico and established ties to the country in spite of their original intentions. In 1996, more than 50 percent of the refugee population were born in Mexico and younger than fourteen years of age, and thus did not share the same emotional ties to Guatemala as their parents. For some Guatemalans, this reality provided sufficient motivation to repatriate so that their cultural and community identities would be preserved in the new generation; for others, this reality compelled them to seek a permanent status in Mexico.

The Mexican government faced the challenge of what to do with the thousands of refugees who were now rendered ineligible for UNHCR protection. Given its stated commitment to *voluntary* repatriation, mass deportation was not an option. Instead, for the first time in its history, the Mexican government created a special program to allow Guatemalans to legalize their status. Under the Migrant Stabilization Program, Guatemalans were allowed to choose between two statuses: the FM-2 (immigrant status) for those who wanted permanent residence or citizenship; or the FM-3 (visitor status)[163] for those who one day hoped to return to their homeland. Both statuses gave the Guatemalans free movement within Mexico, the right to return to Mexico if they traveled outside the country, and certain rights and protections under Mexican law, including the right to work. After two years, those who chose immigrant status would be allowed to apply for Mexican citizenship for themselves and their children (although, theoretically, children born in Mexico were already Mexican citizens).[164] By November 1997, 2,500 Guatemalans had filled out the paperwork to naturalize; and 12,650 had requested forms FM-2 and FM-3 to remain in Mexico. By 2000, some 25,000 Central Americans had regularized their status, including 4,700 who had become naturalized citizens.[165]

3

REFUGEES OR
ECONOMIC MIGRANTS?

The Debate over Accountability in the United States

The Reagan Administration doesn't want to accept us as
refugees because it would be admitting that the military
aid it sends to El Salvador does not help, rather destroys
and creates refugees. I didn't come here because I wanted
to. I had no economic need to come. I left my country
because I had to.

SALVADORAN IMMIGRANT

Marta Ester Paniagua Vides was given a form. She asked
the agents if the form was for voluntary departure and
they assured her it was not. She signed the paper and it
in fact turned out to be Form I-274A. . . . Juan Francisco
Pérez-Cruz, arrested in 1980, did not request asylum
even though informed of it, because the agent told him
that asylum was only for people who were fleeing their
country because they were an enemy of the government
or an assassin. . . . Noe Castillo Núñez, apprehended in
1981, told the INS agents that he was afraid to go back
to El Salvador because he had received death threats.
The agents told Núñez the threats were his problem,
that they did not care what happened to him, and that
he should return because he would be deported anyway.
Núñez was then given some forms and told to "sign
here." The papers were quickly taken away and Núñez
did not know what he signed. He told the agents that
he wanted to apply for asylum, but they told him they
did not know anything about it. . . . Dora Elia Estrada,
arrested in 1980, refused to sign a voluntary departure
form and asked for asylum. The agent who arrested
her told her that political asylum "wasn't given" in the
United States, and that if she did not sign for voluntary
departure she was going to be in detention for a long
time in a jail where there were "only men."

"Evidence concerning INS interference
with the right to apply for asylum"

Like Mexico, the United States became a reluctant host to Central American refugees. By 1987, 88 percent of all Central Americans who chose external migration were either in Mexico or in the United States, and only a small fraction were granted asylum.[1] Between 500,000 and 750,000 Salvadorans, Guatemalans, and Nicaraguans were believed to be in Mexico, and over 1 million in the United States.[2] Migration to Mexico and the United States was not a new phenomenon; Central Americans had traveled to both countries as sojourners and immigrants since the nineteenth century, albeit in much smaller numbers.[3] As a result of the revolutions, their numbers increased exponentially. In the 1980s other factors encouraged migration to these two countries in particular: the relatively open borders; the low cost of an overland journey; and more important, significantly greater stability and economic opportunity than in other neighboring countries.[4]

Only a small percentage of the Central Americans who arrived in the United States came with immigrant visas or refugee status. Some entered with some type of temporary visa, such as a student or tourist visa, and simply stayed once their visas expired, but the majority arrived illegally across the United States–Mexico border. Mexico's refugee policy clearly affected who migrated to the United States and in what numbers. The Salvadorans and Nicaraguans migrated in much larger numbers than the Guatemalans, since unlike the last they had no opportunity to receive protected status in Mexico. The Central Americans who came to the United States were a cross-section of their societies: urban and rural dwellers, factory and agricultural workers, students and professionals, young and old. They included union leaders, former political prisoners, army deserters, and church catechists. Some traveled alone; others came as part of family units.[5] Some had been singled out for persecution in their homeland; others were trying to escape the generalized climate of violence. All were in need of safe haven.

Central Americans who made it to the United States encountered a society that was less than enthusiastic about their arrival. Since the passage of the 1965 Immigration Act, the United States had accommodated millions of immigrants and refugees from a variety of countries—the largest population of newcomers since the first decades of the twentieth century. Americans generally perceived the Central Americans as yet another drain on their fragile economy just barely recovering from the recession of the late 1970s. As Senator Alan K. Simpson, R–Wyoming, the architect of several immigration reform bills, put it, the nation was suffering from "compassion fatigue."[6] The influx of so many people from so many parts of the world contributed to an anti-immigrant backlash that led to the passage of four new pieces of legislation during the 1980s and 1990s to control their numbers.[7]

But for some Americans, the migration of Central Americans presented a moral dilemma. They believed that the United States had a responsibility to assist these displaced people given the role the US government had played in their displacement. Throughout the 1980s, members of one vocal segment of US society called for a reassessment of their country's foreign and immigration policies. They demanded accountability from their government for their actions in Central America and on the United States–Mexico border. And they worked for change—first through protest and civil obedience, lobbying, and the shaping of public opinion, and ultimately through the courts.

ASYLUM OR DEPORTATION?

Economic development was a keystone of US foreign policy in Latin America in the 1980s, to foster geopolitical stability but also to discourage the migration of millions of "feet people" northward to the United States.[8] From 1984 to 1989 the United States committed over five billion dollars to development programs in five countries in Central America (Belize, Honduras, El Salvador, Guatemala, and Costa Rica) "to support the return of economic stability to the region, to establish the foundation for broad-based sustained growth, and to encourage the growth of democracy and democratic institutions."[9] Policymakers also believed that economic development of emigrant-producing countries was the only realistic long-term solution to stemming the flow of migration, even if development might stimulate migration in the short term by raising people's expectations and enhancing their ability to leave.

Officials of the Reagan administration argued that there was little need for Central Americans to travel all the way to the United States, since there were many opportunities for asylum or safe haven south of the United States–Mexico border. During the 1980s the United States contributed 105 million dollars to the UNHCR and the International Committee of the Red Cross to assist refugees, repatriates, and displaced persons in general and in their resettlement elsewhere in the region.[10] Thus, many Central Americans' choice to come to the United States when there were ample opportunities for safe haven elsewhere suggested to administration officials that these migrants were economically rather than politically motivated, and thus were not true refugees. In a 1985 memorandum, for example, one US policymaker stated that Guatemalans did not need a protected status in the United States because Mexico offered sufficient protections: "We note that the UN High Commission for Refugees operates numerous settlements for Guatemalan refugees in southern Mexico, which most of the Guatemalans illegally in the US have chosen to bypass. Guatemalans do not face persecution in Mexico. Nevertheless some of them have decided not to avail themselves of this UN program specifically tailored for their needs, but rather have sought to enter the United States where no such program operates."[11]

The administration's assumption that it could discourage refugees from coming to the United States was as unrealistic as its belief that refugees' needs could be satisfactorily met in other countries or in UNHCR camps. As discussed in chapter 1, the criteria for asylum and safe haven varied across the region. Some countries granted safe haven to one specific national group, but not others. Some restricted the refugees to heavily guarded camps and settlements, while others allowed them to live among the general population. Living conditions varied, as did opportunities for employment, education, and general social welfare. And in countries where the UNHCR was allowed to participate, limited resources meant the commission was able to assist fewer than 10 percent of all those it estimated to be displaced within the region, and then principally in Honduras, Costa Rica, and Mexico.[12] The proximity of the United States, then, and the opportunities available in its society served as a powerful magnet encouraging thousands to risk it all and go to that country, even though their illegal status might subject them to exploitation.

The majority of Central Americans did not qualify for asylum in the United States under the terms of the recently passed 1980 Refugee Act. The 1980 act adopted the United Nations' definition of refugee expanded by the 1967 Protocol[13] in an attempt to standardize the process by which people were officially recognized as refugees and asylees.[14] Prior to 1980, US Cold War policies rewarded those fleeing communist nations. The fact that a person came from Cuba or one of the Eastern bloc countries was often sufficient grounds for automatic entrance into the United States, while those that escaped right-wing authoritarian regimes (usually US allies) had more difficulty proving persecution. The 1980 act tried to make the selection process fairer and more consistent.[15]

Even after the passage of the 1980 act, the majority of those recognized as refugees continued to be from communist nations, but the law made admittance less automatic. A petitioner for asylum now had to prove certain conditions: a refugee was a person who, "owing to a well-founded fear of persecution for reasons of race, religion, nationality, membership of a particular social group or political opinion, is outside the country of his nationality and is unable, or owing to such fear, unwilling to avail himself to the protection of that country."[16] The challenge, then, was to provide evidence of a well-founded fear of persecution, and unfortunately the evaluation of that evidence continued to be politicized. By 1990, over 90 percent of the refugee admissions from abroad came from communist or communist-dominated countries.[17]

Members of the Reagan and Bush administrations clashed with UNHCR officials over this policy. The UNHCR generally favored a more lenient response to the so-called *nonconvention refugees:* those who did not meet the strict definition of the term but who had fled their homes, crossed an international border, and were living in refugee-like conditions. UNHCR officials readily admitted that the 1967 Protocol no longer addressed the realities of today's world. More realistic definitions were offered elsewhere. The Organization of African Unity, for example, defined refugees as "every person who, owing to external aggression, occupation, foreign domination, or events seriously disturbing the public order or nationality, is compelled to leave his place of habitual residence in order to seek refuge in another place outside his country of origin or nationality."[18] And the Intergovernmental Committee for Migration acknowledged two types of refugees: "political refugees"—persons subjected to persecution and violence; and "displaced refugees"—indirect victims obliged to emigrate because of the destruction of their means of subsistence.[19] In May 1981, the UNHCR recommended that all Salvadorans who had left their country since the beginning of 1980 be considered refugees under a prima facie group determination because they had been displaced by political events and were likely to suffer if physically returned to their homeland.[20]

The United States advocated a tougher response during the 1980s. In a letter to the *New York Times,* a spokesperson for the State Department's political asylum division wrote: "It is not enough for the applicant to state that he faces the same conditions that every other citizen faces. [Under the terms of the 1980 Refugee Act we ask,] Why are you different from everyone else in your country? How have you been singled out, threatened, imprisoned, tortured, harassed?"[21] Thus, while in some countries, refugee status was extended simply by membership in a particular group or "class" of people, in the United States the burden of proof was placed on the individual applicant. Asylum applicants had to provide evidence of a "clear probability" of persecution, which was often impossible to prove. The Justice Department regularly rejected asylum petitions of individuals that UNHCR officials, church workers, and legal counsel commonly regarded and referred to as refugees.

In October 1981, the UNHCR charged that the United States was not living up to its responsibilities as a signatory to the UN Protocol, specifically its commitment to *non refoulement,* or no forced return.[22] According to the UNHCR, the United States had failed to grant asylum to any significant number of Salvadorans and was engaged in a "systematic practice" of deporting Salvadorans to their country regardless of the merits of their claims to asylum.[23] UNHCR officials were fully aware of their financial dependence on large donor countries like the United States, so the public criticism was not made easily. Throughout the 1980s, the UNHCR urged the United States to legislate a temporary status other than asylum that would serve as a compromise, offering protection to a group of people who temporarily needed it while allowing the country to maintain its immigration priorities. Such a status would also protect Central Americans from deportation to a war zone and possible death.

Immigration legislation in the United States allowed for such a protected status. Extended Voluntary Departure, or EVD, is a discretionary status given to a group of people when the State Department determines that conditions in the sending country make it is dangerous for them to return. Since 1960, EVD has been granted to Cubans, Dominicans, Cambodians, Vietnamese, Hungarians, Romanians, Iranians, Lebanese, Ethiopians, Afghans, Czechs, Chileans, Ugandans, and Poles. But the Reagan administration resisted the idea of EVD for Central Americans on the grounds that the violence in El Salvador, Nicaragua, and Guatemala was not sufficiently intense or widespread to warrant such an action. Reagan officials also claimed that existing adjudication procedures were sufficient recourse for any "deserving aliens," and disputed the claims that the deportees faced certain death if returned to their homelands.[24] Of course, for the Reagan administration to admit otherwise was to acknowledge that the governments it supported with millions of tax dollars were despotic regimes that violated human rights. The sheer number of Salvadorans also made EVD impossible. According to administration officials, it was one thing to grant EVD to five thousand Poles when martial law was imposed in Poland in 1981; it was quite another to grant EVD to the half-million Salvadorans believed to be in the country by 1983.[25] State and Justice department officials also worried that the promise of EVD would lure even more people to the United States who would then find a way to remain permanently in this country.[26] Thus, while the United States publicly supported safe haven for nonconvention refugees in theory, the Reagan-Bush administrations excluded the Central Americans from any such consideration. From 1983 to 1990, only 2.6 percent of Salvadoran asylum applicants were successful, and only 1.8 percent of Guatemalan applications for the same period were granted.[27]

CRACKDOWN

Immigration reform became a priority for the Reagan administration. The increasing number of undocumented aliens—mostly migrants of the multiracial developing world—signified that current laws and enforcement procedures were inadequate. On March 6, 1981, the administration created a task force to review existing practices, and it submitted its recommendations to Congress in a legislative package.[28] After extensive hearings, Senator Alan Simpson (R-Wyoming) and Representative Romano Mazzoli (D-Kentucky) introduced their own immigration reform bills in March 1983 (S 529, HR 1510), which incorporated many of the administration's proposals. After years of debate and modifications, Congress passed the Immigration Reform and Control Act (IRCA) in 1986 in an attempt to reduce illegal immigration by increasing the border patrol and penalizing employers who knowingly hired undocumented workers.[29] A key provision in the law was an amnesty program that allowed undocumented workers to regularize their status if they could prove that they had entered the country prior to January 1, 1982. Under IRCA's amnesty program: 277,642 Central Americans were able to legalize their status (60 percent of them Salvadorans; 25.4 percent, Guatemalans; and 6 percent, Nicaraguans, with the remaining numbers coming from other Central American countries).[30] However, the majority of Central Americans arrived in the United States after January 1982, making them ineligible.[31]

Long before IRCA was passed, the Justice Department instructed the Immigration and Naturalization Service (INS) and its Border Patrol to increase their surveillance of the United States–Mexico border and expedite the deportation of undocumented aliens.[32] Of particular concern to the Justice Department were the "frivolous" petitions for asylum that bureaucratically tied up the courts. Officials claimed that Central Americans apprehended by Border Patrol agents had little to lose by applying for asylum, since awaiting their hearing could delay their deportation for up to two years. And once the papers were filed and the legal process set in motion, many of them chose to disappear into US society.[33] The goal, then, was to expedite the deportation process. Bail bonds were gradually raised from a hundred dollars to as much as seventy-five hundred dollars per person in some INS districts to prevent their release into society.[34]

Detention centers along the United States–Mexico border filled to capacity with the people the Border Patrol called the OTMs (other than Mexicans). Immigration attorneys and representatives from religious and human rights groups reported a systematic violation of civil liberties on the part of some INS officials. In some detention centers the list of abuses was considerable: women and children were sexually abused; private correspondence was photocopied for government prosecutors; money and property were stolen; phone calls were taped; refugees were denied access to translated legal forms and documents; and many were denied access to legal counsel. Central Americans were regularly tricked into signing deportation papers. One common tactic was to separate family members and tell one spouse that the other had already signed a request for "voluntary departure." Investigators found evidence that some refugees were drugged with tranquilizers and then coerced into signing the I-274A form that waived their right to counsel and a deportation hearing, and then immediately scheduled for voluntary departure. And in particularly tragic cases, information about the deportees was sent to security forces in the homeland, leading to the detention, torture, and murder of some of them.[35]

Abuses at detention centers in Texas and California, especially Port Isabel (popularly known as *el corralón*), Los Fresnos, and El Centro, prompted three lawsuits against the INS in the early 1980s: *Núñez, et al., v. Boldin et al.; El Rescate Legal Services, Inc., et al., v. Executive Office for Immigration Review, et al.;* and *Orantes-Hernández, et al., v. Smith, et al.* US judges hearing these cases ruled in favor of the plaintiffs, ordering the INS to inform detainees of their right to petition asylum, to meet with legal counsel, and to have their legal rights explained in Spanish and English. According to the courts, no one could be deported or coerced to sign voluntary departure forms without being informed of these rights.[36] But over the next few years, the injunctions were repeatedly violated.

PUBLIC CHALLENGES TO US POLICY

Polls conducted during the 1980s revealed that, for most Americans, Central American refugees did not rank high on their list of concerns or priorities. A 1984 CBS News poll revealed that only 25 percent of those interviewed knew which faction the United States supported in El Salvador; and only 13 percent knew that the United States was supporting the Contra rebels in Nicaragua.[37] And even during the height of the Iran–Contra scandal in 1987, only 32 percent of Americans knew that Nicaragua was located in Central America.[38] However, a vocal segment of the US population, reminiscent of the anti-Vietnam War protesters,[39] kept Central America on the front pages of US newspapers. They challenged US refugee policy as a means of protesting US foreign policy in Central America. Indeed, one cannot separate the protests against deportation from the larger cultural protest against US involvement in the region. These Americans argued that the United States had a legal obligation to protect the refugees on the basis of domestic precedent and the international conventions to which it was a signatory, and a moral obligation to do so on the basis of its long history of economic exploitation of the region and the role it currently played in supporting the corrupt military regimes and death squads.

Safe haven for Central Americans was the only option, they argued, because forced return subjected the refugees to harassment, torture, and possibly death. The ACLU and the National Center for Immigrants' Rights, working with the Human Rights Commission in El Salvador, compiled a list of more than one hundred Salvadoran deportees who were murdered after their return in 1981. The ACLU reported that during 1984 there were 119 cases of returnees who were imprisoned, tortured, or murdered.[40] Amnesty International also documented several cases of torture and/or death, including that of twenty-four-year-old Santana Chirino Amaya, deported from the United States to San Salvador and subsequently found tortured and decapitated.[41] While the number of documented murders of deportees seems to have dropped after 1984, thousands of people remained unaccounted for. Some may have returned to Mexico or the United States; others may have relocated to other parts of their country; still others may have met their death at the hands of security police. To refugee advocates, the uncertainty of the deportees' fate in their war-torn homelands was enough evidence that *refoulement* was inhumane. They criticized the Reagan administration for requesting continued aid for El Salvador, to supposedly end the violence, while denying safe haven to the victims of that violence.

During the 1980s, hundreds of articles, books, documentaries and feature films kept Central America in the public consciousness. Think tanks and foundations such as the Inter-American Dialogue and the Carnegie Endowment for Peace commissioned studies that challenged the conclusions of Reagan's National Bipartisan Commission on Central America (the 1984 Kissinger Report). Journalistic accounts such as Joan Didion's *Salvador* and scholarly works such as Walter LaFeber's *Inevitable Revolutions* offered analyses of the conflict for different types of audiences. Television news shows such as *60 Minutes* and *Frontline* aired sympathetic segments on Central America's refugees. Documentaries such as the Academy Award–winning *Americas in Transition,* as well as *Nicaragua: They Will Not Enter, El Salvador. Another Vietnam, They Speak of Hope,* and *In the Name of the People,* among others, portrayed the disastrous consequences of US policy. Hollywood contributed with feature films such as *Under Fire, Salvador, El Norte,* and *Romero* and tried to inform a mass—and generally apathetic—American audience that tended to favor commercial blockbusters like *Rambo* and *Back to the Future.* Even one of the television networks experimented with a Central American theme with its short-lived sitcom *I Married Dora,* which focused on an architect's marriage to an illegal Salvadoran housekeeper to help her avoid deportation.

Dozens of NGOs protested US foreign policy in the Central America, including the Committee in Solidarity with the People of El Salvador

(CISPES), the Washington Office on Latin America; Witness for Peace; the Lawyers' Committee against US Intervention in Central America; Nurses against US Aggression; and the National Central America Health Rights Network. These groups engaged in different types of activism: some collected and transported food and medical supplies for the people of Central America; others sponsored "fact-finding" trips for scholars, legislators, and journalists. They held meetings, rallies, and protests to disseminate information on the wars in Central America, and they organized letter-writing campaigns and testified before Congress. The Washington Office of Latin America, for example, sponsored speaking tours of human rights activists.[42] And the ecumenical Witness for Peace recruited over two thousand Americans to serve as "unarmed human shields" in Nicaragua: groups of volunteers stationed in towns on the Nicaragua-Honduras border to document, and hopefully deter, attacks by the US-funded Contras.[43] In 1984, more than a hundred NGOs participated in a mock trial of Reagan, Bush, Kirkpatrick, and Kissinger, at the UN's Dag Hammerskjold Plaza, to protest the administration's Central America and nuclear policies. They scheduled their protest to coincide with anti-US protests in London and Osaka, to maximize media attention and increase international pressure.[44]

Together with more established international NGOs such as Amnesty International and Americas Watch, these organizations presented a view of the Central American conflict that was quite different from that promoted by the Reagan and Bush administrations. The organizations came under the surveillance of the FBI and other law enforcement agencies, its members harassed and libeled. The FBI interrogated Americans who traveled to Central America; the Customs Department confiscated their diaries and other personal documents; and the IRS audited them or the low-budget advocacy groups they belonged to. On at least fifty occasions, in eleven different cities, the offices of legal aid groups and organizations that challenged administration policies were broken into, their files on refugees, volunteers, and financial donors stolen, their phones tapped and mail intercepted.[45] No one was ever arrested for these activities—indeed the FBI refused to even investigate—but the controversy eventually prompted a congressional investigation. Hearings and declassified documents eventually demonstrated that the CIA, the US State Department, and the FBI collaborated with the Salvadoran National Guard and US-based Salvadoran right-wing activists and security forces to harass Central America activists.[46] In 1988, CISPES and four other organizations filed a class action lawsuit against the FBI, alleging that from March 1983 to June 1985, the FBI spread false information about their group, linking it to Cuban and Salvadoran communists and to assassination attempts and other forms of terrorism, in order to hurt its membership and fund-raising drives.[47]

Religious groups played a central role in the protests of the 1980s: at the grassroots level assisting the refugees; and nationally, as part of an ecumenical movement that lobbied to change policy. As early as 1980, the US Catholic Conference, of over ten thousand members, called on Congress to withhold military aid to El Salvador because its government was "an instrument of terror and repression."[48] Prominent theologians, peace activists, and religious leaders representing a variety of denominations wrote and spoke out against US policy, among them Daniel Berrigan, Elie Weisel, and William Sloane Coffin. Roman Catholic religious orders such as the Maryknolls, the Paulists, and the Jesuits underwrote films and documentaries about Central America, published biographies of church workers assassinated by the death squads, and used their newsletters and periodicals to provide alternative interpretations of events in the region. Religious groups organized petitions and letter-writing campaigns and sent representatives to testify before Congress. A letter to the Subcommittee on Immigration, Refugees, and International Law from the National Council of Churches of Christ stated this general consensus:

> First we hold that the flow of war refugees and asylum-seekers into our country will not cease, no matter what measures are taken along our borders, until the root causes of the flight are addressed. Deep poverty, years of violence and human rights atrocities, political instability and civil war continue to force people to seek safety and stability in the United States. Second, until the root causes of the flow can be addressed, our country must find a way to offer safe haven to Central Americans. . . . Third we would ask that restrictive measures directed against Central American asylum-seekers and war refugees be halted. No person fleeing such conditions should be returned, nor should they be detained. Full due process in asylum adjudication should be observed. In addition, Central Americans should be authorized to work legally, so that they can support their families and themselves with dignity until the day when they can return to their homelands.[49]

Much of their energy focused on the campaign to win EVD status for Central Americans, especially for the Salvadorans, who were believed to be in the most desperate situation.[50] The National Council of Churches of Christ signed a resolution urging *non-refoulement*, temporary safe haven, and fair and expeditious consideration for all those requesting political asylum.[51] Religious groups successfully pressured Western Airlines, under contract with the INS, to end the "death flights" that transported Salvadoran and Guatemalan deportees (the INS turned to the Salvadoran airlines, TACA, instead).[52] Prominent religious leaders also made EVD a personal crusade. Roman Catholic archbishop Joseph Fitzpatrick of Brownsville publicly condemned the human rights violations in INS detention centers and called on President Reagan to grant amnesty to all Central American refugees.[53] William Sloane Coffin, of Manhattan's Riverside Church, chastised the government and American apathy:

> It is an evil thing forcibly to deport innocent civilians to possible detention, torture, and death. Were the US government forcibly returning Soviet Jews to the Soviet Union, or Poles to Poland, neither the Congress nor the American people would stand for it. Why then do so many sit idly by when innocent Salvadorans are being returned to a country whose death squads long ago would have killed Lech Walesa? Why do they tolerate the forceful repatriation of Guatemalans to a government widely viewed as the most brutal in the entire Western hemisphere?[54]

EVD had limited support in the US Congress. On April 7, 1981, the House passed a nonbinding resolution urging that EVD "be granted to El Salvadorans in the US whose safety would be endangered if they were required to return to El Salvador."[55] Two more "sense of Congress" resolutions were passed by late 1983, and eighty-nine members of Congress signed a public letter to the secretary of state and the attorney general requesting that EVD be granted to Salvadoran nationals. In 1983, Senator Dennis DeConcini (D–Arizona) and Representative Joseph Moakley (D–Massachusetts) introduced the first safe haven legislation for Salvadorans, which was debated for the next seven years. The bill passed the House on five different occasions but did not reach the Senate floor until 1990.

Community groups along the United States–Mexico border were at the frontlines of the refugee assistance network and mobilized to provide the Central American refugees with shelter, medical attention, and legal and psychological counseling. The Border Association for Refugees from Central America provided food, shelter, and clothing to the refugees; raised funds to pay the bail bonds of detainees at Port Isabel and other detention centers; and located sponsor families for refugee children alone in this country.[56] Groups such as Proyecto Libertad, El Rescate, the Central American Refugee Center, the Rio Grande Defense Committee, Texas Rural Legal Aid, and the Immigrant and Refugee Rights Project provided free legal counseling and representation. With counsel, refugees could delay deportation for a year or more and, at times, secure release into US society with a work permit while they awaited their hearing. Without legal assistance, detainees were usually deported within a month.

Shelters for the refugees sprang up throughout the Southwest. In the border town of San Benito, Texas, just outside the Brownsville city limits, the Roman Catholic diocese operated Casa Oscar Romero, one of the most important symbols of popular resistance to INS policy. Founded in 1981 by the Missionaries of Jesus, Casa Oscar Romero was a four-room house that initially sheltered a handful of refugees a night, including some detainees who could not be accommodated at the Port Isabel detention center; by 1986, it housed up to six hundred people per night. The Diocese of Brownsville assumed financial responsibility for the shelter, committing an average of sixty thousand dollars a year for operational expenses. Employees and volunteers at Casa Oscar Romero played a key role in the legal battles against the Justice Department in the 1980s.[57] Like CISPES, most of these groups and shelters came under government surveillance. From 1983 to 1985, the FBI monitored their activities and photographed and investigated visitors, clients, office workers, volunteers, and financial donors.[58]

During the 1980s new NGOs emerged to assist the Central Americans who dispersed to towns and cities throughout the country: CASA in Tacoma Park, Maryland, VIVE in Lackawanna, New York, Casa Marianella in Austin, and Casa Juan Diego in Houston were just a handful of organizations that offered counseling, legal aid, job referrals, and other forms of emergency assistance.

THE SANCTUARY MOVEMENT

By the mid-1980s, thousands of Americans were engaged in one of the most important acts of civil disobedience of the late twentieth century—the sanctuary movement—a grassroots resistance movement that protested US foreign policy through the harboring and transporting of refugees, in violation of immigration law.

The movement began, appropriately enough, along the United States–Mexico border. Beginning in 1980, the local press reported a growing number of Central Americans among those apprehended by the Border Patrol.[59] Community groups that assisted immigrants also noticed a steady increase in the number of Central Americans arriving at their offices, asking for help. Those fortunate enough to survive the border crossing told horrible tales of the wars in their homelands: aerial bombardments that destroyed their towns and villages; friends and relatives kidnapped by guerrilla groups or murdered by government security forces; threats of rape, mutilation, and death if they challenged the existing order. Throughout the Southwest, churches, soup kitchens, shelters, and legal aid offices that assisted Mexicans, Chileans, Cubans, and other immigrants stretched already tight resources to assist the needs of the growing number of Central Americans who now arrived on their doorsteps.

It is out of this context that the movement called sanctuary emerged. During the summer of 1981, Jim Corbett, a Quaker goat rancher in Tucson, Arizona, began a personal campaign to assist the Central Americans detained in INS prisons. When his property could no longer accommodate the dozens of refugees he bonded out of prison, he appealed to his friends in the Tucson community for help. Corbett envisioned a network of "safe houses" for the refugees similar to the Underground Railroad that hid escaped slaves in the antebellum period. He traveled to Nogales and other cities in Mexico, and established contacts to assist with his secret network. They agreed to find ways to transport Central Americans across the border to the United States, where they had a slightly better chance of securing asylum. As a longtime resident of the borderlands and fluent in Spanish, Corbett was familiar with the terrain and the various INS checkpoints, and volunteered to direct refugees across the safest routes to sanctuary sites. By the fall of 1981, this new underground movement—the tucson refugee support group—was in place.[60]

As the safe houses filled up, Corbett asked his friend Rev. John Fife, of Southside Presbyterian Church, if the church might serve as a sanctuary site. Like so many churches in the borderlands, Southside was committed to social justice projects in Tucson, among them the bail bond project that raised funds for the Central Americans detained in US prisons. As a member of the Tucson Ecumenical Council Task Force on Central America, Southside church members met regularly to study and discuss the scriptures and liberation theology and to read and learn about the situation in Central America. They discussed the proper course of action for a people of faith, especially in light of the eventual deportation of so many of the refugees whom they bonded out of prison but who were unsuccessful in securing asylum. The congregation carefully debated Corbett's request. They studied the history of sanctuary, both in its Judeo-Christian and American civic forms, and debated the legal consequences of practicing this tradition if they made a commitment to house the refugees. In November 1981, the church session voted in favor of serving as a safe house for the Central American refugees.

Meanwhile, hundreds of miles away, in the San Francisco Bay area, several local church congregations were discussing the same issues and also debating the idea of sanctuary. They, too, voted to establish safe houses for Central American refugees. Some members proposed that they enlist the aid of the news media and make their activities public, both as a means of raising American consciousness about Central America and as a means of combating the INS discourse that labeled them as smugglers and law-breakers.[61] In January 1982, they voted to make a public declaration of sanctuary and contacted the Tucson volunteers to coordinate their actions. On March 24, 1982 (the second anniversary of Archbishop Romero's assassination), Southside Presbyterian and five churches in Berkeley, California, publicly declared themselves to be sanctuaries for Central American refugees. In an open letter to Attorney General William French Smith, the Reverend Fife explained their actions: "We take this action because we believe the current policy and practice of the US government with regard to Central American refugees is illegal and immoral. We believe our government is in violation of the 1980 Refugee Act and international law by continuing to arrest, detain, and forcibly return refugees to terror, persecution, and murder in El Salvador and Guatemala."[62]

During the next few years, over two hundred churches, temples, and synagogues across the country followed suit, representing a variety of denominations: Baptists, Episcopalians, Roman Catholics, Lutherans, Mennonites, Methodists, Presbyterians, Quakers, Unitarians, and conservative and reform Jews. California was home to the largest number of church-declared sanctuaries (one hundred); in the San Francisco Bay area alone, over forty different groups provided legal and charitable assistance to the estimated eighty thousand Salvadorans living in the city.[63] The support network also encompassed hundreds of churches and religious groups in the United States, Mexico, and Canada that assisted the sanctuary sites in their work, either with volunteers or with financial and other material contributions. Thus, the movement was transnational in both composition and influence. Over twenty US religious bodies endorsed the sanctuary movement.[64] A resolution passed by the National Council of Churches of Christ urged member communities to "give serious consideration to the sanctuary movement as an expression and embodiment of the Christian's duty to the suffering, and to afford affirmation and support to those persons and congregations who choose to pursue this difficult path."[65]

For some sanctuary workers, the goal was to hide the refugees until US policy changed or until they were able to return to their countries of origin. For others, the goal was to transport them to Canada, which had a more liberal asylum policy. For those refugees who preferred the latter, Houston and Los Angeles served as "funnel" cities, where refugees congregated to await transport to Canada. It was financially impossible to pay their air fares to Toronto or Montreal (the cities with the largest Central American populations), so the refugees were transported to various safe houses across the country until they reached the United States–Canada border. There they crossed at the relatively unprotected stretches of border, such as the North Dakota–Manitoba boundary line, and were met by Canadian sanctuary workers; or they crossed at busy checkpoints and immediately filed for asylum. By the late 1980s, there were three principal routes to Canada: one route took refugees across the Midwest, with stops in Little Rock, St. Louis, and Chicago before they reached the border crossings at Detroit and Buffalo. Another well-traveled route had refugees fly from Houston to New York City, then take a bus to Plattsburgh, where they crossed the border at Lacolle, Quebec, and then on to Montreal. The third route, took refugees from Los Angeles through San Francisco and Seattle, ending in Vancouver.[66]

Beginning in 1982, the Chicago Religious Task Force on Central America served as coordinator and clearinghouse for much of this vast national network.[67] The CRTF (which eventually formed the National Sanctuary Alliance) distributed manuals (i.e., the *Organizer's Nuts and Bolts*) instructing churches on ways to assist the movement. The CRTF and its member groups organized activities that would guarantee media attention: They organized speaking tours for visiting activists from Central America, who gave eyewitness accounts of what was happening in their countries. They trained refugees for public speaking so that they could give *testimonios*. They organized ecumenical prayer services, candlelight vigils, processions, and caravans to honor the victims of war. They sponsored lectures, concerts, and festivals of Central American arts and crafts. These activities no doubt played a critical role in focusing attention on US policies, but it was the rank-and-file volunteers in individual communities—many of them housewives and retirees—who engaged in the riskiest activities: sheltering refugees or transporting them to safe houses or across the border into Canada.[68] And they worked anonymously and quietly, without the praise of sympathetic journalists—and oftentimes without the approval of the CRTF and other coordinating boards who wished to keep the movement closely supervised.

Those involved in the underground claimed to be following not only a Judeo-Christian tradition but also an American civic tradition. Examples of sanctuary could be found in the American Revolutionary War, the antebellum and Civil War periods, and more recently, during the Vietnam era, when dozens of churches hid conscientious objectors from arrest. Critics of sanctuary, however, claimed that this movement seemed more concerned with challenging US policy in Central America than with addressing the physical and emotional needs of the refugees. If the refugees were their primary consideration, they argued, they could do their work covertly, without the media hoopla and the open confrontation that risked the refugees' arrest by INS agents. One prominent religious leader explained his opposition:

I consider it immoral to practice confrontational civil disobedience where third parties are involved who will share in the punishment if the public authorities choose to act against the one who is practicing civil disobedience. If a priest or minister, after proclaiming publicly that his church will harbor refugees illegally in this country, has his church raided by INS or other federal authorities, it will be the refugees themselves who will suffer the greatest penalty: deportation back to their country, where they may be killed. The priest or minister will likely escape with a light fine or probation.[69]

But as in liberation theology, sanctuary workers believed that the spiritual and the political were inseparable. One could serve the refugees while challenging the political order. The primary goal was to rouse an apathetic population who cared little about the world outside its national borders and who gave tacit support to immoral and illegal government actions.[70] This raising of consciousness, they argued, would ultimately lead to a change in policy.

As the movement expanded, sanctuary workers inevitably disagreed over the organization of the underground and its strategies. Two separate streams emerged within the movement (each with its own set of dissenters). One stream, represented by the Tucson contingent, favored localized consensus, while the other stream, represented by the CRTF, favored a top-down approach, with an elected board setting national goals and policy. One scholar of the movement attributed the divergent views to the Quaker/Congregationalist origins of the Tucson group versus the largely Catholic orientation of the CRTF.[71] Sanctuary workers also disagreed about fundamental questions, such as whether their work was civil disobedience or civil initiative.[72] And they disagreed on which refugees to assist through the underground. Some sanctuary workers, for example, felt that refugees who had lived in Mexico for a period of time before moving to the United States should be automatically disqualified from the underground because they had already found safe haven elsewhere. Others wanted to restrict the underground to those individuals fleeing violence, not the perpetrators (army deserters, for example, who might have played a role in killing their compatriots).[73] And some opposed assisting Nicaraguans for ideological reasons or because they incorrectly assumed that Nicaraguans were either Somozistas or did not need assistance because immigration law favored them.[74] Many sanctuary workers, however, vehemently opposed any litmus test or screening procedures, because in designating some groups as "worthier" than others they would be as guilty as the US government. The disagreements over these various issues were fractious enough to force some groups to sever association with a member group or with national coordinating groups such as the CRTF.[75]

Church groups and other non-governmental organizations offered their own guidelines on sanctuary for those who disagreed with the CRTF's philosophy and/or strategy. The American Friends Service Committee, the Church World Service Immigration and Refugee Program, the Inter-Religious Task Force on El Salvador and Central America, and the Lutheran Immigration and Refugee Service jointly published a manual entitled *Seeking Safe Haven: A Congregational Guide to Helping Central American Refugees in the United States.* It offered practical advice on topics such as organizing a house meeting, releasing refugees from detention centers, legal rights, and the individual and institutional sponsorship of refugees. For those interested in shaping policy, the manual offered advice on lobbying, media work, and public education.

Officials of the Reagan administration tried to discourage the growth of the sanctuary movement by dismissing this civic tradition and reminding activists that the principle of sanctuary was not recognized in common or statutory law. Whenever a church congregation wrote to inquire about the legality of the movement, a Justice Department official emphatically warned that clergy and church workers were not exempt from prosecution. Section 274(a) of the Immigration and Nationality Act identified as a violator anyone who "willfully or knowingly conceals, harbors, or shields from detection . . . any alien . . . not duly admitted by an immigration officer or not lawfully entitled to enter or reside in the United States."[76] Violators faced fines of up to two thousand dollars and/or imprisonment for up to five years for harboring or smuggling, and fines of ten thousand dollars and/or five years imprisonment for conspiracy to harbor. A letter drafted specifically in response to such questions included this reminder:

We are a nation of law. There is an existing statute under which a person can claim and be granted asylum if the individual can prove personal persecution. The statute provides a right to counsel and a hearing in an immigration court, as well as a right to appeal in the Federal courts. We believe that individuals who wish to aid persons from Central America can serve them best by encouraging and assisting them to submit their claims for review within the existing system for asylum adjudications. All claims submitted in accordance with the law receive a full and fair adjudication within the system established for that purpose.[77]

During the 1980s, the work of these religious groups and the influence they held over public opinion posed a serious threat to US policy, and not surprisingly the administration tried to undermine their influence. Just as Kirkpatrick, Haig, and others portrayed some of the assassinated clergy of Central America as guerrilla sympathizers who got what they deserved, Justice Department officials portrayed sanctuary workers and other peace activists as naive and misguided at best, political extremists and terrorists at worst. The conservative Institute for Religion and Democracy branded liberation theology a Marxist plot to undermine capitalism and the geopolitical order. It criticized sanctuary workers for using religion to manipulate the public to support their political agenda, and pressured US churches to sever ties to socially active church groups in Latin America and at home.[78] In Los Angeles and other cities, tax assessors warned churches that they would be stripped of their tax-exempt status if they provided shelter to Central Americans.[79] In congressional testimony, the Center for Constitutional Rights reported a "growing number of . . . FBI visits, IRS audits, customs difficulties, mail tamperings, and break-ins, directed against . . . people involved in the sanctuary movement."[80]

But sanctuary workers were willing to risk their freedom because they believed that they were answering a higher call. When Father Thomas Davis was arrested by the Border Patrol for transporting seven Nicaraguans and six Guatemalans from Laredo to Corpus Christi, Texas, he responded: "I felt we had a special obligation to these people. You have to do something as a Christian. We were caught between the laws of man and the laws of God. I chose the laws of God."[81] The chairperson of the Wellington Avenue Church in Chicago responded to the threats of fines and imprisonment: "Dangerous times call for risky responses. The consequences that may happen to Wellington are minimal in comparison to the pain that happens every day to the people of El Salvador and Guatemala."[82] Sister Darlene Nicgorski, convicted for her sanctuary work in Arizona said: "When all is said and done, I would rather be judged for having helped a refugee than for having defined what one is."[83]

The issue of sanctuary did divide religious congregations, however, as members debated the moral, theological, and legal implications of challenging the government.[84] When clergy took a more liberal stance than their congregations were willing to accept, members defected, which brought the inevitable reprimand from superiors—and in some cases, expulsion—for neglecting their pastoral duties.[85] People of faith looking to the church for guidance were often frustrated, since many churches chose not to speak out on the issue of sanctuary on the advice of their attorneys. As the largest Christian denomination in the border states, and in the country, Roman Catholics found sanctuary particularly confusing and divisive. Governing bodies such as the US Catholic Conference and the National Council of Catholic Bishops condemned US actions in Central America but chose to remain silent on sanctuary—a response some interpreted as tacit approval of the movement.[86] Even Pope John Paul II gave mixed signals to Catholics. During a 1987 visit to the United States, he praised the "great courage and generosity" of those who protected illegal Central Americans from deportation, but when the press interpreted his statement as an endorsement of sanctuary, some church leaders asked him to clarify that he did not endorse lawbreaking.[87] Individual nuns and priests, especially members of the more liberal Maryknoll, Franciscan, and Jesuit orders, were more likely to take a public position on sanctuary, often risking censure from bishops more concerned with protecting the church's uneasy ties with the state.[88]

The Justice Department began its surveillance of the sanctuary movement in 1982, and a number of individuals were indicted soon after. Their penalties varied, depending on the location of the trial and the sympathies of the judge and jury. In 1984, in Brownsville, Texas, Stacey Lynn Merkt, an employee at Casa Oscar Romero, was sentenced to 269 days in prison. She became the first sanctuary worker to be imprisoned (Amnesty International declared her a prisoner of conscience). Jack Elder, the director of Casa Oscar Romero, was convicted on six counts of conspiracy and transporting illegal aliens through south Texas. He served 150 days in a halfway house for parolees. In 1985, Elder's successor at Casa Oscar Romero, Lorry Thomas, was sentenced to two years in prison for transporting a Nicaraguan refugee. The arrests did not stop sanctuary activities, however, and like Merkt and Elder, many of those imprisoned were repeat "offenders."[89]

Refugee workers complained that they were singled out for prosecution because they questioned Reagan's policies on Central America, while the coyotes who smuggled illegal aliens from Mexico for wealthy US ranchers to employ were rarely harassed—a charge that was, of course, denied by the Border Patrol.[90] "It seems strange that with all the illegal aliens coming through the valley every day that the authorities would put the finger on my people and no one else," remarked Bishop Joseph Fitzpatrick of Brownsville.[91] As sanctuary workers were arrested, others emerged to take their place. The Rio Grande Defense Committee and the Chicago Religious Task Force established the Border Witness Program, small groups of volunteers who worked for two-week stretches guiding refugees to the appropriate agencies, volunteering at shelters like Casa Oscar Romero, and monitoring Border Patrol activities at bus stations, airports, and highway checkpoints.[92]

The biggest sting against the sanctuary movement occurred in Tucson, Arizona, in 1984–85 in the covert Operation Sojourner, which led to the indictment of sixteen sanctuary workers. The FBI infiltrated four men, two paid informants and two INS officers, into various sanctuary sites, including Southside Presbyterian Church. The two paid informants, Jesús Cruz and Salomón Delgado, had been previously arrested for smuggling illegal immigrants for a Florida rancher.[93] Posing as concerned volunteers, they gained the trust of the sanctuary workers and attended their meetings, where they taped the conversations. With the one hundred tape recordings gathered over a ten-month period, the Justice Department charged sixteen people, including Corbett and Fife, with seventy-one counts of conspiracy and transporting/harboring illegal aliens.[94] (Charges against five were eventually dropped.) Over eighty other people—refugees and the church workers who had transported them—were arrested as coconspirators.[95]

At the pretrial hearings, US prosecutor Donald Reno introduced a motion to block any evidence relating to the defendants' religious and humanitarian motives, US foreign policy in Central America, human rights abuses in the region, as well as any information on the asylum process— to strengthen the government's case that sanctuary workers were simply smugglers using religion as a cover-up for their criminal actions.[96] (Indeed, the prosecution argued that the defense should not even be allowed to refer to the Central Americans as refugees.) The defense counsel, in turn, introduced a motion to dismiss all charges on the basis of the defendants' constitutionally protected religious beliefs and the illegal infiltration of church activities that violated the separation between church and state.[97] The judge ruled in favor of the prosecution, and the trial began. After six months of evidence and testimonies, the jury found eight of the eleven defendants guilty of various charges, including conspiracy. While deliberating on the sentences, Judge E. H. Carroll received hundreds of letters urging leniency, including one signed by forty-seven members of Congress.[98] In the end, all were given suspended sentences of three to five years probation. (Three years later, a federal appeals court upheld their conviction.)[99]

The Justice Department claimed success. In an interview, INS commissioner Alan Nelson remarked, "Above all, this case has demonstrated that no group, no matter how well-meaning or highly-motivated, can arbitrarily violate the laws of the United States."[100] Prosecutor Reno called the verdict "the death knell for the sanctuary movement."[101] However, if the Justice Department hoped to intimidate sanctuary workers into silence, the plan backfired. The arrests and trial dominated television, radio, and the printed press. Radio networks such as Pacifica and NPR covered the trial, as did international networks such as the BBC. Dozens of magazines, newspapers, and television stations covered the story. Even newspapers like the *Los Angeles Times,* which generally favored tougher immigration controls, criticized the government's infiltration of the movement. One editorial cartoon showed a Border Patrol agent arresting Jesus Christ and his apostles.

The public outcry against Operation Sojourner was significant. "The trial did us a lot of good," said one Arizona sanctuary worker.[102] Over two hundred new sanctuaries emerged during the trial of the eleven activists. By December 1987, the number of sanctuaries had reached 450, including two states that made official pronouncements, twenty-eight cities, 430 distinct religious bodies in thirty-nine states, and over 70,000 active participants.[103] Among the most visible of the new participants was the Reverend Richard Sinner, brother of George Sinner, governor of North Dakota at the time, who felt "called" to transport refugees across the North Dakota–Manitoba border to his contacts in Canada.[104] The Inter-American Symposium on Sanctuary, held in Tucson a week after the arrests, drew over fifteen hundred people rather than the expected two or three hundred.[105] Two hundred representatives from Christian and Jewish congregations traveled to Washington to demand a congressional investigation of the Justice Department's surveillance and intimidation practices; and eighty religious groups filed a lawsuit against the US government. In the years after the trial, no other workers of the sanctuary movement were arrested, partly because members became more savvy about their activities, and partly because the Reagan and Bush administrations could not afford more negative publicity about their Central American policy.[106]

The fallout of Operation Sojourner was felt for years to come and even had a transnational effect. International attention on the Tucson trial revived the sanctuary debate all over Europe, especially as refugees in various countries there appealed for sanctuary to avoid deportation.[107] Sanctuary workers received a number of honors. In December 1986, former president Jimmy Carter and South African bishop Desmond Tutu presented Reverend John Fife the Rothko Chapel Award for Commitment to Truth and Freedom (and six years later, Fife was elected the national leader of the Presbyterian Church USA). Sister Darlene Nicgorski, one of the eight convicted, was named one of *Ms.* magazine's women of the year. In May 1988, four hundred church delegates from forty-two countries met in France and passed a resolution supporting those convicted in Tucson.[108]

In the end, the sanctuary sites of the 1980s assisted only a small percentage of the hundreds of thousands of Central Americans who crossed over to the United States (one source estimated two thousand were assisted),[109] in large part because word spread through the informal immigrant networks that media attention brought government surveillance.[110] But the public debates that resulted from sanctuary ultimately facilitated the legal changes that gave Central Americans certain protections in US society. The sanctuary movement also served Americans, albeit in a very different fashion, by focusing attention on constitutional and philosophical issues important to a democratic society.

THE LEGAL BATTLE FOR ASYLUM

State policies toward the Central American refugees inspired a staggering number of lawsuits during the 1980s and early 1990s. The first lawsuits filed on behalf of the refugees were those trying to address the civil rights violations of detainees in INS prisons. *Noe Castillo Núñez, et al., v. Hal Boldin, et al.,* was a class action suit filed in 1981 on behalf of Salvadorans and Guatemalans detained at the INS facility at Los Fresnos, Texas, who had been denied basic rights, including the right to meet with legal counsel prior to and during all legal proceedings. The court issued an injunction in January 1982 prohibiting the INS from denying detainees their rights.[111]

In the lawsuit *Orantes-Hernández, et al., v. Smith, et al.,* the Salvadoran plaintiffs, representing detainees at INS detention centers at El Centro and Chula Vista, California, issued a nationwide challenge to the adjudication process. These plaintiffs claimed that they had fled political persecution, torture, and death in El Salvador in hopes of finding refuge in the United States, and instead met with "a summary removal process . . . carried out with little or no regard for the procedural or substantive rights of aliens under United States immigration law." They charged the INS with failing to advise detainees of their rights to counsel, to apply for asylum, and to have a hearing before deportation, as well as using coercive tactics to force them to accept "voluntary departure." On April 30, 1982, the court granted the motion for provisional class certification and issued a preliminary injunction against the INS.[112] A permanent injunction was issued in 1988 and upheld in 1990.[113] However, the INS continued to violate the detainees' rights to due process.[114] As late as 1989, attorneys filed class action suits on behalf of Central American refugees. In *El Rescate Legal Services, Inc., et al., v. Executive Office for Immigration Review, et al.,* the plaintiffs charged the Executive Office with failing to provide defendants with full Spanish interpretation of court proceedings, thus depriving them of due process. In November 1989, the court ruled in favor of the plaintiffs.[115]

A 1987 Supreme Court decision in *Immigration and Naturalization Service v. Cardoza-Fonseca* also revised the adjudication process and reinterpreted the 1980 Refugee Act. The case involved a Nicaraguan citizen who entered the country illegally in 1979. The plaintiff testified that her brother, with whom she had fled Nicaragua, had been tortured and imprisoned there because of his political beliefs. Even though she had not been politically active herself, she petitioned for asylum on the grounds that her brother's status and her own opposition to the Sandinista government would cause her to be tortured if she were forced to return. An immigration judge found that she was not entitled to relief because she had failed to establish a "clear probability of persecution." The Board of Immigration Appeals upheld the decision, but the US Court of Appeals, Ninth Circuit, reversed it. Upholding the decision by the appeals court, the Supreme Court ruled that the "well-founded fear" standard of proof for refugee status (section 208[a] of the 1980 Refugee Act) was not equivalent to the "more likely than not" standard required for the withholding of deportation under section 243(h). Congress had used a broader language to determine the category of refugee than it used to define the class of aliens who had a right to relief from deportation.[116] Asylum officers were henceforth advised to evaluate applications in light of general conditions in the country of origin to see if "there is a pattern or practice of persecuting the group of persons similarly situated."[117] To assist in these efforts, the INS established the Resource Information Center to provide adjudicators with information from a wide variety of sources, not just the traditional Department of State bulletins.

None of these lawsuits, however, halted the deportation of Central Americans; they just delayed the inevitable. As one official from the Asylum Policy and Review Unit stated, the avoidance of guerrilla activities did not serve as grounds for asylum.[118] As many as half of all asylum applicants (regardless of country) were unable to retain their own counsel, which made it three times more likely that they would be denied asylum.[119] Salvadorans were regularly deported despite pleas from Salvadoran government officials that accommodating the returnees would destabilize the country. In May 1987, President José Napoleón Duarte personally wrote Ronald Reagan listing several reasons why a stay in deportations was necessary, among them that El Salvador's fragile, war-torn economy had become dependent on the 350–600 million dollars in annual remittances that expatriates sent relatives back home.[120] However, US policymakers remained unmoved. During the Bush administration, the Justice Department announced it was streamlining the adjudication process to expedite deportations. The goal was to interview as many as four hundred asylum applicants a day and decide 95 percent of the cases within three hours of completion of the interview.

At the Harlingen, Texas, office, one of the busiest in the country, at least four INS examiners evaluated the same batch of petitions each day to avoid irregularities that might tie up the courts. In addition, the government terminated its policy of granting one-year work permits to asylum applicants and ordered them to remain in the INS district in which they had originally petitioned for asylum. Those individuals whose petitions were denied were immediately detained until deportation was possible. Detention centers were expanded to accommodate the overflow: at Port Isabel, tents were erected within the prison compound to increase the holding capacity to ten thousand. Of the 617 Central Americans who applied voluntarily for asylum at the Harlingen office between February 21 and April 5, 1989, only 58 were granted asylum.[121] However, this more rigorous enforcement of policy did not discourage Central Americans from crossing the border; it only discouraged them from voluntarily applying for asylum. Between January and May 1989, voluntary asylum applications had dropped from as many as five hundred a day to fewer than ten a day.[122]

The decisions handed down in the various lawsuits against the INS did serve to buttress a larger class action lawsuit against the United States government filed by eighty religious and refugee assistance groups in 1985, with the goal of securing asylum for Salvadorans and Guatemalans. *American Baptist Churches in the USA, et al., v. Edwin Meese III and Alan Nelson* (popularly known as the ABC lawsuit) combined the suits of two separate groups of plaintiffs. The first group represented sanctuary workers who sought an injunction against government interference with their First Amendment right to the free exercise of religion. The second group, the refugee service organizations, sought an injunction against the deportation of Salvadorans and Guatemalans, as well as a "declaratory judgement that persons fleeing war, persecution, and widespread human rights violations in Guatemala and El Salvador are entitled to temporary refuge within the United States until such time as those conditions no longer exist in those countries."[123] The government's motion to dismiss the case was denied in 1987, and the case proceeded through the courts.

In January 1991, a settlement agreement was reached in the ABC lawsuit that further assisted Salvadorans and Guatemalans in their efforts to remain in the United States.[124] Among the requirements of the settlement were: (a) Salvadorans and Guatemalans still in the United States, whether previous petitioners for asylum or not, were entitled to a new adjudication process to be overseen by a newly trained corps of asylum officers; (b) petitioners were entitled to work authorization while they awaited a decision in their case; and (c) asylum officers were not allowed to consider prior denial of asylum in their deliberations, or the petitioner's country of origin, or the State Department's opinions and recommendations, but *were* allowed to consider human rights reports from non-governmental agencies such as Amnesty International. The settlement agreement stipulated that "the fact that an individual is from a country whose government the United States supports or with which it has favorable relations is not relevant to the determination of whether an applicant for asylum [has] a well-founded fear of persecution."[125] The ABC settlement over-turned more than 150,000 cases, granting new trials to Salvadorans who had entered the United States before September 19, 1990 and all Guate-malans who had entered before October 1, 1990.

As a parallel development, Congress passed the omnibus Immigration Act of 1990, which included the statutory basis for safe haven through a *temporary protected status*. Over two hundred thousand Salvadorans living in the United States registered for TPS.[126] One month before their TPS was set to expire on June 20, 1992, Salvadoran president Alfredo Cristiani contacted the Bush administration and requested that the policy be extended until the country was better prepared to deal with the tens of thousands of its countrymen scheduled to return. However, on the expi-ration of TPS, Salvadorans became eligible for a new status, Deferred Enforced Departure (DED), which delayed deportation for one year. In 1993, DED was once again extended—first to December 1994, and then to March 1996. Under the terms of the ABC settlement, Salvadorans were eligible to apply for asylum once their DED status expired.

With TPS, DED, and the new asylum adjudication process, Salvadorans now had more vehicles through which to negotiate their legal stay in the United States. For sanctuary workers, legal counsel, and all those involved in the protests of the 1980s, these developments were a significant vic-tory. Few newspaper articles and editorials focused on the fact that the Nicaraguans and Guatemalans had fewer options. For most Americans, the term *Central American refugee* was synonymous with Salvadorans, who were by far the largest Central American group in the United States and the group believed to be in greatest need of safe haven. That this became the dominant discourse in policy debates demonstrates the importance of lobbying, political patronage, and the media. The next section examines one group's struggles to remain in the United States.

CENTRAL AMERICANS AS PAWNS—AND INSTRUMENTS—
OF POLICYMAKING: NICARAGUANS AS A CASE STUDY

During the 1980s, the US government was not as accommodating of the Nicaraguans as has been generally assumed. This was surprising given the

Reagan administration's obsession with overthrowing the Sandinistas, who they claimed were oppressing the Nicaraguan people. It was also surprising given US asylum preference for those fleeing communist regimes, and the US government, and the Nicaraguans refugees themselves, claimed that they were fleeing an oppressive Marxist regime.

By the end of the decade, close to two hundred thousand Nicaraguans, or 40 percent of their total number in the United States, resided in Dade County, Florida, specifically in the city of Sweetwater, regarded as the heart of "Little Managua."[127] Tens of thousands more settled in Los Angeles, San Francisco, Houston, New York, and other cities. Although the wealthy and upper middle class comprised the earlier arrivals, the majority of those who migrated from Nicaragua were working class, and they represented a wide political spectrum. Existing side by side in the Nicaraguan exile population were members of the Somoza government and the National Guard, the Sandinistas and the Contras, as well as those victimized and uprooted by their policies. Like their fellow Central Americans, the majority of Nicaraguans arrived illegally, or became illegal once their visas expired, and depended on powerful allies to defend their interests.

The principal characteristic that differentiated the Nicaraguan experience in the United States from that of other Central Americans was that Nicaraguans were slightly more successful in securing asylum. From June 1983 to September 1990, not more than 3 percent of Salvadoran and Guatemalan asylum applications were successful (2.6 percent for Salvadorans and 1.8 percent for Guatemalans).[128] In turn, the Nicaraguans had a composite approval rate of 25.2 percent during the period 1983–90. (Those coming from the USSR, in comparison, had an asylum rate of 76.7 percent).[129]

Immediately after the success of the Sandinista revolution, the Carter administration granted Extended Voluntary Departure to Nicaraguans already in the United States, which protected them from immediate deportation and gave them temporary work permits, renewable every six months. Between July 3, 1979, and September 28, 1980, the Nicaraguans qualified for EVD status. However, in 1983, Nicaraguans began receiving notices revoking their work permits. More often than not, those who applied for asylum found their claims rejected.[130] In fiscal year 1984, only 12 percent of asylum applications were approved; and in 1985, 9 percent.[131]

This surprised immigration lawyers, who believed that the Nicaraguans would be allowed to remain in the United States if only because they had so much in common with the Cuban exiles, a group that the US government had legally accommodated in so many ways.[132]

The number of illegal immigrants arriving in the United States during the 1980s increased with each year; in south Florida alone an estimated six hundred new Nicaraguans arrived each week during 1985, traveling on Greyhound buses from Harlingen and Brownsville, Texas.[133] There they hoped to find employment in the large and successful Cuban enclave that had accommodated thousands of legal and illegal immigrants from Latin America and the Caribbean since the 1960s. In Miami, the Nicaraguans organized to protest what they considered to be an unfair policy. "There is a total incongruency between what President Reagan says and what the State Department does," said the cochair of the Nicaraguan Humanitarian Coalition. "Mr. Reagan says that Nicaragua has a dictatorial Communist regime which oppresses our people, and the State Department and the INS say to thousands of Nicaraguans that they were not persecuted at all." In June 1987, a Miami group called the Committee of Poor Nicaraguans in Exile sponsored a trip for over a hundred Nicaraguan children to Washington, D.C., so that the administration "could see exactly who it was they were deporting."[134]

Powerful allies pressured the US government to change its asylum policy. For the Nicaraguans, one ally was found in Perry Rivkind, the district director of the INS in south Florida, who announced in 1986 that he would no longer deport Nicaraguans. "For me it is agonizing to have to reject their applications," he said, "because their asylum claims under present regulations are very hard to prove. Nicaraguans are fleeing Communism. They are a decent, hard-working people who have not given our authorities here any problems."[135]

After the *INS v. Cardoza-Fonseca* decision, Attorney General Edwin Meese initiated the Nicaraguan Review Program: Nicaraguans denied asylum were allowed to reapply for asylum and acquire work authorization pending the review of their cases.[136] Not coincidentally, his announcement came just as the Reagan administration was negotiating with Congress for increased aid to the Contras. Assisting the Nicaraguans in securing asylum reflected and reinforced the general discourse that the Sandinista government was repressive and needed to be overthrown.

According to the US Committee for Refugees, few Nicaraguans whose cases went up for review during this period were deported. By the end of fiscal year 1987, the Nicaraguans' asylum approval rate had shot up to 84 percent.[137] (By 1989, however, when Congress cut off aid to the administration's protégés, asylum approval rates dropped again, this time to 26 percent; and from 1991 to 1993, only 10.7 percent of asylum petitions were approved.)[138]

However, this brief reversal in policy served as a green light urging others to come to the United States. In 1988 the number of Central Americans asking for asylum at border entry points like Harlingen tripled, reflecting the hopes that the United States was becoming more accepting of Central American migration as a whole.[139] Nicaraguan migration into Dade County increased: an estimated fifty thousand new undocumented workers arrived in south Florida from 1988 to 1990.[140] Over four hundred Nicaraguan children enrolled in Dade County public schools each month, enough to fill up six new elementary schools, and they became the largest group of foreign-born children in that school system.[141] In Florida, Nicaraguans received little assistance from the state and local governments, who were reluctant to assist the refugees for fear of attracting even more of them to south Florida. Public school and health service systems were already strained by the thousands of immigrants that arrived each year from all over the Americas. In 1989 in a desperate response to the growing number of homeless refugees, the Miami City government began housing them in Bobby Maduro Stadium, only to shut the stadium down a month later because of overcrowding.[142]

Members of the Nicaraguan community in south Florida were active in asserting their political rights. Imitating the Cuban American lobby, their local role models, the Nicaraguans created dozens of organizations to lobby for their migratory and foreign policy concerns. Members of the Committee of Poor Nicaraguans in Exile demonstrated in front of the White House; the Nicaraguan Solidarity Union staged a hunger strike to demand work authorization; the Coalition for Nicaraguan Civil Rights lobbied the Justice Department for an end to deportations; the Committee of the Nicaraguan Community paid the bail bonds and attorneys of thousands of compatriots held in detention centers along the United States–Mexico border; and the Nicaraguan American National Foundation initiated a letter-writing campaign demanding safe haven.[143] In a community as politically divided as the Nicaraguans, the struggle to acquire a legal status in the United States became one of the few unifying issues. Issues such as the logic or morality of US aid to the Contras were more heatedly contested.

In 1990, many in the Nicaraguan exile population celebrated the news of the Sandinistas' electoral defeat. On the streets of Miami, tens of thousands of Nicaraguans celebrated the victory of Violeta Barrios de Chamorro and her UNO coalition. At a rally at the Orange Bowl, Arnoldo Alemán, the mayor-elect of Managua, enthusiastically told the crowd: "We are waiting for you with open arms. We are going to change Nicaragua, we are going to fulfill the dreams that for years and years we have dreamed."[144] Soon afterward, direct flights were established between Miami and Managua, anticipating the return of the exiles.[145] Representatives of the Chamorro government visited the various exile communities throughout the United States to urge professionals, entrepreneurs, and skilled workers to return, appealing to their nationalism. Aware that the exiles were afraid to forfeit their safety in the United States to face an unknown future in their homeland, the Chamorro government asked the Bush administration to allow exiles to return to Nicaragua without forfeiting the option of one day returning to live and work in the United States.[146]

According to the Nicaraguan Task Force in Miami, some four thousand Nicaraguans returned to their homeland within months of Violeta Barrios de Chamorro's victory. Exiles living elsewhere in the region repatriated in larger numbers: twenty-five thousand Nicaraguans in Honduras and Costa Rica repatriated in the last six months of 1990, and by 1993, seventy-one thousand had returned from those two countries.[147] But the majority of the Nicaraguan exiles in the United States remained doubtful. "We don't know for sure what will really happen," said one man, "and we can't afford to lose what we have here."[148] Exile periodicals expressed concern over the number of Sandinistas in high positions in the Chamorro government; and one Spanish-language weekly regularly warned that civil war still loomed on the horizon.[149] Exiles understandably worried about their safety, especially with the news that many Nicaraguans were assassinated when they tried to reclaim their properties. The assassination of former Contra leader Enrique Bermúdez in Managua and seventy other former Contras over the next year sent a chill through the community, regardless of one's politics.[150] And although the Bush administration pledged forty-seven million dollars to assist the reintegration of the Contra soldiers, no funds were pledged to assist noncombatants in returning home. The UNHCR provided small grants to assist refugees who returned to Nicaragua (fifty dollars for adults and twenty-five dollars for children) if their applications were approved by the government, but the Chamorro government itself was unable to provide any additional assistance. "You have to understand the situation in Nicaragua," said one representative from the Nicaraguan Task Force. "The country is broke. The only people likely to get their fares to Nicaragua paid are those deported by the Immigration and Naturalization Service." Consequently, the Nicaraguan Task Force predicted that only 25 percent of the approximately two hundred thousand Nicaraguans in Miami would ever return home.[151]

By January 1990, 22,167 Nicaraguan asylum applications remained pending, and now that the Sandinistas were out of office, those applications were unlikely to be successful. If Nicaraguans continued with the process and were denied asylum, they would be prevented from reapplying for a period of up to five years. And those who had been granted asylum but who had not adjusted their status to permanent resident were now subject to a revocation of their asylum.[152] Thus, many opted for voluntary departure, which would at least allow them to apply for an immigrant visa one day, if needed.

In 1995, the Clinton administration announced the phasing out of the Nicaraguan Review Program. Those now facing deportation were urged to file for a suspension of deportation if they had lived in the country more than seven years and "were of good moral character"; eight out of every ten applicants who met these conditions won their case. But shortly thereafter, Congress passed the 1996 Illegal Immigration Reform and Immigrant Responsibility Act (IIRIRA), which, among many other provisions for immigration reform, revamped existing deportation and exclusion proceedings and allowed deportation without judicial oversight. To receive cancellation of deportation, applicants now had to demonstrate ten years of continuous residence rather than seven, and provide evidence of "extreme and exceptional hardship" if deported. Not more than four thousand cases could be approved annually.

In response, forty thousand Nicaraguans sued the US government, claiming that they were unfairly deprived of their promised suspension-of-deportation hearings. Once again, a series of allies came to their rescue. A district judge in south Florida ordered an injunction against deportations until a full trial was heard; and later that summer Attorney General Janet Reno froze all deportations in order to give Nicaraguans opportunities to plead their cases.[153] Finally, in 1997, after much lobbying from Cuban-born congressmen Lincoln Díaz-Balart and Ileana Ros-Lehtinen, and other members of the Florida delegation, Congress passed the Nicaraguan Adjustment and Central American Relief Act, which allowed Nicaraguans present in the United States as of December 1, 1995, to adjust their status to that of legal permanent resident. Although the law primarily benefited Nicaraguans, Cubans, and nationals of the former Soviet bloc countries, Salvadorans and Guatemalans benefited to some extent as well: they qualified for "cancellation of removal" under the pre-IIRIRA rules: if they could prove seven years of continual residence in the United States, good moral character, and that deportation would cause extreme hardship to them or a spouse or child who is a US resident.

But, ultimately, the Nicaraguans' success in legalizing their status lay in their ability to manipulate public perceptions of their situation. The US government manipulated the plight of the Nicaraguan exiles to promote and justify a particular foreign policy, but the exiles used that discourse to their benefit. Officials of the Reagan and Bush administrations pointed to the Nicaraguan entrants as proof of the need for US intervention in the region. These were a people fleeing a despotic Marxist government, they argued. The Nicaraguans then used that line of reasoning to demand accommodation from a government reluctant to offer them even temporary protected status. Sympathetic Americans allied themselves to their cause, either because of lingering Cold War sentiments or because they opposed US policy in Central America. It did not matter that their illegal status was a violation of US law. Perceptions became as important as facts. The Salvadorans and the Guatemalans also relied on the circulation of a particular discourse to facilitate the legalization of their status. In the end, the Nicaraguan case study proved that while the Cold War was over and the criteria for acquiring refugee status or asylum had changed somewhat, migration continued to be both a consequence and a tool of foreign policy. And persons wishing to enter the United States must manipulate state discourses in order to pry the door open.

4

HUMANITARIANISM
AND POLITICS

Canada Opens Its Doors to Central America

Living next to you is in some ways like sleeping with an
elephant. No matter how friendly and even-tempered
the beast, one is affected by every twitch and grunt.

PIERRE TRUDEAU

Canada's example of humanitarianism has been the standard against which the US and European governments
have been measured, and found lacking.

US COMMITTEE FOR REFUGEES

If we are regarded as among the best in the world, it
is not because we are perfect, but because the standards
internationally are so low.

CANADIAN COUNCIL FOR REFUGEES

Canada received comparatively smaller numbers of Central American
immigrants than Mexico and the United States did, in large part because
of its more distant geographic location. Salvadorans were the largest group
to migrate to Canada and came to represent almost totally the Central
American refugee crisis, and most had spent some time in other countries before state policies forced them to migrate further north. Canada
officially granted asylum to a larger percentage of those who crossed its
borders than its continental neighbors did. Even after 1986, when domestic concerns forced the Canadian federal government to restrict the number of entrants through a more streamlined admittance procedure, Canada
continued to grant asylum to more than half of all Central American petitioners. While the Canadian government hesitated to criticize US foreign
policy in Central America, refugee policy became the principal means
through which Canadians distinguished themselves politically from the
United States and asserted a distinct role in Central American affairs.

AN OVERVIEW OF CANADIAN IMMIGRATION
AND REFUGEE POLICY

Historically, immigration to Canada was encouraged as an instrument of nation building, just as it was in other former European colonies. Settlers were needed to economically develop the new territories brought into the Canadian confederation and to provide a market for goods produced in the more industrialized areas of the country, namely, Ontario and Quebec. As such, the Departments of Agriculture and Mines and Resources handled all matters related to immigration during this formative period.[1]

By 1930, the descendants of the First Nations and the English and French settlers had been joined by European immigrants, first from northern countries such as Finland, Ireland, Scotland, and Germany, and eventually from the Ukraine, Italy, and other parts of eastern and southern Europe. Land companies also lured American farmers into Canadian prairie lands with a variety of incentives to help populate the region; over one million Americans are believed to have immigrated to Canada between 1910 and 1914, reflecting the porous nature of the United States–Canada border.[2] Until 1930, immigrants accounted for close to a quarter of Canada's population.[3] The volume of immigration never equaled that of its southern neighbor: from 1870 to 1991, the United States accepted 42.2 million immigrants, compared to 5.4 million in Canada. However, the ratio of Canada's admissions to total population was higher than that of the United States: 0.48 as compared to 0.19.[4]

In the twentieth century, Canadian and US immigration policies often mirrored each other, especially in their designs to create the ideal population. Laws passed in Canada from 1906 to 1919 prohibited the entry of criminals, paupers, the infirm, and "any race deemed unsuitable to the climate and requirements of Canada"; the laws also established a lengthy list of categories under which immigrants could be deported.[5] Legislation passed by the US Congress from 1886 to 1927 established similar restrictions on "undesirables," culminating in the restrictive quota laws of the 1920s that limited the entrance of nationals from specific countries to a few hundred per year. Both the United States and Canada gave immigration priority to "white" Europeans from northern and western Europe, who were regarded as industrious, familiar with democratic institutions, and culturally "assimilable." Asian, Jewish, and African origin immigration was heavily restricted, as was the access of these groups to citizenship and economic opportunities. This legal bias in immigration law was not eliminated in both countries until the 1960s, when a "points system" was instituted in its place, giving preference to family reunification and those applicants with skills necessary to their respective economies. As in most nations, Canada and the United States continue to exclude those who pose a medical or security threat, espouse radical ideologies, or may place an excessive burden on the country's social services.

The new laws passed in the 1960s and 1970s opened the door to emigrants from Asia, Africa, Latin America, and the Middle East; and since 1965, immigrants to both countries have come largely from these areas of the world. Back in 1961, 85 percent of Canada's immigration came from Europe and the United States; but by 1993, 42 percent of immigrants were Asian; 26 percent, European; 17 percent came from elsewhere in the Americas; and 15 percent came from Africa and Middle East.[6] The Philippines and Hong Kong became the two leading source countries of immigrants, replacing Great Britain and the United States; and Asia, overall, had replaced Europe as the home region of Canada's new immigrants.[7] By 1990, emigration from Asia accounted for over 40 percent of all immigration to Canada (a trend that continues today); and "Chinese" (Mandarin, Cantonese, and other languages spoken in China and by ethnic Chinese in the diaspora) became the third most-spoken language in Canada, after English and French.[8] Correspondingly, the Asia-Pacific has come to occupy an increasingly important role in Canadian foreign policy.[9]

Canada's Immigration Act of 1976 (which was later replaced by the Immigration and Refugee Protection Act of 2002) provided the framework for refugee policy during the 1980s and 1990s. The law created four classes of immigrants for private or government sponsorship: refugees, family, assisted relatives, and "independent immigrants."[10] In consultation with the provincial governments that accommodated the immigrants, the Immigration Ministry outlined national objectives in five-year planning cycles, and targets were adjusted annually to address the needs and concerns of the individual provinces. The system was designed to be responsive to changes in labor markets and to international crises, as well as public opinion.[11] The Quebec-Canada Accord of 1991 grants the province of Quebec the right and responsibility to select the immigrants and refugees who will settle in that province, and to assume responsibility for the linguistic, cultural, and economic integration services provided to them.[12] Thus, the Quebec-Canada Accord provides the Quebecois with the opportunity to increase their French-speaking population and maintain their unique cultural identity, and ultimately their political influence.[13]

By the 1990s, roughly half of immigrant admissions were family members of Canadian citizens, and one-quarter of the immigrants were selected on humanitarian grounds (i.e., as refugees and displaced persons). The remaining number of immigrants were selected as part of the "independent" class and were evaluated on the basis of their education, age, skills and occupational experience, and language proficiencies.[14] The majority of immigrants to Canada chose Ontario or British Columbia as their principal area of settlement (and continue to do so today).

As in the United States, Canadian legislation did not specifically mention refugees until after World War II, when Canada defined a separate refugee policy as part of an international effort to assist those displaced by war, political upheaval, or oppression. Canada chaired the United Nations committee that drafted the 1951 UN Convention relating to the Status of Refugees, which protected against *refoulement,* but ironically delayed signing the Convention for eighteen years, because, like Mexico, Canadian legislators "feared that signing the Convention would compromise Canadian prerogatives vis-à-vis admission and removal of non-citizens."[15] However, in the interim it served on the Executive Committee of the UNHCR and adopted one of the most generous resettlement policies in the world. Canada accepted over 20 percent of Hungarian refugees (thirty-seven thousand) in 1956 and one-third of Czech refugees in 1968 (twelve thousand). In the 1970s and 1980s, Canada accepted seven thousand Ugandan refugees, six thousand Chileans, eleven thousand Lebanese, and over fifty thousand Southeast Asians. In October 1986, the United Nations honored Canada with the Fridtjof Nansen Medal in recognition of its generous role in refugee resettlement, the first time a country received this award. By the early 1990s, Canada stood second only to Sweden in terms of the ratio of resettled refugees to total population.[16]

It was not until the passage of the Immigration Act that refugees constituted a distinct class of immigrants. Canada accepted not only Convention refugees—that is, those who met the strict definition of "refugee" established by the UN Convention—but also members of "designated classes" who did not meet the strict definition but lived in "refugee-like" conditions. The Immigration Act established three designated classes reflecting the prevailing Cold War ideology of the time: the Latin American political prisoners and oppressed persons class; the Eastern European self-exiled persons class; and the Indochinese class.[17] By the late 1980s, roughly three-quarters of refugees accepted from abroad had been admitted as members of a designated class (some twenty-five thousand people annually).[18] The Canadian government also accepted individuals under a broader "humanitarian" category, which was designed to address specific international crises. Under this category, people who were neither convention refugees nor members of a designated class but were experiencing war, political upheaval, or other negative circumstances in their homeland were eligible for consideration.[19]

The Immigration Act also established an inland determination system to accommodate those who were already inside Canada when they filed for asylum (the so-called landed claims). As transportation became more accessible and affordable in the late twentieth century, individuals could now seek refuge beyond the nations that bordered their own country, and thus by the 1970s, Canada found itself as the country of first or second asylum for a growing number of refugees. When the number of landed claims rose to over four hundred per year, government officials concluded that a separate determination process was needed to assess eligibility. The 1976 Immigration Act and the regulations of 1978 provided the legal framework for this process "to fulfill Canada's international legal obligations concerning refugees and to uphold its humanitarian tradition with respect to the displaced and the persecuted."[20] The Refugee Advisory Status Committee (RSAC) was established to assist the Ministry of Employment and Immigration in this task. Later, when asylum claims increased to four thousand per year in the mid-1980s, new legislation (in 1989) created the more efficient Immigration and Refugee Board to assess claims.[21]

Canada allocated a specific refugee category within its yearly immigration quota (and continues to do so under the 2002 Immigration and Refugee Protection Act). Each year, in consultation with provincial authorities, non-governmental organizations, the UNHCR, and various Canadian interest groups, the immigration minister announced the minimum number of refugees who would be admitted to Canada under government sponsorship. Once admitted into the country, the government assumed financial responsibility for their resettlement for a period of time.

Private groups were allowed to sponsor refugees (a limit was imposed under the 2002 act) as long as they assumed financial responsibility for the costs of resettlement and their accommodation and integration.[22] Indeed, the Canadian government encouraged private sponsorship as a means of meeting its international obligations. Thus, the Canadian system was unique in that private sponsorship played an important role in determining the number of refugees allowed into the country, as well as in determining the areas of the world from which they came. Until the late 1990s, most refugees came from Southeast Asia (Vietnam, Laos, and Cambodia), Central America (El Salvador and Guatemala), Eastern Europe (Poland and Czechoslovakia), and the Middle East (Iran and Iraq).[23]

CANADA AND THE WARS IN CENTRAL AMERICA

In the twentieth century, Canadian identity, cultural orientation, and geopolitical interests slowly shifted from Great Britain and Europe to the Americas. Canada established its own regional foreign policy but concentrated its attention on the United States, especially after World War II, when its southern neighbor emerged as a superpower. The two countries became political allies and maintained similar philosophical approaches to foreign investment, trade, and development. Canada depended on the United States for over half of its import and export trade. In comparison, Canada's commercial investment and trade with Latin America was limited, with a few notable exceptions (Brazil, the Dominican Republic, Guatemala, and Chile). Latin America never figured as prominently in Canadian foreign policy as the United States did, for a variety of cultural and political reasons: there was almost no immigration from Latin America that might have sensitized the Canadian electorate to issues beyond North America; Canadians were largely indifferent to—and ignorant of—the Southern Hemisphere; and policymakers did not view the area with as much strategic interest as the United States did. Canadians regarded Central America and the Caribbean, in particular, as the United States' "backyard," where they could expect to encounter US resistance should they assert a larger political or commercial presence. Indeed, these were some of the factors that influenced the Canadians' decision to remain outside the Organization of American States (OAS) until 1989, when their country's increased visibility in the Contadora peace process made it logical that they play a role in this international body.[24]

Canadian involvement in Central American affairs increased during the administrations of Pierre Trudeau (1968–79, 1980–84), Joseph Clark (1979–80), John Turner (1984), and Brian Mulroney (1984–93). During Trudeau's administration, Parliament reevaluated Canada's relationship to Latin America. A 1982 report recommended making Central America a region of concentration in Canada's foreign policy, independent in tone and substance from the policies of the United States. During this period, the government established a number of new institutions that played an influential role in trade and investment, among them, the Canadian International Development Agency, created in 1968 to oversee aid programs funded through Canadian NGOs, and the Export Development Corporation, created in 1969, to assist Canadian companies in their work overseas. Canada also joined the Inter-American Bank in 1971 and encouraged the formation of the Canadian Association on Latin America to assist Canadian economic expansion in the region.[25] A government trade mission visited several countries to explore commercial opportunities. Trade increased dramatically: from 1974 to 1984, exports to Central America more than doubled, from 64 million to 149 million Canadian dollars; and imports quadrupled, from 53 million to 215 million dollars. Despite the increase, however, trade and investment in Central America accounted for less than 2 percent of Canada's worldwide trade and foreign investment.[26] Canada's growing influence in Central America was best seen in the political arena, and this influence naturally tested the country's relationship with the United States.

Philosophically, the two countries reacted to the Central American crises in very different ways. While the United States preferred to emphasize Cuban-Soviet interference in the region, Canada's position was more in line with the Contadora countries: it viewed the conflicts as home-grown, the logical consequence of the unequal distribution of economic resources and political power. While the United States regarded "protecting" the region as its historical right and duty, using military force if necessary, Canada, like Mexico, opposed foreign meddling in Central American affairs, respecting each country's right to resolve its own domestic problems. Throughout the 1980s and 1990s, Canadian policymakers walked a difficult tightrope: they sought to formulate a Central American policy distinct from the United States, especially with regard to Nicaragua, and at the same time cautiously avoided any condemnation of their ally that might strain their political relationship.

In 1980, under pressure from Canadian NGOs, especially the Inter-Church Committee on Human Rights in Latin America, the government supported a UN resolution that condemned human rights abuses in El Salvador and called upon all governments to refrain from providing military assistance.[27] By 1981, Canada had suspended aid to El Salvador and Guatemala. It cosponsored a UN resolution against Guatemala in response to the continuing human rights abuses, especially the murder of Canadian missionary Joseph Leger by government forces, and the escalated death threats against clerics, missionaries, aid workers, and journalists.[28] Canadian NGOs and church groups pressured the government to do more: specifically, to halt the sale of planes and military hardware by Canadian companies and, more important, to use its diplomatic influence on the United States. But apart from these symbolic gestures, Canadian officials were reluctant to rally international support against their country's ally.

To many Canadians, their government's position seemed inconsistent and contradictory. On the one hand, Canada refused to give asylum to the United States' rightist protégés. In 1979, for example, Canada refused to give asylum to Nicaraguan dictator Anastacio Somoza or his National Guardsmen, and during the 1980s refused to allow former Contra soldiers to immigrate there. Government officials spoke out against the death squads; met with representatives of rebel groups; publicly reiterated their opposition to military aid; and met with Mexican officials to discuss strategies to counter foreign interference. However, on other occasions, Canada seemed to readily accept the Reagan administration's official discourse that the wars in Central America were part of a larger Cuban-Soviet plot to destabilize the Americas, and supported the United States' right to counter that type of foreign intervention with its own. In testimony before the House of Commons, External Affairs Minister Mark MacGuigan stated what was regarded as Canada's official position during the 1980s: "We are prepared to contest the US policy of military aid, but not to protest it; we are prepared to pronounce on it but not to denounce it; we are prepared to criticize it but not to condemn it."[29] Later MacGuigan said, "The United States can at least count on our quiet acquiescence."[30] In 1984, when US mining of Nicaraguan ports was first discovered, Prime Minister Trudeau condemned it as "an act of terrorism," but delayed sending an official protest to Washington, claiming that he "had no evidence" that Reagan had ordered the mining.[31]

Not much changed during the administration of Brian Mulroney. One of Mulroney's major policy objectives was the negotiation of a free trade agreement with the United States, and his administration feared sabotaging this economic venture. Mulroney never officially condemned US military aid to El Salvador or the US embargo on Nicaragua. However, Canada quietly followed its own policy objectives, especially with regard to the Sandinistas. When the United States imposed its trade embargo in 1985, Canada refused to follow suit, and Managua moved its regional trade office from Miami to Toronto. Unlike the United States, which shunned members of the Sandinista government, Canada extended an invitation to Nicaraguan vice president Sergio Ramírez, who visited the country in 1987. That same year, External Affairs Minister Joe Clark toured Central America and announced that Canada would increase its diplomatic presence there with new field offices in Nicaragua, Honduras, and El Salvador. Canada contributed more than forty million dollars to Nicaragua during the 1980s to help address the poverty exacerbated by the Contra war. It also voted in support of the UN resolution supporting the World Court's condemnation of the United States for its violation of Nicaraguan sovereignty.

The United States never penalized Canada for its Central American policies. As one writer analyzed the relationship: "Whether this is because Canada has never been perceived as a threat or embarrassment, whether it is because there is a belief that Canadian policy does not matter and can be ignored in the region, or whether there is an honest sense in the United States that Canada is entitled to its own position—Canada has never been seriously chastised, stifled or pressured by her neighbor over its foreign policy measures in Central America."[32] More likely, the US-Canada relationship was not jeopardized because Canada's Central American policies, with the exception of Nicaragua, supported US objectives. The Mulroney government restored aid to El Salvador and Guatemala in 1985 and 1987, respectively, despite vocal opposition from Canadian NGOs over the continued human rights abuses in those countries.[33] It increased aid to Honduras, despite its role in harboring Contra forces that harassed and murdered Canadian missionaries.[34] Canada also supported the US-backed elections in the region and sent representatives to monitor the electoral process, despite domestic criticism of candidates such as José Napoleón Duarte. And the Canadian government was not particularly sympathetic to dissident voices: when Nobel Peace Prize winner Rigoberta Menchú visited Ottawa, for example, Mulroney refused to meet with her; and three Guatemalan opposition leaders who wished to discuss human rights issues with members of Parliament were refused a visa.[35] However, contrary to the United States, Canada committed itself to the Contadora peace process from the beginning. In 1988, the Canadian government established the House of Commons Special Committee on the Peace Process in Central America, which recommended increased development aid and peace-keeping services to support the Esquipulas II accord; and the following year, Canada participated in the UN Observer Group in Central America to ensure enforcement of the cease fire along the Honduras-Nicaragua border.

As the revolutions escalated, Canada played an important role in relief efforts in the region. Funds from the Canadian International Development Agency were channeled through the UNHCR, the Red Cross, and Canadian NGOs to provide emergency aid such as food, medicine, and clothing as well as assistance in relocation and durable solutions. One Canadian-sponsored project in Honduras, for example, encouraged agricultural self-sufficiency among the Miskito refugees.[36] By the fiscal year 1987, total direct aid to the region had doubled to 55.1 million Canadian dollars.[37] Between 1981 and 1989, Canada contributed over 154 million dollars in bilateral aid to Central America and over 48 million dollars through NGOs.[38] The Canadian government also donated fertilizers and chemicals to assist with agricultural production, and supported the construction of large projects such as power stations and refineries.

As in previous international crises, the Canadian government declared itself willing to accommodate a share of the refugees. The UNHCR's primary goal was to temporarily relocate refugees in neighboring countries to ease the shock of displacement and facilitate repatriation once peace came to the region.[39] Given that most Central Americans were in need of temporary safe haven rather than permanent resettlement, the majority preferred to stay in countries that were closer to home.[40] But the burden of the refugees could not be entirely borne by countries such as Costa Rica, Panama, and Belize, and the UNHCR encouraged the resettlement of a small percentage to other more distant countries, especially if a refugee specifically requested it. During the early 1980s, if Nicaraguans, Salvadorans, and Guatemalans chose to relocate to Canada, they had no consulate they could go to within their own countries to request refugee status; instead they had to travel to the embassy in Costa Rica or patiently await the next visit from a consular official, which was hardly a feasible option for those who feared for their lives. Even after field offices were established in these countries later in the decade, staff shortages meant long waiting periods and irregular screening. At the Canadian office in Guatemala, for example, 80 percent of would-be refugees were turned away at the prescreening stage.[41]

In order to accommodate the refugees from Central America, the Canadian government steadily increased its refugee quota for Latin America, from one thousand in 1981 to two thousand in 1983 and twenty five hundred in 1984. By 1985, roughly two-thirds of the refugee quota was filled up by Central Americans, many of them former residents of Mexican refugee camps or US detention centers. Hundreds more were sponsored privately.[42] During the 1980s, the refugees frequently exceeded the official quotas: the 1986 quota for Latin America, for example, was set at 3,200, but the government sponsored 3,654 refugees from Central America alone.

Under pressure from Canadian NGOs, Canada enacted a series of measures to allow Central Americans to receive protection. In 1981, the government established a moratorium on the deportation of Salvadoran students and visitors. In 1983, when the Constituents Assembly in El Salvador declared a sixty-day amnesty for political prisoners, guerrillas, and exiles who wished to resettle in a new country, Canada sent a team to San Salvador to interview those wishing to emigrate. One hundred thirty-four political prisoners and 139 of their family members were assisted to immigrate to Canada.[43] Canadian consulates in the United States were also instructed to issue visas to Salvadoran refugees who were facing deportation from the United States. Similar measures were enacted for Guatemalans in 1984. Through the UNHCR, Canadian officials facilitated the immigration of Guatemalan refugees already in Costa Rica and Mexico. The moratorium on deportations was expanded to include the Guatemalans, and the government allowed both Guatemalans and Salvadorans to petition for permanent residency without having to leave the country.[44]

Between 1982 and 1987, Canada admitted 15,877 refugees from Central America, the majority of them Salvadoran (11,251). Under a special program, 4,444 family members were allowed entry, bringing the five-year total to 20,955.[45] Salvadorans replaced Chileans as the principal immigrant group from Latin America.[46] Overland migration from Central America also increased as the violence escalated, refugee camps filled up, and restrictive policies were enacted in Mexico and the United States. Most of the landed claimants had spent some time in Mexico and/or the United States before moving on to Canada. The approval rate for Salvadorans' asylum applications was much higher than the United States: between 21 and 60 percent of processed applications were accepted from 1980 to 1986. During the same period, between 28 and 71 percent of processed asylum claims from Guatemalans were accepted.[47] By 1987, 22,283 Salvadorans, 7,700 Guatemalans, and 7,081 Nicaraguans were living legally in Canada.[48]

Refugee policy, critics argued, was an important way to distinguish Canada culturally and politically from the United States. Polls conducted during the 1980s revealed that Canadians opposed US policy by a margin of two-to-one and believed that Canada should pursue policies that were independent from the United States. As one critic of Canadian policy argued: "We, as concerned Canadians, must apply pressure on our government to continue to avoid the double error made by the United States. We must not assume Central Americans are economic migrants. . . . Canada must honour its humanitarian obligations as signatory to the United Nations Convention and Protocol on Refugees."[49] A representative for the Inter-Church Committee for Refugees articulated what became the popular perception of Canada and the United States during the refugee crisis: "The Americans are not living up to their obligations as signatories of the United Nations Protocol [on refugees]. And given the official American position on these people, the Canadian government has taken a courageous stand."[50] The director of Refugee Affairs dressed the government's criticism in more diplomatic language: "The United States has done more for refugees than the rest of the world put together. This situation, I'm afraid, is an anomaly."[51]

A change in US policy, however, forced the Canadian government to adjust its own policies reciprocally. In 1986, the US Congress passed the Immigration Reform and Control Act, which created a series of measures to restrict the number of undocumented workers in the country, among these measures, an expansion of the Border Patrol, tougher status verification criteria, and penalties on employers who knowingly hired undocumented workers. Consequently, Canada experienced a dramatic rise in the number of petitions for asylum when immigrants of many different countries left the United States and traveled northward in search of work and safe haven. The Canadian Consulate in Los Angeles saw a 500 percent increase in the number of Central Americans seeking assistance to go to Canada.[52] Others asked for asylum at border points or entered illegally through the back roads of what was generally regarded as the "longest undefended border in the world."[53] In just one month, January 1987, the number of Salvadorans who arrived at the border of Canada nearly equaled the total number of Salvadoran asylum applicants in the previous year.[54] From December 1986 to February 1987, ten thousand refugees, most of them Central Americans, entered Canada, encouraged in part by the Spanish-language press, immigration lawyers, and sanctuary workers in the United States, who alerted them to Canada's more generous policy.[55] Arriving by the busload, the Canadian press nicknamed the refugees "the bus people."[56] Churches on both sides of the border—between Montana and Alberta, North Dakota and Manitoba, New York and Ontario-Quebec—were flooded with refugees. Salvation Army and Red Cross shelters in Montreal and Toronto filled to capacity, and the Canadian National Exhibition Grounds became an emergency shelter for refugees coming via the United States.[57]

In February 1987, the Canadian government imposed a series of new restrictions to discourage this overland migration. (Ironically, the new policy pronouncements came just weeks after the United Nations awarded Canada the Nansen Medal.) The moratorium on deportations was lifted and the government revoked the automatic permission to work and to receive social services pending ministerial decisions on asylum petitions. Immigration officials at the border of Canada were instructed to send asylum claimants back to wait in the United States; the claimants were given a preliminary hearing date, usually many months away, and told to return at that time. Many of those forced to wait in the United States were then obliged by the INS to sign the voluntary departure form to facilitate automatic deportation by the United States if Canada later rejected the applicant's petition, but in some cases Central Americans were immediately deported.[58] Those who were allowed to stay pending a review were left waiting in halfway houses, homeless shelters, gymnasiums, and churches on the US side of the border in cities such as Detroit, Michigan; Great Falls, Montana; and Plattsburgh, Rochester, Buffalo, and Lackawanna, New York. There they depended on volunteers for emergency aid and protection. Local restaurants and hotels donated food, towels, sheets, and toiletries to churches and shelters housing the refugees. Charitable organizations offered legal and health services. Local businesses offered day jobs. New York governor Mario Cuomo declared Clinton County, New York, a disaster area in order to channel emergency funds to small towns like Plattsburgh.

As part of the new restrictive measures, the Canadian government also announced that nationals from ninety-eight countries (including the countries of Central America) would now require transit visas if they stopped in a Canadian city on the way to another destination. A Salvadoran national traveling by plane from Mexico City to New York via Toronto, for example, was now required to have a Canadian transit visa. Such a measure was designed to prevent visitors whose planes temporarily stopped in Canada from petitioning for asylum during the layover, and applicants considered a potential claimant were frequently denied this transit visa.

The new policies had their desired effect. By March, the number of Central American border entrants to Canada had decreased to 273, and by the end of April, the number was down to 191. Despite the stricter measures, Canada continued to have a generous approval rate: in 1987 the overall acceptance rate was 50 percent compared to 15 percent in other democratic societies.[59] Thus, Canada continued to be an attractive alternative. The goal for refugees, then, was to avoid deportation by the INS while they awaited a ruling by Canadian officials, or conversely, to enter Canada illegally and apply from within.

Immigration Minister Benoit Bouchard assured NGOs that Canada had an "understanding" or verbal agreement with the United States that refugees returned to that country would be protected from deportation if they had filed for asylum with Canadian officials, but the INS contradicted those assertions. A spokesperson for the INS, Duke Austin, told Canadian journalists in Washington: "We have no policy that says because an individual has an application [to Ottawa] that we would hold them indefinitely."[60] A few months later, he put it more bluntly: "If we let in everyone who's supposed to be traveling somewhere else, we'd have all the Mexicans lined up on the border waiting to get in. If somebody wants to go to Canada from Latin America, let them fly. . . . So they have some document in hand—what does it mean? They may change their mind about going to Canada once they're here. They could also be rejected by Canada and we'd end up with them."[61]

The Central American border rush was one of a series of well-publicized events during the late 1980s that forced Canadians to question their immigration policies. During the summer of 1986, 153 Sri Lankan Tamils were picked up off the coast of Newfoundland. Considering it to be an isolated incident, Prime Minister Brian Mulroney responded generously at the time: "Canada was built by immigrants and refugees, and those who arrive in lifeboats off our shores are not going to be turned away. We are not in the business of turning away refugees, and we never will under this government."[62] However, over the next year Canada's self-image as a haven for the oppressed was tested as hundreds of Turks, Portuguese, Brazilians, and Chileans arrived at Montreal's Mirabel Airport requesting asylum.[63] On the heels of the border crisis, a boatload of 174 Sikhs arrived illegally in Nova Scotia in 1987. This last incident proved to be the tipping point prompting "an avalanche of telegrams and telephone calls demanding that [the Sikhs] be sent home to India."[64] Government officials now referred to the would-be asylum seekers as "queue-jumpers" and "economic immigrants trying to take advantage of Canadian generosity." Immigration Minister Bouchard publicly pronounced that "up to seventy-five percent" of asylum claims were false and asserted that Canadians were facing a national emergency.[65] By 1987 even Prime Minister Mulroney did an about-face and referred to the new entrants by the more politically laden term *illegal aliens.*

Immigration dominated the national news in 1987. The language of both journalists and policymakers was sensationalistic and equated immigration with natural disasters: the migrants came as "floods," "hordes," "waves," and "surges." Each news story cited the most recent number of entrants—inflated figures that differed significantly from official government counts. Featured as fact in the pages of newspapers and magazines were rumors of new boatloads of Tamils and Sikhs supposedly en route to Canadian shores.[66] Some in the news media did urge reason. Editorials in the *Toronto Star,* for example, lamented how the terms *refugee* and *illegal* had fused in the public consciousness and criticized Mulroney's use of the term *illegal alien* as an "Americanism" that "appears nowhere in our immigration legislation." Editorials reminded their compatriots that immigration to Canada remained comparatively limited and blamed the national hysteria on the lack of leadership. One writer complained, "For several months, the government has been fueling the anger, and deliberately or inadvertently adding to the public's confusion between genuine refugees and illegal immigrants." Another questioned whether racism had inspired the backlash: "One wonders if there would have been a similar uproar had the refugee claimants been East Europeans rather than turbaned Sikhs."[67]

Regardless of the credibility of some of the claims, the increased number of asylum seekers did focus attention on the limitations of Canada's asylum determination process. The 1976 Immigration Act had created a bureaucratically cumbersome process under the RSAC and the Immigration Appeals Board (IAB) that was adequate in the 1970s when inland applications stood at only two hundred to four hundred per year. The architects of the act never envisioned that one day thousands of people would ask for asylum at border checkpoints at Windsor, Niagara Falls, or Lacolle; nor did it envision a large number of inland claims. In 1985 alone, 18,262 people requested asylum.[68] By the end of the decade a backlog of 121,000 cases existed, and most applicants had to wait an average of three years for a determination on their case.[69]

Refugee advocacy groups (among them the Canadian Council of Churches) had long objected to the RSAC on procedural grounds, because the refugee claimant was unable to have an oral hearing at any stage of the process. Instead, an immigration official presented the claimant's sworn statement to RSAC members for evaluation. If the RSAC's decision was negative, then the claimant could appeal to the Immigration Appeals Board for a reevaluation of his or her case. If the board also ruled negatively, then the claimant could appeal to the Federal Court of Canada, but only on points of law or interpretation. Advocacy groups who urged reform were supported by a 1985 Supreme Court decision, *Singh v. Canada,* which ruled that those seeking asylum were entitled to "fundamental justice" and thus an oral hearing, representation by counsel, and appeals to courts.[70] Unfortunately, the hearings mandated by the *Singh* decision contributed to the backlog.

During the 1980s, the Canada Employment and Immigration Commission (CEIC) established task forces, commissioned outside studies, and consulted NGOs for advice on reforming the system but failed to initiate any radical changes. In 1984, for example, the government commissioned Rabbi Gunther Plaut, a noted humanist and scholar, to advise on a new refugee determination system. The Plaut Report offered a number of recommendations, including the creation of an independent and more streamlined refugee board that guaranteed fair access, expeditious review, and the right to appeal, but the government stalled on its implementation.[71] Legislation was introduced in Parliament in 1985 to increase the number of adjudicators on the IAB, from eighteen to fifty and, in 1986, to create an amnesty program for some twenty thousand landed claimants. However, both were simply Band-Aid measures that did little to address the procedural limitations, the backlog, and the larger issue of increased asylum claims.

On August 11 Mulroney recalled Parliament from summer recess to address the so-called emergency. Two bills were introduced in Parliament to amend the Immigration Act. Bill C-55, which passed in 1988 (and went into effect in January 1989), established a new independent tribunal, the Immigration and Refugee Board (IRB), with a more streamlined system of processing asylum claims.[72] In stage one, petitions for asylum received a preliminary hearing by a two-member panel: an adjudicator from the Immigration Ministry and a member of the Convention Refugee Determination Division of the IRB. Those applying for asylum at United States–Canada border crossings or airports were to be interviewed at the point of entry. Claimants found eligible and credible were allowed to enter the country and granted a work permit while they awaited a final hearing on their case. Only one member of the two-member panel had to support the claim for the case to be referred to the final stage; however, both members of the panel had to concur on the decision to have an applicant "removed" (and removal was to occur within seventy-two hours). At the second stage, a full hearing was to be held before two-member panels of the CRDD. Once again, only one member of the panel had to rule in favor of the claimant in order to receive asylum, and final decisions were to be handed down within a year. One of the most interesting features of the new Immigration and Refugee Board was its Documentation Center/ Resource Library in Ottawa (with five branches across the country), housing a variety of data and information, including country studies and human rights reports compiled by the NGOs, to assist adjudicators in their decision making.[73]

Much more controversial was Bill C-84, which introduced new measures for "detention and deterrence." Among the bill's many provisions was its increase in the criminal penalties on "smugglers" of up to ten years and five hundred thousand dollars per person; its imposition of financial penalties on carriers for every passenger transported without the proper visas and identity documents; its authorization to interdict and turn away ships carrying undocumented aliens without any determination on the passengers' claims to refugee status; and its authorization to detain and remove entrants perceived to pose a security risk. In security-related cases, the new bill essentially denied the accused their rights to due process by barring them, their lawyer, and even the court, from seeing the complete evidence against them if the Canadian Security and Intelligence Service or the Royal Canadian Mounted Police classified the information as sensitive. The bill also allowed the indefinite detention of refugees whose identities could not be proven pending verification of their claims. Refugees could be detained indefinitely as long as an adjudicator agreed that the government was making reasonable efforts to evaluate their case.

The Canadian Civil Liberties Association and a variety of advocacy groups challenged the bill on all of these issues: the turning back of illegal migrants while still at sea constituted *refoulement;* the bill failed to distinguish between professional smugglers and humanitarian groups who assisted refugees and was vague enough to make the latter criminally liable; and the detained were denied due process.[74] Liberal MP (and later immigration minister) Sergio Marchi called the bill "excessive, misguided, very dangerous, very un-Canadian."[75] Trying to put a human face on the problem, one immigration lawyer told the *Toronto Star,* "Soviet dancer Mikhail Baryshnikov [who defected in Toronto in 1974] would have been deported if he had tried to defect under the proposed refugee-screening legislation."[76] The Canadian Hispanic Council, representing two hundred thousand Canadians of Spanish/Latin American origin, publicly rejected Bill C-55 in particular because its members felt the bill discriminated against Central Americans.[77]

One of the most controversial features of C-84 was the "safe third country" provision that allowed immigration officials to return an asylum seeker to a third country if the claimant passed through that country on the way to Canada. Theoretically, such a measure required the government to regularly evaluate the safety of countries or else risk the lives of deportees. In practice, the United States was almost always the third country in the Canadian experience, since most refugees who arrived overland or by air stopped in the United States first. But with its high deportation rates, particularly of Central Americans, Canadian refugee advocates argued that the United States was hardly a safe alternative, although government officials would hesitate to admit it. The United Nations High Commissioner for Refugees Jean-Pierre Hocke expressed his concern in general terms, arguing that this new measure would redirect genuine asylum seekers to territories where their lives were threatened.[78] The Coalition for a Just Refugee and Immigration Policy accused the government of deporting refugees to a third country to get that country to do Canada's "dirty work."[79] The group Amnesty International was even more specific in its criticism, warning Canadian officials that they risked the lives of Central American asylum seekers if they sent them back to the United States to have their refugee claims determined there. This would "increase the risk that Central Americans might be returned against their will to a country where they risk being arbitrarily detained, made to disappear, tortured, or executed."[80]

The parliamentary and public debates over Bills C-55 and C-84 were, in the words of one study, "the most tumultuous and acrimonious . . . in the country's history."[81] Canadian and US refugee advocates blamed the policy shift on the Mulroney government's close ties to the Reagan administration and its desire to fall more in line with US policy in Central America. Lorne Waldeman of the Jesuit Centre for Social Faith and Justice wrote: "For the general public these mythical hordes probably appear in the guise of boatloads of Sikhs or Tamils. But those of us who work with refugees know that the government's prime target is in fact Central Americans."[82] American sanctuary activist Jim Corbett accused the Reagan administration of pressuring Canada to deny asylum to Central Americans. Danny Katz of the Boston-based National Immigration Project explained the pressure: "Canada was a real embarrassment to Reagan. Canada was showing itself to be ethically right when the United States was wrong."[83]

Despite opposition from Amnesty International, the UNHCR, the Canadian Bar Association, the major religious denominations in Canada, and dozens of Canadian NGOs, Bill C-84 passed and became law. Public opinion polls showed that both bills had strong public support.[84] The only major provision to be dropped from C–84 after the parliamentary debates was the interdiction of ships. Several provisions in C–84 were also allowed to expire or were postponed by the government, among them the safe country provision, in part because of pressure from Canadian advocacy groups. Soon after the bill was passed, Immigration Minister Barbara McDougall announced that the ministry would create a committee to advise on the list of so-called safe third countries. She assured critics that the human rights records of each country would be evaluated and steps taken to prevent rejected applicants from going into "international orbit" without a country to go to.[85] However, the Canadian government never released a list of safe third countries, most probably because it could not include the United States.

Over the next five years, the new Immigration and Refugee Board did a competent job addressing the new petitions for asylum. Of the asylum applicants, 95 percent passed the first stage of the process; for some groups, including Salvadorans, the figure was 99 percent.[86] An administrative review was set up to deal specifically with the backlog, which was finally eliminated in 1993 with an overall approval rate of 63 percent.[87] Despite concerns expressed by advocacy groups regarding the fairness of the procedure, 89 percent of asylum cases were ultimately approved during the first years of the new system—a much higher rate than under the RSAC. By mid-1990, the acceptance rate had dropped to 75 percent; and by late 1992, to 61 percent. The overall drop in acceptance rates could be attributed to the high number of Eastern European applicants, whose status changed radically during this period. (In 1989, 76 percent of Eastern Europeans fleeing communism were granted asylum; by mid-1990, after the dismantling of the Soviet bloc, only 16 percent could successfully prove their claim.) Acceptance rates for other groups, including Central Americans, remained high: 77 percent of Salvadorans were accepted at the second hearing.[88] In both stages of the process, legal assistance to the claimant was provided at government expense, and cases that received a negative ruling were immediately appealed. According to former INS director Doris Meissner, Canada had achieved "what no other nation has been able to achieve: a system that is timely and fair."[89]

Once asylum seekers were admitted into the country, the government provided comprehensive refugee assistance. The Adjustment Assistance

Program provided financial aid for food, shelter, clothing, household items, and the incidentals generally needed by refugees during their first year of accommodation in Canada. The CEIC also contracted Canadian NGOs to provide a variety of services, including interpreters, language training, legal advice, occupational and psychological counseling, general information, and community orientation.[90] Financial assistance was also available to help purchase homes.[91] In fiscal year 1988, the government spent close to ninety-five million dollars for settlement, training, and services for those admitted under its refugee and special humanitarian programs—an amount that was much greater than its financial commitment to the UNHCR. After three years of permanent residence, a refugee eighteen or more years of age could apply for citizenship if he or she demonstrated knowledge of one of Canada's languages and of Canadian history, government, and geography. Unlike US policies, which stressed the rapid cultural assimilation of immigrants and refugees to create a "melting pot" society, the 1988 Multiculturalism Act (which passed unanimously) encouraged immigrants to retain their cultural and linguistic heritage. The preamble of the act stated the government's mission to "preserve and enhance the multicultural heritage of Canadians while working to achieve the equality of all Canadians in the economic, social, cultural and political life of Canada."[92]

By January 1987, over fifteen thousand Central Americans were in Montreal and over six thousand were in Toronto, the two most popular cities of settlement. The majority of the Central Americans in Canada were Salvadorans; by the end of the decade, Salvadorans ranked fourth in the number of asylum petitions after Sri Lankans, Somalis, and Iranians.[93] Most of the Salvadorans had undertaken an overland trip to Canada: a 1992 profile of the Salvadorans in Montreal, for example, found that 40 percent had lived in the United States for at least one year before moving to Canada; 33 percent had lived in Mexico for at least six months before moving to Canada; and the rest had chosen Canada as the country of first asylum.[94] Most were young, single males.[95] Like their co-nationals in Mexico and the United States, they had urban working-class backgrounds and an average of ten years of schooling. And as in these other countries, in Canada these young migrants came with a variety of skills and life experiences, or human capital, and eventually occupied important niches in the economy, particularly in the service sector. Over half of Central

American men were employed in construction, manufacturing, and service occupations. One-third of Central American women were employed in service occupations, and another third were employed in managerial, clerical, or professional occupations.[96]

Guatemalans and Nicaraguans were comparatively fewer in number. In 1987, there were 7,700 Guatemalans and 7,081 Nicaraguans in Canada compared to 22,283 Salvadorans.[97] Some attributed the comparatively smaller number of Guatemalans to UNHCR policies that encouraged them to remain closer to their country of origin to facilitate repatriation. Indeed, Guatemalans living in Mexico, Honduras, and Costa Rica were more likely to repatriate in the 1990s than those living in northern countries. The settlement patterns established by the first refugees in the early 1980s, most of whom settled in Mexico, also affected the destinations of those who followed later in the decade. Early Nicaraguan migrants, in turn, settled in the United States and Costa Rica, and their communities served as magnets for those who emigrated later in the decade. Nicaraguans who traveled to Canada found it slightly easier than other Central Americans to receive asylum during the Mulroney years; but as in the United States after the defeat of the Sandinistas in 1990, Nicaraguan petitions were increasingly denied.[98]

CLOSING THE BORDER

Despite the new immigration controls, the number of asylum claims grew dramatically: there were 20,185 asylum petitions in 1989; and three years later the number had doubled to 40,125.[99] Once again, journalists sounded the alarm, portraying Canada as a country under siege. According to Immigration Minister Bernard Valcourt more laws were needed to prevent criminals, terrorists, and potential welfare abusers from entering the country. "It's all right to be softhearted," he said, "but you should not be softheaded."[100]

Bill C-86 was introduced in 1992 to further amend the Immigration Act. This time the goal was to reduce the refugee caseload and streamline the process further to make it more cost-efficient. Given the high approval rates at the first hearing, the bill proposed eliminating this first stage altogether. Instead it gave immigration officers posted at border entries the right to make unilateral decisions over who could have access to the refugee determination process, even though they might have little understanding of the country conditions the petitioners had fled. The bill also established tougher criteria for asylum, resettlement, and detention. Among the new provisions were the fingerprinting and photographing of asylum claimants as a security precaution; expanded rights of search and seizure; an expanded list of criteria by which an applicant might be determined criminally or medically inadmissible; and the resettlement of refugees to underpopulated areas where their skills were needed.[101]

Refugee advocates were outraged at most of the proposals. Under one of the provisions of C-86, for example, applicants could be denied asylum if they had a criminal record in the home country, even if their actions were not recognized as crimes in Canada. In an op-ed, Lorne Waldeman of the Jesuit Centre for Social Faith and Justice wrote: "The scope of this provision is mind-boggling. Activists with groups like Greenpeace would be automatically excluded because of that organization's non-violent civil disobedience policy. Trade unionists would be particularly vulnerable. If a unionist admitted that his organization had, at any time, engaged in an illegal strike or walkout, this would be grounds for exclusion even if no charges were ever laid. People could be excluded from Canada even if the activity they had engaged in was legal in their country—but possibly illegal here."[102] "The bill diminishes us all," said one spokesman for the Canadian Council of Churches.[103] At the parliamentary immigration committee meetings, one immigration lawyer complained: "Virtually the entire world is inadmissible under this act."[104]

The "safe third country" provision was reintroduced in C-86. More specific guidelines for country designation were offered: in order to be declared safe, a country had to be a signatory to the UN Convention, have a positive human rights record, and engage in a bilateral agreement with Canada on refugee determination procedures. Once again, C-86 had potential consequences for Central American refugees: of the 6,637 Salvadorans that filed asylum claims in Canada from 1989 to 1995, 82 percent had entered via the United States.[105] Since one-third to one-half of all asylum applicants entered via the United States, C-86 ensured that the United States continued to buffer Canada from unwanted asylum applicants.[106]

The safe third country provision was a protectionist response not only to developments in the United States but also to asylum policies in the European Union. Throughout the 1980s, member states of the EU enacted a number of policies to discourage refugees from seeking them out as countries of first asylum. These included restrictions on access to citizenship, employment, and educational opportunities. Acceptance rates in EU countries dropped to an all-time low. In Switzerland, for example, acceptance rates dropped from 70 percent in the 1970s to 7 percent in 1989.[107] In addition, the Dublin and Schengen Conventions of 1990[108] established that a signatory could return an asylum applicant to a third country if that third country issued the entry visa or was the first frontier at which the applicant presented him- or herself. The decision to grant asylum was then to be made according to that country's individual statutes. Enforcement of this provision was strict: if on the way to a particular country, an asylum applicant stopped briefly in one country to change planes, he or she was to be returned to that transit point. According to Canadian officials, similar provisions were needed in Canada to stop the practice of "asylum shopping" in North America, as well as to prevent those rejected in the EU from traveling to Canada to take advantage of its more liberal policies.[109] However, as in the EU, bilateral or multilateral agreements were needed with other countries to ensure the safety of the asylum seekers.

Over the forceful objections of Canadian advocacy groups, C-86 passed and became law in 1993. The first attempt to negotiate a bilateral agreement with the United States occurred in 1992 during the Bush and Mulroney administrations, but was shelved when both leaders lost their reelection bids. In January 1995, the United States inserted a safe third country provision into its asylum policy, similar to Canada's. The Justice Department could deport an asylum seeker to a country through which he or she traveled before reaching the United States, if he or she was guaranteed full access to fair asylum procedures in that country, and if that country had an agreement with the United States. In this case, the United States was most concerned with negotiating with Mexico, the country through which a large percentage of asylum seekers traveled. The following month, President Bill Clinton and Prime Minister Jean Chrétien announced their intention to negotiate a border management accord to facilitate trade and prevent drug trafficking, smuggling, and illegal and irregular migration, a logical course after the signing of NAFTA. Article 6 of the proposed Memorandum of Agreement (MOA) with Canada (also known as the Canada–United States Accord on Our Shared Border) stated that any persons who have "arrived in Canada directly from the United States, or in the United States directly from Canada, will have the refugee status claim examined by and in accordance with the refugee status determination system of the country of first arrival."[110] Thus if a Salvadoran traveled to Canada via the United States, he or she would be returned to the United States to have the claim examined there. Exceptions would be made only if the applicant had immediate family in Canada, or had lived there illegally for six months or more.[111]

The MOA elicited heated debate on both sides of the border. In the United States, a coalition of over sixty immigrant advocacy groups asked the Clinton administration to reject the accord with Canada. An editorial in *Refugee Update* argued: "We know of many cases where asylum-seekers have been denied asylum by the US authorities but approved for admission into Canada. Denying these individuals the opportunity to process their claims in Canada will undoubtedly mean that individual asylum-seekers will be denied protection."[112] Others protested the accord because it would add to the US backlog, estimated to be half a million in 1996. Over 30 percent of all refugee claimants in Canada were known to have transited via the United States, and returning them to the United States would add up to fifteen thousand people annually to the backlog and also add to the bureaucratic costs of the asylum determination process.[113] In Canada, the Canadian Council for Refugees led the fight against the MOA, arguing that the "procedural and substantive safeguards [were] lower in the US than in Canada," especially after Congress passed the Illegal Immigration Reform and Immigrant Responsibility Act in 1996.[114] The United States did not consistently recognize the same categories of eligibility as Canada, such as gender-based persecution. The United States also differed from Canada in not offering petitioners work authorization for six months or government-sponsored legal counsel, causing unnecessary hardship. One Canadian scholar complained that the term *shared responsibility* was a euphemism for refusing to process claimants.[115] Another warned of the consequences of allowing Mexico to adjudicate the claims of Central American refugees, where the United States might ultimately return Canada's deportees.[116]

After three years of debate, the Memorandum of Agreement was once again shelved. In December 2002, in the wake of the terrorist attacks of September 11, 2001, Canada and the United States signed a bilateral agreement on border control, which included the safe third country provision and went into effect on December 29, 2004.[117]

CANADIAN ADVOCACY NETWORKS AND CENTRAL AMERICAN IMMIGRATION

Prior to the 1980s, immigration issues did not occupy a prominent position in Canadian public discourse—certainly not comparable to that in the United States. Canada's modest immigration rates (roughly 100,000 per year) did not compare with the United States' yearly entrants of over 750,000, and thus elicited little discussion.[118] The subject attracted concern only when the numbers of immigrants and refugees expanded beyond what was familiar and comfortable, as happened in the 1980s. By the end of that decade, Canadians worried about the strain high numbers of immigrants might place on social services, the educational system, and job opportunities. They also expressed concern about the changing demographics and the impact immigrants might have on Canadian culture or the Canadian "character," notwithstanding the state's commitment to multiculturalism. As one member of Parliament stated, "There's no problem with American citizens or British citizens [immigrating to Canada]—but we are going to have to tighten our doors."[119] Opposition to the new refugee influx seemed to increase almost overnight: in 1989, 31 percent of Canadians felt that too many refugees were admitted; two years later the number had grown to 49 percent. While Canadian anger was largely directed at immigrants and refugees from the Middle East, 35 percent of Canadians also objected to the migration from Latin America.[120] The legislation of the 1980s and 1990s was a political response to these concerns.

As happened in the United States and Mexico, members of a comparatively small but vocal segment of the Canadian population affiliated with churches, charitable organizations, universities, labor groups, and other NGOs used their moral authority to remind the state of its international and humanitarian commitments. They lobbied to keep the border of Canada open and the refugee determination system fair and accessible. On a practical level they argued that current levels of immigration failed to replenish the aging Canadian population, so the country could well afford to accommodate even more of the world's displaced. But philosophically, immigration and refugee policy became a means through which they challenged economic and political practices. Their advocacy was not always successful. According to one writer, Canadian advocacy groups were simply not as influential in shaping state policies as their counterparts in the United States, because in Canada they were "relegated to the margins of political life."[121] But this section argues that the advocacy of scholars, lawyers, aid workers, students, and clergymen, working individually or through non-governmental organizations, was instrumental in shaping Canadian foreign policy and in softening (and in some cases eliminating) the most restrictive measures of refugee legislation.

Central America became a passionate topic for Canadians. According to one writer, Canadians were naturally sympathetic to the countries of Central America because they, too, "must live in the shadow of the US superpower."[122] By the mid-1980s, 30 to 40 percent of the mail received by Prime Minister Mulroney concerned Central America.[123] A 1984 Gallup poll revealed that Canadians opposed US policy in the region by a margin of two to one. Other polls demonstrated that Canadians supported three fundamental positions: first, Canada should pursue a foreign policy independent from the United States, placing human rights at the forefront; second, Canada should work with other nations and international organizations to find a diplomatic resolution to the crisis; and finally, Canada should increase its financial aid in the region to facilitate the political and economic development of the war-torn countries.[124] Much of the advocacy on foreign policy focused on these three points.

Thousands of Canadians traveled to Central America during the 1980s on fact-finding trips for their churches, schools, and organizations. Canadian volunteers worked in refugee camps in Honduras and Mexico; they served as witness-observers in the militarized border zones; and they escorted the deported and repatriated back to their homelands. When they returned to their communities in Canada, their stories and experiences helped to challenge the US news accounts that dominated Canadian press and television.

Grassroots solidarity organizations emerged across Canada; some lasted only a few years in response to a specific issue, such as opposition to the Contra war, and others worked tirelessly throughout the decade, adapting strategies to accommodate changing issues and constituencies. These grassroots organizations often did more for the displaced of Central America than the Canadian government, whose bilateral aid was generally known as "tied aid," requiring Central Americans to use funds to purchase Canadian goods and services.[125] The organizations sponsored "peace caravans," which transported medicines, clothing, food, and agricultural supplies to communities affected by the civil wars. The organizations Horizons and Tools for Peace, for example, raised millions of dollars for food and medical and technical goods to send to Nicaragua.[126] Others staged rallies and demonstrations to protest US policy in Central America and Canada's complicity by failing to distance itself more forcefully from US actions. The protests over diplomatic and immigration policies became intertwined. A 1987 demonstration at Queens Park and the US consulate, for example, attended by over eight hundred protesters, urged the Canadian government to use its influence to end the US-backed Contra war, increase aid and trade with Central America, and open its doors to more refugees.[127]

The Central American advocacy network was dominated by five overlapping sets of non-governmental organizations: aid organizations; the labor movement; the scholarly community; professional associations; and religious groups. The lobbying began immediately after the victory of the Nicaraguan revolution in 1979. Representing over two million members, the Canadian Labour Congress channeled funds to labor groups in Managua to assist them in the transitional period, and lobbied Parliament to recognize and aid the new Sandinista government (especially through the creation of an embassy in Managua). The congress also organized Operation Solidarity, "the largest people-to-people aid operation ever seen in Canada," to assist the Nicaraguan people with food, medical supplies, and tents. Skilled workers from a variety of trade unions raised funds through their own "solidarity drives" and volunteered for "brigades" that traveled to Nicaragua to assist in the reconstruction.[128] Unlike the United States, where labor groups were anti-immigration during the 1980s, Canadian labor groups generally advocated a generous state response to the refugee crisis. In the 1970s, Canadian trade unions had successfully worked with church groups to pressure the government to accept more Chilean refugees from Pinochet's government, and they now extended that pressure to include Salvadorans and Guatemalans. When Canadians complained that the new immigrants took away jobs from citizens, labor groups disputed these claims. In 1987, when Bills C-55 and C-84 were under discussion in Parliament, the president of the Canadian Auto Workers was among those who criticized the proposed legislation and officially refuted the claims that immigrants and refugees took jobs away from Canadians.[129]

Canadian scholars and policy analysts also tried to influence state policies through studies, conferences, and symposia. The Latin American Working Group, founded in the late 1960s, criticized what it perceived as tacit support of human rights abuses. The Centre for Refugee Studies at York University founded its publication, *Refuge,* in 1981 as a forum for discussing such issues as refugee status determination, sponsorship, and resettlement programs. In 1985 the Canadian Institute for International Peace and Security and the Canadian–Caribbean–Central American Policy Alternatives (CAPA) discussed ways that Canada might initiate durable solutions projects in the region. Over the years they brought together government officials, aid workers, and scholars from around the world for conferences and roundtable discussions, subsequently publishing their conclusions and recommendations. One of their most influential publications, consulted by numerous Canadian policymakers during the peace process, was the 1990 study *Between War and Peace in Central America: Choices for Canada.*[130] CAPA and the CCR were among the most persistent pressure groups on Central American policy, particularly in support of Nicaragua and the Central American refugees (one the CCR's presidents during the 1990s was Francisco Rico-Martínez, a Salvadoran refugee).[131] Another network, the Coalition for a Just Refugee and Immigration Policy—representing over two hundred church, labor, ethnic, and human rights groups—was also vocal in its critique of state policies.[132]

Of the various professional associations involved in Central American advocacy, the legal profession was understandably the most active. The number of lawyers working on immigration-related issues increased dramatically after passage of the 1976 Immigration Act, and new associations such as the Refugee Lawyers Association, the Lawyers Committee for Human Rights, and the Quebec Immigration Lawyers Association, as well as the umbrella Canadian Bar Association, were heavily engaged in the parliamentary debates over the proposed legislation of the 1980s.[133] Health care professionals also played an influential role in the debate over immigration. Canadian physicians and nurses associated with Amnesty International, Americas Watch, Médecins sans Frontières, and the various church groups provided firsthand testimony of the consequences of militaristic state policies. In 1982 Toronto-based doctors affiliated with

Amnesty International created the Canadian Centre for Investigation and Prevention of Torture, one of two such centers in the world (the other in Copenhagen), which assisted the more than one thousand victims of torture living in the Toronto area, many of them from Central America.[134] Health care professionals testified in court against the deportation of specific refugees; in 1993, for example, they succeeded in halting the deportation of a Salvadoran woman who was HIV positive on the grounds that she would be denied the health care she needed in order to survive.[135]

As in Mexico and the United States, church groups in Canada played a central role in monitoring and challenging state policies. Using information from Canadian missionaries in the field, coalition groups such as the Inter-Church Committee on Human Rights in Latin America and the Inter-Church Committee on Refugees published information on military maneuvers, death squad activities, human rights abuses, refugees, and displaced persons, which some considered to be far superior to government sources.[136] As one government official told MacFarlane: "It used to be that we could say in External Affairs that we are the people with the expertise. We could say, 'We've got a man down there on the spot who can tell you the way it is.' Now the churches come back and say, 'no, we had a team down there last week, and this is the way it is.'"[137] Church groups vocally opposed aid to repressive regimes in El Salvador and Guatemala, demanding that it be contingent on substantive improvements in human rights; and just as emphatically, they demanded increased aid to Nicaragua to counter US policies. The Inter-Church Committee on Human Rights urged a reassessment of the role Canadian banks and corporations played in sustaining repressive regimes, and urged the establishment of a "code of international corporate conduct" for corporations, banks, and government departments and agencies that would prohibit aid, investment, or credit to any country that persistently violated human rights.[138] The Task Force on the Churches and Corporate Reality succeeded in halting the sale of Canadian aircraft to Guatemala and Honduras in 1982.[139] And individual denominations carried out their own aid projects in Central America.

During the Central American crisis, church groups appealed to the moral and charitable sympathies, as well as the sense of guilt, of their government representatives: they frequently likened the 1980s to World War II, when Canada turned away thousands of Jewish refugees. At the same time, they used the media and the legal system to increase the pressure. One example of this concerned the case of Salvadoran journalist Víctor Regalado. Regalado arrived in Canada in 1980 at the invitation of church and labor groups to speak out against Salvadoran policies. After a brief period, he left for Mexico, but unable to find employment there, he decided to return to live in Canada in 1982; however, during his transit he was stopped at the United States–Mexico border on the grounds that he was a security threat. When he was detained there by US authorities and facing deportation because of his Communist Party affiliation, Canadian church groups and their colleagues in the refugee advocacy network rallied to his cause. They pressured Ottawa until Regalado's case was transferred to Canadian jurisdiction, and then pressured the government to release him pending a ruling on his case.[140]

Speaking against the proposed legislation of the late 1980s were influential mainline denominations and religious groups: the Anglican Church of Canada, B'nai B'rith, the United Church of Canada, the Canadian Jewish Congress, the Inter-Church Committee on Refugees, the Canadian Council of Churches, the Conference of Catholic Bishops, the Jesuit Refugee Service, the Mennonite Central Committee, the Christian Reformed Churches, the Lutheran Refugee Committee, and the Quaker Committee for Refugees. Some opted for a legal course of action: in 1987, the Toronto Refugee Affairs Council, representing twenty-eight church and refugee aid groups, threatened to sue the federal government over the new legislation, claiming that it violated the Canadian Charter of Rights and Freedoms.[141] The Inter-Church Committee on Refugees submitted a brief to the UN Committee for Human Rights, charging that Canada's asylum determination system subjected asylum seekers to "cruel, inhuman, and degrading treatment."[142]

Many individual churches established their own refugee committees and protested at the local level. In February 1987, the Central American Refugee Committee of the Diocese of St. Catharine in Toronto, for example, organized an ecumenical religious service and a demonstration across from the Peace Bridge, which links Detroit and Fort Erie, to protest the proposed legislation. Under the glare of international cameras, hundreds of parishioners, nuns, and clergy publicly chastised their government, chanting and carrying signs saying "Canada, open the door!" and "Shame Bouchard! Minister of Shut Doors."[143] Individual churches were also active in the sponsorship of Central Americans, assuming financial responsibility for hundreds of immigrants, and working extralegally when deemed necessary to assist the undocumented. By the mid-1980s, church workers were actively involved in transnational sanctuary work, transporting refugees across the United States–Canada border, hiding them in safe houses, and securing legal and material assistance for them. Working with clergy, aid workers, and immigration lawyers in Mexico and the United States, Canadians traveled to detention centers, churches, shelters, and halfway houses to encourage refugees to apply for asylum in Canada, or they met the refugees sent to them at airports and border checkpoints. As Canada was the final option for these refugees, they helped them navigate the Canadian legal system to assure that they would receive refuge. The network of sanctuary workers on opposite sides of the United States–Canada boundary line was particularly well developed. The Windsor Central American Refugee Sponsorship Network worked with churches and other groups in Detroit. Vive La Casa, a refugee shelter in Buffalo, New York, worked with a sister shelter, La Casa del Norte, in Fort Erie, Ontario. Clergy in North Dakota transported refugees across the border to their contacts in Manitoba. A refugee program in Montreal, run jointly by the Anglican and Presbyterian churches, worked with churches in Burlington, Vermont.[144]

The extralegal measures that sanctuary workers often took to assist refugees discouraged many Canadians from participation. However, a rival network emerged, euphemistically called the Overground Railroad, for those who wanted to take a more proactive role in refugee assistance but remain within the law. The network consisted of some sixty churches that worked with a Christian community in Comer, Georgia, called Jubilee Partners. Volunteers traveled to detention centers such as Bayview in south Texas, bailed out small groups of refugees interested in moving to Canada, and transported them to the Jubilee Partners' 260-acre compound in Comer. There they remained for several weeks or months, while they received medical and security screening for their immigrant visas. As they waited for the Canadian consulate in Atlanta to process their paperwork, volunteers taught them English and Canadian history and customs. They were instructed on what to expect in Canada: how to deal with the harsh winters; how to secure medical assistance; how to look for employment, and so forth. Some Central Americans were then sent to the Mennonite

Central Committee in Goshen, Indiana, to wait for their visas. Interestingly, Central Americans assisted by the Overground railroad were "legalized" more rapidly than landed claimants, who tended to get caught up in the asylum backlog. If the Canadian consulate ruled an applicant ineligible for an immigrant visa, then the applicant was often referred to sanctuary workers, who assisted him or her in crossing the United States–Canada border and filing for asylum. Indeed, members of the Underground and Overground railroads frequently referred refugees and volunteers to each other. In 1986, 173 Central Americans were assisted by the Overground Railroad.[145]

While many American sanctuary workers welcomed media attention and publicity in order to call attention to US policies, Canadian sanctuary workers were less vocal about their activities during the 1980s. Although the network expanded across the country, prior to 1987 there was only one reported case of a congregation publicly declaring itself a sanctuary. Church workers, for the most part, claimed ignorance of the movement's existence. "We do not want to see RCMP [Royal Canadian Mounted Police] undercover agents infiltrating prayer groups of Canadian churches who are helping refugees [as happened in the United States]," said one participant.[146] However, passage of C-84 changed that. The new law imposed penalties for "assisting undocumented refugees to report to authorities, knowingly contravening or aiding any person to contravene the Immigration Act, and aiding or abetting a person not in possession of a valid visa, passport, or travel document." Suddenly refugee aid workers who were following their conscience were as criminally liable as professional smugglers, facing penalties of five to ten years in prison and fines of up to five hundred thousand dollars. As in the United States, the new penalties did not seem to discourage participants, but rather made them more resolute. As Nancy Pocock, recipient of the Pearson Peace Medal, told a reporter: "If my country tells me that I am a criminal, I'll have to say I'm obeying a higher authority."[147]

Attorneys affiliated with the Canadian Council for Refugees and other coalition groups counseled sanctuary and aid workers on how to do their work within the parameters of the new law. They analyzed the constitutionality of the law in light of Canada's international obligations and the Canadian Charter of Rights and Freedoms, and the defense arguments that could be offered at trial should the government decide to prosecute

sanctuary workers. But they also warned aid workers that they would ultimately have to decide whether they were willing to pay the price for their
beliefs. As Winnipeg lawyer David Matas wrote in one publication:

> Given that the law gives more protection to refugees who enter Canada
> illegally than those who do not, those concerned with the fate of the
> refugees have to ask themselves whether they want to aid refugees in
> circumventing the application of eligibility screening. They have to ask
> themselves whether they want to do what the Sanctuary Movement in
> the US has done. Do they want to give sanctuary and declare sanctuary?
> Do they want to set themselves on a course of violation with both
> the new laws and the old laws in order to protect refugees? The moral
> dimension of the answer to that question I will leave to others to
> answer.[148]

The Canadian sanctuary movement continued well into the next decade.
During the 1990s, sanctuary workers not only assisted in the transporting
of people across the border but also assisted those who had been issued
deportation orders. According to Mary Jo Leddy of the Canadian Council
for Refugees, many of the latter had legitimate claims to asylum, but their
petitions and appeals had been denied because of negligent lawyers, in-
competent translators, or biased board members, many of whom were subsequently disciplined or dismissed. Faced with deportation orders, these
refugees "began showing up in the early mornings and late evenings at the
offices of various advocacy groups," such as Amnesty International, VIGIL,
and Romero House, asking for protection. Sanctuary workers then arranged
for them to be hidden by religious communities and ecumenical groups
in Ontario.[149] The Vigil Network existed in various towns and cities across
Canada: if a refugee was in immediate danger of deportation, network
members were immediately notified so that they could call and telegram
their representatives and organize vigils, demonstrations, and rallies.[150]

REFUGEE POLICY IN THE 1990s

The numbers of immigrants and refugees increased steadily throughout
the 1990s. In 1993, Canada accepted some 25,000 refugees over all, including 13,600 landed claimants.[151] In 1998, Canada admitted 225,000 legal

immigrants and 32,000 refugees, roughly the equivalent of 0.8 percent of its population. (In contrast, the United States admitted 915,900 legal immigrants, or 0.3 percent of its population.)[152] The Immigration and Refugee Board had the highest acceptance rate in the world: 58 percent in 1994, prompting *Maclean's* to ask, "Is Canada a soft touch?"[153]

Many Canadians seemed to think so. Immigration ministers Sergio Marchi and Lucienne Robillard were accused of packing the IRB with liberal adjudicators who were irrationally pro-immigration and who "fast-tracked" applicants from certain countries regardless of the merits of their claims. During the 1990s the print media carried sensationalistic stories of the IRB admitting refugees who should have been rendered ineligible because of their criminal records and who committed new crimes in their host society.[154] A 1998 report by the Canadian Security Intelligence Service acknowledged that most of the world's terrorist cells had "established themselves in Canada, seeking safe haven, setting up operational bases and attempting to gain access to the USA."[155] Polls conducted throughout the decade revealed an increasing intolerance toward immigration and multicultural policies. In eight nationwide polls conducted during 1994–96, roughly half of all Canadians stated that Canada accepted too many immigrants. Not surprisingly, Canadians from Toronto, Montreal, and Vancouver, the chief destination of immigrants, were more likely to favor tougher immigration restrictions. While polls also showed that Canadians were comfortable with the nonwhite demographics of the migration (the largest group came from Hong Kong), almost three-quarters felt that ethnic or racial groups should adapt to the Canadian value system rather than maintain their differences.[156] Even those who favored the current levels of immigration wanted tougher screening of immigrants and refugees, and felt that the government should increase the percentage of people accepted under the "independent," or skilled, class rather than the family class.[157] In 1994 the House of Commons Standing Committee on Citizenship and Immigration recommended a longer residency period before qualifying for citizenship and tougher penalties for illegal immigrants (estimated to number over fifty thousand in the early 1990s), including denying their Canadian-born children the rights of jus soli.[158] A government-commissioned report in 1998 proposed admitting only immigrants who spoke English and French, to reduce language-training costs and to help ensure integration into Canadian life; or conversely, requiring family members of those admitted without the language skills to pay for their relatives' language training.[159]

A tougher refugee policy also had eloquent supporters: "Listening to the statements of immigration lawyers and refugee advocates, one would think that the treatment of refugee claimants in Canada was unusually harsh," wrote policy analyst Daniel Stoffman. "Yet, in fact, no other country comes even close to Canada's willingness to believe the stories of the people who say they are refugees." The real refugees—those stuck in camps without the financial resources to leave the region—were the true victims of international policy, argued Stoffman, and instead of spending over a billion dollars on the refugee determination system, Canada should send more funding to assist the UNHCR.[160] In an op-ed piece in the *National Post,* former ambassador Martin Collacott blamed the state of affairs on Canadian lawyers and advocacy groups who in manipulating Canadian guilt had "succeeded in stretching the definition of refugees to cover cases no other countries would accept." According to Collacott, the fact that Canada had the highest acceptance rate in the world suggested that not all of the entrants were bona fide refugees, and he blamed the increase in applications on the generous welfare package that was available to refugees. Even those who were found excludable found a way to remain in the country, which suggested that the entire refugee determination process needed a comprehensive overhaul.[161]

Critics of the asylum determination process offered a number of recommendations: replacing IRB members, who currently came from all walks of life and were varied in training and expertise, with experienced judges; establishing a "temporary protected status" to serve as a cost-saving alternative to asylum; appointing more judges in the Federal Court to prevent another backlog; and providing accelerated processing and a more rapid removal of those with unfounded claims. Others demanded that the federal government do more to assist the provincial governments with the costs of accommodation. In 1999, then mayor of Toronto, Mel Lastman, criticized Ottawa in very strong language: "The dumping has got to stop. This is a federal responsibility and they're dumping it on us. We want refugees coming to Toronto. We definitely do. But we can't afford to pick up the federal cost."[162]

By the end of the 1990s, the refugee acceptance rate had dropped to 44 percent. According to the UNHCR, Canada had one of the lowest per capita ratios of asylum seekers to population in the industrialized world.[163] Advocacy groups continued to lobby for larger numbers, arguing that Canada could well afford to do more for the world's displaced peoples. "The number of refugees Canada accepts each year is less than a tenth of 1 percent of our population," wrote one member of the Canadian Council for Refugees. "The majority of the world's refugees come from—and remain in—countries of the South."[164] A discussion paper of Employment and Immigration Canada argued the case for increased immigration. First, immigrants were vital to the Canadian economy: they created jobs, provided needed services, consumed more than the average Canadian, and brought funds into the country—as much as 4.5 billion to 6 billion dollars in 1988 alone, more than compensating for the 135 million dollars the government spent each year in services. Second, given that Canada's trade with the Asia-Pacific region now surpassed its trade with Europe, continued immigration from Asia, in particular, would help to create and reinforce these commercial links. And finally, immigration would help to minimize the "shrinking and greying" of the Canadian population, which was already a demographic reality.[165]

Forecasters estimated that the Canadian population would drop dramatically, to twenty-three million, by the middle of the twenty-first century if measures were not taken to replenish the population. Thus, some scholars and policy analysts advocated increasing the immigration rate to 450,000 per year (from its current annual level of 200,000–250,000), especially since roughly 20 percent of immigrants left Canada within ten to fifteen years.[166] However, during 1998 and 1999 Canadian immigration "goals" of 250,000 were unmet; fewer than 174,000 immigrated during that period.[167]

By the start of the next century, Central America's refugees no longer occupied a prominent role in Canadian public discourse. Even though El Salvador and Guatemala continued to be singled out as source countries whose refugees received immigration priority, the number of claimants no longer equaled 1985 figures, the peak year of Salvadoran immigration to Canada. Instead, attention shifted to countries in Africa, Asia, and the Middle East. As a supporter of Esquipulas II, Canada had committed itself to helping find long-term solutions to the Central American refugee crisis, primarily through development assistance and durable solutions.[168] It is unclear how many Central Americans living in Canada actually returned to their homelands after the elections and peace settlements of the 1990s. Like the United States, Canada does not keep a detailed accounting of residents who choose to emigrate or repatriate. However, it is very likely that those who legalized their status in Canada have maintained a transnational existence, investing a variety of capital in both old and new homelands, and blurring the borders in spite of state policies to reinforce them.

CONCLUSION

Shared Responsibility?
Legacies of the Central American Refugee Crisis

> Refugees make easy scapegoats: they are by definition
> foreigners in their country of asylum, they have no
> home to go back to, perhaps as many as half of them
> are children. Perversely, refugees who are virtually
> powerless are regarded as a threat by the powerful.
> Rich countries say they don't want refugees coming
> there; poor countries say, if the rich won't take in
> refugees, how can we be expected to?
>
> CANADIAN COUNCIL FOR REFUGEES

One of the legacies of the refugee crisis in Central America was greater cooperation in immigration matters among Mexico, the United States, and Canada, as well as other countries in the region. Beginning with the 1989 CIREFCA conference in Guatemala City, migration experts from Central and North America met several times over the next decade to discuss issues of mutual concern, including the root causes of migration, the trafficking of immigrants, the protection of human rights, and the accommodation and repatriation of refugees. Since 1996, representatives from eleven countries (Belize, Canada, Costa Rica, El Salvador, Guatemala, Honduras, Mexico, Nicaragua, Panama, the United States, and the Dominican Republic) have met regularly at the Regional Conference on Migration (also known as the Puebla Process) to discuss the "complexity and challenges of international migration movements."[1] Following each meeting, the vice ministers issue a "declaration" and "plan of action" summarizing their conclusions, regional objectives, and timetable for accomplishing these objectives. Recent conferences have focused on issues such as regional consultation before the implementation of immigration policies; transborder cooperation in surveillance; sanctions against trafficking; detention and deportation procedures; challenges in the integration of immigrants in host societies; migrant health issues; and special issues pertaining to women and minors. The Puebla Process has been called a "model for other regions in the world."[2] Similar attempts at policy coordination and information exchange have also been pursued in South America, Europe, and Asia with varying outcomes that, unfortunately, have not always resulted in the protection of migrants and asylum seekers.[3] At all these conferences and negotiations, representatives from non-governmental organizations have advocated on behalf of migrants, refugees, and displaced persons, and have tried to shape the policies of states. Increasingly, governments are turning to NGOs not only as a reliable source of field data but also for creative solutions to very complex problems.

For Mexico, one of the principal legacies of the Central American refugee crisis has been a pronounced interest in its southern border zone. For decades the United States–Mexico border had dominated diplomatic and trade negotiations with the United States, but the wars in Central America, the conflict with Guatemala, the Zapatista rebellion in Chiapas, and the NAFTA negotiations turned the Mexican government's attention southward as well. In the 1990s, the administrations of Carlos Salinas de Gortari and Ernesto Zedillo tried to improve diplomatic and trade relations with their Central American neighbors. In 1996, for example, Zedillo and President Alvaro Arzu, of Guatemala, signed several accords addressing such diverse issues as drug trafficking, extradition, development, and tourism. Both governments cited as a top priority the negotiation of a regional free trade agreement and, in preparation for the increased flow of goods and people, drafted plans to expand and improve highways and to build a bridge linking the border cities of Ciudad Hidalgo and Tecún Umán.[4] As with the NAFTA accords, Mexico's challenge was to find a way to facilitate the flow of capital and labor while protecting political boundaries and ensuring national security.

Control of Mexico's southern border also became a priority because of increased pressure from the United States, which wanted to stem the flow of undocumented Central Americans who transited through Mexico, as well as control drug trafficking.[5] According to the Instituto Nacional de Migración, 170,509 illegal Central Americans were detained in Chiapas in the first trimester of 1991 alone.[6] However, the increased detention and deportation of the undocumented did not deter Central Americans from crossing. From 1996 to 2001, the migration of undocumented Central Americans increased as a result of the ongoing criminal and political violence, as well as natural disasters that disrupted the economy and exacerbated the poverty.[7] Migration from Honduras and Nicaragua increased exponentially as a result of Hurricane Mitch (1998), and from El Salvador after the earthquakes of 2001.[8] By 2004, Salvadoran officials estimated that nearly one-fourth of Salvadorans lived in the United States.[9]

The populations of Guatemalan border towns doubled and tripled in size, as thousands of would-be immigrants from Central America, but also Africa, Asia, and the Middle East, arrived in the late 1990s as part of organized smuggling networks, to cross into Mexico and then possibly on to the United States or Canada. Journalists nicknamed the Guatemalan border town Tecún Umán, "Little Tijuana," because of the hundreds of smugglers and other businesses that emerged to cater to this transient population. In Mexico, one of the newest businesses in the southern border municipalities was the "employment agencies" that promised Mexicans and foreigners alike transportation to, and employment in, the northern *maquiladoras*. Through such agencies undocumented workers secured employment on the United States–Mexico border, which made crossing into the United States easier if they were later laid off.

Like most undocumented workers, Central Americans were vulnerable to exploitation and abuse by gangs, employers, smugglers, and even Guatemalan and Mexican police forces. In the year 2000 over 80 percent of the migrants living at the shelter Casa Albergue del Migrante, in Tapachula, reported that they had been robbed by gang members, petty thieves, and/or Mexican police.[10] According to the Diocese of Tapachula and the Instituto Nacional de Migración, the Salvadoran gang Mara Salvatruchas, which originated in Los Angeles, California, was responsible for many of the robberies, assaults, rapes, and murders of would-be immigrants in the southern border towns.[11] According to some estimates the number of Central Americans who died trying to cross into Mexico exceeded the number of dead along the United States–Mexico border. The Centro de Recursos Centroamericanos estimated that between 1998 and 2002, twenty-five thousand Central Americans were unaccounted for, ten thousand of them Salvadorans.[12] A number of NGOs emerged in the Guatemala-Mexico border zone to deal with the challenges posed by these *transmigrantes*. These included Sin Fronteras, the Casa del Migrante in Tecún Umán, and Casa Albergue del Migrante in Tapachula. Together with older NGOs like the Comité Diocesano de Ayuda a Inmigrantes Fronterizos, they provided temporary housing, food, clothing, small loans, and medical care to hundreds of migrants each month who were deported, left stranded by their smugglers, or abused in some way.

Mexican police were often implicated in the human rights abuses. Migrants accused the police of theft of personal property and identification documents, kidnappings, arbitrary detentions, intimidation, rape, and forced prostitution.[13] Detention centers—the worst said to be located in Ciudad Hidalgo, Tapachula, El Mongito, La Ventosa, and Tehuantepec—were overcrowded. Detainees reported that they received little food, water, and medical attention during their incarceration, and were later crowded into large trucks or buses and transported across the border and simply left there. Mexican law did not offer detainees rights to legal counsel or to petition the courts. And although undocumented workers were to be deported within a reasonable amount of time—usually thirty-six hours—NGOs reported that many were kept for a much longer period and subjected to forced labor, physical and sexual abuse, and extortion.[14]

In 1996, on the recommendation of its human rights commission, the Comisión Nacional de Derechos Humanos, the Mexican government established the special police force Grupo de Protección Betas to provide information and assistance to migrants. The Betas first operated in northern border towns such as Tijuana and Nogales, assisting co-nationals abandoned by their smugglers in the northern deserts, but their presence in southern cities such as Comitán, Tapachula, and Tuxtla Gutiérrez increased in response to reports of human rights abuses. The Betas patrolled bus stations, freight cars, truck stops, and abandoned buildings. Their mission was not to arrest the undocumented but rather to provide them with emergency assistance and direct them to churches, NGOs, and shelters that could offer legal advice and material assistance. However, within months of their founding, the Betas were also accused of corruption. In 1998, the Salvadoran Congress denounced Mexico for its treatment of 132 Salvadorans awaiting deportation, and the California-based immigrant advocacy group El Rescate threatened a formal complaint against Mexico before the Comisión Interamericana de Derechos Humanos for its violation of human rights of Central American migrants.[15]

The United States, in turn, increased its own surveillance of the border with Mexico. Under the terms of the Illegal Immigration Reform and Immigrant Responsibility Act of 1996, the government increased the

Border Patrol by a thousand agents each year. By 2000, over ten thousand agents served in the Border Patrol, most of them along the United States–Mexico border. By 2001, seventy-six miles of new fences were erected along the southwestern border with 130 remote video surveillance systems, and an additional thirty-two miles and 1,100 systems were in the planning stages.[16] As a result, apprehensions of undocumented immigrants were up from 1.14 million in 1992 to 1.64 million in 2000.[17]

The United States also financially underwrote many of the border control initiatives enacted in Mexico and Central America, including the training of border personnel, the purchase of new surveillance equipment, and the transportation of detainees back to their homelands.[18] Central American countries cooperated, primarily through the exchange of information and the coordination of policies. Guatemala, for example, initiated a new policy requiring Salvadorans, Nicaraguans, and Hondurans to carry passports while traveling in Guatemalan territory, and increased the criminal penalties on those that transported or harbored illegal immigrants.[19] During the late 1990s, Nicaragua, Guatemala, and El Salvador carried out separate national campaigns targeting illegal immigration, and thousands were apprehended and deported. These efforts culminated in a joint campaign by fourteen countries in the Western Hemisphere that led to the detention of eight thousand illegal immigrants during the period June 4–20, 2001.[20]

After the terrorist attacks on September 11, 2001, these cooperative ventures acquired more urgency. The United States now sought to prevent the entry not only of drugs and illegal immigrants but also of terrorists, especially when it was discovered that lax screening and the lack of information exchange had allowed the hijackers of 9/11 to enter the United States despite possession of fraudulent passports, false statements on their visa applications, and their listing as security risks in various intelligence data banks.[21] In the wake of the terrorist attacks, the United States, as well as Mexico and Canada, revamped their immigration bureaucracies, increased security personnel at airports and border checkpoints, and enacted new—and highly controversial—detention and deportation procedures. The USA-PATRIOT Act, passed just forty-five days after the 9/11 attacks, expanded the powers of law enforcement agencies to search, monitor, and detain suspected criminals and terrorists; allowed the indefinite detention of noncitizens suspected of a crime; and facilitated their deportation for a number of activities, including those that once fell under the category of free speech. The new Bureau of Customs and Border Protection, in the new Department of Homeland Security, replaced the INS in an attempt to convey a greater sense of security to the general public. The US government made it more difficult for students, tourists, and immigrants from certain nations to receive visas to come to the United States. And under the US–VISIT program,[22] the United States began collecting biometric data on all visitors, including digital fingerprints and photographs, at all ports of entry. According to one Canadian newspaper, the border of the United States became harder to cross than the now-defunct Checkpoint Charlie between East and West Berlin.[23] According to a fact sheet from the Department of Homeland Security, the new security measures would "scrupulously protect the privacy and civil liberties of US citizens and foreign visitors," but civil rights NGOs contested these claims. Dozens of lawsuits have been filed against the government since 2001 for illegal and indefinite detentions, deportations, and violations of civil liberties.[24]

Refugees became a casualty of these new security measures. In 2002 and 2003, admissions sank to fewer than twenty-nine thousand. (In February 2005, the White House promised a close return to the seventy thousand total annual admissions in the years before the 2001 terrorist attacks, but a month later, citing budget restraints, the Bush administration reversed itself, stating that forty-three thousand would be admitted.)[25] A report by the United States Commission on International Religious Freedom revealed extreme disparities in asylum rulings. According to the commission, the probability of securing asylum in the United States depends on the claimant's country of origin, the location where the case is heard, and whether the claimant is represented by counsel. Thus, a refugee from El Salvador has a 5 percent chance of securing asylum, while a Cuban has an 80 percent chance, and an Iraqi, a 60 percent chance. The average claimant has to wait sixty-four days for an immigration judge to rule on the validity of his claim, and if he is represented by counsel, the claimant has a 30 percent better chance of securing a positive ruling.[26] The report also documented the stark conditions in various detention centers around the country, almost twenty years after federal district courts attempted to address these problems. In some areas, detainees are subjected to twenty-four-hour lights that make sleep impossible; overcrowding and a lack of privacy, even to use the toilet; and few opportunities to exercise outdoors.

Equally worrisome to immigration advocacy groups was the omnibus REAL ID Bill, passed by Congress in 2005. The bill has attracted a great deal of media attention because it lays the foundation for a national ID card and prevents undocumented immigrants from securing driver's licenses, but lesser-known provisions address the issue of asylum. Included in the bill, for example, are provisions that increase the burden of proof on asylum seekers, deporting them to the countries they are fleeing if they cannot provide sufficient corroboration of their claims.[27]

As part of its post-9/11 campaign to strengthen the border and national security, the United States increased its diplomatic pressure on Mexico. Intelligence reports showed an increase in the number of Muslim and Arab immigrants to Mexico that heightened State Department concerns. Intelligence reports also revealed that the terrorist group al-Qaeda, responsible for the 9/11 attacks, planned to infiltrate members across the United States–Mexico border. Mexico cooperated with the United States in order to prevent the use of Mexican territory to gain access to or stage actions against its neighbor. The Instituto Nacional de Migración expanded its presence in the southern border zone and began denying visas to nationals of countries the United States has identified as supporting terrorism. As in the United States, would-be immigrants and refugees became the casualties of Mexican obsessions with border control. By 2002, fewer than one-third of asylum applications were successful. Central Americans, trying to escape the poverty and continued violence in their homelands, were especially targeted. By end of 2002, Mexico deported over three thousand Central Americans each week.[28] One critic of Mexico's new policies explained the post-9/11 era: "Anyone with any brains can see that Mexican foreign policy, with regards to migratory issues, tries to accommodate the United States and do its dirty work. . . . Mexico [has] placed the 'tortilla curtain' not at the Rio Grande but at its border with Guatemala to impede the entry of migrants from Central America and the rest of the world."[29]

The United States also increased pressure on Canada, especially in the wake of highly publicized arrests of terrorists caught at the border trying to smuggle explosives into the United States and the discovery of Canada-based terrorist plots to bomb US airports and landmarks.[30] Americans and

Canadians alike blamed such attempts on Canada's more lax immigration and refugee policies, which made Canada, according to one think tank, a haven for the world's terrorists.[31]

Three months after the attacks of September 11, Parliament passed the Anti-Terrorism Act, which, among other features, identified thirty-one groups that had engaged in international terrorism and barred entrance to any of their members. In order to prevent potential terrorists from using the immigration bureaucracy to establish a foothold in North America, Parliament also revamped its immigration law in 2002. The Immigration and Refugee Protection Act provided a stricter set of guidelines for determining immigration and asylum.[32] As in the terms of the previously proposed Memorandum of Agreement, a refugee was now considered ineligible if he or she came to Canada through a designated safe third country. This potentially affected as many as half of the asylum applicants in Canada each year, since most either filed claims at border checkpoints or temporarily stopped in the United States before flying on to Canada.[33] (By comparison roughly two hundred claimants in the United States stopped in Canada first.)[34] Immigrant and refugees advocates opposed the act for a variety of reasons: in associating immigration control with national security, it erroneously equated immigrants with terrorists in the public consciousness; the "safe third country" provision deported claimants to the United States, which was hardly safe because refugees faced discriminatory hearings and unsafe detention and deportation procedures; and there was no appeals process through which rejected claimants might have a chance to plead their case. The Canadian Council for Refugees and other advocacy groups warned that the new law would only increase the number of smuggling networks and illegal immigrants, potentially making Canadian society more vulnerable.[35] They also reminded Canadian citizens that few claimants were ever found ineligible for reasons of security.[36] (In 2004, for example, only one of the 234 claims ruled ineligible was found so for reasons of security.)

In December 2003, the Canadian government announced the creation of a Canadian Border Services Agency and transferred some of the responsibilities of immigration officials to this new agency. Thus an agency entrusted to control the border in the post-9/11 era was also responsible for protecting refugees, two missions that immigration advocates believed were inherently in opposition. The new agency, like the 2003 Statement of Mutual Understanding on Information Sharing, was part of a series of "Smart Border" or "harmonisation" initiatives designed by Canada and the United States to facilitate the sharing of information, complement their admissions and deportation procedures, and control the northern border. (Indeed, some analysts speculated that the United States agreed to the safe third country policy, which increased the US backlog, in exchange for Canada's participation in these initiatives.) As in Mexico, these new measures sometimes resulted in serious civil and human rights violations. The so-called security certificates allowed the Canadian government to detain suspected terrorists without charge or bail on secret evidence that neither they nor their lawyers were allowed to see.[37] According to the government, such measures were necessary in order to protect intelligence sources and, ultimately, national security. One of the most controversial cases of the post-9/11 era involved Maher Arar, a thirty-three-year old Canadian citizen detained by US authorities in 2003 while flying back from a vacation in Tunisia to his home in Canada. On the basis of information shared by Canadian Security Intelligence Service, Arar was detained for suspected ties to the terrorist group al-Qaeda and deported to Syria, his place of birth, where he was held and tortured for ten months before the Canadian government finally admitted a mistake and allowed him to return to Canada. In 2004 Arar sued the service, the Royal Canadian Mounted Police, and the Canadian Border Services Agency for four hundred million dollars.[38]

As a result of all of these new security measures, the number of refugee claims in Canada fell from a record high of 44,063 in 2001 to fewer than half that number in 2003.[39] In 2004, the overall acceptance rate for refugees was also down, to 41 percent—only slightly higher than the US rate of 37 percent (although for some nationalities, such as the Colombians, the acceptance rate in Canada was as high as 81 percent).[40] Despite lobbying by refugee advocates, the government had failed to create a meaningful appeals process by which rejected claimants could seek a reversal of their decision. Articles and editorials in the Canadian press complained that US security priorities were driving policy decisions in Ottawa, and that Canada was neglecting its heritage as a haven for the oppressed.[41] "In our own eyes—and those of recent immigrants—," wrote one journalist, "we are a nation coasting on an outdated reputation."[42] In 2004, the Canadian Council for Refugees asked the Inter-American Commission on Human Rights to investigate Canada for violating the principle of *non-refoulement*. Not surprisingly, participation in sanctuary activities increased as Canadians sought ways to assist refugees who were victimized by the new policies.[43] The Interfaith Sanctuary Coalition, an umbrella group of more than forty church, human rights, labor, and other groups, supported the individuals and families that tried to avoid deportation.[44]

By 2004, then, the number of asylum claims and acceptance rates had dropped in Mexico, the United States, and Canada, although not because the number of refugees had decreased; indeed, in 2004, the World Refugee Survey reported 1.12 million new cases of refugees worldwide, bringing the total number of worldwide refugees to 11.9 million.[45] But the burden of hearing claims and accommodating refugees was increasingly borne by the poorest nations. According to the UNHCR, in 2004 the total number of asylum seekers in the thirty-eight industrialized countries was the lowest since 1988, at 368,000.[46]

The political and economic realities in Central America continued to produce a large migration of unemployed workers and asylum seekers, but it was easier to remain undocumented in the underground economies of Mexico, the United States, and Canada than to secure safe haven, asylum, or some other protected status.

Ironically, these three countries are committed to the free movement of trade. The North American Free Trade Agreement, finalized in 1993, has generated billions of dollars in trade.[47] According to the Migration Policy Institute, the United States' borders with Mexico and Canada, its two largest trading partners, are among the most active in the world: on average 1.2 billion dollars are traded every day with Canada, and $733 million with Mexico. And despite criticism over NAFTA's lack of environmental safeguards and worker protections, the United States is negotiating free trade agreements with several other countries. As the three economies become more integrated, they become more dependent on investments—and labor. In 2001, the US Embassy in Mexico City processed over 2.6 million nonimmigrant visa applications, mostly from nationals who work in the United States.[48] In January 2004, President George W. Bush introduced his controversial guest worker plan, theoretically to control illegal immigration while providing the low-wage labor required by agribusiness and the service sector. Under his proposed plan tens of thousands of workers (most probably from Mexico and Central

America) would be allowed work in the United States (or, in the case of illegal immigrants, remain in the States) on a temporary basis, on the condition that they return to their homelands once their contracts expire. The proposal is, in essence, a new version of the bracero program of the 1940s and 1950s. According to supporters, such a program acknowledges the reality of illegal immigration and its importance to the national economy, allows the administration to meet the labor demands of businesses, but also allows it some symbolic control over who enters and remains in the country. These workers, in turn, join existing immigrant-worker communities that generate billions of dollars in remittances each year. These remittances—ten billion dollars annually to Mexico alone—constitute one of the principal sources of income for many countries in the Americas, and far exceed the development aid provided by the United States, Canada, and other industrial economies.

Thus, Mexico, the United States, and Canada have two parallel and competing goals in the new century: facilitate the free movement of capital while controlling the movement of "undesirables." Decades of immigration restriction measures have demonstrated the difficulties of controlling unwanted migration. Visas, fines on airlines and shipping companies, increased border security personnel, criminal penalties on smugglers, streamlined detention and deportation procedures, and multinational "crackdowns" on illegal immigrants may temporarily reduce the number of immigrants and refugees in a given year, but only until new entry points, transportation networks, and legal loopholes are discovered. And shared information and coordinated policies do not always result in shared responsibility or in the protection of human rights. In matters regarding Central American and other overland migration, Mexico bears the burden of border control, controlling access not only to its own territory but also to the United States and Canada. Thus, the country with a record of serious human rights violations has been entrusted with the responsibility of controlling the migration of undocumented workers and would-be asylum seekers.

Unfortunately, refugees are now subsumed under this general category of "undesirables." The goal of these three countries, as well as others in the region, should be to create and reinforce procedural safeguards that respect the safety and human rights of all migrants. For asylum seekers, these rights include: the right to have their petitions considered in the

country of their choice; the right to humane living conditions and meaningful work or other activity while their petitions are considered; the right
to counsel, a quick hearing, and the public disclosure of any evidence considered against them; and, in the case of a negative ruling, the right to
appeal. Only when these conditions are met can these countries right-
fully be known as havens for the oppressed. Unfortunately, in the post-
9/11 era, strengthening public confidence in the elusive goal of national
security has become more important than defining and protecting refugee rights.

NOTES

INTRODUCTION

Epigraph: Rigoberta Menchú Tum, foreword, *Presencia de los refugiados guatemaltecos en México* (Mexico City: COMAR and UNHCR, 1999), 17. Translation mine. Unless otherwise indicated, all translations in the book are mine.

1. The number of NGOs that operate internationally has grown since World War II. There are at least thirty-five thousand private, not-for-profit organizations with an international focus. According to Boli and Thomas, most are highly specialized, "drawing members worldwide from a particular occupation, technical field, branch of knowledge, industry, hobby or sport, to promote and regulate their respective areas of concern." See John Boli and George M. Thomas, eds., *Constructing World Culture: International Nongovernmental Organizations since 1875* (Stanford: Stanford University Press, 1999), 20.

2. According to Keck and Sikkink, a transnational advocacy network includes "those relevant actors working internationally on an issue, who are bound together by shared values, a common discourse, and dense exchanges of information and services." Margaret E. Keck and Kathryn Sikkink, *Activists beyond Borders: Advocacy Networks in International Politics* (Ithaca, NY: Cornell University Press, 1998), 1–2. According to Risse and Sikkink, advocacy networks serve three purposes: they put norm-violating states on the international agenda; they legitimate the claims of domestic opposition groups, and thus mobilize domestic opposition, social movements, and NGOs in norm-violating countries; and they challenge norm-violating governments by creating a "transnational structure" that

pressures the government from above and below. See Thomas Risse and Kathryn Sikkink, "The Socialization of International Human Rights Norms into Domestic Practices," in Thomas Risse, Stephen C. Ropp, and Kathryn Sikkink, eds., *The Power of Human Rights: International Norms and Domestic Change* (Cambridge: Cambridge University Press, 1998), 5.

3. Risse and Sikkink state that the "diffusion of international norms in the human rights area crucially depends on the establishment and the sustainability of networks among domestic and transnational actors who manage to link up with international regimes to alert Western public opinion and Western governments." See Risse and Sikkink, "International Human Rights Norms," 5.

4. Journalists were a favorite target of right-wing regimes in Central America. In 1979 for example, Nicaraguan National Guardsmen shot ABC journalist Bill Stewart when he stopped to ask a question. Stewart's camera crew, parked in their van off in the distance, captured the entire event on film. That night the assassination was shown on television across the United States. In December 1980, US journalist John Sullivan disappeared from his hotel room in San Salvador; the trunk of his decapitated and dismembered corpse was identified by forensic pathologists in the United States in 1983. The pathologists' postmortem examinations stated that Sullivan's death may have been caused by an explosive device placed inside his mouth. In 1982, Guatemalan security forces murdered three Dutch journalists. Amnesty International, Americas Watch, and Human Rights Watch have documented the killing, disappearance, and torture of dozens of journalists, most of them Central American. See Hubert Campfens, "Guatemalan Refugees in Mexico," *Refuge* 3 (December 1983): 8; and *Voice for Freedom: An Amnesty International Anthology* (London, 1986), 178–180.

5. In Ethiopia in the early 1980s, for example, the migration of over two million people focused international media attention on the catastrophic drought and the Ethiopian government's counterinsurgency campaign. This attention facilitated a massive relief operation and an eventual shift in international policies toward Ethiopia. See William DeMars, "Contending Neutralities: Humanitarian Organizations and War in the Horn of Africa," 101–122 in Jackie Smith, Charles Chatfielf, and Ron Pagnucco, eds., *Transnational Social Movements and Global Politics* (Syracuse, NY: Syracuse University Press, 1997).

6. In May 1987, Salvadoran president José Napoleón Duarte personally wrote Ronald Reagan listing several reasons why a stay in deportations was necessary, among them that El Salvador's fragile, war-torn economy had become dependent on the 350 to 600 million dollars in annual remittances that expatriates sent relatives back home at that time.

7. As part of Plan Sur (Southern Plan), Mexico committed more resources than previously to the detention and deportation of illegals, particularly the *trans-*

migrantes in southern states like Chiapas, who were believed to be heading north-ward toward the United States. The plan is quite controversial, and nationalists charge that Mexico is doing the United States' "dirty work." See, for example, "El Plan Sur y la frontera de la vergüenza," *La Jornada,* August 8, 2001, www.jornada.unam.mx/2001/ago00/010808/mas-guerra.html.

1. THE WARS IN CENTRAL AMERICA AND THE REFUGEE CRISIS

Epigraph: Mark Falcoff, "How to Understand Central America," *Commentary* 78 (September 1984): 30.

1. Perhaps the most obvious example is the CIA's use of Nicaragua as a staging ground for the 1961 Bay of Pigs invasion of Cuba.

2. By the time of the revolution, the majority of the population lived in rural areas, and less than 2 percent of this rural population had access to potable water. Seventy-five percent of Nicaraguan children were malnourished, and one in ten died before one year of age. See Walter LaFeber, *Inevitable Revolutions: The United States in Central America,* 2nd ed. (New York: W. W. Norton, 1993), 11, 162–165; and Douglas V. Porpora, *How Holocausts Happen: The United States in Central America* (Philadelphia: Temple University Press, 1990), 75–76.

3. William M. LeoGrande, *Our Own Backyard: The United States in Central America, 1977–1992* (Chapel Hill: University of North Carolina Press, 1998) 14.

4. When the US Marines withdrew from Nicaragua in 1933, they left in their place a National Guard under the direction of Anastacio Somoza García, who eventually eliminated his opponents and political rivals and assumed control of the government. By the 1970s, the National Guard consisted of five thousand soldiers trained in counterinsurgency tactics. Members of the officer corps were trained at the US Army's School of the Americas. See Porpora, *How Holocausts Happen,* 107; LaFeber, *Inevitable Revolutions,* 67–71.

5. Quoted in Falcoff, "How to Understand Central America," 35.

6. According to LeoGrande, the Somozas and their inner circle financially profited from the devastation. As Managua was rebuilt, all the new construction was made on Somoza land, with Somoza's construction companies, and with money funneled through Somoza's banks. International relief intended for the victims of the earthquake found its way into Somoza coffers; even food was stolen and later sold on the black market at highly inflated prices. See LeoGrande, *Our Own Backyard,* 14–15.

7. The founders of the FSLN named their group in honor of Augusto Cesar Sandino, who beginning in 1925 waged a six-year war against the US Marines occupying Nicaragua. As head of the National Guard, the elder Anastacio Somoza

lured Sandino to Managua on the pretext of negotiating a peace. When Sandino arrived in the city he was assassinated. Inspired by the Cuban revolution, Carlos Fonseca Amador founded the FSLN in 1961 in Havana, Cuba. Fonseca Amador was killed in battle in 1976. After his death, the FSLN split into three principal sections or factions: the Guerra Popular Prolongada, which supported rural-based guerrilla warfare; the Tendencia Proletaria, which worked with the urban proletariat to conduct its war in the cities; and the Tendencia Insurreccional, or Terceristas, which supported traditional military action in both urban and rural areas. Of the three factions, the Terceristas were the most inclusive and willing to work with the moderate opposition. See LeoGrande, *Our Own Backyard,* 17–18; and LaFeber, *Inevitable Revolutions,* 228–229.

8. LeoGrande, *Our Own Backyard,* 22–23.

9. Somoza was assassinated the following year, in Paraguay.

10. LeoGrande, *Our Own Backyard,* 27–29.

11. Alan Riding, "Sandinist Renegade Says CIA Hamstrings Him," *New York Times,* November 15, 1982. Pastora fought against the Somoza regime for eighteen years. When he left the coalition government he vowed to return one day and "rescue" the revolution. In exile he became particularly critical of the US-supported Nicaraguan Democratic Forces (FDN), specifically its inclusion of former National Guardsmen and Somoza supporters such as Enrique Bermúdez and Nicaraguan elites such as Adolfo Calero and Alfonso Robelo. Their presence, he argued, made it improbable that democratically minded Nicaraguans would oust the Sandinistas in the FDN's favor. Instead, Pastora claimed to offer Nicaraguans a "third option" through his organization, the Nicaraguan Democratic Revolutionary Alliance, which advocated a return to the original goals of the Sandinista revolution, including political pluralism and a mixed economy. Pastora settled in Costa Rica, from which he led his own war on the Sandinistas. According to Honey (1994), when the CIA failed to draw Pastora into the Contra network, it tried to eliminate him, first by denying his forces tactical support and ultimately by trying to assassinate him. See also José Melendez, "Ordenó la CIA acabar con Edén Pastora: ARDE," *Excélsior,* June 2, 1984; "Un falso fotografo, posible autor del atentado a Pastora," *Excélsior,* June 5, 1984.

12. Mexico recognized the Castro government in Cuba, for example, and was the only government to refuse to participate in the Organization of American States' economic blockade of the island.

13. See H. Rodrigo Jauberth et al., *The Difficult Triangle: Mexico, Central America, and the United States* (Boulder, CO: Westview Press, 1992). From 1980 to 1991, Mexico provided Central America with 1.3 billion dollars in development assistance. See Juanita Darling, "Mexico Savors Role as Mediator of Central American Conflicts," *Los Angeles Times,* May 4, 1991.

14. According to LeoGrande, López Portillo's peace plan proposed three courses: the United States would cease to threaten Nicaragua with the use of force; the Sandinistas would reduce the size of their armed forces once the Contras had been disarmed; and Nicaragua would sign a nonaggression pact with the United States and its neighbors. LeoGrande, *Our Own Backyard*, 287–289.

15. "Excerpts from Remarks by the Two Presidents," *New York Times*, May 16, 1984. See also Mexico's official position as stated before the United Nations: "Es el público salvadoreño quien debe decidir su destino: México en la ONU," *El Día*, March 11, 1981. According to Donna Rich, Mexico's goal in Nicaragua could be called the "PRI-ization" of the revolution: "an attempt to use moderate forces to co-opt the revolution in order to build an inclusionary authoritarian political system that would be based on a mixed economy, political pluralism and the containment of the Nicaraguan revolution within Nicaraguan territorial boundaries." Donna Rich, *Mexican Policy toward Guatemalan Refugees*, Occasional Paper no. 17, Central American and Caribbean Program, School of Advanced International Studies, Johns Hopkins University, June 1987, 4.

16. Peter MacFarlane, *Northern Shadows: Canadians and Central America* (Toronto: Between the Lines, 1989), 159–161. According to MacFarlane, the United States tried to pressure Canada into accepting Somoza, but the Canadian Office of External Affairs resisted.

17. According to MacFarlane, Ottawa was reluctant to find itself too far from Washington on hemispheric issues (ibid., 173); see also "Condena Canadá el armamentismo en la región," *Unomásuno*, May 2, 1984.

18. As a symbol of this commitment, Carter appointed civil rights activist Andrew Young as US ambassador to the United Nations. In 1977, Congress also approved the creation of the new post of assistant secretary of state for human rights and humanitarian affairs.

19. Lester D. Langley, *America and the Americas: The United States in the Western Hemisphere* (Athens: University of Georgia Press, 1989), 241–242; LeoGrande, *Our Own Backyard*, 30–32; Falcoff, "How to Understand Central America," 35–38.

20. LaFeber, *Inevitable Revolutions*, 209–210, 241.

21. Through the Freedom of Information Act, the National Security Archive, an independent non-government institution at George Washington University, secured and compiled thirty-five hundred documents concerning the Reagan and Bush administrations' perceptions and dealings with the Somoza government, the Sandinistas, and the Contras. See, for example, the February 1, 1984, confidential memorandum, "Themes for Op-Ed Pieces to Be Written by Outside Supporters," item no. NI01969, and the March 1985 unpublished report "The Soviet-Cuban Connection in Central American and the Caribbean," item no. NI01969. The thirty-five hundred documents form part of a microfiche collection enti-

tled "Nicaragua: The Making of US Policy, 1978–1990." See www.gwu.edu/~nsarchive/nsa/publications/nicaragua/nicaragua.html. For information on the NSA's microfiche collections, including those on Central America, see http://nsarchive.chadwyck.com/.

22. The Contras actually consisted of three factions: the Nicaraguan Democratic Forces (FDN), headed by former Guardsman Enrique Bermúdez; the Nicaraguan Democratic Revolutionary Alliance (ARDE), based in Costa Rica, and headed by ex-Sandinista Edén Pastora; and the Nicaraguan Armed Revolutionary Forces. Some soldiers of the FDN and ARDE were Miskito Indians who broke with the Sandinistas when they were relocated from their traditional lands. Of these various Contra factions, the Reagan administration supported the FDN, and this faction was most identified with the term *Contras*.

23. The authorization for the funding to support the Contras came from National Security Decision Directive 17; see LaFeber, *Inevitable Revolutions*, 281. At first, Argentine military officers played a role in training the Contras. After the Falklands/Malvinas War, however, the majority of the Argentine military advisers ceased that work, in gratitude to the Sandinistas for supporting Argentina in the war—and in protest against the United States for siding with Great Britain. Cuban exiles on the CIA payroll also played a role in training the Nicaraguan soldiers, some of them in camps west of Miami, near the Everglades, in violation of the Neutrality Act. See Philip Taubman, "In Exiles' War against Sandinists, Florida is H.Q.," *New York Times,* December 7, 1982; Jo Thomas, "Latin Exiles Focus on Nicaragua as They Train Urgently in Florida," *New York Times,* December 23, 1981; Stuart Taylor Jr., "Latins' Training in US Raises Questions of Criminal and International Law," *New York Times,* December 24, 1981.

24. See Morris H. Morley, *Washington, Somoza, and the Sandinistas: State and Regime in US Policy toward Nicaragua, 1969–1981* (New York: Cambridge University Press, 1994).

25. María Cristina García, *Havana USA: Cuban Exiles and Cuban Americans in South Florida, 1959–1994* (Berkeley: University of California Press, 1996), 122–137.

26. A different CIA publication, "The Freedom Fighter's Manual," instructed Nicaraguans on ways to defy the Sandinistas at home and in the workplace. See LaFeber, *Inevitable Revolutions,* 302–303; Philip Taubman, "Nicaraguan Exile Limits Role of the US," *New York Times,* December 9, 1982.

27. In 1982, opposition to US funding of the Contras from leading congressional Democrats (and at least one Republican) such as Speaker of the House Eugene "Tip" O'Neil (D-Massachusetts); Representatives Clarence Long (D-Maryland) and Edward Boland (D-Massachusetts); and Senators Christopher Dodd (D-Connecticut), Mark Hatfield (R-Oregon), and Edward Kennedy

(D-Massachusetts), led to a compromise amendment to the defense appropriations bill (the first Boland Amendment).

28. Dozens of studies exist on the Iran–Contra affair and the CIA war on the Sandinistas. A short sample includes: Cynthia Arnson, *Crossroads: Congress, the President, and Central America* (University Park: Pennsylvania State University Press, 1993); Robert Busby, *Reagan and the Iran-Contra Affair: The Politics of Presidential Recovery* (New York: St. Martin's Press, 1999); Theodore Draper, *A Very Thin Line: The Iran-Contra Affairs* (New York: Hill and Wang, 1991); Peter Kornbluh, *The Iran-Contra Scandal: The Declassified Story* (New York: New Press, 1993); Lawrence E. Walsh, *Firewall: The Iran-Contra Conspiracy and Cover-up* (New York: W. W. Norton, 1997); and Walsh, *Iran-Contra: The Final Report* (New York: Times Books, 1994). Members of the Reagan administration have offered their own interpretations: see, for example, Oliver North, *Under Fire: An American Story* (New York: Harper Paperbacks, 1992); Elliott Abrams, *Undue Process: A Story of How Political Differences Are Turned into Crimes* (New York: Free Press, 1993).

29. William M. LeoGrande, *Central America and the Polls: A Study of US Public Opinion Polls on US Foreign Policy toward El Salvador and Nicaragua under the Reagan Administration* (Washington, D.C.: Washington Office on Latin America, 1987).

30. A sample of these letters can be read in the declassified files at the Reagan Presidential Library in Simi Valley, California.

31. The Fourteen Families actually consisted of a few thousand people, many of them connected through marriage. See LeoGrande, *Our Own Backyard,* 34.

32. Langley, *America and the Americas,* 237; LeoGrande, *Our Own Backyard,* 34. With six hundred people per square mile in 1980, El Salvador had the highest population density in Latin America.

33. The army was led by General Maximiliano Hernández Martínez, who ruled as dictator until 1944. Tom Barry and Deb Preusch, *The Central America Fact Book* (New York: Grove Press, 1986), 200.

34. This ideological shift was first initiated by Pope John XXIII and his Vatican II Council (1962–65). The Latin American Bishops' Conference in Medellín, Colombia, in 1968, further expounded on issues relating to social justice and helped to popularize liberation theology in the Americas.

35. See, for example, these works by liberation theologians: Gustavo Gutiérrez, *The Power of the Poor in History* (Maryknoll, NY: Orbis Books, 1983); Leonardo Boff, *Introducing Liberation Theology* (Maryknoll, NY: Orbis Books, 1987).

36. Biographies and anthologies of Oscar Romero's writings and speeches include: James R. Brockman, *The Word Remains: A Life of Oscar Romero* (Maryknoll, NY: Orbis Books, 1982); Marie Dennis, Renny Golden, and Scott Wright, *Oscar Romero: Reflections on His Life and Writings,* Modern Spiritual Masters Series

(Maryknoll, NY: Orbis Books, 2000); Raul González Puebla, *El aporte del testimo-nio y martirio de Mons. Oscar Romero a La Teología*, 1st ed. (Quito, Ecuador: Raul González Puebla, 1996); María López Vigil, *Oscar Romero: Memories in Mosaic* (Washington, D.C.: EPICA, 2000); Oscar Romero, *Archbishop Oscar Romero: A Shep-herd's Diary* (London: CAFOD, 1993); Oscar Romero, *La violencia del amor* (Farm-ington, PA: Plough Publishing House, 2001); Oscar Romero, *Voice of the Voiceless: The Four Pastoral Letters and Other Statements* (Maryknoll, NY: Orbis Books, 1985); Jon Sobrino, Germán Schmitz, and Jesús Calderón, *Oscar Romero, profeta y mártir de la liberación* (Lima, Peru: Centro de Estudios y Publicaciones, 1981).

37. Porpora, *How Holocausts Happen,* 89–90.

38. Barry and Preusch, *Central America Fact Book,* 203–204.

39. LeoGrande, *Our Own Backyard,* 48–49. ANSESAL—the Salvadoran National Security Forces—was a centralized intelligence unit staffed by officers from different armed services. It was organized in the 1960s with CIA assistance under the leadership of General José Alberto Medrano. Medrano also founded ORDEN (Democratic Nationalist Organization), which at one point counted a hundred thousand members. When ORDEN was prohibited in 1980, under pres-sure from the United States, it was reorganized under the Nationalist Democratic Front. Barry and Preusch, *Central America Fact Book,* 204–205.

40. US official quoted in the *New York Times,* October 11, 1983, cited in Barry and Preusch, *Central America Fact Book,* 205.

41. According to LeoGrande, the "Miami Six," wealthy Salvadorans living in Florida, funded at least one of these death squads (*Our Own Backyard,* 49–50). In testimony before the US Congress, Robert White, former US ambassador to El Salvador, reported on the links between the exiles and death squad leaders such as D'Aubuisson, Gutierrez, García Vides Casanova, Carranza, and López Nuilla. The Miami exiles were believed to be *latifundistas* who left the country in 1979 and 1980, when they lost much of their land in agrarian reform initiatives. See "Exiliados pobres y asilados ricos de El Salvador en Estados Unidos," *El Día Inter-nacional,* March 8, 1981.

42. LeoGrande, *Our Own Backyard,* 49–50.

43. Since Vatican II, liberal Latin American clerics had discussed ways of mak-ing Catholicism—and Christianity in general—more relevant to the poor of their countries. Liberation theology promoted the idea that the kingdom of God could be achieved here on earth. It encouraged pastoral programs that stressed *comu-nidades de base* of twenty or so people, who read the Bible and discussed ways to apply its teachings to their day-to-day reality. Discussions in these *comunidades de base* stressed Christ's "preferential option for the poor" and *concientizacion*—taking control of your own destiny—even if that meant challenging the existing power

structures. See, for example, Boff, *Introducing Liberation Theology;* and Gutiérrez, *The Power of the Poor in History.*

44. The Jesuit community of El Salvador, for example, was ordered to leave the country forever or else its members would face "extermination." Robert Armstrong and Janet Schenck, *El Salvador: The Face of Revolution* (Boston: South End Press, 1981), 60–62; Penny Lernoux, *Cry of the People* (Garden City: Doubleday, 1980), 76.

45. Americas Watch, *A Year of Reckoning: El Salvador a Decade after the Assassination of Archbishop Romero* (New York: Americas Watch Committee, March 1990), 171–178.

46. LeoGrande, *Our Own Backyard,* 49.

47. Colonel Adolfo Majano, for example, generally regarded as one of the military's most progressive members, was removed from the governing junta (after an assassination attempt failed to permanently remove him). When he refused to take on a diplomatic post as military attaché, he was arrested and forced to leave the country. See ibid., 46–47.

48. LeoGrande provides a detailed discussion of D'Aubuisson's pathology and his rise to power in Salvadoran society. US embassy staff reportedly had a number of nicknames for D'Aubuisson, among them "Blowtorch," in reference to his favorite tool of interrogation (ibid., 49–50). D'Aubuisson and his rightist forces attacked American targets despite US support. In 1981, for example, US ambassador Frederic Chapin accused D'Aubuisson's forces of firing on the US embassy in San Salvador. Regardless, D'Aubuisson enjoyed significant support. As the candidate of the National Republican Alliance Party (ARENA) in the 1984 elections, he received 45 percent of the popular vote. See "El embajador de EU acusa a la derecha del atentado a su sede," *El Día Internacional,* March 5, 1981.

49. Ungo was the vice-presidential candidate denied office in the fraudulent 1972 election. Mayorga was the rector of the Central American University. Zamora was the brother of the slain attorney general.

50. The FMLN was named after the Marxist revolutionary of the 1920s and '30s, most known for organizing the peasant uprising of 1932 that was squelched by *la matanza.*

51. In 1982, for example, the Catholic archdiocese reported 5,397 murders of noncombatants at the hands of the various military forces, but only 46 at the hands of the guerrillas. Porpora, *How Holocausts Happen,* 103. According to MacFarlane, Miguel Obando y Bravo, who replaced Oscar Romero as archbishop of El Salvador, once remarked that death by natural causes was becoming somewhat of a miracle in El Salvador; and one joke circulating the capital city had the government declaring the vulture as the national bird (*Northern Shadows,* 178).

52. In January 1982, the Atlactl battalion was brought to Fort Bragg, North Carolina, for further training, and another five hundred soldiers were trained in Fort Benning, Georgia. Raymond Bonner, *Weakness and Deceit: U.S. Policy in El Salvador* (New York: Times Books, 1984); Porpora, *How Holocausts Happen,* 103; LeoGrande, *Our Own Backyard,* 155.

53. Robert S. Kahn, *Other People's Blood: U.S. Immigration Prisons in the Reagan Decade* (Boulder, CO: Westview Press, 1996), 36.

54. Porpora, *How Holocausts Happen,* 103.

55. The State Department "White Paper" on El Salvador reported that "the insurgency in El Salvador has been progressively transformed into another case of indirect armed aggression against a small Third World country by Communist powers acting through Cuba." See "Communist Interference in El Salvador," Special Report no. 80, United States Department of State, February 23, 1981. The United States' philosophy is also articulated in the 1984 Kissinger Report, produced by President Reagan's appointed twelve-member National Bipartisan Commission on Central America, headed by former secretary of state Henry Kissinger.

56. In response to the announcement, Salvadoran president José Napoleón Duarte called an emergency session of his cabinet to decide whether they would sever diplomatic relations with both countries. "Tratan Duarte y su gabinete de relaciones diplomáticas con México y Francia," *El Día Internacional,* September .3, 1981; press conference with Foreign Minister Jorge Castañeda, *El Día,* September 5, 1981; Ramon Morones, "No somos responsables de que un pueblo se levante: Castañeda," *Excelsior,* September 2, 1981.

57. According to Barry and Preusch: "Washington spent over $10 million and the political section of the US Embassy became the largest in the world during the election process" (*Central America Fact Book,* 208).

58. Quoted in LeoGrande, *Our Own Backyard,* 63–64.

59. Quote cited ibid., 60; from Craig Pyes, "Salvadovar Rightists: The Deadly Patriots," *Albuquerque Journal* (1983).

60. Americas Watch Committee, *El Salvador's Decade of Terror: Human Rights since the Assassination of Archbishop Romero* (New Haven, CT: Yale University Press, 1991), 108.

61. Agrarian reform was first initiated in 1944, when a popular coalition, headed by Juan José Arévalo, took control of the government and briefly ended generations of military dictatorship. In 1950, Arévalo was succeeded by Jacobo Arbenz, who was democratically elected with 65 percent of the vote. In 1954, Arbenz was overthrown in a coup led by military leaders funded and trained by the CIA. Under agrarian reform, the Arbenz government transferred over one million acres of uncultivated land to one hundred thousand landless peasant fam-

ilies. Among the principal losers in this measure was the US-owned United Fruit Company. Although it's unclear whether the company's lost land is calculated in that redistributed acreage, it lost over three hundred thousand acres to expropriation, for which the Arbenz government offered 1.2 million dollars in compensation, based on the company's own tax declarations (the company demanded 16 million dollars in compensation). Not surprisingly, the management of the United Fruit Company, who had important ties to members of the Eisenhower administration, pressured the US government to intervene. Lars Schoultz, *Beneath the United States: A History of U.S. Policy toward Latin America* (Cambridge, MA: Harvard University Press, 1998), 340–345; LaFeber, *Inevitable Revolutions,* 125–127; Langley, *America and the Americas,* 178–182; Barry and Preusch, *Central America Fact Book,* 227.

62. Hiram Ruiz, *El Retorno: Guatemalans' Risky Repatriation Begins,* US Committee for Refugees Issue Paper (Washington, D.C.: US Committee for Refugees, 1993), 3.

63. Guatemalans of European and/or mixed heritage are called *ladinos.* Because of the difficulties of determining who is Indian and who is *ladino,* statistics vary. One study estimated the Maya population to be 47 percent; another put the figure at 65 percent. Twenty different Maya languages are spoken among this indigenous population.

64. Phillip Wearne, *The Maya of Guatemala* (London: Minority Rights Group, 1994), 1–3; LaFeber, *Inevitable Revolutions,* 258.

65. LaFeber, *Inevitable Revolutions,* 255–261.

66. Barry and Preusch, *Central America Fact Book,* 229.

67. Ibid., 231.

68. Ruiz, *El Retorno,* 4.

69. See, for example, Amnesty International, *Guatemala: Massive Extrajudicial Executions in Rural Areas under the Government of General Efraín Ríos Montt* (London: Amnesty International, July 1982).

70. The Guatemalan army blamed the killings on independent paramilitary groups beyond official control, although Amnesty International and Americas Watch have disputed those claims. Amnesty International, *Guatemala: A Government Program of Political Murder* (London: Amnesty International, 1981), 3.

71. See Linda Green, *Fear as a Way of Life: Mayan Widows in Rural Guatemala* (New York: Columbia University Press, 1999), 31; and Barry and Preusch, *Central America Fact Book,* 235. The following excerpt from a 1989 graduation ceremony speech by General Juan José Marroquín Siliezar best articulates the *kaibil* philosophy: "Kaibil officers are trained to forget all humanitarian principles and to become war machines, capable of enduring whatever sacrifice, because from now on, they will be called Masters of War and Messengers of Death." Quoted

Americas Watch Committee, *Messengers of Death: Human Rights in Guatemala, November 1988–February 1990* (New York: Americas Watch Committee, 1990), i.

72. See the *testimonios* in *Caminante*, the newsletter of the Roman Catholic Diocese of San Cristóbal de las Casas, Chiapas. See also Amnesty International's *Guatemala: A Government Program of Political Murder* and *Guatemala: Massive Extra-judicial Executions in Rural Areas under the Government of General Efraín Ríos Montt;* A. J. Good, "Guatemala's Hidden Refugees," *Christian Century* 107 (May 9, 1990): 499–500; Jeremy Adelman, "Guatemalan Refugees in Mexico," *Refuge* 3, no. 2 (December 1983): 7, 10; and Carlos Fazio, *Samuel Ruiz, El Caminante* (Mexico City: Espasa Calpe, 1994), 163–164.

73. Beatriz Manz, *Refugees of a Hidden War: The Aftermath of Counterinsurgency in Guatemala* (Albany: State University of New York Press, 1988).

74. Alan Riding, "Guatemalans Tell of Murder of 300," *New York Times,* October 12, 1982; Adelman, "Guatemalan Refugees in Mexico," 10.

75. According to Fazio, only those who were identified as friends or family members of refugees were pulled out for "Christian burial"; the rest were allowed to continue floating downstream. Fazio, *Samuel Ruiz, El Caminante,* 163–164; "Cerca de 600 Guatemaltecos emigran a nuestro país diariamente," *El Día,* August 2, 1981. Women and children were targeted as readily as men. See, for example, "Guatemala: Matanza de mujeres indígenas," *El Día,* June 7, 1981.

76. Rigoberta Menchú, *I, Rigoberta Menchú: An Indian Woman in Guatemala* (London: Verso, 1998). The book was first published by Editorial Argos Vergara in Barcelona in 1983 with the more appropriate title *Me llamo Rigoberta Menchú y así me nació la conciencia.* Menchú provides a heart-wrenching *testimonio* of the atrocities committed against the Mayas, combining personal memory with her people's collective experience. Her book became controversial when anthropologist David Stoll, confusing *testimonio* with autobiography, challenged the accuracy of her accounts in his book *Rigoberta Menchu and the Story of All Poor Guatemalans* (Boulder, CO: Westview Press, 1988). Sadly, but perhaps appropriately, Menchú's 1992 Nobel Peace Prize was awarded the year of the Columbian quincentenary. It was not the first time a human rights activist received the award. From 1960 to 1979, six of the seventeen peace prizes went to human rights activists or organizations. Ron Pagnucco, "The Transnational Strategies of the Service for Peace and Justice in Latin America," in Smith et al., eds., *Transnational Social Movements and Global Politics,* 134.

77. Brook Larmer, "Guatemala's Indians Become the Battlefield," *Christian Science Monitor,* September 4, 1990, 10; Lydia Chavez, "Guatemala Trying to Win Over 5,000 Indians," *New York Times,* November 20, 1983.

78. Ríos Montt was a member of an evangelical church known as El Verbo (The Word) with ties to the California-based Gospel Outreach. El Verbo was

known for its aggressive evangelization, its pro-Americanism and anticommunism, and alleged ties to the CIA. See MacFarlane, *Northern Shadows,* 185.

79. Manz gives a thorough discussion of the Guatemalan army's control over the indigenous population in *Refugees of a Hidden War.* See also Hubert Campfens, "Guatemalan Refugees in Mexico," *Refuge* 3, no. 2 (December 1983): 7.

80. Inforpress Centroamericana, "Guatemala," in Janie Hampton, ed., *Internally Displaced People: A Global Survey* (London: Earthscarn Publications, 1998), 103–105; Good, "Guatemala's Hidden Refugees," 499–500. According to Inforpress Centroamericana, over half of the displaced were under the age of fifteen, and two hundred thousand children lost one or both parents (104–105).

81. The 1984 document is entitled "Para construir la Paz." See also "Denuncian asesinatos masivos en Guatemala," *Excélsior,* June 10, 1984.

82. "Enfrenta la iglesia de Guatemala al gobierno de Romeo Lucas García," *El Día,* August 14, 1981.

83. Clark Taylor, *Return of Guatemala's Refugees: Reweaving the Torn* (Philadelphia: Temple University Press, 1998), 32; LeoGrande, *Our Own Backyard,* 180.

84. Cecelia Menjívar, *Fragmented Ties: Salvadoran Immigrant Networks in America* (Berkeley: University of California Press, 2000), 41.

85. Ibid., 46. See also Thomas P. Anderson, *The War of the Dispossessed: Honduras and El Salvador, 1969* (Lincoln: University of Nebraska Press, 1981).

86. Germán Martínez Velasco, *Plantaciones, trabajo guatemalteco y política migratoria en la frontera sur de México* (Ocozocoautla de Espinosa, Chiapas: Gobierno del Estado de Chiapas y el Instituto Chiapenco de Cultura, 1994), 89–128. See also Sergio Aguayo, *El éxodo centroamericano: Consecuencias de un conflicto* (Mexico City: Consejo Nacional de Fomento Educativo, 1985), 36.

87. Menjívar reports a Salvadoran presence in the United States in the early twentieth century (*Fragmented Ties,* 41). Terry Repak offers a fascinating discussion of the origins of the Salvadoran community in Washington, D.C., and its suburbs. According to Repak, many of the first "settlers" were nannies and domestic workers brought to D.C. by their employers in the diplomatic corps. This largely female population later sponsored friends and relatives, who, in turn, attracted others to the area. By the 1980 over two hundred thousand Salvadorans had settled in the D.C. area. See Repak, *Waiting on Washington: Central American Workers in the Nation's Capital* (Philadelphia: Temple University Press, 1995).

88. Sidney Weintraub and Sergio Díaz-Briquets, *The Use of Foreign Aid to Reduce Incentives to Emigrate from Central America* (Geneva: International Labour Organisation, 1992), 8.

89. US Comptroller General, *Central American Refugees: Regional Conditions and Prospects and Potential Impact on the United States: Report to the Congress of the United States.* Washington, D.C.: General Accounting Office, July 20, 1984, 41.

90. Four regional conventions address the issue of asylum: the Havana Convention of 1928; the Montevideo Convention of 1933; the 1954 Caracas Convention on Diplomatic Asylum; and the San José Pact of 1969.

91. The UNHCR issues prima facie group determinations in emergencies when the sheer volume of refugees makes individual determinations impossible. Sid L. Mohn, "Central American Refugees: The Search for Appropriate Responses," *World Refugee Survey* (1983): 44.

92. The Cartagena Declaration was adopted at a colloquium entitled "Coloquio sobre la protección internacional de los refugiados en América Central, México y Panamá: Problemas jurídicos y humanitarios," held at Cartagena, Colombia, November 19–22, 1984. The declaration was modeled after the Organization of African Unity's "Convention Governing the Special Aspects of Refugee Problems in Africa" (1969), which defined a refugee as anyone who, "owing to external aggression, occupation, foreign domination, or events seriously disturbing the public order or nationality, is compelled to leave his place of habitual residence in order to seek refuge in another place outside his country of origin or nationality." The text is available at www.refugelawreader.org/index.d2?target=open&id=18.

93. Mohn, "Central American Refugees," 42.

94. Jacqueline María Hagan, "The Politics of Numbers: Central American Migration during a Period of Crisis, 1978–1985," MA thesis, University of Texas at Austin, May 1987, 30–31.

95. Ibid., 15–16. Hagan's thesis examines the biases inherent in international migration data, especially related to Central American refugees. She attributes the variability of the data to: "1) the technical problems associated with tracking a fast-moving and hard-to-detect population; 2) the definitional problem; 3) the different types of migration occurring, and 4) the domestic and foreign policy considerations of all the countries involved in the refugee movements" (112).

96. Gil Loescher, "Humanitarianism and Politics in Central America," *Political Science Quarterly* 103 (Summer 1988): 295; Hagan, "Politics of Numbers," 11.

97. Mohn, "Central American Refugees," 42.

98. Aguayo, *El éxodo centroamericano,* 22; Mohn, "Central American Refugees," 42.

99. Laura O'Dogherty Madrazo, "The Hidden Face of War in Central America," *Current Sociology* 36 (Summer 1988) 95; Americas Watch Committee, *El Salvador's Decade of Terror,* 108; Hector Silva, quoted in Michael Oliver, ed., *The Movement of Peoples: A View from the South* (Ottawa: Group of 78, October 1992), 86.

100. US Comptroller General, *"Central American Refugees,"* ii; UNHCR, "International Conference on Central American Refugees (CIREFCA), Guatemala City, 29–31 May 1989," Information Paper.

101. Sergio Aguayo, *From the Shadows to Center Stage: NGOs and Central Amer-*

ican Refugee Assistance (Washington, D.C.: Hemispheric Migration Project, Center for Immigration Policy and Refugee Assistance, Georgetown University, 1991), 1.

102. According to Patricia Fagen, the government military forces of El Salvador were known to have "interfered with food delivery and medical services, to have bombed places where food has been distributed, or to have arrested persons working with displaced persons. The government . . . is widely accused of absorbing or redirecting large portions of the relief intended for humanitarian purposes." Patricia Weiss Fagen, *Refugees and Displaced Persons in Central America*, Report of the Refugee Policy Group, Washington, D.C., March 1984, 8, 10.

103. Tanya Basok, "Central American Refugees: Resettlement Needs and Solutions," *Refuge* 5 (May 1986): 1.

104. Fagen, *Refugees and Displaced Persons in Central America*, 3.

105. W. Gunther Plaut, *Asylum: A Moral Dilemma* (Toronto: York Lanes Press, 1995). According to Plaut, the US State Department "euphemistically called [them] 'closed camps under the protection of the armed forces'" (117).

106. Martin Barber and Meyer Brownstone, "Relocating Refugees in Honduras," *Refuge* 3 (December 1983): 12.

107. The US State Department pressured the Honduran government to move the camps away from the border in order to prevent them from becoming bases for guerrillas; the Roman Catholic Church, in turn, pressured the government to keep the camps near the border to facilitate the refugees' accommodation, as well as their eventual repatriation. See Plaut, *Asylum*, 117; and Jeremy Adelman, "The Insecurity of El Salvadorean Refugees," *Refuge* 3 (October 1983): 1–4.

108. US Comptroller General, "*Central American Refugees*," iii, Barber and Brownstone, "Relocating Refugees in Honduras," 12–15; Fagen, *Refugees and Displaced Persons in Central America*, 3–5. According to Fagen, the Miskito leadership forcibly recruited young men into the Contras. In response, the UNHCR assumed a more visible role in the region to assure that food and other forms of refugee assistance were not controlled by the Miskito leadership and "subordinated to [their] political agendas" (5–6).

109. Bureau of Refugee Programs, US Department of State, *World Refugee Report* (September 1991), 49–54; UNHCR, "International Conference on Central American Refugees"; Fagen, *Refugees and Displaced Persons in Central America*, 4; Hagan, "Politics of Numbers," 115.

110. Sandra Pentland and Dennis Racicot, "Salvadorean Refugees in Honduras," *Refuge* 5 (May 1986): 3.

111. After another Salvadoran military operation in Cabañas in November 1981, Honduran troops again tried to close the border to refugees. Ibid., 3; See also "Envían soldados salvadoreños a un campamento de refugiados en Honduras,"

El Día Internacional, July 23, 1981; and "Aviones salvadoreños atacan a refugiados en suelo hondureño," *Excélsior,* June 12, 1984.

112. Pentland and Racicot, "Salvadorean Refugees in Honduras," 4; Mohn, "Central American Refugees," 43.

113. Mohn, "Central American Refugees," 42; Pentland and Racicot, "Salvadorean Refugees in Honduras," 4; In November 1985, the International Council of Voluntary Agencies (ICVA), representing forty different relief agencies, met in San José, Costa Rica, to discuss the plight of the refugees in Honduran camps. Not bound by the same restrictions as the UNHCR, the participants agreed to increase the number of staff in the camps for security measures, and to call for a dialogue among the relief agencies, the UNHCR, and the Hondurans to "ensure protection and self-sufficiency of the refugees until their repatriation to a safe El Salvador is possible." See "ICVA Consultation on Refugees and Displaced Persons in Central America," *Refuge* 5 (May 1986): 6.

114. According to Bridget Hayden, however, during the early 1980s, Costa Rican authorities sometimes harassed Salvadorans, searching for evidence of subversion. Hayden, *Salvadorans in Costa Rica* (Tucson: University of Arizona Press, 2003), xii–xiii.

115. By 1984, Costa Rica, Nicaragua, Guatemala, El Salvador, and Panama were the Central American signatories to the UN Convention and Protocol. Costa Rica, Nicaragua, and Panama all had domestic legislation that incorporated the UN definition of refugee and the principle of *non-refoulement.*

116. UNHCR, "International Conference on Central American Refugees"; Gilda Pacheco, *A Decade of Ambiguity: Approaches to Central American Refugee Assistance in the 1980s* (Washington, D.C.: Hemispheric Migration Project, Center for Immigration Policy and Refugee Assistance, Georgetown University, 1991), 5.

117. Hayden, *Salvadorans in Costa Rica,* xii.

118. A study by the National Commission for Refugees found that many of these durable solutions projects—particularly those that trained in mechanics, metallurgy, and painting—had a high failure rate. Tanya Basok examines the various reasons for these failures. See Basok, "How Durable Are the 'Durable Solutions' Projects for Salvadorean Refugees in Costa Rica?" *Refuge* 5 (May 1986): 7–8. See also Pacheco, *A Decade of Ambiguity,* 21–22.

119. Basok examines the many obstacles refugees had to overcome to navigate the government bureaucracy. In order to acquire a work permit, for example, a refugee first had to apply for a permit to the Programa para Refugiados del Instituto Mixto de Ayuda Social, with a supporting letter from a potential employer. Processing the application took three to four months—a period most employers were unwilling to wait—which made the supporting letter difficult to

acquire. Most applications were denied, so while the refugees theoretically had a legal right to work, their ability to do so was blocked by the government bureaucracy. Basok, "How Durable are the 'Durable Solutions' Projects?" 8.

120. UNHCR, "International Conference on Central American Refugees"; Pacheco, *A Decade of Ambiguity,* 5.

121. Hayden (2003) studies the Salvadorans who chose to remain in Costa Rica.

122. Tanya Basok, "The Troubled Road to Repatriation in Central America: Lessons Learned by Refugees in Exile," *Refuge* 13 (March 1994): 11.

123. According to Fagen, the Salvadoran Catholic Archdiocese refused to take US funds for refugee assistance. Unfortunately, the refugees were not protected from attacks from the military, and by 1984, more than a dozen voluntary workers had been arrested and tortured on the grounds that they were aiding subversives. Fagen, *Refugees and Displaced Persons in Central America,* 10.

124. Aguayo, *El éxodo centroamericano,* 74.

125. Bureau of Refugee Programs, *World Refugee Report* (1991); Augusto Morel, *Refugiados Salvadoreños en Nicaragua* (Managua: Asociación de Colectivos de Refugiados Salvadoreños [ACRES], 1991), 169; UNHCR, "International Conference on Central American Refugees"; Fagen, *Refugees and Displaced Persons in Central America,* 3.

126. Jonathan Lemco, *Canada and the Crisis in Central America* (New York: Praeger, 1991), 98. See also Jack Child, *The Central American Peace Process, 1983–1991: Sheathing Swords, Building Confidence* (Boulder, CO: Lynne Rienner, 1992); and Dario Moreno, *The Struggle for Peace in Central America* (Gainesville: University Press of Florida, 1994).

127. Lemco, *Canada and the Crisis in Central America,* 98; Stella Cailoni, "Fracasó el boicoteo contra el grupo de Contadora," *Unomásuno,* May 2, 1984.

128. The assassination of Ignacio Ellacuría, Ignacio Martín Baró, Segundo Montes, Armando López, Joaquin López, and Juan Ramón Moreno occurred on November 16, 1989. The two housekeepers, mother and daughter, were Elba and Celina Ramos. Fr. Segundo Montes, the head of the Human Rights Institute at the Universidad Centroamericana José Simón Cañas, was known for his studies of Salvadoran refugees. Americas Watch Committee, *A Year of Reckoning,* 171–178; see also Teresa Whitfield, *Paying the Price: Ignacio Ellacuría and the Murdered Jesuits of El Salvador* (Philadelphia: Temple University Press, 1995).

129. Child, *The Central American Peace Process.* See also James Dunkerley, *The Pacification of Central America* (London: Institute for Latin American Studies, University of London, 1993).

130. In Nicaragua and El Salvador, for example, per capita income was lower in 1989 than in 1959. Augusto Ramírez Ocampo, "The Question of Displaced

Persons and the Process of Development in Latin America," *In Defense of the Alien,* vol. 12, Proceedings of the 1989 Annual Legal Conference on Immigration and Refugee Policy (Staten Island, NY: Center for Migration Studies, 1989), 47.

131. Most of these actions were committed by the National Police and were directed against journalists, clergy and bishops, and directors of populist organizations. Juan Balboa, "En Guatemala podrá haber paz, pero no respeto a derechos humanos," *La Jornada,* December 22, 1996, www.jornada.unam.mx/1996/dic96/961222/guate.html; Miguel Concha; "De la esperanza a la locura," *La Jornada,* June 30, 1996, www.jornada.unam.mx/1996/jun96/960630/LOCURA02-0.

132. The United Nations and the Catholic Church in Guatemala each established a truth commission. The official four-volume church report, entitled *Guatemala: Nunca más,* cited 150,000 murdered, 150,000 "disappeared," more than 1 million refugees and internally displaced; 200,000 orphans, and 40,000 widows. Nine out of every ten victims were civilians; and in eight out of every ten cases, the acts were attributed to the army and its paramilitary units (Archbishopric of Guatemala, Office of Human Rights, 1998). See also Eduardo Galeano, "Disparen sobre Rigoberta," *La Jornada,* January 16, 1999, www.jornada.unam.mx/1999/ene99/990116/galeano.html.

133. Two months earlier, the first international NGO conference on refugees and displaced persons was held in Mexico. Among the proposals circulated at this conference was a new definition of refugee status. The NGOs proposed that the term should include "persons who have fled their countries because their life, safety or freedom has been threatened by widespread violence, aggression, foreign occupation or domination, and internal conflicts that have caused massive human rights violations." "Mexico: Number of Detained Central American Refugees Tripled," *Inter Press Service,* May 24, 1989, http://web.lexis-nexis.com/universe/.

134. UNHCR, "International Conference on Central American Refugees."

135. See Adolfo Aguilar Zinser, *CIREFCA: The Promises and Reality of the International Conference on Central American Refugees, an Independent Report* (Washington, D.C.: Hemispheric Migration Project, Center for Immigration Policy and Refugee Assistance, Georgetown University, 1991).

136. Patricia Weiss Fagen, "Peace in Central America: Transition for the Uprooted," *World Refugee Survey 1993,* 15, www.refugees.org/world/articles/central america.wrs93.htm.

137. Marvin Ortega and Pedro Acevedo, "Nicaraguan Repatriation from Honduras and Costa Rica," in M. A. Larkin et al., eds., *Repatriation under Conflict in Central America* (Washington, D.C.: Center for Immigration Policy and Refugee Assistance, Georgetown University, 1991), 37; Fagen, "Peace in Central America."

138. Fagen, "Peace in Central America."

2. DESIGNING A REFUGEE POLICY

Epigraphs: Felipe Sánchez Martínez, "Chronology and Entry Zones of the Refugees Entering Chiapas," in *Presencia de los refugiados guatemaltecos en México,* 46. "For this reason we want you to understand . . . ," *Caminante,* no. 31 (February 1984): 3. Translation mine. Luis Ortiz Monasterio, "Labor asistencial de emergencia," in *Presencia de los refugiados guatemaltecos en México,* 53.

1. There is a long but little studied tradition of American migration to Mexico, from African American slaves and Indian tribes fleeing captivity, to the more recent migration of Americans escaping the McCarthy era investigations and the Vietnam War draft.

2. With the exception of the Spanish Republicans, there is little government data on the exact number of exiles/asylees/immigrants from each country. Office of the United States Coordinator for Refugee Affairs, *Country Reports on the World Refugee Situation* (Washington, D.C.: Department of State, 1981), 104; unpublished report in "State Department, US[2]," Box 9, Files of Francis S. M. Hodsoll, President's Task Force on Immigration and Refugee Policy, Reagan Presidential Library; Ortiz Monasterio, "Labor asistencial de emergencia," 48–52; Alonso Urrutia, "Se celebra hoy por primera vez en el mundo el Día Internacional del Refugiado; convoca ONU," *La Jornada,* June 20, 2001, www.jornada.unam.mx/2001/juno1/010620/047n1soc.html.

3. Martínez Velasco, *Plantaciones, trabajo guatemalteco y política migratoria,* 89–128. See also Aguayo, *El éxodo centroamericano,* 36.

4. Rich, *Mexican Policy toward Guatemalan Refugees,* 13.

5. Inda Sáenz-Romero and Juan José Sánchez-Sosa, "Development and Identity of Guatemalan Refugee Children in Mexico: Conditions and Options for Support Interventions," *Refuge* 15, no. 5 (1996): 34; Alan Riding, "Mexicans to Shift Guatemala Exiles," *New York Times,* October 17, 1982.

6. The San José Pact can be found on the Web page of the Organization of American States: www.oas.org/juridico/english/Treaties/b-32.htm.

7. "Fin a los asentamientos de guatemaltecos en la frontera," *Excélsior,* May 10, 1984.

8. Bill Frelick, *Running the Gauntlet: The Central American Journey through Mexico,* Issue Paper, US Committee for Refugees, American Council for Nationalities Service, January 1991, 6; see also Aguayo, *El éxodo centroamericano,* 47–48.

9. Sergio Aguayo and Patricia Weiss Fagen, *Central Americans in Mexico and the United States: Unilateral, Bilateral, and Regional Perspectives* (Washington, D.C.: Hemispheric Migration Project, Center for Immigration Policy and Refugee Assistance, Georgetown University, 1988), 11.

10. Some NGOs excluded Nicaraguans from their assistance programs. See, for example, Laura O'Dogherty's mention of the Programa de Asistencia para los Refugiados Centroamericanos, a Mexican NGO, in O'Dogherty, *Central Americans in Mexico City: Uprooted and Silenced* (Washington, D.C.: Hemispheric Migration Project, Center for Immigration Policy and Refugee Assistance, Georgetown University, 1989), 68 n. 7, and 69 n. 19.

11. Luis Raúl Salvadó, *The Other Refugees: A Study of Non-Recognized Guatemalan Refugees in Chiapas, Mexico* (Washington, D.C.: Hemispheric Migration Project, Center for Immigration Policy and Refugee Assistance, Georgetown University, 1988), 15.

12. On July 1, 1982, Ríos Montt declared a state of siege and sent troops to Quiché, Sololá, San Marcos, and Huehuetenango, which he believed to be rebel bases. Most of the nine thousand families who fled in the July came from Huehuetenango. Alan Riding, "Guatemalan Refugees Flood Mexico," *New York Times,* August 18, 1982; Jeremy Adelman, "Guatemalan Refugees in Mexico," *Refuge* 3, no. 2 (December 1983): 10; Hubert Campfens, "Guatemalan Refugees in Mexico," *Refuge* 3, no. 2 (December 1983): 7.

13. Over half a million indigenous people reside in the state of Chiapas: Tzotziles, Tzeltals, Lacondones, Tojolabales, Cakchiqueles, Zoques, Cho'les, and Mames.

14. Riding, "Mexicans to Shift Guatemala Exiles."

15. Gabino Fraga, "Creación del COMAR," in *Presencia de los refugiados guatemaltecos en México,* 26–30.

16. Cited in Lester Langley, *Mexico and the United States: The Fragile Relationship* (Boston: Twayne Publishers, 1991), 91. Throughout the 1980s, officials of the Secretaría de Gobernación and its Servicios Migratorios continued to regard and refer to the Central Americans as economic migrants, and not political refugees. See, for example, *Caminante* 31 (February 1984): 9.

17. Aguayo and Fagen, *Central Americans in Mexico and the United States,* 5–7.

18. "Conceden asilo político a 46 Guatemaltecos: Otros 1,855 regresaron a su país, informa SG," *Excélsior,* June 22, 1981; Good, "Guatemala's Hidden Refugees," 499–500; Riding, "Mexicans to Shift Guatemala Exiles," 9; Riding, "Guatemalan Refugees Flood Mexico"; Riding, "Guatemalans Evicted in Mexico," *New York Times,* October 29, 1982; Campfens, "Guatemalan Refugees in Mexico," 8.

19. "Mexico y la ONU firman un convenio para ayudar a refugiados políticos: Olivares Santana recalcó la tradicional política de protección a derechos humanos," *Excélsior,* March 4, 1981.

20. See individual reports of the Office of the UNHCR, *UNHCR Assistance Activities.* In 1985, for example, the UNHCR provided over eight million dollars in refugee assistance.

21. Aguayo and Fagen, *Central Americans in Mexico and the United States,* 5–7; Adolfo Aguilar Zinser, "Repatriation of Guatemalan Refugees in Mexico," in Larkin et al., eds., *Repatriation under Conflict in Central America,* 62; Elizabeth Ferris, "The Politics of Asylum: Mexico and the Central American Refugees," *Journal of Inter-American Studies and World Affairs* 26 (August 1984): 369.

22. Ortiz Monasterio, "Labor asistencial de emergencia," 48–52; Aguayo and Fagen, *Central Americans in Mexico and the United States,* 13.

23. Luis Suárez, "Hay en el mundo diez millones de refugiados," *Excélsior,* June 14, 1984.

24. In 1984, for example, Australia accepted fifteen hundred refugees from Central and South America. "Australia aceptará más refugiados," *Excélsior,* June 25, 1984.

25. Roberto Vizcaíno, "Los refugiados confinados en estrecha franja," *Unomásuno,* May 5, 1984.

26. Luis Suárez, "Con el traslado, incólume nuestra práctica de asilo," *Excélsior,* June 13, 1984.

27. Sánchez Martínez, "Chronology and Entry Zones of the Refugees Entering Chiapas," 46.

28. Good, "Guatemala's Hidden Refugees," 499–500; Riding, "Mexicans to Shift Guatemala Exiles," 9; Adelman, "Guatemalans Refugees in Mexico," 11; Americas Watch Committee, *Guatemalan Refugees in Mexico, 1980–1984* (New York: Americas Watch Committee, September 1984), 53–55; Suzanne Fiederlein, "Central American Refugees in Mexico: The Search for a Policy," MA thesis, University of Texas at Austin, May 1985, 79–80.

29. Loescher, "Humanitarianism and Politics in Central America," 299.

30. César Pastor Ortega, "Emergencia en Chiapas," in *Presencia de los refugiados guatemaltecos en México,* 58–60.

31. Ortiz Monasterio, "Labor asistencial de emergencia," 48–52.

32. The intense corruption among immigration officials and agents manifested itself in several ways, including the withholding of wages and excessively charging for the renewal of the FM-8 visa. See Joan Friedland and Jesús Rodríguez y Rodríguez, *Seeking Safe Ground: The Legal Situation of Central American Refugees in Mexico* (San Diego: Mexico-US Law Institute, University of San Diego Law School and the Instituto de Investigaciones Jurídicas, Universidad Nacional Autónoma de México, 1987), 30.

33. In *Caminante* 31 (February 1984): 10.

34. However, the comparatively small number of registered vis-à-vis unregistered refugees was also the result of COMAR's deliberate decision to stop registering new refugees. Ruiz, *El Retorno,* 8.

35. "Bombardeo de Campamentos," *Caminante* 31 (February 1984): 10–12.

36. According to Aguayo, these figures were based only on documented tes-

timonies or cases reported in the Mexican press. Aguayo, *El éxodo centroamericano*, 78.

37. See, for example, the *testimonios* of refugees in *Caminante* 31 (February 1984).

38. According to COMAR, Morales's sympathizers made death threats against aid workers. Aguayo, *El éxodo centroamericano*, 94–95.

39. As one example, in December 1983, sixty men were detained by Mexican authorities. Fifty were eventually released and returned to their settlement emaciated, with burnt soles and other physical signs of torture. Their only source of nourishment was one corn tortilla per day. "Situación general de refugiados," *Caminante* 31 (February 1984): 9.

40. Mario B. Monroy, "¿Qué pasó y qué pasa en Chiapas?" in Mario B. Monroy, ed., *Pensar Chiapas, repensar México: Reflexiones de las ONGs mexicanas sobre el conflicto* (Mexico City: Convergencia de Organismos Civiles por la Democracia, 1994), 48.

41. Human Rights Watch, *Implausible Deniability: State Responsibility for Rural Violence in Mexico* (New York: Human Rights Watch, 1997), 1–3. For a discussion on the Guardias Blancas, see Jan Rus, *Tierra, libertad, y autonomía: Impactos regionales de zapatismo en Chiapas* (Mexico City: Centro de Investigaciones y Estudios Superiores en Antropología Social, 2002). See also Subcomandante Marcos, "Chiapas: The Southeast in Two Winds," August 1992, http://lanic.utexas.edu/project/Zapatistas/0.TXT.

42. Riding, "Guatemalan Refugees Flood Mexico"; Renny Golden and Michael McConnell, *Sanctuary: The New Underground Railroad* (New York: Orbis Books, 1986), 112–113; Fazio, *Samuel Ruiz*, 160–162.

43. Golden and McConnell, *Sanctuary*, 112–113; Fazio, *Samuel Ruiz*, 160–162.

44. In 1977, oil made up 22 percent of all Mexican exports; by 1981, it accounted for 75 percent. By 1982, Mexico owed an estimated eighty-five billion dollars to foreign banks for the development of this industry, but Mexican newspapers celebrated the country's role as a major energy producer. Langley, *Mexico and the United States,* 90–91; Subcomandante Marcos, "Chiapas: The Southeast in Two Winds"; Laura Quintero, "En América Latina, México será líder productor de petroquímicos secundarios," *El Día,* July 22, 1981. See also Onécimo Hidalgo and Mario B. Monroy, "El estado de Chiapas en cifras," in Monroy, ed., *Pensar Chiapas, repensar México,* 25.

45. According to Ferris, in 1980, 29 percent of the Chiapas population was illiterate (compared to 15 percent nationally); 36 percent of homes had electricity (compared to 73 percent nationally); and 4 percent had piped water (71 percent nationally). Little had changed ten years later, when the Zapatista National Lib-

eration Front issued their manifestos. Ferris, "The Politics of Asylum," 365–366. The Tzeltal zone on the Mexico-Guatemala border, where the majority of Guatemalan refugees settled, was of particular strategic value. In this 368-kilometer territory, over thirty thousand families lived, 88 percent of whom were rural *campesinos,* and 85 percent of whom were Indians, mostly Tzeltal, Tzotziles, and Cho'les. See also "Datos de la zona Tzeltal," *Caminante* 33 (May 1984): 48–51.

46. The Zapatista National Liberation Front proposed a variety of reforms in the laws governing land and labor, industry and commerce, social security, and welfare. "Declaration of War," *El Despertador Mexicano,* December 31, 1993, http://lanic.utexas.edu/project/Zapatistas/01.TXT>. For a discussion of the diocese's alleged involvement in inspiring the Zapatista rebellion, see David Fernández, "Chiapas: La iglesia de los pobres y la teología de la liberación en la mira," in Monroy, ed., *Pensar Chiapas, repensar México,* 165–175

47. See, for example, the following articles: "Los campesinos del país, víctimas de la represión," *El Día,* June 15, 1981; "Los indígenas, sin oportunidades políticas," *El Día,* June 15, 1981; Juan Danell, "Monopolizan siete familias de origen alemán la producción de café en el Soconusco," *El Día Internacional,* June 5, 1981; "Han recuperado indígenas de las Huastecas 20 mil hectáreas de manos de los caciques," *Unomásuno,* June 17, 1984. See also Monroy, "¿Qué pasó y qué pasa en Chiapas?" 40. *Caminante,* the diocesan newsletter of San Cristóbal de las Casas, also includes information on squatting, land disputes, agrarian reform, and legal challenges to landholdings.

48. US Comptroller General, *"Central American Refugees,"* ii; Ferris, "The Politics of Asylum," 377; Adelman, "Guatemalan Refugees in Mexico," 11.

49. By 1985, Vallejo had stepped down as director of both units amid charges of irregularities. Aguayo, *El éxodo centroamericano,* 95–97.

50. Arturo Sotomayor, "Refugiados en la frontera: Cuidemos nuestra integridad territorial," *Unomásuno,* June 1, 1984.

51. These political parties included the Partido Socialista Unificado de México, the Partido Democrático Mexicano, the Partido Revolucionario de los Trabajadores, and the Partido Popular Socialista. Ferris, "The Politics of Asylum," 375; see also Mario Alberto Reyes and Ubaldo Díaz, "Apoyo de cinco partidos a la protesta contra la incursión de Guatemaltecos," *Unomásuno,* May 5, 1984; "Crítica medida sobre refugiados," *Unomásuno,* May 12, 1984.

52. Reflecting on the role of *La Jornada,* Luis Ortiz Monasterio wrote: "It would be unfair at this point in time to fail to recognize the historic role that *La Jornada* played in those first days when the refugees arrived. Their reflections and spirit of solidarity helped shape a public mood that facilitated the giving of assistance to our Central American brothers, precisely in those days of economic

uncertainty because of the debt crisis." "De refugiados: Lecciones para la era del posmercado," *La Jornada*, August 17, 1999, www.jornada.unam.mx/1999/ago99/990817/monasterio.html.

53. Among Guatemala's historical grievances was the illegal seizure of Guatemalan territory in the nineteenth century. More recent disputes concerned the trade deficit; illegal fishing in Guatemalan territorial waters; the mistreatment of Guatemalan braceros; and the housing of Guatemalan rebels and their sympathizers on Mexican soil. According to Adrián Lajous, Mexico was Guatemala's own *coloso del norte*. Lajous, "México en Centroamérica," *Excélsior*, June 8, 1984.

54. Ibid., my translation.

55. Riding, "Guatemalan Refugees Flood Mexico."

56. Three Guatemalan groups sent a communiqué to *Prensa Latina* threatening to assassinate López Portillo for, among many reasons, harboring Guatemalan guerrillas and supporting the independence of Belize. The three groups were the League for the Protection of Guatemala, the Guatemalan Anti-Mexican League, and the Commandos for the Recuperation of Belize. See Abraham García Ibarra, "De ajusticiamientos y terrorismo informativo," *El Día*, September 3, 1981; "Amenazan asesinar a López Portillo grupos terroristas guatemaltecos," *Excélsior*, September 2, 1981; press conference with Foreign Minister Jorge Castañeda, *El Día*, September 5, 1981.

57. Quinto Informe de Gobierno, printed in *El Día*, September 2, 1981. See his comments on international relations there.

58. The deportations allegedly provoked the resignation of COMAR director Gabino Lafragua. "Piden al gobierno Mexicano firmar la Convención de Ginebra sobre refugiados," *El Día*, August 14, 1981. See also Americas Watch Committee, *Guatemalan Refugees in Mexico, 1980–1984*, 52–53; Ferris, "The Politics of Asylum," 368; Aguayo, *El éxodo centroamericano*, 62–63.

59. Riding, "Mexicans to Shift Guatemala Exiles," 9; "Detuvo Guatemala a tres helicopteristas Mexicanos," *Excélsior*, June 5, 1984.

60. Riding, "Mexicans to Shift Guatemala Exiles," 9.

61. *Caminante* 31 (February 1984): 10–11; Campfens, "Guatemalan Refugees in Mexico," 8; Marlise Simons, "Guatemala Asks Refugees to Return," *New York Times*, June 12, 1983.

62. The Diocese of San Cristóbal's official position is stated in "Postura de la Diocesis," *Caminante* 39 (June-July 1985): 1–7. The diocese recognized the government's right to decide the most convenient area of settlement, but this right "was mediated by respect for the human rights of the refugees" (2).

63. *Caminante* 31 (February 1984): 11–13.

64. Rafael Medina and Miguel González, "Atacan un campamento de refugiados en Chiapas: Murieron acribillados 6 exiliados chapines en ejido Las Deli-

cias," *Excélsior*, May 2, 1984. See also Ricardo Alemán and Roberto Vizcaíno, "Ataque a refugiados en Chiapas: Culpan a tropas guatemaltecas," *Unomásuno*, May 2, 1981; and "Comunicado de la diócesis de San Cristóbal," *Caminante* 33 (May 1984): 1–3.

65. Miguel Almar, "A quienes lo han olvidado: La masacre de El Chupadero," *Caminante* 38 (March-May 1985): 3–6; "Cartas de asilados en las que piden que no se las traslade," *Excélsior*, June 14, 1984; Rafael Medina and Miguel González, "'Los Pintos,' autores de la masacre," *Excélsior*, May 3, 1984; "Enérgica protesta de México al Gobierno de Guatemala," *Excélsior*, May 4, 1984; Ricardo Alemán, "Soldados guatemaltecos mataron a los refugiados, dicen testigos," *Unomásuno*, May 3, 1984; Roberto Vizcaíno, "Desapareció el campamento de El Chupadero," *Unomásuno*, May 4, 1984; Roberto Vizcaíno, "Campesinos de Chiapas huyen de la frontera," *Unomásuno*, May 6, 1984; Roberto Vizcaíno, "3 mil refugiados que salvaron la vida se hacinan en Las Delicias," *Unomásuno*, May 7, 1984.

66. "Contradicciones de una decisión," *Caminante* 33 (May 1984): 8–9. See the following articles by Rafael Medina and Manuel González in the May 5, 1984, edition of *Excélsior:* "No hay necesidad de reforzar la tropa en Chiapas: Castellanos"; "Respeto a México por parte de Guatemala"; and "Delincuentes subversivos los responsables: Méndez M." See also Vizcaíno, "Desapareció el campamento de El Chupadero."

67. Leonardo Franco, "Un episodio contovertido en la historia del refugio: La reubicación a Campeche y Quintana Roo," in *Presencia de los refugiados guatemaltecos en México,* 77–80; Suárez, "Con el traslado, incólume nuestra práctica de asilo"; "Fin a los asentamientos de guatemaltecos en la frontera," *Excélsior*, May 10, 1984; Ricardo Alemán, "Un problema para la seguridad de México, la situación en Guatemala," *Unomásuno*, May 12, 1984; "Tentativa de COMAR para que los refugiados Guatemaltecos acepten viajar a Campeche," *Unomásuno*, June 13, 1984.

68. "Contradicciones de una decisión," 7–8.

69. Loescher, "Humanitarianism and Politics in Central America," 300–301; Roberto Santiago, "Suministro parcial de alimentos a refugiados," *Unomásuno,* June 12, 1984.

70. "Comunicado de la Diocesis de San Cristóbal," *Caminante* 33 (May 1984): 1–2.

71. Vizcaíno, "Desapareció el campamento de El Chupadero"; Samuel Ruiz García, "Comunicado de prensa," *Caminante* 38 (March-May 1985): 2. Americas Watch also criticized the UNHCR for failing to aggressively defend the rights of refugees. Americas Watch Committee, *Guatemalan Refugees in Mexico, 1980–1984.*

72. "Contradicciones de una decisión," 7.

73. Letter from the San Caralampio camp to Paul Hartling, UNHCR, reprinted in *Caminante* 38 (March-May 1985): 7–8; letter from *ejidatarios* of Paso Hondo

to COMAR, reprinted in *Caminante* 38 (March–May 1985): 12; "Carta de asilados en las que piden que no se los traslade," *Excélsior*, June 14, 1984.

74. Jeanette Becerra Acosta, "Se asegurará la integridad de los refugiados
guatemaltecos," *Unomásuno*, May 16, 1984.

75. "La reubicación y los refugiados de Chiapas," *Caminante* 40 (August–
September 1985): 1–8; "Representantes de refugiados examinan los nuevos asentamientos," *Unomásuno*, May 21, 1984; Ruiz García, "Comunicado de prensa," 2;
"Comisión de visita a Campeche y Quintana Roo," *Caminante* 39 (June–July
1985): 7–8.

76. Carlos Velasco Molina, "Mantener a los refugiados aislados sería una dis-
criminación," *Excélsior*, June 3, 1984.

77. "Se reubicará a los refugiados políticos guatemaltecos," *Excélsior*, May 11,
1984.

78. Gonzalo Martínez Maestre and Roberto Vizcaíno, "Reubicarán en Campeche a 46 mil refugiados," *Unomásuno*, May 10, 1984.

79. Adolfo Aguilar Zinser, "Algunas preguntas sobre los refugiados," *Unomásuno*, June 6, 1984, 3.

80. "'Acción laudable' de autoridades reubicar a refugiados, dice el obispo de
Campeche," *Unomásuno*, May 17, 1984.

81. "La reubicación y los refugiados de Chiapas," 1–2.

82. "Se niegan a viajar a Campeche 2 mil 503 refugiados que habitaban en Las
Delicias," *Unomásuno*, June 11, 1984.

83. Ruiz García, "Comunicado de prensa," 2; letter from the San Caralampio
camp to Paul Hartling, UNHCR, reprinted in *Caminante* 38 (March–May 1985):
7–8; Fazio, *Samuel Ruiz* 163–165; Roberto Santiago, "Suministro parcial de alimentos a refugiados," *Unomásuno*, June 12, 1984; "Se niegan a viajar a Campeche
2 mil 503 refugiados que habitaban en Las Delicias," 3.

84. Cited in Golden and McConnell, *Sanctuary*, 120; see also Americas Watch
Committee, *Guatemalans in Mexico 1980–1984;* "Entrevista a Don Samuel," *Caminante* 33 (May 1984): 3–4.

85. Aguilar Zinser, "Algunas preguntas sobre los refugiados," 3.

86. In Quintana Roo the refugees formed the settlements of Los Lirios, Los
Ranchos, and Maya Balám y Cuchumatán; in Campeche they formed the settlements of Quetzal Edzná, Maya Tecún, Los Laureles, and Santo Domingo. See
Rosa Elvira Vargas, "Partió de México el último grupo de los repatriados," *La Jornada*, 29 July 1999, www.jornada.unam.mx/1999/jul99/990729/retorno.html.
According to Laura Carrera Lugo, most of those who relocated to Campeche
were mestizos. Carrera Lugo, "Creación de nuevos asentamientos en Campeche
y el programa multianual," in *Presencia de los refugiados guatemaltecos en México*, 88.

87. See, for example, Fazio, *Samuel Ruiz*, 163–165.

88. "Tentativa de COMAR para que los refugiados guatemaltecos acepten viajar a Campeche," *Unomásuno,* June 13, 1984.

89. Ricardo Epifanio Pérez Hernández, "Mayas de Guatemala refugiados: Nuestra organización y participación," in *Presencia de los refugiados guatemaltecos en México,* 62–68; Carrera Lugo, "Creación de nuevos asentamientos en Campeche y el programa multianual," 88–98.

90. On January 16, 1986, the Guatemalan refugees in Quintana Roo reportedly presented the seed from their first crop to the Mexican *ejido* farmers, to express their gratitude to the Mexican citizens who had so graciously welcomed them. Leonardo Franco, "Un episodio controvertido en la historia del refugio: la reubicación a Campeche y Quintana Roo," in *Presencia de los refugiados guatemaltecos en México,* 81; Faustino Sánchez Martínez, "Recepción y autosuficiencia de refugiados en Quintana Roo, 1984–1989," in *Presencia de los refugiados guatemaltecos en México,* 84.

91. Ruiz, *El Retorno,* 6; Friedland and Rodríguez y Rodríguez, *Seeking Safe Ground,* 33.

92. In their 1991 report, Joan Friedland and Jesús Rodríguez y Rodríguez lamented the "serious gaps in information about refugees in Mexico" and the "serious conflicts [that] exist in the information that has been gathered." These authors go on to write: "Few independent studies have been conducted. Newspapers are often the only source of information, in part because some of them are the government's preferred forum for making policies known" (*Seeking Safe Ground,* xii).

93. Ibid., 24.

94. Aguayo, *El éxodo centroamericano,* 137.

95. Survey compiled by the Comité de Servicio de los Amigos, Mexico, DF, cited in Aguayo, *El éxodo centroamericano,* 151.

96. The reasons for migration are cited in the surveys of the Comité de Servicio de Amigos, the Comisión de Refugiados en México, and the Comité Mexicano de Solidaridad con el Pueblo Salvadoreño, cited in Aguayo, *El éxodo centroamericano,* 146–147.

97. Edelberto Torres-Rivas, *Report on the Condition of Central American Refugees and Migrants* (Washington, D.C.: Center for Immigration Policy and Refugee Assistance, Georgetown University, July 1985), 24; Mohn, "Central American Refugees," 44; Loescher, "Humanitarianism and Politics in Central America," 304.

98. Survey, Comité de Servicio de los Amigos, México, DF, cited in Aguayo, *El éxodo centroamericano,* 42–43, 154.

99. *Caminante* 31 (February 1984): 8–9.

100. See, for example, the various surveys of Salvadorans cited in Aguayo, *El éxodo centroamericano,* 139–143. See also Aguayo and Fagen, *Central Americans in*

Mexico and the United States, 5–7. Central Americans were reported in Oaxaca, Hermosillo, Tampico, Puebla, Veracruz, and the oil ports of Coatzacoalcos, Minatitlán, and Salina Cruz. Friedland and Rodríguez y Rodríguez, *Seeking Safe Ground,* 20.

101. O'Dogherty, *Central Americans in Mexico City,* 63–65.

102. Sáenz-Romero and Sánchez-Sosa, "Development and Identity of Guatemalan Refugee Children in Mexico," 34–35.

103. Bill Frelick, "Mexico Deports 80,000 in First Six Months of 1990," *Refugee Reports* 11, no. 9 (September 28, 1990): 2, 14–16.

104. Mohn, "Central American Refugees," 43.

105. Frelick, *Running the Gauntlet,* 18.

106. Formerly the Comité de Servicio de los Amigos, or Friends Service Committee.

107. Some agencies, like Vluchteling, were tolerated even though they did not have official state permission to operate in Mexico City. Friedland and Rodríguez y Rodríguez, *Seeking Safe Ground,* 41.

108. Aguayo, *El éxodo centroamericano,* 49.

109. Ibid., 148.

110. "Llegó a 21.8% la inflación este año," *Unomásuno,* May 5, 1984; "En 4 meses, aumentos de 37% a los básicos," *Unomásuno,* June 5, 1984.

111. See, for example, Aguayo, *El éxodo centroamericano,* 51, 114.

112. Torres-Rivas, *Report on the Condition of Central American Refugees and Migrants,* 24.

113. Indeed, as early as 1982 the Secretaría de Gobernación reportedly sent out a circular forbidding the passage of Central Americans with tourist visas to the United States–Mexico border, and suspicion that they intended to cross into the United States was sufficient grounds for detention. Friedland and Rodríguez y Rodríguez, *Seeking Safe Ground,* 43, 49.

114. Frelick, "Mexico Deports 80,000 in First Six Months of 1990," 1–2; Susan Gzesh, "So Close to the United States, So Far from God: Refugees and Asylees under Mexican Law," *World Refugee Survey 1995,* www.refugees.org/world/articles/mexicanlaw_wrs95.htm.

115. See, for example, the testimony of Antonio Sánchez Meraz in *Presencia de los refugiados guatemaltecos en México,* 40–42.

116. The Dioceses of San Cristóbal, Tapachula, and Cuernavaca, together with an ecumenical Christian committee in Mexico City, established the Christian Coordinator for Aid to Guatemalan Refugees. Aguilar Zinser, "Repatriation of Guatemalan Refugees in Mexico," 78.

117. Torres-Rivas, *Report on the Condition of Central American Refugees and Migrants,* 66; Aguayo, *From the Shadows to Center Stage,* 6. According to Aguayo,

the Diocese of Tehuantepec also created a committee to oversee assistance to refugees, but the committee was short-lived, as was the attempt by all three dioceses to coordinate their emergency assistance through the umbrella organization Coordinator for Guatemalan Refugee Assistance.

118. The twenty-fifth anniversary edition of *Presencia de los refugiados guatemaltecos en México,* a compilation of essays commemorating the arrival, accommodation, and repatriation of the Guatemalan refugees by COMAR and the UNHCR, rarely mentions the church groups who played so important a role in refugee aid. See also Jean Meyer (with Federico Anaya Gallardo and Julio Ríos), *Samuel Ruiz en San Cristobal* (Mexico City: Editores Tusquets, 2000), 73; and Rich, *Mexican Policy toward Guatemalan Refugees,* 16. According to Friedland and Rodríguez y Rodríguez, the Comité de Ayuda a Refugiados Guatemaltecos was one of the few NGOs permitted to work in Chiapas (*Seeking Safe Ground,* 31).

119. "El Obispo Samuel Ruiz, una institución en Chiapas," *Caminante* 31 (February 1984): 26–28.

120. *Caminante* 31 (February 1984): 26–27.

121. Torres-Rivas, *Report on the Condition of Central American Refugees and Migrants,* 66.

122. "Postura de la Diócesis," *Caminante* 39 (June–July 1985): 4.

123. *Caminante* also included articles and news updates on the wars in Central America and the peace process; liberation theology; human rights abuses in Chiapas and Central America; worker rights, the agrarian reform movement, and other social and political developments in Chiapas.

124. The Permanent Commissions consisted of six permanent and two supplemental representatives elected by direct vote by the registered refugees in Chiapas, Campeche, and Quintana Roo. Aguilar Zinser, "Repatriation of Guatemalan Refugees in Mexico," 74.

125. Rich, *Mexican Policy toward Guatemalan Refugees,* 14.

126. Cited in Golden and McConnell, *Sanctuary,* 120.

127. Library of Congress Country Studies, "Mexico: Church-State Relations," http://lcweb2.loc.gov/cgi-bin/query/D?cstdy:2:./temp/~frd_pBa8::. According to the Mexican Constitution, the church lacked any legal status. Thus all weddings performed in a church were not legal, and all church buildings were owned and had to be authorized by the state. The church was also forbidden from participating in primary and secondary education and establishing religious orders. All religious ceremonies had to occur within church buildings, and the clergy were mandated to wear secular clothing outside of church rituals. During the administration of Carlos Salinas de Gortari, the legislature relaxed several of these provisions. See also Pamela Voekel, *Alone before God: The Religious Origins of Modernity in Mexico* (Durham, NC: Duke University Press, 2002); and Roberto Blan-

carte, *Historia de la Iglesia Católica en México* (Mexico City: Colegio Mexiquense: Fondo de Cultura Económica, 1992).

128. According to Lona Reyes, the most progressive bishops were in Oaxaca, Chiapas, Hermosillo, Ciudad Juárez, Chihuahua, and Tarahumara. Aurora Berdejo, "La iglesia Mexicana, profundamente conservadora: Arzobispo Lona Reyes," *Excélsior*, August 2, 1981.

129. Fazio, *Samuel Ruiz*, 166; see also Fernández, "Chiapas: La iglesia de los pobres y la teología de la liberación en la mira," 165–175. According to Fernández, church groups that are committed to service to the poor are called the "parallel church" (166). See also Aguilar Zinser, "Repatriation of Guatemalan Refugees in Mexico," 91.

130. Fazio, *Samuel Ruiz*, 177. According to Laura O'Doherty, a politically conscious church and its increased hostility toward the government presented a far greater threat to the government than the refugee problem. Cited in Rich, *Mexican Policy toward Guatemalan Refugees*, 29.

131. Center for Human Rights Fray Bartolomé de las Casas, named after the famed sixteenth-century Franciscan who defended the rights of the indigenous peoples in the Americas.

132. According to the Secretaría de Gobernación, 26,218 indigenous people were imprisoned nationally during this period, of which only 6,848 obtained their freedom. The majority were imprisoned in Oaxaca, Veracruz, Puebla, and Chiapas. Monroy, "¿Qué pasó y qué pasa en Chiapas?" 47.

133. Quoted in Fernández, "Chiapas: La iglesia de los pobres y la teología de la liberación en la mira," 168.

134. Ibid., 168–169.

135. "Samuel Euiz se hace acreedor al Nuremberg," *La Jornada,* November 13, 2000, www/jornada.unam.mx/2000/novoo/001113/005n2pol.html.

136. Ann Crittenden, *Sanctuary, A Story of American Conscience and the Law in Collision* (New York: Weidenfeld and Nicolson, 1988), 82.

137. Ibid., 82.

138. Because of the small number of beds, residents were allowed to stay at the shelter a maximum of three days. According to *Refugee Reports,* in January 1989, the shelter had five hundred residents, but by April only ten because of the tougher US policies. *Refugee Reports,* May 19, 1989, 13.

139. Amnesty International, *Mexico: Human Rights in Rural Areas* (London: Amnesty International Publications, 1986), 1.

140. Ibid., 6.

141. Monroy, "¿Qué pasó y qué pasa en Chiapas?" 47.

142. Jean-François Durieux, "Capturing the Central American Refugee Phe-

nomenon: Refugee Law-Making in Mexico and Belize," *International Journal of Refugee Law* 4 (1992): 301.

143. Plaut, *Asylum,* 116; Bill Frelick, "Mexico Deports 80,000 in First Six Months of 1990," *Refugee Reports* 11, no. 9 (September 28, 1990): 6.

144. Gzesh, "So Close to the United States, So Far from God," 5–6.

145. Frelick, "Mexico Deports 80,000 in First Six Months of 1990," 7.

146. Ibid., 7.

147. In 2001 Mexico became a member of the Executive Committee of the UNHCR, and in 2002 became the ninety-second member of the International Organization for Migration (IOM). The IOM was founded in 1951 as an inter-governmental organization to resettle European displaced persons, refugees, and migrants. With offices and operations on every continent, the IOM helps governments deal with rapid humanitarian responses to sudden migration flows; re-integration programs; training in migration management and other assistance work; information and education on migration; and many other programs. www.iom.int/en/who/main_mission.shtml.

148. According to Kuhner, before March 2002, if an asylum seeker filed with the UNHCR before he or she was detained by authorities, he or she was likely to be released into UNHCR custody. Gretchen Kuhner, "Detention of Asylum Seekers in Mexico," *Refuge* 20 (May 2002): 59–60.

149. See the 2001 country report for Mexico at the Web site of the U.S. Committee for Refugees and Immigrants, at www.refugees.org.

150. Kuhner, "Detention of Asylum Seekers in Mexico," 59.

151. Guatemalan officials, in turn, reported that as many as seven thousand refugees returned in 1984. Aguilar Zinser, "Repatriation of Guatemalan Refugees in Mexico," 68–69. See also "Comisión de visita a Campeche y Quintana Roo," *Caminante* 39 (June-July 1985): 7.

152. The Permanent Commissions represented an estimated 80 percent of the registered Guatemalan refugees in Mexico. Representing the unregistered refugees was the Asociación de Refugiados Dispersos Guatemaltecos. Dennis Gallagher and Janelle M. Diller, *CIREFCA: At the Crossroads between Uprooted People and Development in Central America* (Washington, D.C.: Commission for the Study of International Migration and Cooperative Economic Development, March 1990), 7; Barbara Zerter, "Canadian Consortia Supports [sic] Guatemalan Return," *Refuge* 13, no. 10 (March 1994): 25; Ruiz, *El Retorno,* 11; Aguilar Zinser, "Repatriation of Guatemalan Refugees in Mexico," 75; Patricia Weiss Fagen, "Peace in Central America: Transition for the Uprooted," *World Refugee Survey 1993,* 13, www.refugees.org/world/articles/centralamerica.wrs93.htm.

153. Loescher, "Humanitarianism and Politics in Central America," 301–302.

154. Americas Watch Committee, *Messengers of Death,* 1–5.

155. Aguilar Zinser, "Repatriation of Guatemalan Refugees in Mexico," 70; Loescher, "Humanitarianism and Politics in Central America," 302–303; Brian Egan and Alan Simmons, "Refugees and the Prospects for Peace and Development in Central America," *Refuge* 13, no. 10 (March 1994): 8.

156. Fagen, "Peace in Central America," 13.

157. According to the US Committee for Refugees, "Guatemalan refugees refer to their planned collective repatriations as *retornos,* or "returns." They use the term *repatriación,* or "repatriation," to refer to UNHCR-assisted repatriation by individual families." Ruiz, *El Retorno,* 1.

158. Fagen, "Peace in Central America," 4, 14.

159. "Coordination of NGOs and Cooperatives for the Accompaniment of the Population Victimized by the Internal Armed Conflict."

160. See, for example, Project Accompaniment, sponsored by over a dozen Canadian NGOs. Zerter, "Canadian Consortia Supports Guatemalan Return," 25. In Chicago, the National Coordinating Office on Refugees and Displaced of Guatemala was one of many groups to emerge in the United States "to coordinate information, advocacy and support activities." Ruiz, *El Retorno,* 14.

161. This quote was cited in Beth Abbott, "Project Accompaniment: A Canadian Response," *Refuge* 13, no. 10 (March 1994): 26.

162. In October 1995, soldiers massacred eleven returnees, celebrating the first anniversary of their return to Guatemala, and the archbishop's Office of Human Rights continued to report hundreds of extrajudicial killings. Julianne E. Lindsey, "Peace Dividend or Broken Promise for Guatemala's Internally Displaced?" *Refugee Reports* 18, no. 5 (1997), www.refugees.org/world/articles/guatemala_rr97_5.htm; press release, "US Committee for Refugees Condemns Killing of Returned Guatemalan Refugees," October 6, 1995, www.refugees.org/news/press_releases?1995/100695.htm.

163. Under the general category of nonimmigrants are a tourist (FM-T), transmigrant (FM-6); visitor, usually for purposes of business (FM-3); asylee (FM-10); and student (FM-9).

164. Article 30 states that Mexican citizens are those born in Mexican territory, regardless of their parents' nationality; those born abroad whose parents, or at least one of them, are of Mexican nationality; and those born on vessels or aircraft that fly the Mexican flag or are registered in Mexico. For this reason, prior to 1996, the children of refugees were not given birth certificates so that their parents could not then obtain the FM-2. Friedland and Rodríguez y Rodríguez, *Seeking Safe Ground,* 30.

165. Frelick, *Running the Gauntlet,* 11; Alonso Urrutia, "México y la UE apoyan planes de refugiados guatemaltecos," *La Jornada,* October 18, 2000, www.jornada

.unam.mx/2000/octoo/001018/016n1pol.html; Elio Henríquez, "Empezó en Chiapas el plan para integrar a los refugiados guatemaltecos," *La Jornada,* June 17, 1998, www.jornada.unam.mx/1998/jun1998/980517/plan.html; Tania Molina Ramírez, "Desplazados, al lado invisible de la guerra," *La Jornada,* October 7, 2001, www.jornada.unam.mx/2001/octo1/011007/mas-desplazado.html.

3. REFUGEES OR ECONOMIC MIGRANTS?

Epigraphs: "The Reagan Administration doesn't want to accept us as refugees . . . ," quoted in *Los Angeles Times,* March 9, 1987; "Evidence concerning INS interference," *Orantes-Hernández, et al., v. Richard Thornburgh, et al.* (1990).

1. Aguayo and Fagen, *Central Americans in Mexico and the United States,* 1–2.

2. Linda S. Peterson, *Central American Migration: Past and Present* (Washington, DC: Center for International Research, US Bureau of the Census, CIR Staff Paper no. 25, November 1986), 7–19. An estimated 225,000 Guatemalans, 881,000 Salvadorans, and 205,000 Nicaraguans were living in the United States by 1985.

3. Between 1951 and 1978, 235,200 Central Americans immigrated to the United States. Aguayo, *El éxodo centroamericano,* 51. See also Menjívar, *Fragmented Ties.*

4. Aguayo and Fagen, *Central Americans in Mexico and the United States,* 1–2.

5. Aurora Camacho de Schmidt, "US Refugee Policy and Central America," *Christianity and Crisis* 49 (September 25, 1989): 283.

6. John Ellement, *States News Service,* April 22, 1985, www.lexis-nexis.com. See also John Mintz, "Lost Dreams and Mourning; Many Prosper Here, but Others Are Mired in Poverty," *Washington Post,* April 18, 1985.

7. These were the 1980 Refugee Act, the 1986 Immigration Reform and Control Act, the 1990 Immigration Act, and the 1996 Illegal Immigration and Immigrant Responsibility Act.

8. Bob Woodward, *VEIL: The Secret Wars of the CIA, 1981–1987* (New York: Simon and Schuster, 1987), 340. Examinations of refugee policy by Washington think tanks forecasted how particular economic policies might deflect migration to the United States. See, for example, the conclusions and recommendations offered by the Refugee Policy Group in Fagen's *Refugees and Displaced Persons in Central America.*

9. Jonathan Moore, "Developing Solutions for Central American Refugee Problems," *Department of State Bulletin* 89 (August 1989): 87. According to Moore, the US coordinator for Refugee Affairs, the US aid programs in the five countries targeted areas with significant refugee returns and displaced populations. Projects included water supply, rehabilitation of rural roads and bridges, microenterprise credit, primary health care, employment generation, housing, agricul-

tural assistance, family planning services, municipal development, sanitation, feeding programs, forestry, irrigation, soil conservation, and primary education.

10. Ibid., 87–88.

11. Memorandum for Robert M. Kimmitt from Raymond F. Burghardt, May 23, 1985, in "Guatemala 4/4," Box 91176, Latin American Affairs Directorate: Record, Ronald Reagan Presidential Library.

12. US Comptroller General, *"Central American Refugees: Regional Conditions and Prospects and Potential Impact on the United States,"* 40. UNHCR refugee estimates were always much higher than those of the US State Department. For example, in 1984, the State Department estimated 118,000 to 143,460 Central American refugees were in the region. The UNHCR, on the other hand estimated 321,854. The UNHCR had assisted 87,517 of this total number.

13. The 1967 Protocol expanded the definition of refugee drafted by the 1951 UN Convention relating to the Status of Refugees. The United States became a signatory to the Protocol on November 1, 1968.

14. US immigration law distinguishes between refugees and asylees. Refugees must apply for protection from outside the United States, usually from a third country; if they are already within the United States and petition—and are granted—asylum, they are asylees. Both groups have the same status under American law. One year after immigrants are granted asylum/refugee status, they may apply for legal permanent resident status, at which point their cases are reviewed to determine whether conditions of their source country have changed sufficiently to merit withdrawing asylum/refugee status. Letter from John D. Evans, director of the Resource Information Center, US Department of Justice, to the Immigration and Refugee Board of Canada, Ottawa, December 15, 1994.

15. The president must consult with Congress on the specific number and source countries of refugees to be admitted each year. However, the final number is left to presidential discretion. Throughout most of the 1980s, the number of refugees admitted annually exceeded the fifty thousand quota.

16. US Comptroller General, *"Central American Refugees: Regional Conditions and Prospects and Potential Impact on the United States,"* 41.

17. Deborah Anker, "US Immigration and Asylum Policy: A Brief Historical Perspective," *In Defense of the Alien,* vol. 13, Proceedings of the 1990 Annual Legal Conference on Immigration and Refugee Policy (Staten Island, NY: Center for Migration Studies, 1990), 80.

18. Moore, "Developing Solutions for Central American Refugee Problems," 87–88.

19. Peterson, *Central American Migration,* 3.

20. Mohn, "Central American Refugees," 44.

21. Laura Dietrich, "Political Asylum: Who Is Eligible and Who Is Not," *New York Times,* October 2, 1985.

22. Article 33 of the Convention lists the right to *non-refoulement:* no expulsion of refugees to the frontiers or territories where their lives or freedom would be threatened for reasons of race, religion, nationality, political belief, or membership in a particular social group.

23. Mohn, "Central American Refugees," 44.

24. "Judge Refuses Summary Judgment on EVD," *Refugee Reports* 10 (October 20, 1989): 9.

25. "Why Poles but Not Salvadorans?" *New York Times,* May 31, 1983.

26. In May 1983, the State Department advised that the United States not grant the Salvadorans EVD "because it would encourage further illegal immigration to the US from El Salvador." The possibility of asylum granted from other countries that Salvadorans passed through on their way to the United States should also exempt them from consideration, officials argued. Mohn, "Central American Refugees," 46. State department officials also used the refugee exodus as an excuse for expanding US military aid in the region. Secretary of State Alexander Haig warned that the United States might be flooded with refugees if radical trends in El Salvador and other countries were not stopped. Bernard Gwertzman, "Haig Fears Exiles from Latin Areas May Flood the US," *New York Times,* February 23, 1982.

27. "Refugees Admitted to the United States by Nationality, FY 82–95," *Refugee Reports,* December 31, 1995, 10–11.

28. The task force warned of the "demographic consequences" of Latin American immigration. See Gary MacEoin and Nivita Riley, *No Promised Land: American Refugee Policies and the Rule of Law* (Boston: Oxfam America, 1982). For the legislative package to Congress, see "Immigration Reform: White House IGA Position Analysis," n.d., Case file 253900, Box FG006–01, Reagan Presidential Library.

29. The bill ultimately passed was the Simpson-Rodino Bill, which became P.L. 99–603. IRCA targeted the problem of undocumented migration in three principal ways: (1) imposed fines on employers who hired undocumented workers (but deferred the enforcement of penalties for employment of seasonal agricultural workers); (2) increased the border patrol by sixteen hundred new agents; and (3) imposed harsher criminal penalties on those who transported or harbored illegal aliens. IRCA's failure to control illegal immigration led to the passage of a new immigration control act in 1996, the Illegal Immigration and Immigrant Responsibility Act.

30. Weintraub and Díaz-Briquets, *The Use of Foreign Aid to Reduce Incentives to Emigrate from Central America,* 9.

31. Paul Glickman, "United States: Salvadoran Refugees Overlooked by Immigration Law," *Inter-Press Service*, February 16, 1987, http://web.lexis.nexis .com universe/printdoc.

32. Studies show, however, that over half of undocumented workers in the United States came into the country legally and became "illegal" by staying once their visas expired. Thus, the Illegal Immigration and Immigrant Responsibility Act targeted this specific population.

33. Jane Applegate, "Idealism of the '60s Reborn in Pleas for Immigrants," *Los Angeles Times,* June 1, 1986; US Comptroller General, *Central American Refugees: Regional Conditions and Prospects and Potential Impact on the United States,"* 38; Elliott Abrams, "Letter to the Editor," *Wall Street Journal,* March 15, 1985.

34. Following the guidelines established by the Board of Immigration Appeals, bond amounts were theoretically determined by such factors as family ties, length of residence in a community, and employment history (ironically rewarding those who had managed to escape "the system" for a period of time). But according to Markley, bond amounts for Central American detainees were arbitrary, varying within and across INS districts. Jennifer Jo Markley, "Bonds in the Asylum Context: The Treatment of Central American Refugees in Texas," MA thesis, University of Texas at Austin, December 1990, 97–112.

35. *Refugee Reports* 10 (May 19, 1989): 8; Gelbspan (1991) and MacEoin and Riley (1982), cite the case of Ana Estela Guevara Flores, a Salvadoran maid arrested by the INS in San Antonio, carrying "subversive literature" (copies of Archbishop Romero's sermons). Convinced that she was the guerrilla leader Comandante Norma Guevara, FBI agents reported their suspicions to security police in El Salvador. However, in 1986, a federal circuit court ruled that Guevara Flores was not the FMLN leader and had demonstrated a "well-founded fear of persecution."

36. Kahn, *Other People's Blood,* 14–18. Kahn based his study on interviews with more than three thousand refugees in the United States, as well as his work as a legal assistant in four detention centers from 1984 to 1987: Port Isabel and Laredo, Texas; Oakdale, Louisiana; and Florence, Arizona. According to Kahn, the worst abuses occurred in Laredo and Oakdale. See also Mohn, "Central American Refugees," 45.

37. However, 57 percent of those interviewed guessed that the cause of the unrest in Central America was poverty and human rights abuses, and not Soviet-Cuban intervention. Mark Falcoff, "How to Understand Central America," *Commentary* 78 (September 1984): 30–31.

38. LeoGrande, *Central America and the Polls.*

39. Throughout the 1980s, protestors drew parallels between El Salvador and Vietnam. For many, the Reagan administration's rhetoric about El Salvador and its incremental involvement were eerily similar to the actions that led to US

involvement in the Vietnam War. Flora Lewis, "Vietnam and Salvador—a Battle for Hearts and Minds," *New York Times*, February 21, 1982; "Preocupación de que se produzca otro Vietnam," *El Día*, March 4, 1981.

40. "Despite a Crackdown, 7 Guatemalans Are Smuggled into US," *New York Times*, January 20, 1985; Loescher, "Humanitarianism and Politics in Central America," 306.

41. Ann Crittenden, *Sanctuary, a Story of American Conscience and the Law in Collision* (New York: Weidenfeld and Nicolson, 1988), 364–365; Mohn, "Central American Refugees," 44.

42. Founded in 1974 by Protestant and Catholic agencies, the Washington Office on Latin America "is a nonprofit policy, research and advocacy organization working to advance democracy, human rights and social justice in Latin America and the Caribbean." The organization "facilitates dialogue between governmental and non-governmental actors, monitors the impact of policies and programs of governments and international organizations, and promotes alternatives through reporting, education, training and advocacy." As part of their public education campaign, members have testified before Congress, arranged meetings between human rights activists and church and government officials, and arranged speaking tours. Information on current activities can be found on their Web site, www.wola.org. For a general discussion of humanitarian activism in Latin America, especially the organization called Service for Peace and Justice, see Ron Pagnucco, "The Transnational Strategies of the Service for Peace and Justice in Latin America," in Smith et al., eds., *Transnational Social Movements and Global Politics*, 123–138.

43. Porpora, *How Holocausts Happen*, 191–193.

44. "Simulacro de juicio contra Reagan en NY," *Excélsior*, June 10, 1984; "Condenas a la política de EU en Centroamérica y al armamentismo," *Unomásuno*, June 10, 1984.

45. The Center for Constitutional Rights established the Movement Support Network, which set up a hotline for political groups to report any type of harassment. Ross Gelbspan, *Break-ins, Death Threats and the FBI. The Covert War against the Central America Movement* (Boston: South End Press, 1991); "Break-ins at Sanctuary Churches and Organizations Opposed to Administration Policy in Central America," *Hearings before the Subcommittee on Civil and Constitutional Rights*, Committee on the Judiciary, House of Representatives, 100th Congress, 1st session, February 19 and 20, 1987; Laurie Becklund, "Burglars or Snoopers? Break-ins in 11 cities Are Aimed at Churches, Groups Involved in the Sanctuary Movement," *Los Angeles Times*, January 30, 1986; Ross Gelbspan, "FBI to Probe Theft at Contra Foes' Office," *Bergen Record*, January 8, 1987; David Kowalewski, "The Historical Structuring of a Dissident Movement: The Sanctuary Case," *Research in Social Movements, Conflicts, and Change* 12 (1990): 100.

46. See Gelbspan, *Break-ins, Death Threats and the FBI*.

47. *Committee in Solidarity with the People of El Salvador (CISPES), et al., v. William F. Sessions, et al.*, 929 F.2d 742 (D.C. Cir. 1991). The appeals court ruled that since the FBI had acknowledged inappropriate actions and subsequently relinquished all files to the National Archives, the plaintiffs could no longer allege continued damage. See also "Group Falsely Linked to Terrorism Sues FBI," *Bergen Record*, November 30, 1988.

48. Thomas C. Kelly, the general secretary of the US Catholic Conference wrote: "The position of our Conference is taken because of the information coming to us from the Church in El Salvador. Rather than a view of a beleaguered government caught between extremists of the left and right, the picture we receive is that the military arm of government in El Salvador is itself an instrument of terror and repression, quite unable to win the political support needed to govern in peace." Letter from Thomas C. Kelly to Clarence D. Long, chairman of the Foreign Operations Subcommittee, March 24, 1980, in Carter Presidential Library, Staff Offices, Special Assistant to the President, Esteban Torres, Box 18, File "El Salvador 1/31/80–12/10/80." For a complete account of the Catholic Conference's position on Central America, see "USCC Policy towards Central America: A Synthesis," Washington, D.C., February 24, 1985, Catholic Archives of Texas.

49. "Central American Asylum Seekers," *Hearing before the Subcommittee on Immigration, Refugees, and International Law of the Committee of the Judiciary, House of Representatives*, 101st Congress, 1st session, March 9, 1989, appendix 1, 267.

50. Among those that came out in public support for EVD were the Lutheran Immigration and Refugee Services, the American Council for Nationalities Services, the International Rescue Committee, the National Council of Churches, the US Catholic Conference, the ACLU, and the National Lawyers Guild.

51. "Resolution on Refugee Protection and Sanctuary," *Migration News* 4 (1985): 49. The Maryknoll order of nuns, who lost two nuns to violence in Central America, issued a public statement in support of the Salvadorans and Guatemalans who had been forced to flee because of "the brutal policies of their own security forces supported by escalating military aid from the United States." See "Franciscans Endorse Sanctuary Movement," *Florida Catholic*, March 29, 1985.

52. Activists purchased and then used their shares in the airlines to force a stockholder vote. According to Gelbspan, this incident led to the FBI probe of sanctuary workers and other religious activists involved in Central America advocacy. Kowalewski, "The Historical Structuring of a Dissident Movement," 100; Gelbspan, *Break-Ins, Death Threats and the FBI*, 102.

53. "Brownsville Bishop Asked Amnesty for Refugees," *Texas Catholic*, April 8, 1983.

54. William Sloane Coffin, "The Tasks Ahead," in Gary MacEoin, ed., *Sanctuary: A Resource Guide for Understanding and Participating in the Central American Refugees' Struggle* (San Francisco: Harper and Row, 1985), 177.

55. Mohn, "Central American Refugees," 44.

56. *Refugee Reports* 10 (August 31, 1989): 12. The Border Association for Refugees from Central America was one of the most important legal advocates in the Texas Rio Grande Valley. Founded in 1981 by Chad Richardson, a professor at the University of Texas–Pan American in Edinburgh, the association united people from all walks of life—clergy, students and professors, lawyers and retirees.

57. *Refugee Reports* 10 (May 19, 1989): 12. The first director of Casa Oscar Romero was Rosemary Smith, a church social worker who served in San Salvador for sixteen years. Smith was visiting the United States when the four American church workers were raped and murdered. On the advice of friends, Smith remained in the United States and committed herself to work on behalf of the Central American refugees.

58. Kahn, *Other People's Blood,* 55.

59. In a particularly tragic case, in 1980 a group of twenty-six men and women were found in the Sonoran Desert, where they had been abandoned by their "coyote"; nearly half of them died, and thirteen were arrested by the INS and sent to a jail in Tucson to await deportation. Three were never found.

60. The name appears in lowercase because Jim Corbett and his fellow Quakers envisioned a network rather than a formal, more authoritarian organization. Hilary Cunningham, *God and Caesar at the Rio Grande: Sanctuary and the Politics of Religion* (Minneapolis: University of Minnesota Press, 1995), 28.

61. Ibid., 30–31.

62. Quoted in Gary MacEoin, "A Brief History of the Sanctuary Movement," in Gary MacEoin, ed., *Sanctuary,* 21.

63. Peter Applebome, "Sanctuary Movement: New Hopes after Trial," *New York Times,* May 6, 1986.

64. For a list of endorsers (by 1985), see MacEoin, "A Brief History of the Sanctuary Movement," 26.

65. "Resolution on Refugee Protection and Sanctuary," 49.

66. Dale Brazao, "Church Groups Guide Refugees to Canada," *Toronto Star,* March 17, 1987.

67. The CRTF, a coalition of religious and social action groups, formed largely in response to the murders of the four American women in El Salvador in 1980. Cunningham, *God and Caesar at the Rio Grande,* 39.

68. Charles Austin, "More Churches Join in Offering Sanctuary for Latin Refugees," *New York Times,* September 21, 1983.

69. Statement on the Sanctuary Movement, Ad Hoc Committee on Migra-

tion and Tourism, National Conference of Catholic Bishops, November 16, 1983, in vertical file "Sanctuary Movement," Catholic Archives of Texas; Gerard E. Sherry, "Symposium Focuses on Sanctuary for Refugees," *Our Sunday Visitor,* February 24, 1985, 4.

70. The rhetoric of sanctuary supported this idea. "Sanctuary is a very public statement that is more symbolic than it is designed to solve the direct needs of refugees," said one activist. Kendall Wills, "Churches Debate Role as Sanctuary," *New York Times,* June 16, 1985.

71. Cunningham, *God and Caesar at the Rio Grande,* 42. The author discusses at some length the divergent views of these two streams and the rift that almost threatened the movement. See also, Miriam Davidson, *Convictions of the Heart: Jim Corbett and the Sanctuary Movement* (Tucson: University of Arizona Press, 1988), 84–85.

72. Those who viewed their work as civil initiative claimed that it was the government—not they—who was breaking the law; and thus they had a civic responsibility to force a change in government policy.

73. Cunningham, *God and Caesar at the Rio Grande,* 166–170; see also Susan Bibler Coutin's discussion of the screening process in chapter six of *The Culture of Protest: Religious Activism and the US Sanctuary Movement* (Boulder, CO: Westview Press, 1993); Davidson, *Convictions of the Heart,* 131–132.

74. Wills, "Churches Debate Role as Sanctuary," 35.

75. The tucson refugee support group, for example, severed its association with the CRTF. Cunningham gives an excellent account of the various strategies and ideologies within the movement. See *God and Caesar at the Rio Grande,* 171–175.

76. "Sanctuary for Illegal Aliens," memorandum from Wilfred R. Caron to Monsignor Hoye, United States Catholic Conference, November 10, 1983, in vertical file "Sanctuary Movement," Catholic Archives of Texas.

77. Draft of a response letter to Sister Mary Ryan, n.d., in IM 566041–570165, WHORM Subject File-Immigration, Reagan Presidential Library.

78. Kowalewski, "The Historical Structuring of a Dissident Movement," 95. The institute was founded in Washington, D.C., in 1981.

79. Glenn F. Bunting and Paul Feldman, "Assessor Threatens Tax Status of Churches That Provide Asylum," *Los Angeles Times,* February 1988.

80. "Break-ins at Sanctuary Churches and Organizations Opposed to Administration Policy in Central America." See also Gelbspan, *Break-ins, Death Threats and the FBI.*

81. Ron Hamm, "Sanctuary Movement Raises Hard Political Questions," *National Catholic Register,* February 12, 1984, 7.

82. Quoted in Mohn, "Central American Refugees," 46.

83. Dan Walter, "Courage in the Sanctuary; Nun Says She Must Aid Refugees," *Bergen Record,* April 1, 1986.

84. See, for example, Ari L. Goldman, "U.S. Clerics Debating Ethics of Giving Sanctuary to Aliens," *New York Times,* August 23, 1985.

85. See, for example, Kathy Boccella, "Controversial Priest Ousted in Hempstead," *Newsday,* May 29, 1988, 2.

86. In its report on policy recommendations, the US Catholic Conference wrote: "Because the US government has not yet granted the desired moratorium on deportations . . . some US Christians have adopted a tactic of non-violent civil disobedience to challenge the government's actions. . . . This movement has become a matter of controversy within the Church in the US, with some bishops supporting, some opposing direct participation in the sanctuary movement. Up to the present, the movement has had very little effect on the public policy but it has become a symbolically important focus for many Christians opposing aspects of US policy. The US Bishop's Conference has taken no official position regarding the Sanctuary Movement." *USCC Policy Towards Central America,* 13.

87. Don Schanche and J. Michael Kennedy, "Pope Lauds Sanctuary for Central Americans," *Los Angeles Times,* September 14, 1987.

88. Despite the silence of their national body, some Roman Catholic bishops could not remain quiet, much to the concern of administration officials cognizant of their influence on Catholic opinion. Joseph Fitzpatrick of the Brownsville Diocese was one of the most vocal supporters of sanctuary and other acts of civil disobedience. He contributed to the bail bonds of sanctuary workers who were detained by the INS, and testified at their trials. On one occasion, Fitzpatrick paid twenty-seven thousand dollars of his own personal savings to finance the bail bonds of two sanctuary workers. The group Concerned Citizens for Church and Country accused him of being no better than a "coyote," and ran ads in three newspapers in the Rio Grande Valley demanding a Vatican investigation of Fitzpatrick and another sanctuary sympathizer, Archbishop Patricio Flores of San Antonio. Archbishops Raymond Hunthausen of Seattle and Rembert Weakland of Milwaukee also eloquently supported sanctuary; and after the Justice Department began its persecution of church workers, others followed suit with Hunthausen and Weakland, including Bishops Joseph Fiorenza of Galveston-Houston, Manuel D. Moreno of Tucson, Thomas J. O'Brien of Phoenix, and Jerome J. Hastrich of Gallup, New Mexico. Opponents to sanctuary were also well represented. Bishops Enrique San Pedro and René Gracida of the Corpus Christi Diocese publicly discouraged Catholics from engaging in any type of sanctuary work. Gracida disbanded his diocesan social justice group when it came out in support of the movement. See vertical file "Sanctuary Movement," Catholic

Archives of Texas. David Sedeno, "He Keeps Working for the Poor, Oppressed," *Houston Chronicle,* March 2, 1985.

89. Merkt was granted an early release from prison because of complications in her pregnancy, which allowed her to serve eighty-three days of her sentence under house arrest. "Sanctuary Activist Gets Early Prison Release," *Los Angeles Times,* April 18, 1987. Sue Fahlgren, "Elder Gets 150 Days in Halfway House," *Corpus Christi Times,* March 28, 1985. Other arrests included that of Philip Willis-Conger of the Tucson Ecumenical Council Task Force, in 1984, but his case was dismissed on a technicality. In 1986, in New Mexico, journalist and poet Demetria Martínez and Lutheran minister Glen Remer-Themert were arrested and indicted by a federal grand jury for conspiring to smuggle Central American refugees. As the first journalist indicted on a sanctuary case, Martínez became a cause célèbre, attracting unwanted media attention to the Justice Department's crackdown. The two were acquitted in 1988. Victor Valle, "Poet or Smuggler?" *Los Angeles Times,* May 26, 1988; Catherine Robbins, "Sanctuary Movement Gains a Court Hearing on Its Principles," *New York Times,* June 7, 1988.

90. "Bishop Says Sanctuary Figures Singled Out for Prosecution," *Houston Chronicle,* December 10, 1984.

91. Dick Stanley, "Brownsville Bishop Pays Bail to Free 2 Sanctuary Workers," *Austin American Statesman,* December 13, 1984.

92. Rio Grande Defense Committee newsletter, in vertical files, Catholic Archives of Texas.

93. "Sanctuary Activists Convicted," *Bergen Record,* May 2, 1986.

94. Ronald Ostrow, "Clergy, Nuns Charged with Alien Smuggling," *New York Times,* January 15, 1985; Stephanie Overman, "Refugee Crisis Challenges US Policy," *Florida Catholic,* January 25, 1985; Sherry, "Symposium Focuses on Sanctuary for Refugees," 4; Wayne King, "Use of Informers Questioned in Inquiry on Aliens," *New York Times,* March 2, 1985.

95. Wayne King, "Church Members Will Press Sanctuary Movement," *New York Times,* January 23, 1985.

96. Wayne King, "Trial Opening in Arizona in Alien Sanctuary Case," *New York Times,* October 21, 1985; Mark Turner, "Sanctuary Evidence Suppression Sought," *Arizona Daily Star,* March 29, 1985.

97. Coutin, *The Culture of Protest,* 134–136.

98. Crittenden, *Sanctuary,* 335.

99. "Sanctuary Co-founder Gets Probation," *Los Angeles Times,* July 2, 1986; "Court Upholds Conviction of Arizona Sanctuary Workers," *Los Angeles Times,* March 30, 1989.

100. "Sanctuary Activists Convicted," *Bergen Record,* May 2, 1986.

101. "Despite Prosecutions, Sanctuary Movement Is Still Vital, Growing, Its Activists Insist," *Los Angeles Times,* July 11, 1987.

102. Jay Matthews, "Refugees' Underground Railway to Canada," *Washington Post,* October 15, 1987.

103. These cities included Berkeley and Los Angeles, California; Cambridge, Massachusetts; Madison, Wisconsin; Ithaca and Rochester, New York; New York City; St. Paul, Minnesota; and Chicago, Illinois. Victor Merina, "Cities vs. INS," *Los Angeles Times,* November 17, 1985. According to Kowalewski, Catholics provided 17.4 percent of the sanctuaries, while Unitarians, Quakers, and Jewish sites were somewhat overrepresented in terms of their proportions of US believers. See Kowalewski, "The Historical Structuring of a Dissident Movement," 103; Davidson, *Convictions of the Heart,* 85.

104. Interestingly, Sinner seems to have attracted more media attention in Canada than in his own country. "Dakota Priest Feels Compelled to Help Refugees Reach Canada," *Toronto Star,* March 13, 1987.

105. Sherry, "Symposium Focuses on Sanctuary for Refugees," 4.

106. In July 1987, for example, the Border Patrol stopped Ken Kennon and Rabbi Joseph Weizenbaum with a group of refugees near the border, but the Patrol let the two men go without even taking fingerprints. Davidson, *Convictions of the Heart,* 160.

107. See, for example, Edith Lederer, "Sri Lanka Activist Revives Debate in England over Sanctuary Movement," *Los Angeles Times,* November 20, 1988.

108. Nicgorski faced twenty-five years in prison, but was given a suspended sentence and five years probation. See Michael McAteer, "Church Sanctuary for Refugees?" *Toronto Star,* December 26, 1987, "Despite Prosecutions, Sanctuary Movement Is Still Vital, Growing, Its Activists Insist," *Los Angeles Times,* July 11, 1987; "Sanctuary Movement Activist Elected Leader of Presbyterians," *Houston Chronicle,* June 6, 1992; Kowalewski, "The Historical Structuring of a Dissident Movement," 100–102; Davidson, *Convictions of the Heart,* 160.

109. See Crittenden, *Sanctuary.*

110. Wills, "Churches Debate Role as Sanctuary," 35; Hamm, "Sanctuary Movement Raises Hard Political Questions," 1, 7; Applebome, "Sanctuary Movement: New Hopes after Trial."

111. *Noe Castillo Núñez, et al., v. Hal Boldin, et al.,* 537 F. Supp. 578 (1982).

112. *Crosby Wilfredo Orantes-Hernández, et al., v. William French Smith, et al.,* 541 F. Supp. 351 (1982).

113. *Crosby Wilfredo Orantes-Hernández, et al., v. Edwin Meese III, et al.,* 685 F. Supp. 1488 (1988); *Crosby Wilfredo Orantes-Hernández, et al., v. Richard Thornburgh, et al.,* 919 F. 2d 549 (1990); Bill Frelick and Hiram Ruiz, "Detention and Deter-

rence in Texas: Central Americans in INS Proceedings," *Refugee Reports* 10 (May 19, 1989): 2–4; *Refugee Reports* 10 (November 17, 1989): 7.

114. *Orantes-Hernández, et al., v. Thornburgh, et al.* The decision was upheld in 1991 and 1992.

115. *El Rescate Legal Services, Inc., et al., v. Executive Office for Immigration Review, et al.,* 727 F. Supp. 557 (1989); 941 F.2d 950 (1991); 959 F.2d (1992).

116. *Immigration and Naturalization Service v. Luz Marina Cardoza-Fonseca,* 480 US 421; 107 S. Ct. 1207; 94 L. Ed. 2d 434 (1987). See also Deborah Anker, "INS v Cardoza-Fonseca, One Year Later: Discretion, Credibility, and Political Opinion," *In Defense of the Alien,* vol. 11, Proceedings of the 1988 Annual Legal Conference on Immigration and Refugee Policy (Staten Island, NY: Center for Migration Studies, 1988), 120–130; and Anker, "US Immigration and Asylum Policy," 82–83.

117. Elizabeth Hull, "United States Asylum Process: Problems and Proposals," *In Defense of the Alien,* vol. 16, Proceedings of the 1994 Annual Legal Conference on Immigration and Refugee Policy (Staten Island, NY: Center for Migration Studies, 1994), 117–118.

118. The Asylum Policy and Review Unit was established by the attorney general in April 1987 to "insure that senior levels in both the Office of the Deputy Attorney General and the Immigration and naturalization Service (INS) had the opportunity to review denials of applications for asylum." Henry Curry, "US Asylum Adjudications," *In Defense of the Alien,* vol. 13, Proceedings of the 1990 Annual Legal Conference on Immigration and Refugee Policy (Staten Island, NY: Center for Migration Studies, 1990), 65–69.

119. Hull, "United States Asylum Process," 118.

120. José Napoleón Duarte, letter to President Ronald Reagan, May 1987, in File CO 046, Box 475126, Reagan Presidential Library.

121. *Refugee Reports* 10 (May 19, 1989): 3.

122. Bill Frelick and Hiram Ruiz, "Detention and Deterrence in Texas: Central Americans in INS Proceedings," *Refugee Reports* 10 (May 19, 1989): 1.

123. *American Baptist Churches in the USA, et al., v. Edwin Meese III and Alan Nelson,* 666 F. Supp. 1358 (N.D. Calif. 1987).

124. *American Baptist Churches in the USA, et al., v. Richard Thornburgh, et al.,* 760 F. Supp. 796 (N.D. Calif. 1991). The settlement affected all Guatemalans in the United States as of October 1, 1990, and all Salvadorans in the United States as of September 19, 1990 (except for those detained as felons).

125. Tracy Wilkinson, "US Agrees to Reopen 150,000 Asylum Cases," *Los Angeles Times,* December 20, 1990.

126. According to Frelick and Kohnen, applying for TPS was expensive and

probably deterred some refugees from applying. Salvadorans had to pay 75 dollars to register and 60 dollars every six months to secure work authorization until they reached the 225 dollar family cap. If applicants could not understand the forms, they had to hire a lawyer to assist them. Fee waivers were granted to families whose income met federal poverty guidelines, but the National Refugee Rights Project filed a class action suit against the INS charging that Salvadorans earning as little as fifty dollars a month were not granted fee waivers. Bill Frelick and Barbara Kohnen, "Filling the Gap: Temporary Protected Status," *Journal of Refugee Studies* 8 (1995): 347.

127. *La Prensa Centroamericana,* June 6–12, 1989, 10.

128. "Asylum Cases Filed with INS District Directors Approved and Denied, by Selected Nationalities," *Refugee Reports* 11 (December 21, 1990): 12.

129. Ibid.

130. George Volsky, "Group Would Aid Nicaraguans Here," *New York Times,* August 28, 1985.

131. George Volsky, "Nicaraguans in Miami Hoping for a Future as a Legal Resident," *New York Times,* April 22, 1986. Only 1,192 Nicaraguans were ever granted refugee status from 1980 to 1993. See "Refugees Admitted to the United States by Nationality, FY 80–93."

132. The Cuban Adjustment Act of 1966, for example, essentially allowed illegal Cuban immigrants to avoid deportation and legalize their status in the United States by eliminating the requirement that they apply for an immigrant visa from their homeland or from a third country. For a discussion of the various ways the US government legally accommodated Cuban immigrants, see my *Havana USA.*

133. Volsky, "Group Would Aid Nicaraguans here."

134. Ibid.

135. "Double Standard for Refugees?" *Time,* April 28, 1986, 34.

136. *Refugee Reports* 10 (January 27, 1989): 2; Aguayo and Fagen, *Central Americans in Mexico and the United States,* 37.

137. "Following Nicaraguan Elections, Mixed Prospects for Refugees," *Refugee Reports* 11 (April 27, 1990): 1.

138. Ibid.; *Refugee Reports* 14 (December 31, 1993): 12.

139. *Nica Actividades,* December 24–31, 1988 (a Nicaraguan exile periodical available at the Otto Richter Library, University of Miami).

140. David Hancock, "Desperate Nicaraguans Move On," *Miami Herald,* June 11, 1990.

141. Celia W. Dugger, "Refugee Numbers May Dip," *Miami Herald,* March 5, 1990.

142. Hancock, "Desperate Nicaraguans Move On."

143. "Nicaragua Asks US to Ease Limits on Refugee Travel," *Miami Herald,* March 5, 1990"; *La Prensa Centroamericana,* May 22–28, 1989, June 12–15, 1989, September 14–21, 1989.

144. Sandra Dibble, "Exiles Cheer Victory, Hope for Change," *Miami Herald,* March 5, 1990.

145. *La Prensa Centroamericana,* July 13, 1990.

146. "Nicaragua Asks US to Ease Limits on Refugee Travel"; *La Prensa Centro-americana,* December 7–13, 1990.

147. Marvin Ortega and Pedro Acevedo, "Nicaraguan Repatriation from Honduras and Costa Rica," in Larkin et al., eds., *Repatriation under Conflict in Central America,* 37; Patricia Weiss Fagen, "Peace in Central America," cited in Egan and Simmons, "Refugees and the Prospects for Peace and Development in Central America," 8.

148. *Refugee Reports* 11 (April 27, 1990): 1.

149. *La Prensa Centroamericana,* December 6, 1990.

150. *La Prensa Centroamericana,* February 22–28, 1991, July 5–11, 1991.

151. *Refugee Reports* 11 (April 27, 1990): 1–2.

152. Ibid., 2–3.

153. My interview with Janet Reno, November 6, 2003; Andes Viglucci, "A Victory for Nicaraguans," *Miami Herald,* June 25, 1997; "Reno to the Rescue," *Miami Herald,* July 12, 1997.

4. HUMANITARIANISM AND POLITICS

Epigraphs: National Press Club, Washington, D.C., March 1969. Cited in *The Globe and Mail,* October 16, 1999; Bill Frelick, "Refugees Can't Be Slotted into Neat Categories," *Toronto Star,* July 14, 1987; Canadian Council for Refugees, "Introduction," *State of Refugees in Canada,* November 2002, 2, www.web.net/~ccr/state .html#Introduction.

1. In 1867, the confederation consisted of Nova Scotia, New Brunswick, and Canada (Ontario and Quebec). Within a decade they were joined by Prince Edward Island, British Columbia, Rupert's Land, and the Northwest Territories. Ninette Kelley and Michael Trebilcock, *The Making of the Mosaic: A History of Canadian Immigration Policy* (Toronto: University of Toronto Press, 1998).

2. Ibid., 124–125. See also Bruno Ramírez, "Canada and the United States: Perspectives on Migration and Continental History," *Journal of American Ethnic History* 20 (Spring 2001): 50–70.

3. Viviane Renaud and Rosalinda Costa, "Immigrants in Quebec," *Canadian Social Trends,* Catalogue 11–008E (Ottawa: Statistics Canada, Summer 1995), 10–11.

4. *Facts and Figures: Immigration Overview, 1998* (Ottawa: Citizenship and Immigration Canada, 1999), 2; Harry R. Clarke and Lee Smith, "Labor Immigration and Capital Flows: Long-Term Australian, Canadian, and United States Experience," *International Migration Review* 30 (Winter 1996): 925–949.

5. Kelley and Trebilcock, *The Making of the Mosaic,* 137.

6. Doris M. Meissner et al., *International Migration Challenges in a New Era: A Report to the Trilateral Commission,* no. 44 (New York, Paris, and Tokyo: Trilateral Commission, 1993), 21–22.

7. Constantine Passaris, "The Role of Immigration in Canada's Demographic Outlook," *International Migration* 36 (1998): 97.

8. Jane Badets and Tina W. L. Chui, *Canada's Changing Immigrant Population* (Ottawa: Statistics Canada and Prentice-Hall Canada, 1994), 13. See also "Chinese Is Third after English, French in Canada," *Migration World* 26, nos. 1–2 (1998): 8.

9. The Department of Foreign Affairs and International Trade has a subdivision on Asia-Pacific affairs, the "first-ever geographically based allocation of ministerial responsibilities." G. Bruce Doern and John Kirton, "Foreign Policy," in G. Bruce Doern, Leslie A. Pal, and Brian W. Tomlin, eds., *Border Crossings: The Internationalization of Canadian Public Policy* (New York: Oxford University Press, 1996), 252.

10. The "family class" consists of immediate relatives such as spouse, children, and parents; the "assisted relatives class" includes siblings, grandparents, and aunts and uncles. Sponsorship of family and assisted relatives is open to citizens and permanent residents, and sponsors must assume financial responsibility for the immigrant for up to ten years.

11. Meissner et al., *International Migration Challenges in a New Era,* 17.

12. By the 1980s, many regarded Quebec as having the best assistance programs for immigrants. David H. Bai, "Canadian Immigration Policy: Twentieth-Century Initiatives in Admission and Settlement," *Migration World* 29, no. 3 (2001): 9–10; Meissner et al., *International Migration Challenges in a New Era,* 17–20; *International Migration Policies* (New York: Department of Economic and Social Affairs, Population Division, United Nations, 1998), 75; Renaud and Costa, "Immigrants in Quebec," 12; Charles D. Smith, "Trials and Errors: The Experience of Central American Refugees in Montreal," *Refuge* 5 (May 1986): 10.

13. Francophones constitute 84.5 percent of the Quebec population. Given the lower birth rates in Quebec (the lowest in Canada), increasing the French-speaking population is of immediate concern. Almost 90 percent of immigrants in Quebec live in Montreal. Renaud and Costa, "Immigrants in Quebec," 9–10; see also Arnold Panitch and Jeanne Marie Cragin, "Immigrating to Quebec: The Demographic Challenges of a Province Experiencing Low Fertility," *Migration World* 19, no. 4 (1991): 3–4.

14. Meissner et al., *International Migration Challenges in a New Era,* 17; Renaud and Costa, "Immigrants in Quebec," 9–10.

15. Joseph Bissett, "Canadian Policy on Refugees and Asylum Seekers," in *In Defense of the Alien,* vol. 9, Proceedings of the 1986 Annual National Legal Conference on Immigration and Refugee Policy (Staten Island, NY: Center for Migration Studies, 1987), 113–121.

16. Bai, "Canadian Immigration Policy," 9–10; Gerald H. Stobo, "The Canadian Refugee Determination System," *Texas International Law Journal* 29 (Summer 1994): 384; Howard Adelman, "Humanitarianism and Self-Interest: Canadian Refugee Policy and the Hungarian Refugees," in Peter R. Baehr and Geza Tessenyi, eds., *The New Refugee Hosting Countries: Call for Experience-Space for Innovation* (Utrecht: SIM, December 1991), 106; Lemco, *Canada and the Crisis in Central America,* 155; "Canada," *World Refugee Report, 1989* (Washington, D.C.: Bureau for Refugee Programs, Department of State, 1989), 108.

17. To qualify for either of the last two designated classes, individuals had to be outside their area of origin and not permanently resettled.

18. Tom Clark, "Human Rights versus Immigration Controls: A Canadian Profile," *World Survey: 1988 in Review* (US Committee for Refugees, 1988), 84–85; C. Michael Lanphier, "Asylum Policy in Canada: A Brief Overview," in Howard Adelman and C. Michael Lanphier, eds., *Refuge or Asylum: A Choice for Canada* (Toronto: York Lanes Press, 1990), 82.

19. "Canada," *World Refugee Report, 1989,* 108; Stobo, "The Canadian Refugee Determination System," 384; William Bauer, "Refugees, Victims, or Killers: The New Slave Trade?" *International Journal* 52 (Autumn 1997): 678; Meissner et al., *International Migration Challenges in a New Era,* 20.

20. Canada Employment and Immigration Commission, *New Directions: A Look at Canada's New Immigration Act and Regulations* (Hull: Minister of Supply and Services, 1978), 13.

21. The RSAC consisted of immigration officials as well as private citizens appointed by the minister of employment and immigration. A representative of the UNHCR attended RSAC sessions to ensure that Canada fulfilled its obligations as signatory to the UN Convention and Protocol. Gerald E. Dirks, *Controversy and Complexity: Canadian Immigration Policy during the 1980s* (Montreal: McGill-Queen's University Press, 1995), 78–79.

22. The Canadian sponsor must be a group of five individuals, usually of a faith-based community, ethnic association, or union. See David Matas (with Ilana Simon), *Closing the Doors: The Failure of Refugee Protection* (Toronto: Summerhill Press, 1989), 218–219.

23. Target Groups Project, *Immigrants in Canada: Selected Highlights* (Ottawa: Minister of Supply and Services Canada, 1990), 40.

24. Canada was excluded from the Pan-American Union, a predecessor to the OAS, because of its imperial ties to Great Britain. See chapter 2, "Canada and the OAS," in Lemco, *Canada and the Crisis in Central America;* see also MacFarlane, *Northern Shadows.*

25. The Trudeau government was particularly interested in developing its relationship with Mexico and Cuba. MacFarlane, *Northern Shadows,* 134–135.

26. Trade declined during 1984–89 as a result of Central American political instability and foreign debt. Lemco, *Canada and the Crisis in Central America,* 3, 55.

27. MacFarlane, *Northern Shadows,* 171–172.

28. Leger was a lay missionary engaged in social welfare work. See "Enfrenta la iglesia de Guatemala al gobierno de Romeo Lucas García," *El Día,* August 14, 1981.

29. At a 1981 meeting with US secretary of state Alexander Haig, MacGuigan read the State Department's "White Paper" on El Salvador, which documented the military support of Salvadoran rebels by foreign powers, namely, Nicaragua. Following that meeting, MacGuigan toned down his criticisms. See Liisa North and CAPA, eds., *Between War and Peace in Central America. Choices for Canada* (Toronto: Between the Lines, 1990), 205.

30. Antoine Char, "Canada: Quiet Opposition to US Policy in Central America," *Inter Press Service,* April 17 1984, http://web.lexis-nexis.com/universe/.

31. "Canada: No Protest to Washington over Mining of Nicaragua's Ports," *Inter Press Service,* April 13, 1984, http://web.lexis-nexis.com/universe/.

32. Lemco, *Canada and the Crisis in Central America,* 14.

33. When six Jesuits and their two housekeepers were brutally assassinated in El Salvador in November 1989, Canada suspended aid to that country once again.

34. The Contras were believed to be responsible for the 1986 murder of Father William Arsenault, a Catholic priest from Quebec involved in social welfare work in Honduras.

35. Dave Todd, "Ottawa Cancels Visas for Three Guatemalans," *Toronto Star,* November 21, 1992.

36. "Agencies Get $276,000 to Help Settle Refugees," *Toronto Star,* January 5, 1989.

37. The largest percentage of funding went to Honduras. North and CAPA, eds., *Between War and Peace in Central America,* 96–97.

38. Lemco, *Canada and the Crisis in Central America,* 65–66, 71. Canadian International Development Agency, *Summary of Canadian Aid to Central America* (Ottawa, 1986, 1988, and 1989), in North and CAPA, eds., *Between War and Peace in Central America,* 101.

39. In 1981, in a speech before Parliament, Canada's minister of employment and immigration, Lloyd Axworthy, stated that Canada's policy toward Central Americans was designed in consultation with the UNHCR. As a signatory to the

Convention on Refugees, Canada committed itself to uphold the UNHCR's goals and policies; and in the case of the Central Americans, the UNHCR's preference was to relocate displaced persons to neighboring countries rather than to distant third countries, unless they specifically asked to migrate there. Given that there was no tradition of migration to Canada from these nations, it was unlikely that large numbers would seek to come to Canada. See Dirks, *Controversy and Complexity*, 72–73.

40. Charles D. Smith, "Lessons from Latin American Exiles," in Adelman and Lanphier, eds., *Refuge or Asylum,* 99, 103–104.

41. Arch Mackenzie, "Canada's Refugee Policy Reflects Bias, Study Says," *Toronto Star,* July 11, 1988.

42. However, the private sponsorship of Central Americans never equaled that of Indochinese refugees. Ann Finlayson, "The Underground Railroad to Canada," *Maclean's,* May 13, 1985, 44; Paul Watson, "Canada 'Rescuing' 200 Salvadorans," *Toronto Star,* June 8, 1989; Rosie DiManno, "Crackdown on Refugees Protested; Keep Borders Open for Persecuted, Fort Erie Gathering Urges," *Toronto Star,* February 23, 1987.

43. During the amnesty period, El Salvador released approximately 550 prisoners and Canada accepted one-fifth of these. See "Canada Accepts 134 Freed Salvadoran Political Prisoners," *Refuge* 3 (October 1983): 4; Canada Employment and Immigration Commission, *Refugee Perspectives, 1984–1985* (Hull: Refugee Affairs Division, Policy and Program Development Branch, 1985).

44. See Lemco, *Canada and the Crisis in Central America,* 153; Howard Adelman and David Cox, "Overseas Refugee Policy," in Howard Adelman et al., eds., *Immigration and Refugee Policy: Australia and Canada Compared,* vol. 1 (Toronto: University of Toronto Press, 1994), 280.

45. In 1985, El Salvador produced the second-largest number of refugees to Canada after Vietnam. Canadian Council for Refugees, "Top Two Countries of Permanent Residence," *Resettlement Statistics,* November 6, 1996, 2, www.webb .net/%7Eccr/stat3a.htm#top. See also Lemco, *Canada and the Crisis in Central America,* 159.

46. Fernando G. Mata, *The Four Immigrant Waves from Latin America to Canada: Historical, Demographic and Social Profiles,* graduate research paper, York University, January 1985, cited in Howard Adelman, *A Survey of Postwar Refugee Intakes and Developments in Canadian Refugee Policy,* report prepared for the CEIC (Toronto: Centre for Refugee Studies, York University, August 1990), 30.

47. R. A. Girard, "Canadian Refugee Policy: Government Perspectives," in Adelman and Lanphier, eds., *Refuge or Asylum ,* 119.

48. Cited in Brian Egan and Alan Simmons, "Refugees and the Prospects for Peace and Development in Central America," *Refuge* 13 (March 1994): 5.

49. Smith, "Trials and Errors," 12.

50. Finlayson, "The Underground Railroad to Canada," 43.

51. Ibid.

52. Marita Hernández, "Many in US Turn to Canada," *Los Angeles Times,* March 9, 1987.

53. Rosie DiManno, "Aid Group Consider a New Underground Railroad," *Toronto Star,* February 24, 1987.

54. Gil Loescher, *Beyond Charity: International Cooperation and the Global Refugee Crisis* (New York: Oxford University Press, 1993), 108.

55. Joseph Bissett, "Canada's Refugee Determination System and the Effect of US Immigration Law," in *In Defense of the Alien,* vol. 10, Proceedings of the 1987 Annual National Legal Conference on Immigration and Refugee Policy (New York: Center for Migration Studies, 1988), 62–63; "Central Americans Pour into Canada Seeking New Homes," *Toronto Star,* January 14, 1987; Arch Mackenzie, "U.S. Crackdown on Refugee Claims Swelling Numbers Coming to Canada," *Toronto Star,* January 15, 1987.

56. The *Toronto Star* reported that the refugees were taking advantage of Greyhound's two-for-one sale. David Lord, "Fearful Central Americans Hoping for New Life in Canada," *Toronto Star,* January 16, 1987; Herbert H. Denton, "Illegal Aliens Flee U.S. for Refuge in Canada; 'Bus People' Influx Spurred by U.S. Law," *Washington Post,* February 23, 1987.

57. Laurie Monsebraaten, "CNE Dorm to House 140 Latin Refugees Starting March 1," *Toronto Star,* February 20, 1987; Denton, "Illegal Aliens Flee U.S. for Refuge in Canada."

58. Tom Clark, "Human Rights versus Immigration Controls: A Canadian Profile," *World Refugee Survey: 1988 in Review* (Washington, D.C.: US Committee for Refugees, 1988), 84; Hernández, "Many in US Turn to Canada," 1.

59. Daniel Stoffman, "Making Room for Real Refugees," *International Journal* 52 (Autumn 1997): 576; Lemco, *Canada and the Crisis in Central America,* 155.

60. Editorial, "Refugee Policy Doubts," *Toronto Star,* February 25, 1987.

61. Olivia Ward, "US Is Blocking Refugees to Canada," *Toronto Star,* October 18, 1987.

62. Editorial, "Be Calm on Refugees," *Toronto Star,* August 1, 1987.

63. David Hatter, Matthew Horsman, and Philip Mathias, "Refugees: Tough Choices," *Financial Post,* July 20, 1987.

64. Aileen Ballantyne and Clyde Sanger, "When the Boat Comes In," *Guardian* (London), August 14, 1986; John F. Burns, "Sikhs Wade Ashore in Canada Clutching Attache Cases," *New York Times,* July 19, 1987.

65. Brian McAndrew and Dale Brazao, "Ottawa to Stem Refugee Flood," *Toronto Star,* February 20, 1987; "Canada Cracks Down on Refugees, Begins Deportations

to U.S.," *Inter-Press Service,* February 20, 1987, http//web.lexis.nexis.com; Olivia Ward, "Refugee Bills Are Weighted to Security," *Toronto Star,* August 18, 1987.

66. See, for example: Arch MacKenzie, "Ottawa Plans Strategy to Control Refugee Flood," *Toronto Star,* February 11, 1987; Michael Hanlon, "Hunted Vessel Left Dutch Port with Just Crew Official Says," *Toronto Star,* August 3, 1987; Arch MacKenzie, "Changes to Refugee Bill Just Tinkering, Critics Say," *Toronto Star,* June 4, 1988.

67. Editorial, "Be Calm on Refugees"; Frank Jones, "PM's Phrase Is 'Alien' to Canada," *Toronto Star,* August 6, 1987; Ward, "Refugee Bills Are Weighted to Security."

68. "Refugee Entries Restricted," *Facts on File,* February 27, 1987, 130 G3.

69. Stobo, "The Canadian Refugee Determination System," 418; Edward Opoku-Dapaah, "Integration of Landed Refugee Claimants in Canada: Toward an Explanatory Model," *Refuge* 13 (February 1994): 11.

70. *Singh v. Canada* [1985], Minister of Employment and Immigration, 14 C.R.R., SCC 13. Harbhajan Singh and six other refugees appealed to the Supreme Court when the Federal Court of Canada dismissed their application for a judicial review of the decision handed down by the Immigration Appeals Board. The petitioners argued that they had been denied a full oral hearing in the refugee determination process. The judges ruled in their favor, arguing that refugees were entitled to the same protections accorded to Canadian citizens. April 4, the anniversary of the judgment, is celebrated in Canada as Refugee Rights Day.

71. According to the Plaut Report (1986), the Refugee Board was to be guided by certain fundamental principals: (a) Canada is morally and legally bound not to return Convention refugees who are within its borders to the land of their persecution. (b) Refugee determination is not an immigration matter. Immigration and refugee determination converge only in the person of the refugee claimant. (c) Refugee determinations must be made by an independent decision-making body. (d) The system must meet Canadian standards of natural justice and comply with the country's legal standards of procedural fairness. (e) The government must assume the good faith of the claimant. (f) The process must be expeditious. (g) And the focus of the claims process should always be on the potential refugee, not on misuse of the system. See Lanphier's discussion of the Plaut Report in "Asylum Policy in Canada," 82. See also Bissett, "Canadian Policy on Refugees and Asylum Seekers," 116–117.

72. The IRB replaced the Immigration Appeals Board. The IRB is made up of the Convention Refugee Determination Division and the Immigration Appeal Division. Meissner et al., *International Migration Challenges in a New Era,* 23.

73. "Canadian Asylum Rates at 75 percent, Government Seeks to Streamline Process," *Refugee Reports* (October 26, 1990): 15.

74. In the bill anyone who "knowingly organizes, induces, aids or abets or attempts to organize, induce, aid or abet the coming into Canada" of a person without valid documents is guilty of the offense—perhaps even if he or she were leading the claimant to a border guard. Mary Janigan et al., "Saying No," *Maclean's,* August 24, 1987, 10.

75. Arch Mackenzie, "Refugees' Lives Threatened by New Bill, MPs Warned," *Toronto Star,* August 19, 1987.

76. Arch MacKenzie, "Refugee Bill Puts Lives in Danger Lawyer Says," *Toronto Star,* September 4, 1987.

77. "Bill Will Close Door to Canada," *Toronto Star,* July 15, 1987.

78. Janigan et al., "Saying No," 8.

79. M. Rose and S. Aikenhead, "New Policy, New Protests," *Maclean's,* May 18, 1987, 16, reported in Kelley and Trebilcock, *The Making of the Mosaic,* 419; see also David Hatter, Matthew Horsman, and Philip Mathias, "Refugees: Tough Choices," *Financial Post,* July 20, 1987, 1.

80. "Canada's More Restrictive Asylum System in Place," *Refugee Reports* (January 27, 1989): 10–11.

81. Kelley and Trebilcock, *The Making of the Mosaic,* 386.

82. Lorne Waldman, "Canada's Doing It Right in Central America," *Toronto Star,* November 5, 1987.

83. Ward, "US Is Blocking Refugees to Canada"; Kelly Toughill, "Refugee Policy Called Death Sentence for Many," *Toronto Star,* October 25, 1987.

84. Janigan et al., "Saying No," 8.

85. Arch MacKenzie, "Altered Bill on Refugees Tightens Entry," *Toronto Star,* June 3, 1988.

86. See "Canadian Asylum Rates at 75 percent, Government Seeks to Streamline Process," *Refugee Reports* (October 26, 1990): 12–15.

87. Smith, "Trials and Errors," 10.

88. The Iranians (91 percent), Lebanese (72 percent), Somalis (94 percent), and Sri Lankans (90 percent) were also among the highest. "Canadian Asylum Rates at 75 Percent," 14.

89. Stobo, "The Canadian Refugee Determination System," 385; Meissner et al., *International Migration Challenges in a New Era,* 24.

90. During the 1990s, inadequate funding made it difficult to keep a stable body of personnel and maintain consistent services, and thus the quality of services varied from city to city. For a description of services available to refugees and immigrants, see Canadian Council for Refugees, *Best Settlement Practices: Set-*

tlement Services for Refugees and Immigrants in Canada (Montreal: Canadian Council for Refugees, February 1998).

91. Jeff Crisp and Clive Nettleton, eds., *Refugee Reports, 1984* (London: British
Refugee Council, 1984); "Canada," *World Refugee Report, 1989,* 109–110.

92. However, a 1993 poll revealed that 72 percent of Canadians surveyed
believed ethnic or racial groups should "adapt to the Canadian value system rather
than maintain their differences." Brian Bergman, "Pride and Prejudice," *Maclean's,*
November 7, 1994, 32. For a discussion of the Multiculturalism Act, see: Fernando G. Mata, "The Multiculturalism Act and Refugee Integration in Canada,"
Refuge 13 (February 1994): 17; and Perry Romberg, "Service Delivery to Refugees and Immigrants: Toward an Integrated Approach," *Refuge* 13 (February
1994): 27.

93. "Canada," *World Refugee Report, 1989,* 108.

94. André Jacob, "Adaptation of Salvadoran Refugees in Montreal," *Migration
World* 20 (January–February 1992): 21–24.

95. Smith, "Trials and Errors," 10–11; see also Francine Juteau, "Divorce and
the Migration Process among Salvadorians in Montreal," in Satya P. Sharma et
al., eds., *Immigrants and Refugees in Canada: A National Perspective on Ethnicity, Multiculturalism, and Cross-Cultural Adjustment* (Saskatoon: University of Saskatchewan
Press, 1991), 282.

96. A 1991 study of 15,950 Central American men revealed that they were
employed in the following occupational categories: managerial and administra-
tive-related (4.6 percent); professional and related (8.7 percent); clerical and related
(7.9 percent); sales (3.4 percent); service (20.3 percent); primary (agriculture, mining, etc.) (6.6 percent); processing (11.9 percent); product fabricating (13.9 per-
cent); construction trades (9.7 percent); and other (12.9 percent). Thirty percent
of Central American women were in service occupations (as compared to 31 percent of southern European women). The employment distribution of 11,435
Central American women among occupational categories was as follows: managerial (3.5 percent); professional (12.5 percent); clerical (17.6 percent); sales (5.1
percent); service (29.9 percent); primary (5.6 percent); processing (3.6 percent);
product fabricating (15.0 percent); construction (0.7 percent); other (6.4 percent).
See Badets and Chui, *Canada's Changing Immigrant Population,* 57–60.

97. Cited in Egan and Simmons, "Refugees and the Prospects for Peace and
Development in Central America," 5.

98. MacKenzie, "Canada's Refugee Policy Reflects Bias, Study Says"; Luisa
D'Amato, "Second K-W Family Faces Deportation," *Kitchener-Waterloo Record,*
May 11, 1992.

99. Immigration and Refugee Board, "Asylum Claims to Canada, 1984 to June

1993," *Immigration Board Statistical Summary* (Ottawa: Immigration and Refugee Board, July 19, 1993).

100. Glenn Allen, "Beefing Up the Border," *Maclean's*, August 31, 1992, 13.

101. The bill also required Convention Refugee Determination Division panelists to give a unanimous decision in certain cases, rather than the standard one affirmative vote. Such cases included applicants who arrived without the proper identity documents; those who migrated from a country regarded as safe; and those who returned to the country of persecution for any given time during the application process.

102. Lorne Waldman, "Draconian Refugee Bill a Tory Stop to Reform," *Toronto Star*, August 19, 1992.

103. Quoted in Allen, "Beefing Up the Border," 14.

104. Quoted ibid., 12.

105. "Canada, United States Draft Agreement on Returning Asylum Seekers," *Refugee Reports* (November 30, 1995): 9.

106. In 1994, one-third of the twenty-two thousand asylum applicants in Canada entered via the United States. "Canada and the United States Consider Returning Transiting Asylum Seekers," *Refugee Reports* (March 31, 1995): 12. Complicating matters was the 1993 decision *Nguyen v. Canada,* in which the court ruled that denying access to the refugee determination procedure was not a violation of the principles of fundamental justice embodied in the Charter. According to Nazaré Albuquerque Abell, "Thus asylum seekers do not possess a substantive right to have their claims determined in Canada, but do have sufficient procedural safeguards to ensure that their rights to life, liberty, and security of person are protected by the procedural guarantees of fundamental justice." See Abell, "Safe Country Provisions in Canada and in the European Union: A Critical Assessment," *International Migration Review* 31 (Fall 1997): 580.

107. Henry Kram, "Western Nations Are Raising Barriers to Refugees," *New York Times,* March 27, 1989; Daniel Stoffman, "The High Costs of Our Refugee System," *Toronto Star,* September 21, 1992.

108. The Convention Determining the State Responsible for Examining Applications for Asylum Lodged in One of the Member States of the European Communities (Dublin, 1990) and the Gradual Abolition of Checks at their Common Borders (Schengen, 1990) sought to eliminate duplicate applications for asylum in the various member states of the EU. If the applicant held several visas, the state that issued the visa with the longest period of validity was responsible for assessing the claim.

109. Abell, "Safe Country Provisions in Canada and in the European Union," 570; Janigan et al., "Saying No," 8.

110. Canada also tried to negotiate an agreement with European nations but was similarly unsuccessful. "Canada–United States of America: Discussions on Responsibility-Sharing for Asylum Seekers Adjourned," *International Journal of Refugee Law* 10 (January/April 1998): 256; Abell, "Safe Country Provisions in Canada and in the European Union," 583–588.

111. "Canada, United States Draft Agreement on Returning Asylum Seekers," *Refugee Reports* (November 30, 1995): 8–10.

112. Elizabeth Ferris, "The Backlash against Immigrants in the USA and the Canadian-US Memorandum of Agreement," *Refugee Update* 28 (Spring 1996): 4.

113. Ibid., 4.; Bill Frelick, "Refugee Ping-Pong, North American Style," *Chicago Tribune,* September 5, 2002, in e-mail from Janet Dench, CCR listserve, September 5, 2002.

114. "Canada, United States Draft Agreement on Returning Asylum Seekers," 10; "Canada–United States of America: Discussions on Responsibility-Sharing for Asylum Seekers Adjourned," *International Journal of Refugee Law* 10 (January/April 1998): 256; Ferris, "The Backlash against Immigrants in the USA," 4; "North America–Immigration: Groups Oppose New US-Canadian Pact," *Inter-Press Service,* March 19, 1996, http://web.lexis-nexis.com; "Canada and the United States Consider Returning Transiting Asylum Seekers," *Refugee Reports* (March 31, 1995): 12.

115. Adelman and Cox, "Overseas Refugee Policy," 271.

116. Abell, "Safe Country Provisions in Canada and in the European Union," 587. The Canadian Council for Refugees dubbed the agreement "None Is Too Many" in reference to the response given by a Canadian official in 1945 to the question of how many Jewish refugees Canada should accept. Canadian Council for Refugees, "Safe Third Country," *State of Refugees in Canada,* November 2002. http://www.web.net/~ccr/state.html#Introduction.

117. Several groups will be exempted from these provisions, including unaccompanied minors, those with relatives in Canada, and those from countries to which Canada does not deport. In 2004 this list included Zimbabwe, Burundi, Congo, Liberia, Afghanistan, Iraq, Rwanda, and Haiti.

118. During the 1990s, roughly two hundred thousand people immigrated to Canada each year. *Facts and Figures: Immigration Overview, 1998,* 2.

119. "Tory MP Wants Visa Requirement for People Fleeing Central America," *Toronto Star,* January 20, 1987.

120. Robert Holton and Michael Lanphier, "Public Opinion, Immigration and Refugees," in Adelman et al., eds., *Immigration and Refugee Policy,* 132.

121. Lemco, *Canada and the Crisis in Central America,* 147–151.

122. Ibid., 14.

123. Ibid., 147–148.

124. Ibid., 70; North and CAPA, eds., *Between War and Peace in Central America*, 51.

125. Eighty percent of bilateral aid funds must be used for the purchase of Canadian goods and services. See Lemco, *Canada and the Crisis in Central America*, 65–66, 71.

126. North and CAPA, eds., *Between War and Peace in Central America*, 51.

127. The demonstration was organized by the Toronto Anti-Intervention Coalition. "Protest War in Nicaragua, Canada Urged," *Toronto Star*, June 7, 1987.

128. MacFarlane, *Northern Shadows*, 164–167.

129. Janice Turner, "Hundreds Condemn 'Draconian' Policies to Thwart Refugees," *Toronto Star*, March 9, 1987.

130. The Canadian Institute for International Peace and Security was created by Parliament in 1984. North and CAPA, eds., *Between War and Peace in Central America*, 11–15.

131. The CCR was established in 1977, and its membership represents over 180 agencies and organizations "involved in the settlement, sponsorship, and protection of refugees and immigrants." According to its mission statement, the CCR advocates for the rights of refugees and immigrants through media relations, government relations, research, and public education. Canadian Council for Refugees, "Mission Statement," www.web.ca/~ccr/aboutccr.htm. Before immigrating to Canada in 1990, former CCR president Francisco Rico-Martínez was a law professor and human rights investigator in El Salvador. Together with his wife, he later operated Hamilton House, a shelter for refugee women in Toronto. Carol Thiessen, "Refugees Enrich Canadian Society," *Canadian Mennonite*, October 25, 1999, in Lexis-Nexis database, http://web.lexis-nexis.com. See also Lemco, *Canada and the Crisis in Central America*, 70–71; Bauer, "Refugees, Victims, or Killers," 689.

132. Janice Turner, "Bill Could Force Refugee Aid Groups to Go Underground," *Toronto Star*, August 14, 1987.

133. Kelley and Trebilcock, *The Making of the Mosaic*, 389.

134. Christopher S. Warren, "Salvaging Lives after Torture," *New York Times*, August 17, 1986, 18.

135. "Deportation Stalled for Woman with HIV," *Kitchener-Waterloo Record*, July 31, 1993.

136. The Inter-Church Committee on Human Rights in Latin America began as an ad-hoc committee on Chile in response to the human rights violations that followed the 1973 coup against Salvador Allende's government, but later its focus also included Argentina, Brazil, and Uruguay. In 1977 the committee was renamed to reflect its mission to examine human rights abuses throughout Latin America. It is an ecumenical coalition of nine major national church bodies including the

Anglican, Lutheran, Presbyterian, Roman Catholic, and United Churches, as well as religious orders and groups affiliated with the Roman Catholic Church, such as the Scarboro Foreign Mission Society, the Canadian Religious Conference, and the Upper Canada Province of the Jesuit Fathers. ICCHRLA, "Submission to the 36th Session of the United Nations Commission on Human Rights (1980)," in John R. Williams, ed., *Canadian Churches and Social Justice* (Toronto: Anglican Book Centre and James Lorimer and Company, 1984), 230, 241–242; see also Dirks, *Controversy and Complexity,* 73.

137. Interview of David Bickford by Peter MacFarlane, included in MacFarlane, *Northern Shadows,* 166.

138. ICCHRLA, "Submission to the 36th Session of the United Nations Commission on Human Rights (1980)," 246–247.

139. Lemco, *Canada and the Crisis in Central America,* 147.

140. In 1987, the Supreme Court of Canada finally cleared the way for Regalado's deportation, but the delay had bought him critical time. In 1982, a Salvadoran journalist with his history would have been assassinated if sent back to his country. "Court Upholds Plan to Deport Salvadoran Journalist," *Toronto Star,* January 30, 1987; MacFarlane, 200–201.

141. The Canadian Charter of Rights and Freedoms, drafted in 1982, provides a list of rights and privileges afforded to every resident of Canada. Dale Brazao, "Church Groups May Go to Court over Refugee Curbs," *Toronto Star,* February 21, 1987.

142. "Canadian Asylum Rates at 75 percent, Government Seeks to Streamline Process," *Refugee Reports* (October 26, 1990): 15.

143. DiManno, "Crackdown on Refugees Protested."

144. Finlayson, "The Underground Railroad to Canada," 44; Agnes Bongers, "For Isaac, It's Like Being Born Again," *Hamilton Spectator,* November 26, 1991; "Dakota Priest Feels Compelled to Help Refugees Reach Canada," *Toronto Star,* March 13, 1987.

145. Lindsay Scotton, "Refugees Take Overground Railroad," *Toronto Star,* January 24, 1987: Nadine Epstein, "Refugees Find Sanctuary in Canada," *Christian Science Monitor,* December 30, 1986, 3.

146. Michael McAteer, "Church Sanctuary for Refugees?" *Toronto Star,* December 26, 1987, A1.

147. Janigan et al., "Saying No," 10; MacKenzie, "Refugees' Lives Threatened by New Bill, MPs Warned"; Lois Sweet, "'Mama Nancy's House Known for Warmth, Love," *Toronto Star,* November 20, 1987; Matas (with Simon), *Closing the Doors,* 223.

148. David Matas, "Canadian Sanctuary," n.d., photocopied article found in Resource Centre, Immigration and Refugee Board, Ottawa.

149. Quoted in Plaut, *Asylum,* 135–136.

150. Matas (with Simon), *Closing the Doors,* 218.

151. "Canada: Less Welcome," *Economist,* November 5, 1994, 42; Anthony Wilson-Smith, "Is Canada a Soft Touch?" *Maclean's,* November 7, 1994, 28; "Unwelcome Aliens," *Economist,* November 15, 1997, 37.

152. "Canadians Clash over Cost of Diversity," *Migration World* 26, no. 3 (1998): 9.

153. Stoffman, "Making Room for Real Refugees," 576; Anthony Wilson-Smith, "Is Canada a Soft Touch?" *Maclean's,* November 7, 1994, 28.

154. Wilson-Smith, "Is Canada a Soft Touch?" 28.

155. Andrew Phillips, "Trouble on the Border," *Maclean's,* August 3, 1998, 31.

156. In 1993, the majority of immigrants settled in Ontario (54 percent) followed by Quebec (19 percent), British Columbia (14 percent) and Alberta (9 percent). Sixty percent of all immigrants lived in Toronto, Montreal, and Vancouver. Paul Kaihla, "Canada's Changing Face," *Maclean's,* December 30, 1996, 38; Brian Bergman, "Pride and Prejudice," *Maclean's,* November 7, 1994, 32; "Battling over Immigration," *Maclean's,* February 14, 1994, 17; Chris Wood, "A New Chill in Relations," *Maclean's,* February 3, 1997, 33; *Vancouver Sun,* October 12, 1999, in e-mail from Janet Dench, CCR listserve (York University), October 12, 1999; Meissner et al., *International Migration Challenges in a New Era,* 21-22.

157. In 1993, family immigrants made up 53 percent of the total number of immigrants, and even Immigration Minister Sergio Marchi proposed slimming this percentage down to 45, since one family sponsor in seven reneged on his commitment to guarantee support for his family member, thus costing the government seven hundred million dollars a year in welfare assistance to the sponsored family members. "Canada: Less Welcome," *Economist,* November 5, 1994, 42; "Unwelcome Aliens," *Economist,* November 15, 1997, 37.

158. Kelley and Trebilcock, *The Making of the Mosaic,* 387

159. "Canadians Clash over Cost of Diversity," 9.

160. In 1991, Canadian contributions to the UNHCR were 50.7 million dollars. Stoffman, "The High Costs of our Refugee System."

161. From 1989 to 1991, only 20 percent of unsuccessful claimants were actually removed. These figures do not include those who left voluntarily or who were not returned because of the instability of their countries. Kelley and Trebilcock, *The Making of the Mosaic,* 435; Martin Collacott, "Canada Is a Great Country—for Refugees," *National Post,* n.d., in e-mail from N. Gitanjali Lena, CCR listserve, August 14, 2001.

162. John Spears, "No Room for Refugees, Mayor Says," *Toronto Star,* October 13, 1999, in e-mail from Janet Dench, CCR listserve (York University), October 13, 1999.

163. In the first half of the 1990s an average of thirty thousand claims were made each year. In 1998, under twenty-five thousand claims were filed. E-mail from Janet Dench, CCR listserve (York University), "Migrants—Qs and As," October 13, 1999. See also UNHCR, "The State of the World's Refugees" (1993), cited in Abell, "Safe Country Provisions in Canada and in the European Union," 577. By 1993, the Canadian per capita ratio of asylum seekers to population is, according to the UNHCR, "among the lowest in the industrialized world and cannot compare with the reception rates in many poor countries."

164. E-mail from Janet Dench, CCR listserve (York University), "Migrants—Qs and As," October 13, 1999.

165. Bai, "Canadian Immigration Policy," 11.

166. "How Many and What Immigrants Canada Needs?" *Central News Agency,* January 23, 1989, http;//web.lexis-nexis.com.

167. Allan Thompson, "Caplan Expected to Reject Pleas for Immigration Hike," *Toronto Star,* n.d., forwarded in e-mail from Janet Dench, CCR listserve (York University), October 30, 1999.

168. North and CAPA, eds., *Between War and Peace in Central America,* 132.

CONCLUSION

Epigraph: Canadian Council for Refugees, "Introduction," *State of Refugees in Canada,* November 2002, 2, www.web.net/~ccr/state.html# Introduction.

1. Mexico initiated the first meeting, in Puebla. Since 1996, the Regional Conference on Migration has met in Panama City, Ottawa, San Salvador, Washington, D.C., San José, Antigua, and Cancún. See www.crmsv.org. A similar conference, the South American Migration Dialogue, sponsored by the International Organization for Migration, has brought together twelve South American nations since 1999, as well as international and regional organizations, to discuss migration issues.

2. "Fifth Regional Conference on Migration held in Washington, D.C.," *US Newswire,* March 28, 2000, www.lexis-nexis.org.

3. Other examples of plans of action include the Dublin and Schengen agreements of the European Union; Southeast Asia's Comprehensive Plan of Action for the repatriation of Indochinese refugees; the Commonwealth of Independent States' "plan of action" regarding migration within or from the former Soviet Union; and the South American Migration Dialogue. Melanie Nezer, "The Puebla Process: US Migration Controls Move South of the Border," *World Refugee Survey 1999,* 1–2, www.refugees.org/world/articles/wrs99_migrationcontrols .htm.

4. Elena Gallegos, "Zedillo: México y Guatemala buscan construir una 'fron-

tera ejemplar,'" *La Jornada,* September 10, 1996, www.jornada.unam.mx/1996/
sp96/960910/zedilloguate.txt.

5. Ten drug cartels from Colombia and Mexico operate on the Tecún Umán–
Ciudad Hidalgo border. Kyra Núñez, "México se integra a la Organización Internacional de las Migraciones," *La Jornada,* June 4, 2002, www.jornada.unam
.mx/2002/jun02/020604/041n1soc.php?.

6. An estimated 40 percent of the undocumented Central Americans were
Guatemalans. See María Cristina Renard, "La frontera escondida," *La Jornada,*
October 22, 2000, www.jornada.unam.mx/2000/octo0/001020/mas-frontera
.html.

7. By February 2005, an increase in political crimes was reported, including
the assassination of labor leaders, intellectuals, and journalists. See www.crispaz
.org/news/list/2005.

8. Following the earthquakes, the United States granted Salvadorans TPS until
March 2005.

9. Salvadoran immigrants sent an estimated 2.1 billion dollars in remittances
to relatives in 2003. Susan Coutin, "The Odyssey of Salvadoran Asylum Seekers," *NACLA Report on the Americas* 37, no. 6 (May/June 2004), in e-mail from
Alejandro Segura Loarte, CCR listserve, May 17, 2004.

10. Renard, "La frontera escondida."

11. Many of the gang members were former Salvadoran military deported from
the United States. They were easily identifiable by the "MS" tattoo on their arms.
Alma E. Muñoz, "Ex militares Salvadoreños, azote de migrantes," *La Jornada,* May
9, 1997, www.jornada.unam.mx/1997/may97/970509/militares.html; Juan Balboa, "Tecún Umán, Guatemala, emporio de polleros," *La Jornada,* May 4, 1997,
www.jornada.unam.mx/1997/may97/970504/polleros.html.

12. The Centro de Recursos Centroamerianos is located in El Salvador. The
Guatemalan consulate in Tapachula reported that at least a hundred nationals went
missing every year. Núñez, "México se integra a la Organización Internacional
de las Migraciones"; Alberto Najar, "El costo de cuidar el patio trasero," *La Jornada,* February 9, 2003, www.jornada.unam.mx/2003/feb03/030209/mas-najar
.html.

13. Friedland and Rodríguez y Rodríguez, *Seeking Safe Ground,* 32.

14. Frelick, *Running the Gauntlet,* 14–16.

15. "Abusos en México contra migrantes, acusa el Congreso de El Salvador,"
La Jornada, July 26, 1998, www.jornada.unam.mx/1998/jul98/980726/salvador
.html; Alberto Najar, "El costo de cuidar el patio trasero," *La Jornada,* February
9, 2003, www.jornada.unam.mx/2003/feb03/030209/mas-najar.html.

16. Donald Kerwin, "Migrant Crossing Deaths, Immigrant Families, and Low-
Wage Laborers on the US–Mexico Border," *In Defense of the Alien,* vol. 24, Pro-

ceedings of the 2001 Annual Legal Conference on Immigration and Refugee Policy (Staten Island, NY: Center for Migration Studies, 2001): 62–63.

17. Ibid., 63.

18. In 1993, for example, the United States reimbursed Mexico 424,000 dollars for deporting Chinese nationals interdicted at sea, heading for the United States. Gzesh, "So Close to the United States, So Far from God."

19. Nezer, "The Puebla Process: US Migration Controls Move South of the Border," 3–4.

20. Georgina Saldierna, "Operative internacional logró el arresto de casi 8 mil ilegales," *La Jornada*, June 28, 2001, www.jornada.unam.mx/2001/jun01/010628/046n1soc.html; Velia Jaramillo, "Mexico's 'Southern Plan': The Facts," *World Press Review* 48 (September 2001), www.worldpress.org/0901feature22.html.

21. According to the 9/11 Commission's investigations, as many as fifteen of the nineteen hijackers could have been intercepted by border authorities. Richard A. Clarke, "Ten Years Later," *Atlantic Monthly,* January/February 2005, 64 n. 6.

22. The US Visitor and Immigrant Status Indicator Technology (US-VISIT).

23. CNN also reported that police officers across the United States were now carrying handheld wireless computers to access information on suspected criminals from large commercial databases. See Catherine Solyom, "US Drops Red, White, and Blue Curtain," *Gazette,* August 27, 2004, in e-mail from Janet Dench, CCR listserve, August 27, 2004; Paul Weinberg, "Homeland Security beyond US Borders," *OneWorld,* July 15, 2004, in e-mail from Janet Dench, CCR listserve, July 16, 2004.

24. US Department of Homeland Security, "Fact Sheet: Vision for 21st Century Immigration and Border Management System," January 25, 2005, in e-mail from Alejandro Segura Loarte, CCR listserve, January 26, 2005.

25. The proposed budget for fiscal year 2006 includes funding for the Refugee Corps, within the Department of Homeland Security, and increased funding for resettlement-related assistance. Tom Hamburger and Peter Wallsten, "Refugees' Tales Heard by Powerful Audience of One," *Los Angeles Times,* February 14, 2005, in e-mail from Janet Dench, CCR listserve, February 14, 2005; Refugee Council USA, "Fewer Refugees Being Rescued," in e-mail from Janet Dench, CCR listserve, March 22, 2005.

26. Nina Bernstein and Marc Santora, "Asylum Seekers Treated Poorly, U.S. Panel Says," *New York Times,* February 8, 2005, in e-mail from Janet Dench, CCR listserve, February 8, 2005.

27. The bill broadens the definition of a terrorist organization and makes it easier to deport long-term, permanent residents for providing nonviolent humanitarian support to organizations regarded as terroristic. The bill is opposed by a broad coalition of faith-based organizations and other refugee advocates.

28. Kuhner, "Detention of Asylum Seekers in Mexico," 59; Juan Balboa, "Pre-ocupa a las autoridades de Chiapas la migración masiva hacia Estados Unidos," *La Jornada,* December 22, 2002, www.jornada.unam.mx/2002/dec02/021222/005n1pol.php?; US Committee on Refugees, "Country Report: Mexico" (2002), www.refugees.org/world/countryrpt/amer_carib/mexico.htm.

29. Alberto Najar, "El costo de cuidar el patio trasero," *La Jornada,* February 9, 2003, www.jornada.unam.mx/2003/feb03/030209/mas-najar.html.

30. "Sgro to Curb Refugee Claimants' Appeals," *Toronto Star,* July 26, 2004, in email from Janet Dench, CCR listserve, July 26, 2004; Andrew Duffy, "False Travel Papers Curtailed," *National Post,* December 28, 2004, in e-mail from Janet Dench, CCR listserve, December 28, 2004.

31. According to the Mackenzie Institute, which monitors political violence and terrorism, Canada was home to ten thousand terrorists. Canadian legislators were hesitant to act, claimed the report, because front groups for these terrorist organizations courted politicians and guaranteed them the "ethnic vote." David Pugliese, "10,000 Terrorists in Canada: A Report," *Ottawa Citizen,* July 9, 2003, in e-mail from Janet Dench, CCR listserve, July 9, 2003.

32. The new law established two categories of refugees: "source country," for individuals who were facing persecution in a specific number of countries and are still in their country of origin (El Salvador and Guatemala were two of the six "source countries"); and "country of asylum," for individuals who were affected by civil war, armed conflict, or massive violation of human rights. Refugees could receive protection through either a resettlement program, where, in consultation with the UNHCR and other international organizations, they were identified abroad and resettled in Canada; or through in-land claims after they arrived in Canada or at a border entry point.

As in the 1976 Immigration Act, the government established a target for government-assisted refugees and a "range" for the privately sponsored. (In 2002, the range for the latter was established at twenty-nine hundred to forty-two hundred, while the official government target was set at seventy-five hundred.) A back-log of fifty-three thousand cases existed by the end of 2002, and the new law also sought ways to address this problem. "Canada's Refugee Policies in Flux," http://news.bbc.co.uk/1/hi/wprld/americas/3078743.stm. See also Canadian Council for Refugees, "Resettlement Program," *State of Refugees in Canada,* November 2002, p. 7, www.web.net/~ccr/state.html#Introduction.

33. Some in-land claims are the exception. If an applicant has lived for a period of time in Canada and/or has family members who reside legally, his or her application will be processed in Canada. Potential claims were also discouraged through several additional measures: visa requirements; document checks before boarding aircraft; and fines on airlines and ships for bringing refugee claimants to Canada.

Canadian Council for Refugees, "Interdiction," *State of Refugees in Canada,* November 2002, p. 15, www.web.net/~ccr/state.html#Introduction.

34. Sue Bailey, "New Rules Shut Out Refugees: Advocates," Canadian Press, December 22, 2004, in e-mail from Mary Boyce, CCR listserve, December 23, 2004.

35. Canadian Council for Refugees, "Ten Reasons Why Safe Third Country Is a Bad Deal," n.d., from e-mail circulated on December 23, 2004, arguments based on text found at www.web.net/~ccr/10reasons.html.

36. In 2003, for example, over thirty thousand claims were made, but only one claimant was found ineligible on the basis of security inadmissibility. See Canadian Council for Refugees, "CCR Decries Security Policy's Impact on Refugees," April 28, 2004, in e-mail from Janet Dench, CCR listserve, April 28, 2004.

37. In 2004, five Muslim men, in Montreal, Ottawa, and Toronto, had been detained from eighteen months to four years without charge or bail. "Action against Security Certificates," in e-mail from No One Is Illegal Vancouver, CCR listserve, December 8, 2004; Andrew Duffy, "Testing Time for Justice," *Gazette,* December 13, 2004, in e-mail from Janet Dench, CCR listserve, December 13, 2004.

38. Sean Gordon, "CSIS Role in Arar Case Scrutinized," *Ottawa Citisen,* December 23, 2003; Francine Dubé, "Arar Sues Canada for $400M over Syria Ordeal," *National Post,* April 22, 2004.

39. Victor Malarek, "Refugee Claimant Totals Drop," *Globe and Mail,* September 13, 2002, in e-mail from Janet Dench, CCR listserve, September 14, 2002.

40. "IRB Statistics, Jan-June 2004," n.d., in e-mail from Janet Dench, CCR listserve, August 11, 2004.

41. Paul Weinberg, "Homeland Security beyond US Borders," *OneWorld,* July 15, 2004, in e-mail from Janet Dench, CCR listserve, July 16, 2004.

42. Carol Goar, "We Cannot Let Immigrants Fail," *Toronto Star,* April 14, 2004.

43. Since 1993, some 250 people have sought and received sanctuary when their claims were rejected. Allison Hanes, "Cops Storm Church," *Montreal Gazette,* March 6, 2004; "Sanctuary under Fire," *Globe and Mail,* July 27, 2004.

44. In March 2004, a provincial court judge issued an arrest warrant for a man given sanctuary inside a church in Quebec City, the first time such an action had been taken by Canadian authorities. However, the move was so unpopular that Immigration Minister Judy Sgro later offered reprieves to several individuals sheltered in churches throughout Canada. Ingrid Peritz, "Deportation Orders Stayed in Two Sanctuary Cases," *Globe and Mail,* December 15, 2004; Jonathan Fowlie, "Archbishop Weighs In on Deportation Row," *Vancouver Sun,* March 25, 2005, in e-mail from Janet Dench, CCR listserve, March 5, 2005.

45. According to the World Refugee Survey published in 2004, refugee and

asylum seekers totaled 11.9 million worldwide, and internally displaced persons totaled 23.6 million. Canadian Council for Refugees, "Overview of Canadian Refugee System," *State of Refugees in Canada,* November 2002, p. 6, www.web .net/~ccr/state.html#Introduction. Other sources placed the number as high as twenty-one million. Alonso Urrutia, "Refugiados, 'radiografía de nuestros errores': ONU," *La Jornada,* June 21, 2001, www.jornada.unam.mx/2001/jun01/010621/ 016n1pol.html.

46. The top receiving nation was France, with 61,600 asylum seekers. The United States came second, with 52,000. However, using a per capita formula, the top receiving nations were Cyprus, Austria, Sweden, Luxembourg, and Ireland. UNHCR press release, March 1, 2005, in e-mail from Nanda Na Champassak, CCR listserve, March 1, 2005.

47. David Armstrong, "Free-Trade Pact Touted as a Way to Cut Loss of Jobs," *San Francisco Chronicle,* January 4, 2004.

48. Kevin Jernegan, "A New Century: Immigration and the US," *Migration Information Source,* February 2005, www.migrationinformation.org/Profiles/.

SELECTED BIBLIOGRAPHY

COLLECTIONS, ARCHIVES, AND LIBRARIES

Nettie Lee Benson Latin American Collection, University of Texas at Austin
Biblioteca Central, Universidad National de México
George H. W. Bush Presidential Library, College Station, Texas
James E. Carter Presidential Library, Atlanta, Georgia
Catholic Archives of Texas, Austin
Immigration and Refugee Board, Documentation Centre, Ottawa
Lauinger Library, Georgetown University
Library of Congress, Washington, D.C.
National Archives of Canada, Ottawa
National Security Archives, George Washington University, Washington, D.C.
John T. Olin Library, Cornell University
Ronald Reagan Presidential Library, Simi Valley, California

NEWSPAPERS

El Día (Mexico City)
Excélsior (Mexico City)
Florida Catholic
La Jornada (Mexico City)
La Prensa Centroamericana
Los Angeles Times

Miami Herald
New York Times
South Texas Catholic
Texas Catholic
Toronto Star
Universal (Mexico City)
Unomásuno (Mexico City)

NEWSLETTERS AND OTHER PUBLICATIONS

Annual Report (Immigration Appeal Board [Canada]), 1986–88
Refuge (Centre for Refugee Studies, York University)
Refugee Reports (U.S. Committee for Refugees)
Refugees (United Nations High Commissioner for Refugees)
Refugee Update (Jesuit Refugee Service/Canada)

ARTICLES AND ESSAYS

Abbott, Beth. "Project Accompaniment: A Canadian Response." *Refuge* 13, no. 10 (March 1994): 26.

Abell, Nazaré Albuquerque. "Safe Country Provisions in Canada and in the European Union: A Critical Assessment." *International Migration Review* 31 (Fall 1997): 569–590.

Adelman, Howard. "Humanitarianism and Self-Interest: Canadian Refugee Policy and the Hungarian Refugees." In Peter R. Baehr and Geza Tessenyi, eds., *The New Refugee Hosting Countries: Call for Experience-Space for Innovation*, 98–108. Utrecht: SIM, December 1991.

———. "The Safe Third Country in Canadian Legislation." *European Journal of International Migration and Ethnic Relations* 21, no. 22 (1994): 71–94.

Adelman, Jeremy. "Guatemalan Refugees in Mexico." *Refuge* 3, no. 2 (December 1983): 10.

Allen, Glenn. "Beefing Up the Border," *Maclean's,* August 31, 1992, 12–14.

"Anglican Church Studies Refugee Problem." *New Belize* 13, no. 4 (November 1983): 8–13.

Badgley, Kerry. "'As Long as He Is an Immigrant from the United Kingdom': Deception, Ethnic Bias, and Milestone Commemoration in the Department of Citizenship and Immigration." *Journal of Canadian Studies* 33, no. 3 (Fall 1998): 130–144.

Bai, David H. "Canadian Immigration Policy: Twentieth-Century Initiatives in Admission and Settlement." *Migration World* 29, no. 3 (2001): 9–13.

Barber, Martin, and Meyer Brownstone. "Relocating Refugees in Honduras." *Refuge* 3 (December 1983): 12–15.

Basok, Tanya. "Central American Refugees: Resettlement Needs and Solutions." *Refuge* 5 (May 1986): 1.

———. "How Durable Are the 'Durable Solutions' Projects for Salvadorean Refugees in Costa Rica?" *Refuge* 5 (May 1986): 7–9.

———. "The Troubled Road to Repatriation in Central America: Lessons Learned by Refugees in Exile." *Refuge* 13 (March 1994): 11–12.

Bauer, William. "Refugees, Victims, or Killers: The New Slave Trade?" *International Journal* 52 (Autumn 1997): 677–694.

"Border Rule May Imperil Canada Ties." *Migration World* 25, no. 5 (1997): 9.

Buckner, Phillip. "The Peopling of Canada." *History Today* 43 (November 1993): 48–54.

Burns, Allan F. *Maya in Exile: Guatemalans in Florida.* Philadelphia: Temple University Press, 1993.

Camacho de Schmidt, Aurora. "U.S. Refugee Policy and Central America." *Christianity and Crisis* 49 (September 25, 1989): 283–286.

Campfens, Hubert. "Guatemalan Refugees in Mexico." *Refuge* 3, no. 2 (December 1983): 7.

"Canada–United States of America: Discussions on Responsibility-Sharing for Asylum Seekers Adjourned." *International Journal of Refugee Law* 10 (January/April 1998): 256.

"The Canadian Approach to the Settlement and Adaptation of Immigrants." *ICMC Migration News* no. 2 (1986): 14–25.

"Canadians Clash over Cost of Diversity." *Migration World* 26, no. 3 (1998): 9.

Carozza, Paolo G. "From Conquest to Constitutions: Retrieving a Latin American Tradition of the Idea of Human Rights." *Human Rights Quarterly* 25 (2003): 281–313.

"Chinese Is Third after English, French in Canada." *Migration World* 26, nos. 1–2 (1998): 8.

Clarke, Harry R., and Lee Smith. "Labor Immigration and Capital Flows: Long-Term Australian, Canadian, and United States experience." *International Migration Review* 30 (Winter 1996): 925–949.

Durieux, Jean-François. "Capturing the Central American Refugee Phenomenon: Refugee Law-Making in Mexico and Belize." *International Journal of Refugee Law* 4 (1992): 301–325.

Egan, Brian, and Alan Simmons. "Refugees and the Prospects for Peace and Development in Central America." *Refuge* 13 (March 1994): 4–10.

Fagen, Patricia Weiss. "Peace in Central America: Transition for the Uprooted."

World Refugee Survey 1993, www.refugees.org/wprld/articles/centralamerica _wrs93.htm.

Ferris, Elizabeth G. "The Churches, Refugees, and Politics." In Gil Loescher and Laila Monahan, eds., *Refugees and International Relations,* 159–178. New York: Oxford University Press, 1989.

———. "The Politics of Asylum: Mexico and the Central American Refugees." *Journal of Inter-American Studies and World Affairs* 26 (August 1984): 357–384.

Fisher, Marc. "Home, Sweetwater Home." *Mother Jones* 13 (December 1988): 34–40.

Fontaine, Louise. "Immigration and Cultural Politics: A Bone of Contention between the Province of Quebec and the Canadian Federal Government." *International Migration Review* 29 (Winter 1995): 1041–1048.

Frelick, Bill, and Barbara Kohnen. "Filling the Gap: Temporary Protected Status." *Journal of Refugee Studies* 8 (1995): 339–363.

Good, A. J. "Guatemala's Hidden Refugees." *Christian Century* 107 (May 9, 1990): 499–501.

Gzesh, Susan. "So Close to the United States, So Far from God: Refugees and Asylees under Mexican Law." *World Refugee Survey 1995,* www.refugees.org/ world/articles/mexicanlaw_wrs95.htm.

Hamm, Ron. "Sanctuary Movement Raises Hard Political Questions." *National Catholic Register,* February 12, 1984.

Howland, Todd, et al. "Safe Haven for Salvadorans in the Context of Contemporary International Law: A Case Study in Equivocation." *San Diego Law Review* 29 (November-December 1992): 671–699.

Inforpress Centroamericana. "Guatemala." In Janie Hampton, ed., *Internally Displaced People: A Global Survey,* 103–107. London: Earthscarn Publications, 1998.

Jacob, André. "Adaptation of Salvadoran Refugees in Montreal." *Migration World* 20 (January-February 1992): 21–24.

Jensen, Rita Henley. "They've Been Working on the Underground Railroad." *Eastern Oklahoma Catholic,* February 17, 1985.

Keller, Bill. "Interest Groups Focus on El Salvador Policy." *Congressional Quarterly Weekly Report* 40 (1982): 895–900.

Kirkpatrick, Jeane. "Dictatorships and Double Standards." *Commentary* 68 (November 1979): 34–45.

———. "U.S. Security and Latin America." *Commentary* 71 (January 1981): 29–40.

Kowalewski, David. "The Historical Structuring of a Dissident Movement: The Sanctuary Case." *Research in Social Movements, Conflicts, and Change* 12 (1990): 89–110.

Kuhner, Gretchen. "Detention of Asylum Seekers in Mexico." *Refuge* 20 (May 2002): 58–64.

Kulig, Judith. "Family Life among El Salvadorans, Guatemalans, and Nicaraguans: A Comparative Study." *Journal of Comparative Family Studies* 29, no. 3 (Autumn 1998): 469–479.

Larmer, Brook. "Guatemala's Indians Become the Battlefield." *Christian Science Monitor*, September 4, 1990, 10–11.

Loescher, Gil. "Humanitarianism and Politics in Central America." *Political Science Quarterly* 103 (Summer 1988): 295–320.

Madrazo, Laura O'Dogherty. "The Hidden Face of War in Central America." *Current Sociology* 36 (Summer 1988): 93–106.

Mata, Fernando G. "The Multiculturalism Act and Refugee Integration in Canada." *Refuge* 13 (February 1994): 17–20.

Mohn, Sid L. "Central American Refugees: The Search for Appropriate Responses." *World Refugee Survey* (1983): 42–47.

Moore, Jonathan. "Developing Solutions for Central American Refugee Problems." *Department of State Bulletin* 89 (August 1989): 87–88.

Nezer, Melanie. "The Puebla Process: US Migration Controls Move South of the Border." *World Refugee Survey 1999*, www.refugees.org/world/articles/wrs99_migrationcontrols.htm.

Opoku Dapaah, Edward. "Integration of Landed Refugee Claimants in Canada: Toward an Explanatory Model." *Refuge* 13 (February 1994): 10–15.

———."Persons Needing Protection: A Reflection on Canada's Role." *Refuge* 16 (June 1997): 29–31.

Panitch, Arnold, and Jeanne Marie Cragin. "Immigrating to Quebec: The Demographic Challenges of a Province Experiencing Low Fertility." *Migration World* 19, no. 4 (1991): 3–4, 13–14.

Passaris, Constantine. "The Role of Immigration in Canada's Demographic Outlook." *International Migration* 36 (1998): 93–101.

Pentland, Sandra, and Dennis Racicot. "Salvadorean Refugees in Honduras." *Refuge* 5 (May 1986): 3–5.

Ramírez, Bruno. "Canada and the United States: Perspectives on Migration and Continental History." *Journal of American Ethnic History* 20 (Spring 2001): 50–70.

"Resolution on Refugee Protection and Sanctuary." *Migration News* 4 (1985): 49.

Rodríguez, Néstor P. "Undocumented Central Americans in Houston: Diverse Populations." *International Migration Review* 21 (Spring 1987): 4–26.

Romberg, Perry. "Service Delivery to Refugees and Immigrants: Toward an Integrated Approach." *Refuge* 13 (February 1994): 27.

Sherry, Gerald E. "Sanctuary Movement at Odds with Government." *Our Sunday Visitor*, February 17, 1985, 4.

———. "Symposium Focuses on Sanctuary for Refugees." *Our Sunday Visitor*, February 24, 1985, 4.

Smith, Charles D. "Trials and Errors: The Experience of Central American Refugees in Montreal." *Refuge* 5 (May 1986): 10–12.

Stobo, Gerald H. "The Canadian Refugee Determination System." *Texas International Law Journal* 29 (Summer 1994): 383–426.

Stoffman, Daniel. "Making Room for Real Refugees." *International Journal* 52 (Autumn 1997): 575–580.

Wallace, Steven P. "The New Urban Latinos: Central Americans in a Mexican Immigrant Environment." *Urban Affairs Quarterly* 25 (December 1989): 239–264.

Zerter, Barbara. "Canadian Consortia Supports Guatemalan Return." *Refuge* 13, no. 10 (March 1994): 25–26.

BOOKS, DISSERTATIONS, AND THESES

Abrams, Elliott. *Undue Process: A Story of How Political Differences Are Turned into Crimes.* New York: Free Press, 1993.

Adelman, Howard, ed. *Legitimate and Illegitimate Discrimination: New Issues in Migration.* Toronto: York Lanes Press, 1995.

———, ed. *Refugee Policy: Canada and the United States.* Toronto: York Lanes Press, 1991.

Adelman, Howard, and C. Michael Lanphier, eds. *Refuge or Asylum: A Choice for Canada.* Toronto: York Lanes Press, 1990.

Adelman, Howard, Allan Borowski, Meyer Burstein, and Lois Foster, eds. *Immigration and Refugee Policy: Australia and Canada Compared.* Vols. 1 and 2. Toronto: University of Toronto Press, 1994.

Aguayo, Sergio. *El éxodo centroamericano en México: Consecuencias de un conflicto.* Mexico City: Consejo Nacional de Fomento Educativo, 1985.

Aguayo, Sergio, and Patricia Weiss Fagen. *Central Americans in Mexico and the United States: Unilateral, Bilateral, and Regional Perspectives.* Washington, DC: Hemispheric Migration Project, Center for Immigration Policy and Refugee Assistance, Georgetown University, 1988.

Anderson, Thomas P. *The War of the Dispossessed: Honduras and El Salvador, 1969.* Lincoln: University of Nebraska Press, 1981.

Armstrong, Robert, and Janet Schenck. *El Salvador: The Face of Revolution.* Boston: South End Press, 1981.

Arnson, Cynthia. *Crossroads: Congress, the President, and Central America.* University Park: Pennsylvania State University Press, 1993.

Barry, Tom, and Deb Preusch. *The Central America Fact Book.* New York: Grove Press, 1986.

Blancarte, Roberto. *Historia de la Iglesia Católica en México.* Mexico City: Colegio Mexiquense and Fondo de Cultura Económica, 1992.

Boff, Leonardo. *Introducing Liberation Theology*. Maryknoll, NY: Orbis Books, 1987.

Boli, John, and George M. Thomas, eds. *Constructing World Culture: International Nongovernmental Organizations since 1875*. Stanford: Stanford University Press, 1999.

Bonner, Robert. *Weakness and Deceit: U.S. Policy in El Salvador*. New York: Times Books, 1984.

Brands, H. W. *The Devil We Knew: Americans and the Cold War*. New York: Oxford University Press, 1993.

Brockman, James R. *The Word Remains: A Life of Oscar Romero*. Maryknoll, NY: Orbis Books, 1982.

Burns, F. Allan. *Maya in Exile: Guatemalans in Florida*. Philadelphia: Temple University Press, 1993.

Busby, Robert. *Reagan and the Iran-Contra Affair: The Politics of Presidential Recovery*. New York: St. Martin's Press, 1999.

Castro, Max, ed. *Free Markets, Open Societies, Closed Borders? Trends in International Migration and Immigration Policy in the Americas*. Miami: North-South Center Press, 1999.

Child, Jack. *The Central American Peace Process, 1983–1991: Sheathing Swords, Building Confidence*. Boulder, CO: Lynne Rienner, 1992.

Clarkson, Stephen. *Canada and the Reagan Challenge: Crisis and Adjustment, 1981–85*. Toronto: James Lorimer and Company, 1985.

Coatsworth, John H. *Central America and the United States: The Clients and the Colossus*. New York: Twayne, 1994.

Compher, Vic, and Betsey Morgan, eds. *Going Home: Building Peace in El Salvador; The Story of Repatriation*. New York: Apex Press, 1991

Coutin, Susan Bibler. *The Culture of Protest: Religious Activism and the U.S. Sanctuary Movement*. Boulder, CO: Westview Press, 1993.

— —. *Legalizing Moves: Salvadoran Immigrants' Struggle for U.S. Residency*. Ann Arbor. University of Michigan Press, 2000.

Crittenden, Ann. *Sanctuary, a Story of American Conscience and the Law in Collision* New York: Weidenfeld and Nicolson, 1988.

Cunningham, Hilary. *God and Caesar at the Rio Grande: Sanctuary and the Politics of Religion*. Minneapolis: University of Minnesota Press, 1995.

Davidson, Miriam. *Convictions of the Heart: Jim Corbett and the Sanctuary Movement*. Tucson: University of Arizona Press, 1988.

Dennis, Marie, Renny Golden, and Scott Wright. *Oscar Romero: Reflections on His Life and Writing*. Modern Spiritual Masters Series. Maryknoll, NY: Orbis Books, 2000.

Díaz-Briquets, Sergio, and Sidney Weintraub, eds. *The Effects of Receiving Country Policies on Migration Flows*. Series on Development and International Migration in Mexico, Central America, and the Caribbean Basin, vol. 6. Boulder, CO: Westview Press, 1991.

Dirks, Gerald E. *Controversy and Complexity: Canadian Immigration Policy during the 1980s.* Montreal: McGill-Queen's University Press, 1995.

Doern, G. Bruce, Leslie A. Pal, and Brian W. Tomlin, eds. *Border Crossings: The Internationalization of Canadian Public Policy.* New York: Oxford University Press, 1996.

Draper, Theodore. *A Very Thin Line: The Iran-Contra Affairs.* New York: Hill and Wang, 1991.

Dunkerley, James. *The Pacification of Central America.* London: Institute for Latin American Studies, University of London, 1993.

Ebeling, Richard M., and Jacob G. Hornberger. *The Case for Free Trade and Open Immigration.* Fairfax, VA: Future of Freedom Foundation, 1995.

Fazio, Carlos. *Samuel Ruiz, El Caminante.* Mexico City: Espasa Calpe, 1994.

Ferris, Elizabeth G. *The Central American Refugees.* New York: Praeger, 1987.

Fiederlein, Suzanne. "Central American Refugees in Mexico: The Search for a Policy." MA thesis, University of Texas at Austin, May 1985.

Findling, John E. *Close Neighbors, Distant Friends: United States–Central American Relations.* Westport, CT: Greenwood Press, 1987.

Finkel, Alvin. *Our Lives: Canada after 1945.* Toronto: James Lorimer and Company, 1997.

Fisher, Julie. *Non-Governments: NGOs and the Political Development of the Third World.* West Hartford, CT: Kumarian Press, 1998.

García, María Cristina. *Havana USA: Cuban Exiles and Cuban Americans in South Florida, 1959–1994.* Berkeley: University of California Press, 1996.

Gelbspan, Ross. *Break-ins, Death Threats and the FBI: The Covert War against the Central America Movement.* Boston: South End Press, 1991.

Golden, Renny, and Michael McConnell. *Sanctuary: The New Underground Railroad.* Maryknoll, NY: Orbis Books, 1986.

González Puebla, Raul. *El aporte del testimonio y martirio de Mons Oscar Romero la teología.* 1st ed. Quito, Ecuador: Raul González Puebla, 1996.

Green, Linda. *Fear as a Way of Life: Mayan Widows in Rural Guatemala.* New York: Columbia University Press, 1999.

Gutiérrez, Gustavo. *The Power of the Poor in History.* Maryknoll, NY: Orbis Books, 1983.

Hagan, Jacqueline María. *Deciding to Be Legal: A Maya Community in Houston.* Philadelphia: Temple University Press, 1994.

———. "The Politics of Numbers: Central American Migration during a Period of Crisis, 1978–1985." MA thesis, University of Texas at Austin, May 1987.

Hamilton, Nora, and Norma Stoltz Chinchilla. *Seeking Community in a Global*

City: Guatemalans and Salvadorans in Los Angeles. Philadelphia: Temple University Press, 2001.

Hathaway, James C., and John A. Dent. *Refugee Rights: Report on a Comparative Survey.* Toronto: York Lanes Press, 1995.

Hawkins, Freda. *Canada and Immigration: Public Policy and Public Concern.* Kingston: McGill-Queen's University Press, 1988.

Hawley, Mary Christina. "Private Resettlement of Central American Refugees in the United States: A Response of the Episcopal Church." MA thesis, University of Texas at Austin, August 1991.

Hayden, Bridget A. *Salvadorans in Costa Rica.* Tucson: University of Arizona Press, 2003.

Hesse, Jurgen. *Voices in Exile: Refugees Speak Out.* White Rock, British Columbia: Thinkware Publishers, 1994.

Honey, Martha. *Hostile Acts: US Policy in Costa Rica in the 1980s.* Gainesville: University Press of Florida, 1994.

Jauberth, H. Rodrigo, Gilberto Castañeda, Jesús Hernández, and Pedro Vuskovic. *The Difficult Triangle: Mexico, Central America, and the United States.* Boulder, CO: Westview Press, 1992.

Kahn, Robert S. *Other People's Blood: U.S. Immigration Prisons in the Reagan Decade.* Boulder, CO: Westview Press, 1996.

Keck, Margaret E., and Kathryn Sikkink. *Activists beyond Borders: Advocacy Networks in International Politics.* Ithaca, NY: Cornell University Press, 1998.

Kelley, Ninette, and Michael Trebilcock. *The Making of the Mosaic: A History of Canadian Immigration Policy.* Toronto: University of Toronto Press, 1998.

Knowles, Valeroe. *Strangers at Our Gates: Canadian Immigration and Immigration Policy, 1540–1997.* Toronto: Dundurn Press, 1997.

Kornbluh, Peter. *The Iran-Contra Scandal: The Declassified Story.* New York: New Press, 1993.

LaFeber, Walter. *Inevitable Revolutions: The United States in Central America.* 2nd ed. New York: W. W. Norton, 1993.

Langley, Lester D. *America and the Americas: The United States in the Western Hemisphere.* Athens, GA: University of Georgia Press, 1989.

———. *Mexico and the United States: The Fragile Relationship.* Boston: Twayne Publishers, 1991.

Larkin, Mary Ann, Frederick C. Cuny, and Barry N. Stein, eds. *Repatriation under Conflict in Central America.* Washington, D.C.: Center for Immigration Policy and Refugee Assistance, Georgetown University, 1991.

Lemco, Jonathan. *Canada and the Crisis in Central America.* New York: Praeger, 1991.

LeoGrande, William M. *Our Own Backyard: The United States in Central America, 1977–1992.* Chapel Hill: University of North Carolina Press, 1998.

Leonard, Thomas M. *Central America and the United States: The Search for Stability.* Athens, GA: University of Georgia Press, 1991.

Lernoux, Penny. *Cry of the People.* Garden City: Doubleday, 1980.

Loescher, Gil. *Beyond Charity: International Cooperation and the Global Refugee Crisis.* New York: Oxford University Press, 1993.

———. *The UNHCR and World Politics: A Perilous Path.* New York: Oxford University Press, 2001.

Loescher, Gil, and Laila Monahan, eds. *Refugees and International Relations.* New York: Oxford University Press, 1989.

Loescher, Gil, and John Scanlon. *A Calculated Kindness: Refugees and America's Half-Open Door, 1945–Present.* New York: Free Press, 1986.

López Vigil, María. *Oscar Romero: Memories in Mosaic.* Washington, D.C.: EPICA, 2000.

Lorentzen, Robin. *Women in the Sanctuary Movement.* Philadelphia: Temple University Press, 1991.

Loucky, James, and Marilyn M. Moors. *The Maya Diaspora: Guatemalan Roots, New American Lives.* Philadelphia: Temple University Press, 2000.

MacDonald, Mandy, and Mike Gatehouse. *In the Mountains of Morazan: Portrait of a Returned Refugee Community in El Salvador.* London: Latin American Bureau, 1995.

MacEoin Gary. *The People's Church: Bishop Samuel Ruiz and Why He Matters.* New York: Crossroad Publishing Company, 1996.

———, ed. *Sanctuary: A Resource Guide for Understanding and Participating in the Central American Refugees' Struggle.* San Francisco: Harper and Row, 1985.

MacEoin, Gary, and Nivita Riley. *No Promised Land: American Refugee Policies and the Rule of Law.* Boston: Oxfam America, 1982.

MacFarlane, Peter. *Northern Shadows: Canadians and Central America.* Toronto: Between the Lines, 1989.

Manz, Beatriz. *Refugees of a Hidden War: The Aftermath of Counterinsurgency in Guatemala.* Albany: State University of New York Press, 1988.

———. *Repatriation and Integration: An Arduous Process in Guatemala.* Washington, D.C.: Center for Immigration Policy and Refugee Assistance, Georgetown University, 1988.

Markley, Jennifer Jo. "Bonds in the Asylum Context: The Treatment of Central American Refugees in Texas." MA thesis, University of Texas at Austin, December 1990.

Martínez Velasco, Germán. *Plantaciones, trabajo guatemalteco y política migratoria en la frontera sur de México.* Ocozocoautla de Espinosa, Chiapas: Gobierno del Estado de Chiapas y el Instituto Chiapenco de Cultura, 1994.

Matas, David (with Ilana Simon). *Closing the Doors: The Failure of Refugee Protection*. Toronto: Summerhill Press, 1989.

McDaniel, Judith. *Sanctuary: A Journey*. Ithaca, NY: Firebrand Books, 1987.

Menchú, Rigoberta. *I, Rigoberta Menchú: An Indian Woman in Guatemala*. London: Verso, 1998.

Menjívar, Cecilia. *Fragmented Ties: Salvadoran Immigrant Networks in America*. Berkeley: University of California Press, 2000.

Meyer, Jean (with Federico Anaya Gallardo and Julio Ríos). *Samuel Ruiz en San Cristóbal*. Mexico City: Editores Tusquets, 2000.

Mitchell, Christopher, ed. *Western Hemisphere Immigration and United States Foreign Policy*. University Park: Pennsylvania State University Press, 1992.

Monroy, Mario B., ed. *Pensar Chiapas, repensar Mexico: Reflexiones de las ONGs Mexicanas sobre el conflicto*. Mexico City: Convergencia de Organismos Civiles por la Democracia, 1994.

Montes Mozo, Segundo, and Juan José García Vásquez. *Salvadoran Migration to the U.S.: An Exploratory Study*. Washington, D.C.: Hemispheric Migration Project, Center for Immigration Policy and Refugee Assistance, Georgetown University, 1988.

Morel, Augusto. *Refugiados Salvadoreños en Nicaragua*. Managua: Asociación de Colectivos de Refugiados Salvadoreños (ACRES), 1991.

Moreno, Darío. *The Struggle for Peace in Central America*. Gainesville: University Press of Florida, 1994.

———. *US Policy in Central America: The Endless Debate*. Miami: Florida International University Press, 1990.

Morley, Morris H. *Washington, Somoza, and the Sandinistas: State and Regime in US Policy toward Nicaragua, 1969–1981*. New York: Cambridge University Press, 1994.

Mosley, Don (with Joyce Hollyday). *With Our Own Eyes: The Dramatic Story of a Christian Response to the Wounds of War, Racism, and Oppression*. Scottsdale, Pennsylvania: Herald Press, 1996.

Nackerud, Larry G. *The Central American Refugee Issue in Brownsville, Texas: Seeking Understanding of Public Policy Formulation from within a Community Setting*. San Francisco: Mellen Research University Press, 1993.

North, Liisa, and CAPA, eds. *Between War and Peace in Central America: Choices for Canada*. Toronto: Between the Lines, 1990.

North, Oliver. *Under Fire: An American Story*. New York: Harper Paperbacks, 1992.

O'Dogherty Madrazo, Laura. *Central Americans in Mexico City: Uprooted and Silenced*. Washington, D.C.: Hemispheric Migration Project, Center for Immigration Policy and Refugee Assistance, Georgetown University, 1989.

Out of the Ashes: The Lives and Hopes of Refugees from El Salvador. London: El Salvador Committee for Human Rights and Guatemala Committee for Human Rights, War on Want Campaigns, Ltd., 1985.

Pacheco, Gilda. *A Decade of Ambiguity: Approaches to Central American Refugee Assistance in the 1980s.* Washington, D.C.: Hemispheric Migration Project, Center for Immigration Policy and Refugee Assistance, Georgetown University, 1991.

———. *Nicaraguan Refugees in Costa Rica: Adjustment to Camp Life.* Washington, D.C.: Hemispheric Migration Project, Center for Immigration Policy and Refugee Assistance, Georgetown University, 1989.

Pastor, Robert A. *Condemned to Repetition: The United States and Nicaragua.* Princeton, NJ: Princeton University Press, 1987.

Pedraza, Silvia. *Political and Economic Migrants in America: Cubans and Mexicans.* Austin: University of Texas Press, 1985.

Plaut, W. Gunther. *Asylum: A Moral Dilemma.* Toronto: York Lanes Press, 1995.

Porpora, Douglas V. *How Holocausts Happen: The United States in Central America.* Philadelphia: Temple University Press, 1990.

Presencia de los refugiados guatemaltecos en México: 50 años de la creación del Alto Comisionado de las Naciones Unidas para los Refugiados (ACNUR). Mexico City: Comisión Mexicana de Ayuda a Refugiados Secretaría de Gobernación and the Alto Comisionado de las Naciones Unidas para los Refugiados, 1999.

Repak, Terry A. *Waiting on Washington: Central American Workers in the Nation's Capital.* Philadelphia: Temple University Press, 1995.

Risse, Thomas, Stephen C. Ropp, and Kathryn Sikkink, eds. *The Power of Human Rights: International Norms and Domestic Change.* Cambridge: Cambridge University Press, 1998.

Romero, Oscar. *Archbishop Oscar Romero: A Shepherd's Diary.* London: CAFOD, 1993.

———. *La violencia del amor.* Farmington, PA: Plough Publishing House, 2001.

———. *Voice of the Voiceless: The Four Pastoral Letters and Other Statements.* Maryknoll, NY: Orbis Books, 1985.

Romero, Oscar A., and James R. Brockman. *The Violence of Love: The Pastoral Wisdom of Archbishop Oscar Romero.* San Francisco: Harper and Row, 1988.

Rus, Jan. *Tierra, libertad, y autonomía: Impactos regionales de zapatismo en Chiapas.* Mexico City: Centro de Investigaciones y Estudios Superiores en Antropología Social, 2002.

Saénz Carrete, Erasmo. *Un servidor público nacional e internacional con las refugiadas y los refugiados.* Mexico City: Potrerillos Editores, SA, 1994.

Salvadó, Luis Raúl. *The Other Refugees: A Study of Non-recognized Guatemalan Refugees in Chiapas, Mexico.* Washington, D.C.: Hemispheric Migration Project,

Center For Immigration Policy and Refugee Assistance, Georgetown University, 1988.

Santiago, Jorge S. *Seeking Freedom: Bishop Samuel Ruiz in Conversation with Jorge S. Santiago.* Translated from the Spanish and edited by Michael Andraos. Chiapas: San Cristóbal de las Casas and Toronto Council of the Canadian Catholic Organization for Development and Peace, 1999.

Schoultz, Lars. *Beneath the United States: A History of U.S. Policy toward Latin America.* Cambridge, MA: Harvard University Press, 1998.

Seeking Safe Haven: A Congregational Guide to Helping Central American Refugees in the United States. Philadelphia: American Friends Service Committee et al., 1983.

Sharma, Satya P., Alexander M. Ervin, and Deirdre Meintel, eds. *Immigrants and Refugees in Canada: A National Perspective on Ethnicity, Multiculturalism, and Cross-Cultural Adjustment.* Saskatoon: University of Saskatchewan Press, 1991.

Singer, Audrey L. "Central American Immigrants in the United States, 1980: A Socioeconomic Profile." MA thesis, University of Texas at Austin, May 1988.

Smith, Jackie, Charles Chatfielf, and Ron Pagnucco, eds. *Transnational Social Movements and Global Politics.* Syracuse, NY: Syracuse University Press, 1997.

Sobrino, Jon, Germán Schmitz, and Jesús Calderón. *Oscar Romero, profeta y mártir de la liberación.* Lima, Peru: Centro de Estudios y Publicaciones, 1981.

Suárez-Orozco, Marcelo M. *Central American Refugees and U.S. High Schools: A Psychosocial Study of Motivation and Achievement.* Stanford: Stanford University Press, 1989.

Taylor, Clark. *Return of Guatemala's Refugees: Reweaving the Torn.* Philadelphia: Temple University Press, 1998.

Teitelbaum, Michael. *Labor Migration North: The Problem for US Foreign Policy.* New York: Council on Foreign Relations, 1985

Tomsho, Robert. *The American Sanctuary Movement.* Austin: Texas Monthly Press, 1987.

Tulchinsky, Gerald, ed. *Immigration in Canada: Historical Perspectives.* Toronto: Copp Clark Longman, 1994.

Tushnet, Mark. *Central America and the Law: The Constitution, Civil Liberties, and the Courts.* PACCA Series on the Domestic Roots of United States Foreign Policy. Boston: South End Press, 1988.

Voekel, Pamela. *Alone before God: The Religious Origins of Modernity in Mexico.* Durham, NC: Duke University Press, 2002.

Walsh, Lawrence E. *Firewall: The Iran-Contra Conspiracy and Cover-up.* New York: W. W. Norton, 1997.

———. *Iran-Contra: The Final Report.* New York: Times Books, 1994.

Weintraub, Sidney, and Sergio Díaz-Briquets. *The Use of Foreign Aid to Reduce Incen-*

tives to Emigrate from Central America. Geneva: International Labour Organisation, 1992.

Whitfield, Teresa. *Paying the Price: Ignacio Ellacuría and the Murdered Jesuits of El Salvador.* Philadelphia: Temple University Press, 1995.

Williams, John R., ed. *Canadian Churches and Social Justice.* Toronto: Anglican Book Centre and James Lorimer and Company, 1984.

Woodward, Bob. *VEIL: The Secret Wars of the CIA, 1981–1987.* New York: Simon and Schuster, 1987.

Wroe, Ann. *Lives, Lies and the Iran-Contra Affair.* London: I. B. Tauris and Company, 1991.

REPORTS, HEARINGS, LEGAL CASES, AND PROCEEDINGS

Adelman, Howard. *A Survey of Postwar Refugee Intakes and Developments in Canadian Refugee Policy.* Report prepared for the CEIC. Toronto: Centre for Refugee Studies, York University, August 1990.

Aguayo, Sergio. *From the Shadows to Center Stage: NGOs and Central American Refugee Assistance.* Washington, D.C.: Hemispheric Migration Project, Center for Immigration Policy and Refugee Assistance, Georgetown University, 1991.

Aguilar Zinser, Adolfo. *CIREFCA: The Promises and Reality of the International Conference on Central American Refugees, an Independent Report.* Washington, D.C.: Hemispheric Migration Project, Center for Immigration Policy and Refugee Assistance, Georgetown University, 1991.

American Baptist Churches in the USA, et al., v. Edwin Meese III and Alan Nelson. 666 F. Supp. 1358 (N.D. Calif. 1987).

American Baptist Churches in the USA, et al., v. Edwin Meese III and Alan Nelson. 712 F. Supp. 756 (N.D. Calif. 1989).

American Baptist Churches in the USA, et al., v. Richard Thornburgh, et al. 760 F. Supp. 796 (N.D. Calif. 1991).

American Bar Association Coordinating Committee on Immigration. *Lives on the Line: Seeking Asylum in South Texas: A Report.* Washington, D.C.: American Bar Association, June 1989.

Americas Watch Committee. *El Salvador's Decade of Terror: Human Rights since the Assassination of Archbishop Romero.* New Haven, CT: Yale University Press, 1991.

———. *Guatemalan Refugees in Mexico, 1980–1984.* New York: Americas Watch Committee, September 1984.

———. *Human Rights in Guatemala: No Neutrals Allowed.* New York: Americas Watch Committee, November 1982.

———. *Human Rights in Nicaragua: Reagan, Rhetoric and Reality.* New York: Americas Watch Committee, July 1985.

———. *Messengers of Death: Human Rights in Guatemala, November 1988–February 1990.* New York: Americas Watch Committee, 1990.

———. *A Year of Reckoning: El Salvador a Decade after the Assassination of Archbishop Romero.* New York: Americas Watch Committee, March 1990.

Amnesty International. *Guatemala: A Government Program of Political Murder.* London: Amnesty International, 1981.

———. *Guatemala: Massive Extrajudicial Executions in Rural Areas under the Government of General Efraín Ríos Montt.* London: Amnesty International, July 1982.

———. *Mexico: Human Rights in Rural Areas.* London: Amnesty International, 1986.

Anker, Deborah. "INS v Cardoza-Fonseca, One Year Later: Discretion, Credibility, and Political Opinion." *In Defense of the Alien,* vol. 11, 120–130. Proceedings of the 1988 Annual Legal Conference on Immigration and Refugee Policy. Staten Island, NY: Center for Migration Studies, 1988.

———. "US Immigration and Asylum Policy: A Brief Historical Perspective." *In Defense of the Alien,* vol. 13, 74–85. Proceedings of the 1990 Annual Legal Conference on Immigration and Refugee Policy. Staten Island, NY: Center for Migration Studies, 1990.

Aubry, Andrés. *Los obispos de Chiapas.* Chiapas: Apuntes de Lectura 12–15, Instituto de Asesoría Antropológica para la Región Maya, A.C., May 1990.

———. *Los padres dominicos remodelan a Chiapas a su imagen y semejanza.* Chiapas: Apuntes de Lectura 8, Instituto de Asesoría Antropológica para la Región Maya, A.C., October 1988.

Badets, Jane, and Chui, Tina W. L. *Canada's Changing Immigrant Population.* Ottawa: Statistics Canada and Prentice-Hall Canada, 1994.

Berryman, Angela. *Central American Refugees: A Survey of the Current Situation.* Philadelphia: American Friends Service Committee, May 1983.

Bissett, Joseph. "Canada's Refugee Determination System and the Effect of US Immigration Law." In *In Defense of the Alien,* vol. 10, 57–64. Proceedings of the 1987 Annual National Legal Conference on Immigration and Refugee Policy. Staten Island, NY: Center for Migration Studies, 1988.

———. "Canadian Policy on Refugees and Asylum Seekers." In *In Defense of the Alien,* vol. 9, 113–121. Proceedings of the 1986 Annual National Legal Conference on Immigration and Refugee Policy. Staten Island, NY: Center for Migration Studies, 1987.

"Break-ins at Sanctuary Churches and Organizations Opposed to Administration Policy in Central America." *Hearings before the Subcommittee on Civil and Constitutional Rights.* Committee on the Judiciary, House of Representatives, 100th Congress, 1st session, February 19 and 20, 1987.

Bureau for Refugee Programs, US Department of State. *World Refugee Report* (September 1991): 49–54.

"Canada." *World Refugee Report, 1989,* 108–110. Washington, D.C.: Bureau for Refugee Programs, Department of State, 1989.

Canada Employment and Immigration Commission. *New Directions: A Look at Canada's New Immigration Act and Regulations.* Hull: Minister of Supply and Services, 1978.

———. *Refugee Perspectives, 1984–1985.* Hull: Refugee Affairs Division, Policy and Program Development Branch, 1985.

Canadian Council for Refugees. *Best Settlement Practices: Settlement Services for Refugees and Immigrants in Canada.* Montreal: Canadian Council for Refugees, February 1998.

———. *Interdicting Refugees.* Montreal: Canadian Council for Refugees, May 1998.

"Central American Asylum Seekers." *Hearing before the Subcommittee on Immigration, Refugees, and International Law.* Committee of the Judiciary, House of Representatives, 101st Congress, 1st session, March 9, 1989.

Centro América: Refugiados, repatriados y desplazados: Documentos e informes de la Conferencia International sobre refugiados Centraoamericanos (CIREFCA, Guatemala, 29–31.5.89). Guatemala City: Panorama Centroamericano/Temas y documentos de Debate no. 21, May-June 1989.

Clark, Tom. "Human Rights versus Immigration Controls: A Canadian Profile." In *World Refugee Survey: 1988 in Review,* 84–85. US Committee for Refugees, 1988.

Comisión para la Defensa de los Derechos Humanos en Centroamérica. *Los horizontes del éxodo: El proceso de reintegración de los retornados salvdoreños y guatemaltecos.* San José, Costa Rica: CODEHUCA, 1994.

Committee in Solidarity with the People of El Salvador (CISPES), et al. v. William F. Sessions, et al. 929 F.2d 742 (D.C. Cir. 1991).

Crisp, Jeff, and Clive Nettleton, eds. *Refugee Report, 1984.* London: British Refugee Council, 1984.

Curry, Henry. "US Asylum Adjudications." *In Defense of the Alien,* vol. 13, 65–69. Proceedings of the 1990 Annual Legal Conference on Immigration and Refugee Policy. Staten Island, NY: Center for Migration Studies, 1990.

El Rescate Legal Services, Inc., et al., v. Executive Office for Immigration Review, et al. 727 F. Supp. 557 (C.D. Calif. 1989).

El Rescate Legal Services, Inc., et al., v. Executive Office for Immigration Review, et al. 941 F.2d 950 (9th Cir. 1991).

El Rescate Legal Services, Inc., et al., v. Executive Office for Immigration Review, et al. 959 F.2d 742 (9th Cir. 1992).

Enos, Don, et al. *Displaced Persons in El Salvador: An Assessment.* Washington, D.C.:

Bureau for Latin America and the Caribbean, Agency for International Development, March 1984.

"An Evaluation of Democracy in Nicaragua." *Hearing before the Subcommittee on the Western Hemisphere.* Committee on International Relations, House of Representatives, 104th Congress, 1st session, November 8, 1995.

"Extension of the Legalization Program." *Hearing before the Subcommittee on Immigration, Refugees, and International Law.* Committee on the Judiciary, House of Representatives, 100th Congress, 2d session, March 30, 1988.

Facts and Figures: Immigration Overview, 1998. Ottawa: Citizenship Immigration Canada, 1999.

Fagen, Patricia Weiss. *Refugees and Displaced Persons in Central America.* Report of the Refugee Policy Group. Washington, D.C., March 1984.

Fagen, Patricia Weiss, and Sergio Aguayo. *Fleeing the Maelstrom: Central American Refugees.* Occasional Paper no. 10, Central American and Caribbean Program, School of Advanced International Studies, John Hopkins University, March 1986.

Frelick, Bill. *The Back of the Hand. Bias and Restructionism towards Central American Asylum Seekers in North America.* Issue Brief, US Committee for Refugees, American Council for Nationalities Service, October 1988.

———. *Running the Gauntlet: The Central American Journey through Mexico.* Issue Paper, US Committee for Refugees, American Council for Nationalities Service, January 1991.

Friedland, Joan, and Jesús Rodríguez y Rodríguez. *Seeking Safe Ground: The Legal Situation of Central American Refugees in Mexico.* San Diego: Mexico-US Law Institute, University of San Diego Law School and the Instituto de Investigaciones Jurídicas, Universidad Nacional Autónoma de México, 1987.

Gallagher, Dennis, and Janelle M. Diller. *CIREFCA: At the Crossroads between Uprooted People and Development in Central America.* Washington, D.C.. Commission for the Study of International Migration and Cooperative Economic Development, March 1990.

Gatehouse, Mike. *Uprooted: The Displaced People of Central America.* Working Papers on Refugees, vol. 2, no. 3. London: British Refugee Council/Queen Victoria House, April 1986.

Hull, Elizabeth. "United States Asylum Process: Problems and Proposals." *In Defense of the Alien,* vol. 16, 114–129. Proceedings of the 1994 Annual Legal Conference on Immigration and Refugee Policy. Staten Island, NY: Center for Migration Studies, 1994.

Human Rights Watch. *Implausible Deniability: State Responsibility for Rural Violence in Mexico.* New York: Human Rights Watch, 1997.

Immigration and Naturalization Service v. Luz Marina Cardoza-Fonseca. 480 US 421; 107 S. Ct. 1207; 94 L. Ed. 2d 434 (1987).

Immigration and Refugee Board. "Asylum Claims to Canada, 1984 to June 1993." *Immigration Board Statistical Summary*. Ottawa: Immigration and Refugee Board, July 19, 1993.

Immigration Statistics." *Ontario Ministry of Citizenship,* vol. 11. Toronto: Ministry of Citizenship, 1993.

Inter-American Commission on Human Rights. *Report on the Situation of Human Rights in the Republic of Guatemala*. Washington, D.C.: Organization of American States, 1981.

International Migration Policies. New York: Department of Economic and Social Affairs, Population Division, United Nations, 1998.

Jonas, Susanne. *Transnational Realities and Anti-Immigrant State Policies: Issues Raised by the Experience of Central American Immigrants and Refugees in a Trinational Region*. Santa Cruz: Chicano/Latino Research Center, Working Paper no. 7, University of California at Santa Cruz, 1996.

Kerwin, Donald. "Migrant Crossing Deaths, Immigrant families, and Low-Wage Laborers on the US–Mexico Border." *In Defense of the Alien,* vol. 24, 61–84. Proceedings of the 2001 Annual Legal Conference on Immigration and Refugee Policy. Staten Island, NY: Center for Migration Studies, 2001.

LeoGrande, William M. *Central America and the Polls: A Study of U.S. Public Opinion Polls on U.S. Foreign Policy toward El Salvador and Nicaragua under the Reagan Administration*. Washington, D.C.: Washington Office on Latin America, 1987.

Loescher, Gil. *Refugee Movements and International Security*. Adelphi Papers 268. London: International Institute for Strategic Studies, 1992.

MacDonald, Brian, ed. *Canada, the Caribbean, and Central America*. Proceedings of the Canadian Institute of Strategic Studies. Toronto: CISS, 1986.

Meissner, Doris M., Robert D. Hormats, Antonio Garrigues Walker, and Shijuro Ogata. *International Migration Challenges in a New Era: A Report to the Trilateral Commission,* no. 44. New York, Paris, and Tokyo: Trilateral Commission, 1993.

Montes, Segundo. *El Salvador 1987: Salvadoreños refugiados en los Estados Unidos*. San Salvador: Instituto de Investigaciones e Instituto de Derechos Humanos de la Universidad Centroamericana de El Salvador, 1987.

Navarrete, Emma Liliana, and Marta G. Vera Bolaños. *Diagnóstico de la evolución demográfica en el Estado de México, 1990*. Mexico City: Consejo Estatal de Población, Gobierno del Estado de México, 1992.

Núñez, et al., v. Hal Boldin, et al. 537 F. Supp. 578 (S.D. Tex., Brownsville Div., 1982).

Oliver, Michael, ed. *The Movement of Peoples: A View from the South*. Ottawa: Group of 78, October 1992.

Orantes-Hernández, et al., v. Edwin Meese III, et al. 685 F. Supp. 1488 (C.D. Calif. 1988).

Orantes-Hernández, et al., v. William French Smith, et al. 541 F. Supp. 351 (C.D. Calif. 1982).

Orantes-Hernández, et al., v. Richard Thornburgh, et al. 919 F.2d 549 (9th Cir. 1990).

Peterson, Linda S. *Central American Migration: Past and Present.* Washington, D.C.: Center for International Research, US Bureau of the Census, CIR Staff Paper no. 25, November 1986.

Ramírez Ocampo, Augusto. "The Question of Displaced Persons and the Process of Development in Latin America." *In Defense of the Alien,* vol. 12, 44–49. Proceedings of the 1989 Annual Legal Conference on Immigration and Refugee Policy. Staten Island, NY: Center for Migration Studies, 1989.

"Refugee Problems in Central America." Staff report prepared for the use of the Subcommittee on Immigration and Refugee Policy, Committee of the Judiciary, US Senate, September 1983. Washington, D.C.: Government Printing Office, 1984.

Refugees and Others of Concern to UNHCR: 1998 Statistical Overview. Geneva: United Nations High Commission for Refugees, July 1999.

Renaud, Viviane, and Rosalinda Costa. "Immigrants in Quebec." *Canadian Social Trends,* Catalogue 11–008E. Ottawa: Statistics Canada, Summer 1995.

Rich, Donna. *Mexican Policy toward Guatemalan Refugees.* Occasional Paper no. 17, Central American and Caribbean Program, School of Advanced International Studies, Johns Hopkins University, June 1987.

Ruiz, Hiram. *El Retorno: Guatemalans' Risky Repatriation Begins.* US Committee for Refugees Issue Paper. Washington, D.C.: US Committee for Refugees, 1993.

Singh v. Canada. [1985] Minister of Employment and Immigration. 14 C.R.R,. SCC 13.

Target Groups Project. *Immigrants in Canada: Selected Highlights.* Ottawa: Minister of Supply and Services Canada, 1990.

Teitelbaum, Michael. *U.S. Response to Refugees and Asylum-Seekers.* International Migration Working Paper Series, Center for International Studies, Massachusetts Institute of Technology, 1995.

Tenneriello, Bonnie. *Uncertain Return: Refugees and Reconciliation in Guatemala.* Washington, D.C.: Washington Office on Latin America, May 1989.

Torres-Rivas, Edelberto. *Report on the Condition of Central American Refugees and Migrants.* Washington, D.C.: Center for Immigration Policy and Refugee Assistance, Georgetown University, July 1985.

UNHCR. "International Conference on Central American Refugees (CIREFCA), Guatemala City, 29–31 May 1989." Information Paper.

United National General Assembly. *Situation of Human Rights in Guatemala.* Report of the Economic and Social Council, no. A/38/485. November 4, 1983.

"USCC Policy towards Central America: A Synthesis." Washington, D.C., February 24, 1985. Catholic Archives of Texas.

US Committee on Refugees. "Country Report: Mexico," 2002. www.refugees
.org/world/countryrpt/amer_carib/mexico.htm.

US Comptroller General. *Central American Refugees: Regional Conditions and Prospects and Potential Impact on the United States: Report to the Congress of the United States.* Washington, D.C.: General Accounting Office, July 20, 1984.

Wearne, Phillip. *The Maya of Guatemala.* London: Minority Rights Group, 1994.

INDEX

ABC lawsuit, 111–12

Abell, Nazaré Albuquerque, 223n106

Abrams, Elliott, 18

abuses, at detention centers, 91, 92

Adjustment Assistance Program (Canada), 138–39

advocacy networks, 3–4, 5, 8, 10–11, 12, 71–72, 160, 164; in Canada, 134, 136, 138, 144–52

African-American slaves, as migrants to Mexico, 187n1

Africans, as Canadian immigrants, 120, 121

agrarian reform: in El Salvador, 178n61; in Guatemala, 26

agricultural laborers, refugees as, 45, 48–49, 62, 65

aircraft, Canadian sale to Guatemala and Honduras, 148

airlines, protests against, 96, 206n52

Alba Palacios, Jesús, 61, 73

Alemán, Arnoldo, 116

Allende, Salvador, 225n136

Al-Qaeda, 163, 165

Alta Verapaz, Guatemala, Maya migrants from, 47

American Baptist Churches in the USA, et al., v. Edwin Meese III and Alan Nelson, 111, 212n123

American Civil Liberties Union (ACLU), 92, 206n50

American Convention on Human Rights. *See* San José Pact of 1969

American Council for Nationalities Services, 206n50

American Friends Service Committee, 103

American Indians, as migrants to Mexico, 187n1

American Revolutionary War, sanctuaries during, 101

Americans, as migrants to Mexico, 187n1

Americas in Transition (documentary), 93

Americas Watch, 3, 19, 75, 94, 147, 170n4

amnesty, for Central American refugees, 59, 91, 135

Amnesty International, 19, 75, 76, 93, 94, 111, 137, 147, 148, 152, 170n4
Anglican Church of Canada, 149, 150
ANSESAL. *See* Salvadoran National Security Forces (ANSESAL)
Anti-Communist Forces for Liberation, 22
Arab immigrants, to Mexico, 163
Arana Osorio, Carlos ("Butcher of Zacapa"), 27
Arar, Maher, 165
Arbenz Guzmán, Jacobo, 26, 178n61
ARENA. *See* National Republican Alliance Party (ARENA)
Arévalo, Juan José, 178n61
Argentina: in Contadora Support Group, 40; Contra training by, 174n23
Arias Plan, 41
Arias Sánchez, Oscar, 41
Armed Forces of Liberation, 22
Armed Forces of National Liberation, 21–22
Arsenault, William, 217
Arzu, Alvaro, 158
Asians, as Canadian immigrants, 120, 121, 155
asylees, vs. refugees, 101
asylum: in Canada, 119, 123, 135, 136, 143; deportation vs., 178n61; legal battle for, 108–12; persons granted, 46, 78, 162, 166
Asylum Policy and Review Unit, 110, 212n118
Atlacatl battalion, 24, 178n52
Austin, Duke, 132–33
Australia, Central Americans in, 51, 189n24
Axworthy, Lloyd, 217n39

bail bonds, for refugees, 91, 204n34
Baja Verapaz, Guatemala, Maya migrants from, 47
Baptist Church, refugee aid of, 100
Bartlett, Manuel, 62

Baryshnikov, Mikhail, 136
BBC, 107
Belize: peace efforts of, 43; refugees in, 43; US aid to, 43
Bermúdez, Enrique, 116
Berrigan, Daniel, 95
Between War and Peace in Central America: Choices for Canada, 147
Bill C-55 (Canada), 135, 136, 137, 146
Bill C-84 (Canada), 136–38, 146, 151
Bill C-86 (Canada), 140–42
Black Christ, 41
B'nai B'rith, 149
Board of Immigration Appeals, 109, 204n34
Bobby Maduro Stadium, as homeless shelter, 115
Boland Amendment, 19
border, refugee detention on, 31
Border Association for Refugees from Central America, 97, 207n56
border control, of US and Canada, 144
Border Patrol, 91, 98, 104, 105, 106, 107, 131, 161
"border visitors," 47–65, 77
Border Witness Program, 106
Bouchard, Benoit, 132, 133, 149
Brazil: in Contadora Support Group, 40; as refugees in Canada, 133
British Columbia, immigrants in, 122, 227n156
Brownsville, Texas, 97, 105
Brzezinski, Zbigniew, 18
Bureau of Customs and Border Protection, 162
Bush, George W., 94, 166
Bush administration: Central American policies of, 4, 10, 20, 29–30, 78, 88, 90, 94, 110, 112, 117, 118, 142, 173n21; immigration policy of, 162

caciques (power brokers), 54
Calderón, Rafael, 39
Calero, Adolfo, 172n11
California, detention centers in, 92

Caminante, 71

Campeche, refugee camps in, 9, 60, 61, 62, 63, 64, 65, 72, 79, 194n86

campesinos, 56, 59, 64; Mayas as, 45; persecution of, 29, 74, 76; refugee aid by, 69

Campora, Héctor, 44

Canada: advocacy networks in, 144–52, 155; American immigration to, 120; border closing of, 140–44; Central American policy and aid of, 42, 145, 200n160; Central American refugees in, 1, 2, 8, 11, 45, 51, 68, 78, 119–56; Central American wars and, 124–40; Guatemalan policy of, 29–30; immigrant classes of, 121–22, 215n10; immigrant families in, 227n157; immigration and refugee policy of, 2, 24, 120–24, 130, 152–56; languages of, 121; refugee jobs in, 139–40, 222n96; refugee response of, 6, 7, 119–56; refugees in, 130, 152–53; refugee sponsors in, 216n22; sanctuary movement in, 100, 152, 166; solidarity groups of, 145–46; Somoza policy of, 173; terrorist cells in, 163–64, 231n31

Canada Employment and Immigration Commission (CEIC), xv, 134–35

Canada–United States Accord on Our Shared Border, 142–43

Canadian Association on Latin America, 125

Canadian Auto Workers, 146–47

Canadian Bar Association, 137, 147

Canadian Border Services Agency, 164–65

Canadian-Caribbean-Central American Policy Alternatives (CAPA), 147

Canadian Centre for Investigation and Prevention of Torture, 148

Canadian Charter of Rights and Freedoms, 149, 151, 226n141

Canadian Civil Liberties Association, 136

Canadian Council for Refugees (CCR), xv, 119, 143, 147, 151, 152, 155, 157, 164, 165, 225n131

Canadian Council of Churches, 134, 141, 149

Canadian Hispanic Council, 136

Canadian Institute for International Peace and Security, 147, 225n130

Canadian International Development Agency, 125, 128

Canadian Jewish Congress, 149

Canadian Labour Congress, 146

Canadian National Exhibition Grounds, as shelter, 131

Canadian Religious Conference, 225n136

Canadian Security and Intelligence Service, 136, 153, 165

Caracas Convention on Diplomatic Asylum (1954), 182n90

Cardoza y Aragón, Luis, 44

Carnegie Endowment for Peace, 93

Carrasco, Bartolomé, 61

Carroll, E. H., 107

Cartegena Declaration, 33, 46, 77, 182n92

Carter, Jimmy, 17, 21, 108, 173n18

Carter administration: Salvadoran policy of, 23–24; Sandinistas and, 18

CASA, 97

Casa Albergue del Migrante (shelter), 159

Casa Juan Diego (shelter), 75, 97

Casa Marianella (shelter), 97

Casa Oscar Romero (shelter), 97, 105, 106, 207n57

Casey, William, 18

Casteñada de la Rosa, Jorge, 58

Castillo Nuñez, Noe, 84

Castro, Fidel, 44

Castro government, Mexico and, 172n12

Catholic Bishop's Conference of Guatemala, 33

Catholic Church: human rights activism of, 29, 42–43, 57, 60, 64, 95, 96, 185n128, 197n127, 206n48;

Catholic Church *(continued)*
in Mexico, 72; opposition to, 74;
refugee aid of, 39, 48–49, 97, 99,
209n88, 225n135; role in Central
American politics, 21, 23, 63, 95;
Salvadoran persecution of, 24, 25, 28,
177n51; sanctuary movement and,
105; truth commission of, 186n132
Catholic Diocese of Brownsville, 97,
209n88
Catholic Diocese of Cuernavaca,
196n116
Catholic Diocese of San Cristóbal de las
Casas, 53, 56, 57, 59, 61, 63, 66, 69,
70, 71, 72, 192n62
Catholic Diocese of Tapachula, 69, 159,
196n116
Catholic Diocese of Tehuantepec, 69,
196n117
Catholic Relief Services, 35, 76
CBS News, 92
CCR. *See* Canadian Council for
Refugees (CCR)
CCS. *See* Comité Cristiano de
Solidaridad (CCS)
CEAR. *See* Comisión Nacional para la
Atención de Repatriados, Refugiados,
y Desplazados (CEAR)
CEIC. *See* Canada Employment and
Immigration Commission (CEIC)
Center for Constitutional Rights, 104,
205n45
Center for Human Rights Fray
Bartolomé de las Casas, 73, 198n131
Central America: human rights abuses
in, 1, 3, 197n123; migration from, 7,
31–32; peace efforts in, 42, 43;
poverty in, 42, 159, 204n37; refugee
crisis in, 2; wars in, 1, 2, 7, 13–43
Central American Refugee Center, 97
Central American Refugee Committee
of the Diocese of St. Catharine in
Toronto, 149
Central American Revolutionary
Workers' Party, 22

Central Americans: as Canadian
immigrants, 121; as pawns, 112–18
Central American University, professors
murdered at, 42, 185n128
Central Intelligence Agency (CIA), 94;
Contras and, 18, 19, 174nn23,26,
175n28
Centre for Refugee Studies at York
University, 147
Centro de Derechos Humanos, 74
Centro de Estudios y Promoción Social,
68
Centro de Recursos Centroamericanos,
159, 229n12
Cerezo, Vicente, 79, 80
Cerro Hueco prison, 74
Cervantes Arceo, Hipólito, 54
Chajul refugee camp, 64
Chamorro, Pedro Joaquin, 15, 16
Chamorro, Violeta Barrios de, 16, 20,
42, 116, 117
Chapin, Frederic, 177n48
Chiapas: economy of, 54, 56, 190n44; as
former Guatemalan territory, 48,
192n53; Guatemalans in, 28, 32, 45,
49, 50, 61, 70, 83; human rights
abuses in, 70, 73, 158, 197n123;
indigenous peoples of, 55, 188n13;
Maya march in, 74; poverty in, 52,
54–55, 70, 159, 190n45; refugee
camps in, 9, 30, 31, 51, 64, 70;
Salvadorans in, 66–67, 69; *transmigrantes* of, 170n7
Chicago Religious Task Force on
Central America (CRTF), xv; refugee
aid by, 102, 103, 106, 207n67, 208n75
children, of refugees, 79, 83, 200n164
Chile: immigrants from, 122, 130, 133,
146; refugees from, 11
Chileans, community aid to, 98
Chimaltenango, Guatemala, Maya
migrants from, 47
Chirino Amaya, Santana, 93
Christian denominations, sanctuary
work of, 98–108

Christian Reformed Churches, 149

Chrétien, Jean, 142

Chuj Indians: massacre of, 28; as migrants to Mexico, 47

churches, as religious aid workers. *See* Catholic church; religious aid workers; *names of church denominations*

Church World Service, 3, 19, 35

Church World Service Immigration and Refugee Program, 103

Cienegüita refugee camp, 60

CIREFCA. *See* International Conference on Central American Refugees (CIREFCA)

CISPES. *See* Committee in Solidarity with the People of El Salvador (CISPES)

Ciudad Cuauhtémoc, Chiapas, 53–54, 60

Ciudad Hidalgo: as border city, 158; refugee mistreatment in, 160; refugee sanctuaries in, 66, 75; Salvadorans in, 66

civil initiative, sanctuary work as, 208n72

civil rights, violation of, 108

civil rights movement, 5

Civil War, sanctuaries during, 101

Clark, Joseph, 125, 127

Clarke, Maura, 23

clergy, Salvadoran persecution of, 23

Clinton, Bill, 142

Clinton administration, Central American policy of, 117

CNN, 230n23

Coalition for a Just Refugee and Immigration Policy, 137, 147

Coalition for Nicaraguan Civil Rights, 115

Cobán, as repatriation station, 81

coffee, as Salvadoran export, 20

Coffin, William Sloane, 95, 96

Cold War, 5, 14, 18, 87, 118, 123

Collacott, Martin, 154

Colomancagua refugee camp, 36, 37–38

Colombia: in Contadora Group, 40; refugee policy of, 9

Comalapa, refugee camps in, 51

COMAR. *See* Mexican Committee for Refugee Assistance (COMAR)

Comisión Nacional de Derechos Humanos, 73, 75, 160

Comisión Nacional para la Atención de Repatriados, Refugiados, y Desplazados (CEAR), xv, 79, 80, 81

Comisiones Permanentes de Representantes de Refugiados Guatemaltecos en México, 71

Comité Cristiano de Solidaridad (CCS), xv, 71

Comité de Ayuda a Refugiados Guatemaltecos, 76

Comité del Distrito Federal de Ayuda a Refugiados Guatemaltecos, 68, 197n118

Comité Diocesano de Ayuda a Immigrantes Fronterizos, 69, 159–60

Comité Mexicano de Solidaridad con el Pueblo Salvadoreño, 57

Commandos for the Recuperation of Belize, 192n56

Commission for Human Rights, 81

Committee in Solidarity with the People of El Salvador (CISPES), xv, 93–94, 95, 97

Committee of Poor Nicaraguans in Exile, 114, 115

Committee of the Nicaraguan Community, 115

communism, in Central America, 95, 113, 114

"compassion fatigue," 86

comunidades de base (faith communities), 3, 21, 176n43

Concerned Citizens for Church and Country, 209n88

concientizacion, 176n43

Conference of Catholic Bishops, 29, 149

Conferencia Episcopal Mexicana, 60

Congregationalists, as sanctuary
 workers, 102
CONONGAR. *See* National Coordinator of NGOs Assisting Refugees in
 Mexico (CONONGAR)
Constituents Assembly (El Salvador),
 129
Contadora Group, members of, 9, 40
Contadora peace proposal, 46, 63, 125,
 128
Contadora Support Group, 40
Contras, 113, 126, 127; action of, 19, 34,
 36, 37, 47; composition of, 174n22;
 demobilization of, 42; murder by,
 217n34; murder of, 116; US aid to,
 18–19, 40, 41, 92, 94, 114, 116, 117,
 146, 174nn23,27
Convention on Territorial Asylum
 (1954), 46
Convention Refugee Determination
 Division (CRDD; Canada), 135,
 223n101
Coordinación de ONGs y Cooperativas
 para el Accompañimiento de la
 Población Damnificada por el
 Conflicto Armado Interno, 82
Corbett, Jim, 98–99, 106, 137, 207n60
corruption: of immigration officials, 52,
 189n32; of Mexican bureaucracy, 73;
 in Nicaragua National Guard, 14, 15,
 17; of police, 67
Costa Rica, 129; at Esquipulas meeting,
 41; Guatemalans in, 140; Nicaraguans
 in, 32, 34, 116; refugee policy of, 36,
 38, 41; refugees in, 1, 8, 16, 35, 39, 40,
 87, 184n114; repatriation from, 43, 80;
 US aid to, 86; war effects on, 13, 18
counterinsurgency, 53
Cristiani, Alfredo, 112
Cristiano de Solidaridad (CCS), 69
CRTF. *See* Chicago Religious Task
 Force on Central America (CRTF)
Cruz, Jesús, 106
Cuba, 95; Central American wars and,
 13, 16, 19, 125; exiles from, 114, 118,

162; OAS blockade of, 172; US
 policy on, 17, 88
Cuban Adjustment Act (1966), 213n132
Cuban American lobby, 115
Cubans, community aid to, 98
Cuomo, Mario, 132
Customs Department, 94
Czechoslovakia, immigrants from, 122,
 124

Dalgado, Salomón, 106
D'Aubuisson, Roberto, 23, 25, 42,
 177n48
Davis, Thomas, 104
"death flights," 96
death squads, 3, 5, 42, 92, 95; in El
 Salvador, 20–26
DeConcini, Dennis, 96
Deferred Enforced Departure (DED),
 xv, 112
De la Madrid, Miguel, 17, 50, 56, 60,
 61
Democratic Nationalist Organization
 (ORDEN), xvi, 22, 176n39
demographic consequences of Latin
 American immigration, 203n28
Department of Homeland Security, 162
Departments of Agriculture and Mines
 and Resources (Canada), 120
deportation: of Guatemalans, 58, 73;
 from Mexico, 163; of Salvadorans, 69,
 196n103
detainment, of refugee supporters, 74
detention, of refugees, 91
detention centers, poor conditions of,
 160
Diaz-Balart, Lincoln, 118
Didion, Joan, 93
displaced refugees, definition of, 88
documentaries, on refugees, 93
documentation, of human rights abuses,
 3–4
Documentation Center/Resource
 Library (Canada), 135–36
Dominicans, investigation of, 74

Donovan, Jean, 23
drugging, of refugees, 91
drug trafficking, 158, 220n3, 229n5
Duarte, José Napoléon, 24, 25, 110, 128, 170n7, 178n56, 212n120
Dublin and Schengen Conventions (1990), 142, 222n108, 228n3
"durable solutions," for refugees, 36, 52, 69–70, 76

earthquakes, in El Salvador, 159, 229n8
Eastern bloc refugees, 88, 123, 124, 138
Echevarría Castellot, Eugenio, 62
economic migrants, refugees as, 84–118
Eisenhower administration, Salvadoran policy of, 178n61
ejidatarios, 53, 59, 61, 195n90
El Amitillo refugee camp, 36
El Chupadero refugee camp: attack on, 59, 60, 61; relocation of, 64
Elder, Jack, 105, 210n89
El Heraldo, 56
"eligibility committee," 77–78
Ellacuría, Ignacio, murder of, 185n128
El Mongito, refugee mistreatment in, 160
El Mozote massacre, 24
El Norte (film), 93
El Quiché, Guatemala, Maya migrants from, 47
El Rescate, 97, 160
El Rescate Legal Services, Inc., et al., v. Executive Office for Immigration Review et al., 92, 109, 212n115
El Salvador, 41; advocacy groups in, 3; at Esquipulas meeting, 41; expatriate remittances to, 170n5, 229n9; human rights abuses in, 1, 93, 126; poverty in, 42, 185n130; refugees from, 1, 2, 6, 9–10, 11, 26, 33, 34–35, 129, 155; refugees in, 40; repatriation from, 43; repatriation to, 43; US aid to, 25–26, 41, 86, 92, 93, 127, 162; US embargo on, 23; wars in, 1, 8, 13, 16, 18, 20–26. *See also* Salvadorans

El Salvador: Another Vietnam (documentary), 93
El Verbo, 180n78
emergency aid, for refugees, 76
"employment agencies," for refugees, 159
Episcopalians, refugee aid of, 100
Esquipulas, Guatemala, peace meeting at, 41
Esquipulas II accords, 41, 43, 76, 80, 128, 155
Estrada, Dora Elia, 84
Ethiopia, migration from, 170n5
"ethnocide," 64
Europe, Central American wars and, 13, 16
European Economic Community, refugee aid by, 80
European Union (EU), 141–42
Evangelical Committee for Development and Emergency, 38
excludable refugees, 70
Export Development Corporation, 125
Extended Voluntary Departure (EVD), xv, 89, 96, 113, 203n26, 206n50

Farabundo Martí Front for National Liberation (FMLN), xvi, 18, 23, 42, 177n50; FDR merger with, 23, 24
FDN. *See* Nicaraguan Democratic Forces (FDN)
FDR. *See* Revolutionary Democratic Front (FDR)
Federal Bureau of Investigation (FBI), 94, 95, 97, 104, 106, 206n52
Federal Court of Canada, 134
"feet people," as term for refugees, 10, 86
Fife, John, 98, 106, 108
Fiorenza, Joseph, 209n88
Fitzpatrick, Joseph, 96, 106, 209n88
Flores, Patricio, 209
Florida, Nicaraguans in, 113, 115
FMLN. *See* Farabundo Martí Front for National Liberation (FMLN)
FM-T (tourist) visa, 66, 200n163

FM-2 visa, 83, 200
FM-3 visa (visitor), 46, 62, 83, 200n163
FM-6 visa (transmigrant), 200n163
FM-8 visa (border visitor), 50
FM-9 visa (student), 46, 200n163
FM-10 visa (asylee), 46, 200n163
Fonseca Amador, Carlos, 171n7
Ford, Ita, 23
Ford administration, Nicaragua politics
    and, 13–14
foreign policies, effects on population
    displacement, 8
Fourteen Families, as El Salvador elite,
    20, 175n31
France: asylum seekers in, 233n46;
    Salvadoran policy of, 24–25
Franciscans, refugee activism of, 105
Francophones, in Canada, 122, 215n13
Freedom of Information Act, 173n21
Frente, 25
frijoles y fusiles program, 27
Frontline, 93
Front of United Popular Action, 21
FSLN. *See* Sandinista National
    Liberation Front (FSLN)
"funnel cities," for refugee, 100

Gallegos, Rómulo, 44
gangs, refugees as prey of, 159, 229n11
Garcia, Romeo Lucas, 27, 53
Garcia Márquez, Gabriel, 44
General Population Law (Mexico), 76–
    77
Gerardi, Juan, murder of, 43
globalization, development of, 5
González, Oscar, 51, 63
González Garrido, José Patrocino, 73, 74
González Martínez, Héctor, 63
Gospel Outreach, 59
Government of National Reconstruc-
    tion (Nicaragua), 15
Gracida, René, 209n88
grassroots NGOs, 76
Grupo de Lima. *See* Contadora Support
    Group

Grupo de Protección Betas, 160
Guadalajara, Salvadoran migrants in, 67
Guajiniquil refugee camp, 36
Guardias Blancas (White Guards), 54, 74
Guarita refugee camp, 36
Guatemala, 16; advocacy groups in, 3; at
    Esquipulas meeting, 41; human rights
    abuses in, 1, 42–43; NGOs in, 82;
    Nicaraguan refugees in, 39; refugees
    from, 1, 6, 9, 11, 33, 129; refugees in,
    40, 161; repatriation to, 43, 81,
    200n162; Salvadoran refugees in, 32,
    39; scorched earth policies of, 26–30;
    US aid to, 86; wars in, 1, 8, 13, 158
Guatemala-Mexico border, migrant
    settlements near, 47, 48, 159, 190n45
Guatemalan Anti-Mexican League,
    192n56
Guatemalan Church in Exile, 29
Guatemalan Commission on Human
    Rights, 60
Guatemalan Human Rights Commis-
    sion, 82
Guatemalan National Revolutionary
    Unity (URNG), xvi, 27, 42, 79, 82
Guatemalan Refugee, 44
Guatemalans: asylum for, 113; as asylum
    seekers, 78, 104; lawsuits involving,
    111, 112; in Mexico, 45, 47, 85,
    199n152; refugee camps for, 36–38; as
    refugees in Canada, 129, 130, 140,
    155; repatriation of, 78, 81; status of,
    118; in US, 90
Guerra Popular Prolongada, 171n7
guerrillas: in El Salvador, 20, 21–22, 23;
    in Guatemala, 47
guest worker plan, 166–67
Guevara, Norma, 204n35
Guevara Flores, Ana Estela, 204n35

Hagan, Jacqueline María, 182nn94,95
Haig, Alexander, 18, 25, 104
Harlingen, Texas, INS reviews at, 110–11
"harmonisation" initiative, 165
Hastrich, Jerome J., 209n88

Havana Convention (1928), 182n90
health care professionals, views on
    immigration, 147–48
Hernández, Fidel Sánchez, 21
Hernández Martínez, Maximiliano,
    175n33
HIV, refugee with, 148
Hocke, Jean-Pierre, 137
homeland security, effects on US
    immigration, 162
Honduras: asylum seekers from, 78;
    Canadian aid to, 128, 145, 217n37; at
    Esquipulas meeting, 41; Guatemalan
    refugees in, 140; migrants to Mexico
    from, 45; Nicaraguans in, 116;
    refugee policy of, 36, 183n107;
    refugees in, 1, 8, 15, 30–31, 34, 35,
    36, 37, 40, 87, 159, 184nn112,113;
    repatriation from, 43, 80; Salvadoran
    refugees in, 32; US aid to, 86; war
    effects on, 13, 16, 18, 41
Honduras-Nicaraguan border: cease fire
    on, 128; Contra maps on, 36
Hong Kong, immigrants from, 121, 153
Horizons and Tools for Peace, 146
House of Commons Special Commit-
    tee on the Peace Process in Central
    America, 128
House of Commons Standing Commit-
    tee on Citizenship and Immigration,
    153
Houston: as "funnel city," 100;
    Nicaraguans in, 34
Huehuetenango, Guatemala: European
    aid to, 80; Maya migrants from, 47, 79
humanitarianism, politics and, 119–56
human rights abuses, in Central
    America, 4, 25, 33, 38, 42–43, 60, 62,
    75–76, 80, 92, 96, 106, 126, 147, 160,
    225n135
human rights activists: in Central
    America, 3, 33–34; in Mexico, 167
Human Rights Commission (El
    Salvador), 92
Human Rights Ombudsman, 81

Human Rights Watch, 75, 170n4
Hungary, immigrants from, 122
Hunthausen, Raymond, 209
Hurricane Mitch, 159

I, Rigoberta Menchú, 28
ID cards, US bill proposing, 163
"illegal alien," as term for refugee, 133–
    34
illegal aliens, in Mexico, 47–65
Illegal Immigration Reform and
    Immigrant Responsibility Act (1996)
    (IIRIRA), xvi, 117, 143, 160, 204n32
I Married Dora (TV sitcom), 93
Immigrant and Refugee Rights Project,
    97
Immigration Act (1965; US), 85
Immigration Act (1976; Canada), 121,
    122–23, 134, 135, 140, 147, 231n32
Immigration Act (1990; US), 201
Immigration and Nationality Act, 103
Immigration and Naturalization Service
    (INS), 69, 84, 91, 92, 96, 98, 106, 107,
    108, 114, 117, 131, 132, 138, 162; suits
    against, 109, 111, 212n115
Immigration and Naturalization Service v.
    Luz Marina Cardoza-Fonseca, 109,
    114, 212n116
Immigration and Refugee Board (IRB),
    xvi, 123, 135, 138, 153, 154,
    220nn71,72
Immigration and Refugee Protection
    Act (2002; Canada), 121, 123, 164,
    231n32
Immigration Appeals Board (IAB;
    Canada), 134, 135, 220n72
Immigration Ministry (Canada), 121, 135
immigration officials, corruption of, 52,
    189n32
immigration policy, 8; of Canada, 120–
    24; of US, 2, 92–97, 120, 201nn8,9
immigration reform, US policy for, 5, 90
Immigration Reform and Control Act
    (IRCA; 1986), xvi, 2, 10, 11, 90, 91,
    110, 130, 201n7, 203n29

Impacto, 56
Independencia, refugee camps in, 51
indigenous peoples: of Chiapas, 55,
  188n13; imprisonment of, 198n132
Inevitable Revolutions (LaFeber), 93
Institute for Religion and Democracy,
  104
Instituto Nacional de Migración, 77,
  158, 159, 163
Inter-American Bank, 125
Inter-American Commission on
  Human Rights, 165–66
Inter-American Development Agency, 26
Inter-American Dialogue, 93
Inter-American Symposium on
  Sanctuary, 107
Inter-Church Committee on Human
  Rights in Latin America, 126, 148,
  225n136
Inter-Church Committee on Refugees,
  130, 148, 149
Interfaith Sanctuary Coalition, 166
Internal Revenue Service (IRS), 104
International Commission on Human
  Rights, 74
International Committee of the Red
  Cross, 19, 39, 58–59, 86–87, 128, 131
International Conference on Central
  American Refugees (CIREFCA), xv,
  43, 76, 157
International Council of Voluntary
  Agencies (ICVA), 184n113
International Monetary Fund, 26
International Organization for Migra-
  tion (IOM), xvi, 199n147, 228n1
International Rescue Committee,
  206n50
Inter-Religious Task Force on El
  Salvador and Central America, 103
In the Name of the People, 93
IOM. *See* International Organization
  for Migration (IOM)
Iran-Contra affair, 20, 92, 175n28
Iranians, as refugees in Canada, 139,
  221n88

Iraqis, US asylum for, 162
IRB. *See* Immigration and Refugee
  Board (IRB)
IRCA. *See* Immigration Reform and
  Control Act (IRCA; 1986)
I-274A form, 91
Ixcán refugee camp, 59, 64

Jambor, Pierre, 52
Jecalteca Indians, as migrants to Mexico,
  47
Jesuit Centre for Social Faith and
  Justice, 137, 141
Jesuit Refugee Service, 149
Jesuits: investigation of, 74; murder of,
  41, 217n33; refugee activism of, 95,
  105; Salvadoran expulsion of, 23,
  177n44
Jews: as Canadian immigrants, 120, 148;
  refugee aid of, 100
John XXIII, Pope, 175n34
John Paul II, Pope, 105
journalists, murder of, 170n4
Jubilee Partners, 150
judicial review, of refugee status, 78
junta, in El Salvador, 22, 23

kaibiles, 53, 64, 179n71
Kanjobal Indians, as migrants to
  Mexico, 47
Katz, Danny, 137
Kazel, Dorothy, 23
Kelly, Thomas C., 206
Kirkpatrick, Jeane, 18, 25, 94, 104
Kissinger, Henry, 94, 178n55
Kissinger Report (1984), 93

La Casa del Norte, 150
ladinos: definition of, 179n63; as
  migrants to Mexico, 45
LaFeber, Walter, 93
Lafragua, Gabino, 192n58
La Jornada, 57, 191n52
Lancandón jungle, refugee camps in, 52
land-lease program, for refugees, 71

La Prensa (Nicaragua), 15
Las Delicias refugee camp, 59, 60, 64
Las Margaritas refugee camps, 51, 52
Lastman, Mel, 154
latifundistas, 176n41
Latin American Bishops' Conference
    (1968), 175n34
Latin American Working Group, 147
La Trinitaria refugee camps, 51, 60
La Unión, 71
La Ventosa, refugee mistreatment in, 160
La Virtud refugee camp, 36
law breakers, as refugee label, 98
Lawyers' Committee against US
    Intervention in Central America, 94
Lawyers Committee for Human Rights,
    147
League for the Protection of
    Guatemala, 192n56
Lebanon, immigrants from, 122, 221n88
Leddy, Mary Jo, 152
leftist movements, in Latin America, 16
legal aid groups, FBI investigation of, 94
legal counseling, for refugees, 97
Leger, Joseph, 126, 217n28
liberation theology, 21, 102, 104, 176n43
"Little Managua," Sweetwater as, 113
Loma Bonita refugee camp, 64
Lona Reyes, Arturo, Bishop, 61, 73
López, Armando, murder of, 185n128
López, Joaquin, murder of, 185n128
López Portillo, José, 16–17, 49, 50, 56,
    58, 173n14, 192n36
Los Angeles: as "funnel city," 100;
    Nicaraguans in, 34
Los Angeles Times, 107
Los Hernandez refugee camp, 36
Lutheran Church, refugee aid of, 100
Lutheran Immigration and Refugee
    Service, 103, 206n50
Lutheran Refugee Committee, 149

MacFarlane, Peter, 148
MacGuigan, Mark, 126
Maclean's, 153

Magaña, Alvaro, 25
Majano, Adolfo, 177n47
Mama Maquin, 71
Mam Indians, as migrants to Mexico, 47
Managua, earthquake in, 14, 171n6
Mapastepec, refugees in, 54
maquiladoras, 159
Mara Salvatruchas, refugees as prey of,
    159
Marchi, Sergio, 136, 153, 227n157
Marroquín Siliezar, Juan José, 179n71
Martí, Farabundo, 44
Martí, José, 44
Martín Baró, Ignacio, murder of,
    185n128
Martínez, Demetria, 210n89
Marxism, 72, 104, 113, 118
Maryknoll order: refugee activism of,
    95, 105, 206n51; Salvadoran persecu-
    tion of, 23
Matamoros, refugee sanctuary in, 75
la matanza, 20, 177n50
Matas, David, 152
Maya Indians: in Guatemala, 26–27, 29;
    languages of, 70, 179n63; Mexican
    camps for, 9, 30, 47, 70; persecution
    of, 27–28, 29, 180nn76,77; protest
    march of, 74; as refugees, 31, 45
Mayorga, Roman, 23, 177n49
Mazzoli, Romano, 90
McCarthy era, 187n1
McDougall, Barbara, 138
Médecins sans Frontières, 137
Medellín Conference (1968), 70
Medrano, José Alberto, 176n39
Meese, Edwin, 114
Meissner, Doris, 138
Mejía Victores, Oscar, 27, 35, 53, 58
Memorandum of Agreement (MOA),
    142–44
Menchú Tum, Rigoberta, 1, 28, 81, 128,
    180n76
Menjívar, 181n87
Mennonite Central Committee, 149,
    150–51

Mennonites, refugee aid of, 100
Merkt, Stacy Lynn, 105, 210n89
Mesa Grande refugee camp, 36
mestizos, in Mexico, 31
Methodist Church, refugee aid of, 100
Mexican Committee for Refugee
  Assistance (COMAR), xv, 49, 50, 51,
  54, 56, 58, 61, 63, 64, 67, 72, 192n58;
  possible corruption in, 52, 189n32;
  refugee repatriation and, 78, 79
"Mexicanization" of refugee children,
  79, 200
Mexicans, community aid to, 98
Mexico: American migrants to, 187n1;
  border control by, 167; Canadian
  workers in, 145; Central American
  refugees in, 1, 2, 8–9, 28, 44–83, 85,
  87; 1917 Constitution of, 55; in
  Contadora Group, 40; exiles in, 44;
  Guatemalan migrants in, 45, 47–65,
  140, 199n152; immigration policies
  of, 2; Muslim immigrants to, 163;
  NGOs in, 76, 79; Nicaraguan
  migrants in, 47; peace efforts of, 43;
  Plan Sur of, 170n7; police brutality
  in, 160; refugee aid of, 100, 129;
  refugee conference in, 186n133;
  refugee expulsion by, 49–50,
  196n103; refugee legacy of, 158;
  refugee policy of, 2, 6, 9–10, 30,
  44–83; repatriation from, 43, 79;
  Salvadoran policy of, 24; Salvadorans
  in, 32, 33, 35, 66–69; war effects on,
  13, 16
Mexico City: Nicaraguan migrants in,
  47; refugee outmigration from, 68;
  Salvadoran migrants in, 67, 68
Miami, Central American migrants in,
  31, 34, 44
Miami Six, 176n41
Middle East, immigrants from, 144
Midwest, refugee crossing of, 99
Migrant Stabilization Program, 83
Migration Policy Institute, 166
military regimes, corrupt, 5

Ministry of Employment and Immigra-
  tion (Canada), 123
Miskito Indians, 37, 128, 183n108; in
  Contras, 174n22
missionaries, in Central America, 3
Missionaries of Jesus, 97
Moakley, Joseph, 96
model villages, 18
Monterrey, Salvadoran migrants in, 67
Monterroso, Augusto, 44
Montes, Segundo, murder of, 185n128
Montevideo Convention (1933), 182n90
Morales, César, 54
Moreno, Juan Ramón, murder of,
  185n128
Moreno, Manuel D., 209n88
motion pictures, on refugee problem,
  93
Movement Support Network, 205n45
Movimiento Mexicano de Solidaridad
  con el Pueblo de Guatemala, 57, 61
Ms. magazine, 108
Mulroney, Brian, 125, 127, 128, 133–34,
  135, 137, 140, 142, 145
Muslim immigrants: in Canada, 232n37;
  in Mexico, 163

NAFTA. See North America Free Trade
  Agreement (NAFTA)
Nansen Medal, 122, 131
National Bank of Mexico, 55
National Bipartisan Commission on
  Central America (1984 Kissinger
  Report), 93
National Center for Immigrants' Rights,
  92
National Central American Health
  Network, 94
National Commission for Refugees, 38,
  184n118
National Coordinator of NGOs
  Assisting Refugees in Mexico
  (CONONGAR), xv, 76, 77
National Council of Catholic Bishops,
  105

National Council of Churches of Christ, refugee activism of, 95, 96, 99, 206n50
National Immigration Project, 137
Nationalist Democratic Front, 176n39
National Lawyers Guild, 206n50
National Opposition Union (Unión Nacional Opositora, UNO), xvi, 20, 42, 116
National Peace Fund, 81
National Post, 154
National Refugee Rights Project, 212n126
National Republican Alliance Party (ARENA), xv, 42, 177n48
National Sanctuary Alliance, 101
National Security Decision Directive 17, 174n23
Nelson, Alan, 107
Neruda, Pablo, 44
news media, refugee reporting of, 56, 57, 62–63, 74, 92, 107, 165, 191n52
New York, Central American migrants in, 31
New York Times, 49, 89
NGOs. *See* non-governmental organizations (NGOs)
Nguyen v. Canada, 223n106
Nicaragua: advocacy groups in, 3; Canadian aid to, 127, 146; at Esquipulas meeting, 41; human rights abuses in, 1; poverty in, 42, 171n2, 185n130; refugees from, 1, 6, 33, 34, 39–40, 129, 159; refugees in, 40, 102; repatriation to, 43; Sandinista revolution in, 13–20; US aid to, 20; US presence in, 14, 127; wars in, 1, 8, 13
Nicaragua: They Will Not Enter (documentary), 93
Nicaragua-Honduras border, peacekeeping along, 42, 94
Nicaraguan Adjustment and Central American Relief Act, 118
Nicaraguan American National Foundation, 115

Nicaraguan Armed Revolutionary Forces, 174n22
Nicaragua National Guard, 113, 126; corruption in, 14, 15, 17; journalist targets of, 170n4
Nicaraguan Democratic Forces (FDN), xvi, 172n11, 174n22
Nicaraguan Democratic Front, 34
Nicaraguan Democratic Movement, 16
Nicaraguan Democratic Revolutionary Alliance (ARDE), 174n22
Nicaraguan Humanitarian Coalition, 114
Nicaraguan Review Program, 114, 117
Nicaraguans: aid to, 104, 105; case study on, 112–18; lawsuits involving, 110, 117–18; in Mexico, 45, 85; as refugees in Canada, 130, 140; repatriation of, 80
Nicaraguan Solidarity Union, 115
Nicaraguan Task Force, 116, 117
Nicgorski, Diane, 104, 108, 211n108
Nobel Peace Prize, 41, 81, 128
Noe Castillo Núñez, et al., v. Hal Boldin, et al., 92, 108, 211n111
Nogales, refugee sanctuary in, 75
nonconvention refugees, 32, 88
non-governmental organizations (NGOs), xvi, 33, 158; in Canada, 123, 125, 126, 127, 128, 129, 132, 135, 136, 137, 144, 145, 200n160; in Central America, 19, 35, 78, 188n10; Central American peace efforts of, 43, 186n133, 200n160; effects on international policies, 4, 8; growth of, 169n1; in Guatemala, 82, 159; in Mexico, 76, 79, 159; policy protests of, 93–94, 160; refugee programs and aid of, 39, 47, 51, 67, 68, 81, 97, 159, 162
non-refoulement (no forced return), of refugees, 32, 36, 50, 96, 166
North America Free Trade Agreement (NAFTA), xvi, 10, 142, 166
North Dakota–Manitoba border, as refugee crossing, 100, 107, 150

NPR, 107
Nueva Estrella, 71
Nuevo Iztlán refugee camp, 60
Nuremberg Human Rights Award, 75
Nurses against US Aggression, 94

OAS. *See* Organization of American
States (OAS)
Oaxaca, refugees in, 61, 76
Obando y Bravo, Miguel, 177n51
O'Brien, Thomas J., 209n88
Ocosingo refugee camps, 52, 59
oil, role in Mexican economy, 54, 73,
190n44
Ontario, immigrants in, 122, 227n156
ONUCA. *See* United Nations Observer
Mission in Central America
(ONUCA)
Operation Sojourner, 106, 107, 108
Operation Solidarity, 146
Orantes-Hernández, et al., v. Smith, et al.,
92, 109
ORDEN. *See* Democratic Nationalist
Organization (ORDEN)
Organization for the Liberation from
Communism, 22
Organization of African Unity, 88
Organization of American States
(OAS), xvi, 74, 124–25, 219n24
Organizer's Nuts and Bolts, 101
Ortiz Monasterio, Luis, 44, 57–58,
191n52
Osaka, anti-US protest in, 94
Other Than Mexicans (OTMs), 91
Our Lady of Guadalupe, 41
Ovaciones, 56
Overground Railroad, refugee transport
by, 150
OXFAM, 35, 76

Pacifica, 107
Padrón Rotsaert, Joel, 74
Panama: in Contadora Group, 40;
refugee policy of, 9; refugees in,
34

Pan-American Union, 217
Paniagua Vides, Marta Ester, 84
Partido Acción Nacional, 56
Partido Democrático México, 191n51
Partido Popular Socialista, 191n51
Partido Revolucionario de los Traba-
jadores, 191n51
Partido Socialista Unificado de México,
191n51
Pastora Gomez, Edén, 16, 172n11,
174n22
patrullas de autodefensa civil, 27
Paulist order, refugee activism of, 95
peace, Central American plans for, 41,
47, 63
peace accords, of Central America, 40–
43, 80–81, 82
Peace Bridge, 149
peace caravans, 5
Pearson Peace Medal, 151
PEMEX, 54
peones, 53
People's Revolutionary Army, 21
People's Revolutionary Block, 21
Pérez-Cruz, Juan Francisco, 84
Permanent Commissions, 71, 79, 80,
197n124
Peru, in Contadora Support Group,
40
Petén, Guatemala, Maya migrants
from, 47
Philippines, immigrants from, 121
Pinochet, Augusto, 146
Plan Chiapas, 56
Plan Sur (Southern Plan), of Mexico,
170n7
Plaut, Gunther, 135
Plaut Report, 135, 220n71
Pocock, Nancy, 151
"points system," for immigrants to
Canada, 121
polas de desarrollo, 28
Poles, EVD granted to, 90
political exiles, in Mexico, 44
political refugees, definition of, 88

Popular League of February 28, 21
Popular Liberation Forces, 21
Port Isabel detention center, 97
Portugal, refugees from, 133
Presbyterian Church, 108, 150; refugee
aid of, 100
*Presencia de los refugiados guatemaltecos en
México* (UNCHR), 65, 197n118
Prigione, Girolamo, 74–75
"Procedure for the Establishment of a
Strong and Lasting Peace in Central
America," 41
Programa de Asistencia para los
Refugiados Centroamericano, 76
Programa para Refugiados del Instituto
Mixto de Ayuda Social, 184n119
protest march, of Maya Indians, 74
Protocol (1967), 88
Proyecto Libertad, 97
Puebla Process, 157–57, 228n1
Puerto Rico refugee camp, 54, 64

Quaker Committee for Refugees, 149
Quakers, refugee aid by, 98, 99, 102,
103, 207n60
Quebec: immigrant aid of, 215n12;
immigrants in, 227n156
Quebec-Canada Accord (1991), 121–22
Quebec Immigration Lawyers Associa-
tion, 147
Quetzaltenango, Guatemala, Maya
migrants from, 47
Quick Impact Program, 81–82
Quintana Roo refugee camps, 9, 60, 61,
62, 63, 64, 65, 72, 79, 194n86, 195n90

radio networks, refugee news on, 107
Ramírez, Bishop, 73
Ramírez, Hermenegildo, 61
Ramírez, Sergio, 127
Ramos, Elba and Celina, murder of,
185n128
Reagan, Ronald, 94, 110, 114, 170n5
Reagan administration: Canada and,
137; Central American policies of, 4,

6, 10, 18, 19, 29–30, 40, 41, 57, 68,
78, 84, 86, 88, 90, 93, 94, 105, 118,
126, 173n21; Salvadoran policies of,
25; sanctuary movement and, 103;
Sandinistas and, 16, 114
REAL-ID Bill, 163, 230n27
"reception areas," for refugees, 36
refoulement, 93, 122, 136
Refuge, 147
Refugee Act (1980), 87, 99, 110, 201n7
Refugee Advisory Status Committee
(RSAC), xvi, 123, 134, 138, 216n21
refugee advocacy, 3, 4–6
refugee assistance, 32
refugee camps, 9, 30, 31, 145
Refugee Corps, 230n25
refugee crisis, results of, 157–68
Refugee Lawyers association, 147
refugee policy, of Canada, 120–24
Refugee Rights Day (Canada), 220n70
refugees: from Central America, 30–40;
children of, 79, 83, 200n164;
definition of, 88, 122–23; economic
influences of, 6, 48; as economic
migrants, 65, 84–118; economic
remittances of, 5–6, 170n5, 229n9;
employment of, 39; financial aid for,
70–71; "Mexicanization" of children
of, 79; as naturalized citizens, 83;
persecution of, 58, 60, 76, 82, 98, 159,
183n102, 200n162; poor health of, 52,
55; repatriation of, 43, 78–83, 157;
sanctuary movement for, 98–108;
UN definition of, 32; vs. asylees, 101
Refugee Update, 143
Regalado, Victor, 149, 226n140
Regional Conference on Migration,
157, 228n1
religious aid workers: in Canada, 131,
147, 148, 149; in Central America, 3,
4, 69, 95, 98–103; Central American
aid work of, 75, 98–108; persecution
of, 54, 74, 104, 126, 127, 207n57,
209n88, 217n33; sanctuary movement
of, 98–108. *See also* Catholic Church

religious objectors, 101
Remer-Themert, Glen, 210n89
remittances, of refugees, 5–6, 170n5, 229n9
Reno, Donald, 106, 107
Reno, Janet, 118, 214n153
reorientation, of Guatemalan prisoners, 28
Repak, Terry, 181n87
repatriation, of refugees, 43, 78–83, 140
Resource Information Center (INS), 110
retornos, 81, 82; persecution of, 92–93
Revolutionary Democratic Front (FDR), xvi, 23
revolutions, in Central America, 44, 85
Rico-Martinez, Francisco, 147
right-wing activists, of Salvador, 94–95
Rio Grande Defense Committee, 97, 106
Ríos Montt, Efrain, 27, 29, 35, 53, 58, 180n78, 188n12
Riverside Church, 96
Rivkind, Perry, 114
Robelo, Alfonso, 16, 172n11
Robillard, Lucienne, 153
Romero, Carlos Humberto, 172n11
Romero, Oscar Arnulfo, Archbishop, 4, 21, 23, 99, 175n36, 177n51
Romero (film), 93
Romero House, 152
Ros-Lehtinen, Ileana, 118
Rothko Chapel Award for Commitment to Truth and Freedom, 108
Royal Canadian Mounted Police, 136, 151, 165
RSAC. *See* Refugee Advisory Status Committee (RSAC)
Ruiz García, Samuel, as refugee advocate, 57, 61, 70–73, 74–75, 198n120

"safe third country," 136–37, 141–44, 164
Salinas de Gortari, Carlos, 158

Salvadoran Catholic Archdiocese, refugee aid of, 39, 185n123
Salvadoran National Guard, 94
Salvadoran National Security Forces (ANSESAL), xv, 22, 176n39
Salvadorans: asylum for, 113, 131; in Canada, 119, 130, 138, 139, 218nn43,45; cross-border migration of, 30; labor value of, 45; lawsuits involving, 111–12; in Mexico, 45, 66–69, 85, 160, 195n100; persecution of, 92–93, 96; refugee camps for, 36–39, 88; as refugees in Canada, 129, 130, 131, 155, 218n43; repatriation of, 80; status of, 112, 118; in US, 90, 159, 203n26
Salvador (book), 93
Salvador (film), 93
Salvation Army, 131
San Antonio (Honduras) refugee camp, 36
San Benito, Texas, 97
San Caralampio Huanacaston refugee camp, 64
Sánchez Martínez, Felipe, 44
Sánchez Meraz, Antonio, 196n115
sanctuaries, for refugees, 69–78, 75
sanctuary movement, 4, 7, 98–108, 152; opponents to, 105, 106, 209n88
Sandinista National Liberation Front (FSLN), xvi, 172n11; history of, 15–16, 171n7
Sandinistas, 109, 113, 114, 127, 146; CIA war on, 20, 175n28; Contadora support of, 40–41; defeat of, 43, 116, 117, 140; refugee camps of, 40; war with Somoza dictatorship, 34, 47, 113
Sandino, César Augusto, 44, 171n7
San Francisco, Central American migrants in, 31
San Francisco Bay area, refugee aid of, 99
San José Pact of 1969, 46, 182n90, 187n6
San Marcos, Guatemala, Maya migrants from, 47

Sano, Seki, 44
San Pedro, Enrique, 209n88
Scarboro Foreign Mission Society, 225n136
"scientific killings," in Guatemala, 28
scorched earth policies, of Guatemalan army, 26–30, 45
Secretaría de Gobernación, 46, 49, 50, 59, 61, 62, 66, 73, 196n113
Secretaría de Relaciones Exteriores, 49, 58, 76
Secretarías de Defensa and Gobernación, 58
security certificates, 165, 232n37
Seeking a Safe Haven: A Congregational Guide to Helping Central American Refugees in the United States, 103
Seminario Bautista, 68
September 11 terrorist attack, 8, 12, 143, 161–64, 168, 230n27
Serrano Elías, Jorge, 81
Service for Peace and Justice, 205n42
Servicio, Desarrollo, y Paz, 68, 76
Servicios Migratorios, 49, 51, 56, 58, 69
Sikhs, as refugees in Canada, 133, 134, 137
Simjoval, Catholic persecution in, 74
Simpson, Alan K., 86, 90
Simpson-Rodino bill, 203n29
Sin Fronteras, 78, 159
Singh v. Canada, 134, 220n70
Sinner, George, 107
Sinner, Richard, 107, 211n104
60 Minutes, 93
"Smart Border" initiative, 165
Smith, Rosemary, 207n57
Smith, William French, 99
smuggling, of refugees, 98, 106, 136, 210nn89,94
social justice, in El Salvador, 21, 176n43
Soconusco region: Maya Indian refugees in, 31; Salvadorans in, 45
"solidarity committees," 57
Sololá, Guatemala, Maya migrants from, 47

Somalis, as refugees in Canada, 221n88
Somoza Debayle, Anastacio, 13, 126, 171n7, 172n11
Somoza Debayle, Luis, 13
Somoza family, as Nicaragua dictators, 13–20, 47, 102
Somoza García, Anastacio, 13, 34, 171n4
Sonoran Desert, refugee loss on, 207n59
"source country," of refugees, 231n32
South American Migration Dialogue, 228n1
Southeast Asians, as Canadian immigrants, 122, 124
Southside Presbyterian Church (Tucson), refugee shelter in, 75, 99, 106
Southwest, refugee shelter in, 97
Soviet Union, Central American wars and, 13, 16
Spain, Central American policy of, 42
Sri Lankans, as refugees in Canada, 139
Statement of Mutual Understanding on Information Sharing (2003), 164–65
Stewart, Bill, 170n4
Stoffman, Daniel, 154
Subcommittee on Immigration, Refugees, and International Law, 95
"subversive literature," 204n35
Sullivan, John, 170n4
Summa, 56
Support Program for Voluntary Repatriation in Huehuetenango, 79
Supreme Court of Canada, 226n140
Switzerland, EU and, 142

Tabasco refugee camp, 60
TACA, 96
Talismán, Salvadorans in, 66
Tamils, as refugees in Canada, 133, 137
Tapachula: Betas in, 160; refugee camps in, 51, 56, 66, 75, 160
Task Force on the Churches and Corporate Reality, 148
tatik (father in faith), 70
techo, tortillas y trabajo program, 27

Tecún Umán: as border city, 158, 159, 229n3; Salvadorans in, 66

Tegucigalpa Bloc, 41

Tehuantepec, refugee mistreatment in, 160

Tela, Honduras, peace meeting at, 42

Televisa, 56

television programs: on Central America, 93; on refugees, 93

temporary protected status (TPS), xvi, 112, 229n8

Tendencia Insurreccional (Terceristas), 171n7

Tendencia Proletaria, 171n7

terrorist attacks, of September 11, 8, 12, 143, 161–64, 230n27

terrorist cells, in Canada, 153, 165

Tesoro, El Salvador, peace meeting at, 42

testimonies, from refugees, 101

Texas: detention centers in, 92; North American immigrants in, 56

Texas Rural Legal Aid, 97

They Speak of Hope (documentary), 93

Thomas, Lorry, 105

"tied aid," 146

Tijuana, Betas in, 160

"the time of mass terror," 28

Toronto Refugee Affairs Council, 149

Toronto Star, 133, 136

Torres Arcieniega, Diana, 49

"tortilla curtain," 163

Totonicapan, Guatemala, Maya migrants from, 47

TPS. *See* temporary protected status (TPS)

transmigrantes, in Mexico, 10, 65, 159, 170n7

transmigration, of Central Americans to US, 10, 57, 65, 159, 170n7

transnationalism, of Canadian immigrants, 156

transnational structures, of advocacy groups, 169n2

Tribunal Federal de Justica Fiscal y Administrativa, 78

Trotsky, Leon, 44

Trudeau, Pierre, 11, 119, 125, 127, 217n25

Truman administration, Nicaragua politics and, 13–14

truth commission, 186n132

Tucson Ecumenical Council Task Force on Central America, 99, 210n89

tucson refugee support group, 98–99, 102, 207n60, 208n75

Turks, as refugees in Canada, 133

Turner, John, 125

Tuxtla Gutiérrez, Betas in, 160

Uganda, immigrants from, 122

Under Fire (film), 93

Underground Railroad, refugee aid as, 98, 211n102, 218n42

"undesirables," border control of, 167

Ungo, Guillermo, 23, 177n49

UNHCR. *See* United Nations High Commissioner for Refugees (UNHCR)

Unitarian Church, refugee aid of, 100

United Church of Canada, 149

United Fruit Company, 178n61

United Nations: Central American peace efforts of, 43; truth commission of, 186n132

United Nations Committee for Human Rights, 149

United Nations Convention against Torture, 76

United Nations Convention and Protocol (1951), 9, 32, 39, 46, 203n22; signatories of, 36, 38, 39, 46, 50, 76, 77, 122, 130, 141

United Nations High Commissioner for Refugees (UNHCR), xvi, 3, 32, 33, 34, 39–40, 72, 166, 182n91, 184n113; Canadian agreements with, 123, 128, 137, 154, 217n39, 231n32; Mexican agreement with, 50, 61, 199n147; refugee aid of, 46, 50, 52, 65, 66, 69–70, 78, 79–80, 81, 82, 87,

89, 117, 188n20; refugee camps of, 9, 10, 35–36, 37, 38; refugee relocation by, 9, 10, 35–36, 37, 38, 51; US aid to, 86

United Nations Observer Group in Central America, 128

United Nations Observer Mission in Central America (ONUCA), xvi, 42

United States: Central American policy of, 92–97, 201nn8,9; Central American refugees in, 1, 8, 10, 31, 45, 68, 70, 84, 91, 204n36; foreign policy of, 6; immigration policies of, 2; legal immigrants in, 153; refugee aid of, 100. *See also* Bush administration; Reagan administration

United States-Canada border, 120, 132, 135, 150, 162; control of, 144; economic activity across, 166

United States-Mexico border: control of, 158, 161, 163; economic activity across, 166; policies affecting, 11, 47; refugee aid near, 75, 97, 151; refugee crossing of, 57, 85, 91, 149, 159; refugee detention on, 31; sanctuary movement on, 98

UNO. *See* National Opposition Union (Unión Nacional Opositora, UNO)

Unomásuno, 62–63

Upper Canada Province of the Jesuit Fathers, 225n136

URNG. *See* Guatemalan National Revolutionary Unity (URNG)

Uruguay, in Contadora Support Group, 40

USA-PATRIOT Act (2001), 161–62

US Catholic Conference, 95, 105, 206nn48,50, 209n86

US Commission on International Religious Freedom, 162

US Committee for Refugees, 77, 115, 119

US Congress, 96, 112, 114, 120

US Court of Appeals, 109

US Justice Department, 89, 90, 91, 103,

105, 106, 107, 115, 142, 202n14, 209n88

USSR, refugees from, 113

US State Department, 80, 90, 94, 110, 114, 163; refugee definitions of, 90

US Visitor and Immigrant Status Indicator Technology (US-VISIT), 162, 230n22

Valcourt, Bernard, 140

Vallejo, Mario, 56, 191n49

Vatican, in Ruiz protest, 74–75

Vatican II Council (1962–65), 70, 175n34

Venezuela: in Contadora Group, 40; refugee policy of, 9

Veracruz refugee camp, 60

Vietnam War, 19, 92, 101; El Salvador compared to, 93, 204n39; protests against, 5

VIGIL, 152

Vigil Network, 152

"visitors program," for refugees, 38

Vive La Casa (Buffalo), 150

Vluchteling, 68, 76, 196n107

voluntary departure, 91, 92, 109

voluntary repatriation, 83

Waldeman, Lorne, 137, 141

Walesa, Lech, 96

Washington, D.C., Salvadorans in, 181n87

Washington Office on Latin America, 94, 205n42

Watergate scandal, 19

Weakland, Rembert, 209n88

Wellington Avenue Church (Chicago), 104

West Germany, Central American policy of, 42

White, Robert, 24, 176n41

White Hand, 22

"White Paper" on El Salvador, 178n55, 217n29

White Warriors Union, 22
Willis-Conger, Philip, 210n89
Windsor Central American Refugee
    Sponsorship Network, 150
Witness for Peace, 94
World Bank, 26
World Food Program, 80
World Refugee Survey, 166, 232n45
World War II, 122, 124, 148

Young, Andrew, 173n18

Zamora, Mario, 23
Zamora, Rubén, 23, 177n49
Zapatista National Liberation Front,
    190n45, 191n46
Zapatista rebellion, 55, 56, 73, 76, 158
Zapatistas, Ruiz as mediator for, 75
Zedillo, Ernesto, 158

Compositor: BookMatters, Berkeley
Text: 10.75/14 Bembo
Display: Bembo
Printer and binder: Maple-Vail Manufacturing Group